THE CONSTITUTIONAL RIGHTS, PRIVILEGES, AND IMMUNITIES OF THE AMERICAN PEOPLE

THE CONSTITUTIONAL RIGHTS, PRIVILEGES, AND IMMUNITIES OF THE AMERICAN PEOPLE

The Selective Incorporation of the Bill of Rights, the Refined Incorporation Model of Akhil Reed Amar, Dred Scott, National Citizenship and Its Implied Privileges and Immunities, the Second Amendment Right, and Much More

Arnold T. Guminski

iUniverse, Inc.
New York   Bloomington

The Constitutional Rights, Privileges, and Immunities of the American People

iUniverse books may be ordered through booksellers or by contacting:

iUniverse
1663 Liberty Drive
Bloomington, IN 47403
www.iuniverse.com
1-800-Authors (1-800-288-4677)

ISBN: 978-1-4401-2589-8 (sc)
ISBN: 978-1-4401-2588-1 (dj)
ISBN: 978-1-4401-2590-4 (ebook)

Library of Congress Control Number: 2009923049

Printed in the United States of America

iUniverse rev. date: 05/01/2009

For Annegret

My beloved wife and best friend

"Neither slavery nor involuntary servitude, except as a punishment for crime whereof the party shall have been duly convicted, shall exist within the United States, or any place subject to their jurisdiction."

U.S. CONST. amend. XIII, § 1 (1865)

"Congress shall make no law respecting an establishment of religion, or prohibiting the free exercise thereof; or abridging the freedom of speech, or of the press; or the right of the people peaceably to assemble, and to petition the Government for a redress of grievances."

U.S. CONST. amend. I (1791)

"No person shall ... be deprived of life, liberty, or property, without due process of law ..."

U.S. CONST. amend. V (1791)

"All persons born or naturalized in the United States and subject to the jurisdiction thereof, are citizens of the United States, and of the State wherein they reside. No State shall make or enforce any law which shall abridge the privileges or immunities of citizens of the United States; nor shall any State deprive any person of life, liberty, or property, without due process of law; nor deny to any person within its jurisdiction the equal protection of the laws."

U.S. CONST. amend. XIV, § 1 (1868)

Table of Contents

Preface: Why This Book Was Written

Before I explain why this book was written, I had better explain what this book is about. What I hope to accomplish is to propose, in a somewhat polemical way, the essentials of a general theory of the constitutional rights of the American people (i.e., the citizens of the United States). This theory *should be* accepted by the Supreme Court as being the most textually plausible model of the relevant constitutional provisions, and sufficiently harmonious with the lower order judicial doctrines concerning concrete legal issues that any general theory should adequately explain and harmonize.[1] In addition, very importantly, the general theory proposed in this book fully coheres with the principles of popular sovereignty and republicanism, federalism and national unity, and separation of powers that inform the Constitution as a charter of powers for the American commonwealth and a charter of rights and liberties for the American people. Keep in mind that the general theory of constitutional rights as expounded in this book is not an historical treatise. Nor is it a systematic treatise on what is the constitutional law as determined by the Supreme Court and other appellate courts, with modestly proposed criticisms and suggestions about how it might be improved concerning this or that detail.

However unlikely it is that the Court would adopt the general theory of this book, I believe it is not an idle enterprise to advocate what ideally should be constitutional law concerning this or that matter. For instance, witness how the Court had (following the adoption of the Fourteenth Amendment) first declared that the First Amendment freedoms of speech and the press were not protected at all against state abridgment by the Fourteenth Amendment, but then later ruled that they were fully protected by that amendment. Another relevant and glaring example is how the Court first adhered to the separate-but-equal doctrine in issues pertaining to racial discrimination, but later repudiated that doctrine.[2] While the reader might be disposed to reject the general theory of this book as a whole, he or she might well find merit in some of the ideas expounded herein. Alternatively, the reader may value this book if only because of its possible soporific qualities.

I strongly hold that judicial review is essential to the proper functioning of our constitutional order. It is much better than not that the Supreme Court rules on constitutional issues, even though, like all human institutions, it is fallible and even sometimes abuses its authority. However, justices, like all judges, usually work within constraints—such as the doctrine of *stare decisis*, so generally (but not without exception) needful to ensure stability in the law. Settled judicial doctrines are not lightly to be overturned simply because, by hindsight, one concludes that it would have been better had the Court adopted a different doctrine. A justice, quite understandably, will ordinarily not actively seek a reversal of a precedent unless he is assured of support from some colleagues. The members of the Court bring to the bench their respective fundamental beliefs about what constitutes the good society. So the reader is asked to keep in mind that, although at times I sharply criticize the Court for such-and-such decisions, my overall intention is not to personally censure its members simply for holding what I believe are erroneous opinions. In this, my enterprise, I am encouraged by the words of Justice David J. Brewer, delivered in his Lincoln Day address of 1898:

> It is a mistake to suppose that the Supreme Court is either honored or helped by being spoken of as beyond criticism. On the contrary, the life and character of its justices should be the objects of constant watchfulness by all, and its judgments subject to the freest criticism. The time is past in the history of the world when any living man or body of men can be set on a pedestal and decorated with a halo. True, many criticisms may be, like their authors, devoid of good taste, but better all sorts of criticism than no criticism at all. The moving waters are full of life and health; only in still waters is stagnation and death.[3]

The Constitution of the United States, as originally adopted in 1788, did not include provisions prohibiting infringements by the United States (or by the states) of such essential substantive rights as religious freedom, freedom of speech and of the press, or of all those procedural rights encompassed by the right not to be deprived of life, liberty, or property without due process of law. Amendments I–VIII (the Bill of Rights) were adopted in 1791 to remedy the defect.[4] Nevertheless, quite correctly, the Supreme Court has consistently ruled that the provisions of the Bill of Rights do not apply to the states. Following the Civil War, the Thirteenth Amendment, abolishing slavery and involuntary servitude (save as punishment for crime), was adopted in 1865. In 1868, the Fourteenth Amendment was adopted.[5] Section 1 of that amendment provides that: "All persons born or naturalized in the United States and subject to the jurisdiction thereof, are citizens of the United States, and of the State wherein they reside. No State shall make or enforce any law which shall abridge the privileges or immunities of citizens of the United States; nor shall any State deprive any person of life, liberty, or property, without due process of law; nor deny to any person within its jurisdiction the equal protection of the laws." There is virtually universal agreement that the adoption of the Fourteenth Amendment effected the incorporation of at least some rights specified in the Bill of Rights. But, which specific rights? And by what constitutional provision?

Thus, before the adoption of the Fourteenth Amendment, it was not a violation of the United States Constitution for any state to violate religious freedom, or freedom of speech or of the press, or to deprive persons within its jurisdiction of rights encompassed by only the specific right of the due process clause. However, the Court has since ruled that the Fourteenth Amendment due process clause incorporates most rights specified in the Bill of Rights, and thus each such incorporated right is as fully protected against violations by the states as it is against violations by the United States.

Let us, for example, take for granted that the First Amendment prohibits Congress from enacting a law forbidding the publication of atheist propaganda in what would otherwise be in the lawful exercise of its powers. But before 1868 a state law that forbade the publication of atheist propaganda would not have violated the Constitution. However, the comity clause in the original Constitution (art. IV, § 2, cl. 1) provides that the citizens of each state shall be entitled to the privileges and immunities of the citizens of the several states. This provision has been judicially construed such that were state A's constitution, for example, to prohibit the state from abridging freedoms of religion and expression in religious matters of its citizens, then citizens of other states, while present in state A, would be equally protected concerning the same matter. Nevertheless, the comity clause itself does not protect the citizens of state A against violations of that state's constitutional provisions securing freedom of religion or expression in religious matters.

When we examine the meaning, purposes, functions, scope, and limits of a particular right protected by the United States Constitution, we are concerned with a *special* theory of that right. One could, of course, write a more- or less-extensive treatise setting forth the special theory about every major particular right secured by the Constitution. However, this book is not a treatise that systematically expounds a special theory of any constitutional right. I discuss the special theory of any right only insofar as it is relevant to the purpose of this book, which is to set forth a general theory of the constitutional rights, privileges, and immunities of the American people. This book explores the structure and interrelationships of constitutional rights. To do so, we discuss some aspects of some special theories of constitutional rights in order to insure a sufficient universe of discourse. My strategy is to show that the sound formulation of the special theory of any particular constitutional right presupposes, in part, a sound formulation of the general theory of constitutional rights.

Proper to a special theory of religious freedom would be to ascertain what are, and what are not, the components of that right. Does the right of religious freedom encompass as a component the right not to be criminally prosecuted for the bona fide use of a particular drug (such as peyote) in the course of a religious ritual in a place of public worship? Does the right of freedom of the press include as a component the right to freely publish pictorial pornography? These are important and interesting questions. Nevertheless, I shall certainly maintain (at least for the purposes of argument) some things about various rights, because it seems to me, there must be some outside parameters or markers of what we mean, for example, by *religious freedom* to develop a satisfactory general theory of constitutional rights of the American people. However, proper to the general theory of constitutional rights would be an inquiry about why religious freedom may be constitutionally abridged neither by the United States nor by the several states. Nevertheless, the general theory of constitutional rights that I propose is rather open-textured with respect to many concrete issues pertaining to what should or should not be embraced by some special theory of any particular constitutional right.

What are the *constitutional rights of the American people?* They are all those legal rights that are secured or granted by the Constitution for the American people (and, in some cases, for persons other than American citizens, depending upon the nature of the particular right in question) against violations by the United States—even though some particular right is not also protected by the Constitution against violations by the states. And so, for example, the freedoms of speech and of the press were, before the adoption of the Fourteenth Amendment, constitutional rights of the American people by virtue of the First Amendment, even though the Constitution did not then prohibit their violation by the states. The right of a person not to be deprived of life, liberty, or property without due process of law was also a constitutional right of the American people by virtue of the Fifth Amendment due process clause before the Fourteenth Amendment was adopted. However, now it is also a right of all persons subject to the jurisdiction of the United States that is secured against violations by any state. The reader will notice that section 1 of the Fourteenth Amendment prohibits the states from denying the equal protection of the laws to any persons within their respective jurisdictions. There is no constitutional provision that expressly prohibits the United States from denying the equal protection of the laws to any persons within their respective jurisdiction. Let us assume, just for the sake of exposition, that the right of a person not to be denied the equal protection of the laws is not a component of any specific constitutional right fully protected against violation by the United States.[6] Then, according to my usage, the constitutional right not to be denied the equal protection of the laws would not belong to the class of the *constitutional rights of the American people*. Rather, it would be one of *constitutional rights of the peoples of the several states.*

I make frequent reference in this book to specific rights in the Constitution. For example, freedom of speech is a specific right; that is, the First Amendment expressly specifies this right. Yet it is possible for one specific right to be a component of another specific right. For example, the specific right of the just compensation clause of the Fifth Amendment is judicially held (and rightly so) to be a component of the specific right of the Fourteenth Amendment due process clause. According to the current doctrine of the Supreme Court, the specific right of the Fourteenth Amendment due process clause incorporates the specific rights of the free exercise, free speech, free press, and the assembly-petition clauses. The specific right of the free speech provision in the First Amendment is the freedom of speech. The specific right of the due process clause of the fifth or Fourteenth Amendment is the right not to be deprived of life, liberty, or property without due process of law. Each specific right consists of component rights. Thus, for example (assuming the Court's current doctrine), the specific right of the Fourteenth Amendment due process clause has as a component the right that freedom of speech not be abridged.

In speaking of *specific rights*, I must at the outset present the reader with a terminological qualification. I shall refer at times to the specific right of the free exercise clause. A commonly held opinion appears to be that what we generally understand as religious freedom is identical with the specific right of the free exercise clause. However, suppose it is not; and, indeed, this is the current doctrine of the Supreme Court.[7] It then follows that religious freedom is not a right specified as such in the First Amendment, although the specific right of the free exercise clause would be a major component. However, it is nevertheless true that religious freedom is secured against all abridgments by the First Amendment because the term also encompasses all other freedom-rights in matters of religion that are the components of other rights specified in the First Amendment and all those freedom-rights in religious matters entailed by the establishment clause. Thus, whatever components of the specific rights of free speech and free press are freedom-rights concerning religious matters, then these components are also components of the right of religious freedom secured by the First Amendment against abridgment by Congress. Given the foregoing, I shall frequently indulge (for the sake of convenience) in the practice of referring to religious freedom as a specific right (adding, at times, "of the First Amendment") in the interest of brevity. It seems to me a legitimate practice because it would be quite natural to impute, for the sake of convenience and economy of expression, to the free exercise clause the protection of all the components of the right of religious freedom.

The terms *rights*, *privileges*, and *immunities* are ambiguous. So are composite terms such as *privileges and immunities,* as used in the comity clause (art. 4, § 2, cl. 1) in the original Constitution, or *privileges or immunities,* as used in the privileges or immunities clause of the Fourteenth Amendment. Generally, when I use the term *rights*, I shall use it often in a generic sense. However, I shall frequently also use the term *rights* in much more limited senses when I discuss the privileges and immunities of American citizens. For, in my view, although freedom of speech and the specific right of the just compensation clause (Fifth Amendment) are both *rights* in a generic sense, freedom of speech is a *privilege* (i.e., a legal freedom) but not a *right* in the stricter sense in which the specific right of the just compensation clause is a *right* in some stricter sense.

Constitutional privileges (i.e., freedoms) are best understood as pertaining to certain domains in which one is constitutionally free to do or not do x. Constitutional immunities (i.e., freedom-from rights) are best understood as pertaining to certain domains in which one is constitutionally exempt from a burden, disadvantage, or obligation typically based upon status or class membership. Freedoms and freedom-from rights belong to the class of so-called *natural rights* insofar as this term is understood in the social compact theory of government.[8] But, as I see it, some *natural rights* (as so understood) are neither freedoms nor freedom-from rights. Constitutional *rights* (in one stricter sense) include (but are not limited), to use the words of James Madison, "positive rights, which may seem to result from the nature of the social compact." Thus, for example, "[t]rial by jury cannot be understood as a natural right, but a right resulting from a social compact which regulates the action of the community, but is essential to secure the liberty of the people as any right of the pre-existent rights of nature."[9] So, indeed, some constitutional rights of the American people are positive rights. All the components of the specific rights of the Third, Fourth, Fifth, Sixth, Seventh, and Eighth Amendments are constitutional rights, but not privileges or immunities, of the American people because each is either essentially or predominantly procedural or remedial, or pertains to law enforcement or the administration of justice, or specially provides for the security of person or property. The class of constitutional rights (in a stricter sense) includes the right of civil parties to sue and be sued in federal courts,[10] the "Privilege of the Writ of Habeas Corpus,"[11] the personal rights entailed by the prohibitions against bills of attainder and ex post facto laws by the Congress and the states,[12] and immunities from discrimination concerning the political right to vote based upon race, color, or previous condition of servitude,[13] sex,[14] failure to pay poll tax or other tax,[15] age of less than eighteen years.[16] There are others. However, some constitutional *rights* of the American people (according to the Court's current doctrine) are not secured against abridgment by the states—such as the specific right of the Fifth Amendment grand jury clause and that of the Seventh Amendment (jury trial in civil cases). It should be noted that some constitutional rights, privileges, and immunities of the American people are exclusively theirs, whereas others are not. Thus, for example, religious freedom is a constitutional privilege of the American people that is not exclusively theirs.

The constitutional privileges and immunities of the American people are especially important freedoms and freedom-from rights that are fully secured by the Constitution against abridgment by the United States. These freedoms and freedom-from rights are secured, in my opinion, against abridgment by the states via the privileges or immunities clause. Most obviously, the freedoms of the First Amendment are constitutional privileges (in the requisite sense) because they are secured against abridgments by Congress for important public policy reasons, in addition to the need to sufficiently protect whatever components of these rights are among the essential badges and incidents of free persons as such, and thus proximately sounding in human dignity. The privileges or immunities clause presupposes that, before the adoption of the Fourteenth Amendment, there were privileges and immunities of American citizens that could not be constitutionally abridged by the United States—even though they could then be constitutionally abridged by the individual states.

According to the Court, the First Amendment freedoms (as well as some other freedoms and freedom-from rights) are secured against abridgment by the states via the due process clause of the Fourteenth Amendment. These freedoms as well as some other rights, according to the Court, are secured against abridgment because the fundamental constitutional principles underlying our civil and political institutions are embodied, as it were, by the due process clause of the Fourteenth Amendment, and these fundamental constitutional principles warrant, if not require, very broad and sweeping limitations upon the scope of governmental powers.

Although I do not believe that the Fourteenth Amendment due process clause incorporates any First Amendment freedom, I believe that there are substantive rights pertaining to religion and expression that are protected by the due process clauses independently of the First Amendment and the privileges or immunities clause of the Fourteenth Amendment. The substantive aspects of the due process clauses pertain to those fundamental rights, privileges, and immunities of free persons as such that obtain by virtue of that universal civil freedom established by the Thirteenth Amendment's abolition of slavery and involuntary servitude. Such rights are proximately based upon the dignity of free persons as rational, social, and moral agents. Because, in my opinion, the due process clauses are not charged with incorporating the freedoms of the First Amendment, the role of the due process clauses vis-à-vis their substantive aspects should remain important but relatively modest—given federalism, the separation-of-powers principle, and the republican and secular form of our governments as essential features of our political institutions.

A textualist approach, when considering the Bill of Rights synoptically with section 1 of the Fourteenth Amendment, easily leads to the conclusion that the most probable hypothesis about the meaning of the Fourteenth Amendment's first section is that the freedoms specified in the First Amendment are the only specific rights in the Bill of Rights incorporated by the privileges or immunities clause. However, according to the Court, the due process clause of the Fourteenth Amendment incorporates the First Amendment freedoms and most other personal rights secured in the Bill of Rights. Nevertheless, the selective incorporation theory of the Court has many serious analytical defects. Surely, there is sufficient evidence to show that one important original understanding of the founders of the Fourteenth Amendment was that the privileges or immunities clause incorporates the First Amendment freedoms. And there is no substantial evidence whatsoever that there was any original understanding that the due process clause of the Fourteenth Amendment incorporates any First Amendment freedom or any other right specified in the Bill of Rights other than those understood to be also already embodied by the Fifth Amendment due process clause.

In speaking of the founders' original understanding of the Constitution (or the amendments thereto), we are not speaking of only the framers' intent. Evidence of such intent is, of course, relevant, but not exclusively so, in determining the intent of the founders since, for example, ratification of a proposed amendment by the legislatures or conventions of three-quarters of the states is constitutionally required. As Justice Joseph Story so wisely counseled about the interpretation of constitutional provisions, "The people make them, the people adopt them, the people must be supposed to read them, with the help of common-sense, and cannot be presumed to admit in them any recondite meaning or any extraordinary gloss."[17] He cautions that "[i]n the first place ... every word employed in the Constitution is to be expounded in its plain, obvious, and common sense, unless the context furnishes some ground to control, qualify, or enlarge it."[18]

One essential question for us is, by what theory does this incorporation most credibly obtain? And, thus, another is, what are the constitutional rights of the American people other than those of the First Amendment that are incorporated by the privileges or immunities clause? In large measure, the construction of a sound general theory of the constitutional rights of the American people involves consideration of issues pertaining to the credibility of the Constitution and of the Supreme Court for the general public. Failure to hold to a sound general theory of constitutional rights hinders the evolution of constitutional law in wholesome ways. For example, because the Court holds that it is the Fourteenth Amendment due process clause that incorporates the First Amendment freedoms, there has been and continues to be a very marked tendency for the Court to invest the due process clauses with a much greater potency than they should ideally have in a democratic republic.

I do not claim that the general theory of the constitutional rights of the American people outlined in this book is radically novel. Indeed, I regard it as a development of the contributions of such scholars as Charles Fairman, Howard Graham, Earl M. Maltz, and

Jacobus tenBroek, who also maintained some version of the thesis that the privileges or immunities clause incorporates some but not all rights specified in the Bill of Rights.

Even during the time I attended law school (1953–56), I had become very troubled by how the Supreme Court had eventually come to adopt the doctrine that the Fourteenth Amendment incorporates some but not all rights specified in the Bill of Rights, thus making them fully secure against all infringements by the states. The Supreme Court, having virtually neutered the privileges or immunities clause in the famous *Slaughter-House Cases*[19] of 1873, eventually came to use the Fourteenth Amendment's due process clause as the vehicle of incorporation of some rights specified by the Bill of Rights. Very early on, I concluded that the Court's theory of incorporation is seriously riddled with flaws. I marveled, and still do, about how many people who pride themselves as civil libertarians so docilely accept the Court's official theory of incorporation, instead of being scandalized by it, since it offers an intellectually and polemically insecure foundation for the constitutional rights of the American people. How is it possible for the Fourteenth Amendment due process clause to be regarded as the vehicle of incorporation of the freedoms secured against abridgment by the First Amendment? Ostensibly, the due process clauses of the Fifth and Fourteenth Amendments are equivalent in meaning. Yet, surely, the specific right of the due process clause of the Fifth Amendment does not incorporate religious freedom or freedom of speech or of the press. This is surely bizarre and should be mystifying to all thoughtful citizens. Moreover, although a due process clause appears both in the Bill of Rights and in section 1 of the Fourteenth Amendment, the privileges or immunities clause has presently an essentially unimportant function in constitutional law.

Very early on also, I concluded that the most probable model is to regard the privileges or immunities clause of the Fourteenth Amendment as the vehicle of selective incorporation of the Bill of Rights. I came to hold that the only specific rights in the Bill of Rights that are incorporated by the privileges or immunities clause are the freedoms of the First Amendment. However, some but not all rights secured in the Bill of Rights are components of the due process clause of Fourteenth Amendment (and, therefore, also that of the Fifth Amendment due process clause). But, of course, there are (and in a sense there must be) some constitutional rights of the American people not secured by the First Amendment that are embraced by the privileges or immunities clause. In the course of my legal and historical studies, I discovered what appears to have been much neglected: that the term *privileges or immunities of citizens of the United States* has an ancestral line found in some treaties and statutes of the United States in force before the adoption of the Fourteenth Amendment. This ancestral line, I believe, provides compelling evidence that confirms the thesis that the privileges or immunities clause incorporates some rights specified in the Bill of Rights.

In 1985, I authored an article in which I criticized the Court's theory in detail, proposed an alternative selective incorporation theory, presented the evidences of the true ancestral line of the privileges or immunities clause, and insisted upon the equivalence of the due process clauses of the Fifth and Fourteenth Amendments, and that these clauses have substantive aspects.[20] Since then, I have continued to study the relevant issues, especially since my retirement in 1993 from the district attorney's office of Los Angeles County. Unfortunately, I have not been able to get a very long article (the basis of this book) published in law journals. Time marches on, so I have decided to extend my article to more thoroughly address the issues covered by my 1985 article, because so much has happened since its publication.

Part I of this book focuses upon rights specified in the Bill of Rights. Part II considers in detail whether national citizenship, before the Civil War, was paramount and superior, and what constitutional rights other than the First Amendment freedoms are secured by the Constitution against abridgement by the United States and should be deemed incorporated by the privileges or immunities clause. Especially important in Part II is the exposition of the thesis that freedom from racial and other ethnic discrimination is a constitutional immunity of the American people grounded in the notion of national citizenship embodied in the citizenship clause of the Fourteenth

Amendment. Part III addresses the procedural and substantive aspects of the due process clauses. Part IV recites the textualist and nontextualist reasons for accepting the general theory of this book.

Hopefully, no reader will be unduly alarmed by the general theory of the constitutional rights of the American people proposed in this book. It is, as I say, rather open-textured within fairly broad limits about the concrete details of the special theory of each such right. The most knotty problems pertain to the establishment clause of the First Amendment, which will need careful examination. With a bit of tweaking and poking, most current doctrines concerning particular constitutional rights about concrete issues can be harmonized with the general theory expounded in my book. However, I maintain that it is very important to have a sound general theory, because otherwise the evolution of constitutional law is attended with anomalous and even bizarre features. Among the chief anomalies has been how the Fourteenth Amendment due process clause has recurrently been assigned a grossly inflated meaning to accommodate the incorporation of the establishment clause, the First Amendment freedoms, and some other rights specified in the Bill of Rights. Indeed, such incorporation via the Fourteenth Amendment due process clause was only possible because the Court had already inflated the substantive aspects of the due process clauses to accommodate the so-called liberty of contract, which proved to be a serious impediment to enacting rational legislation in the domain of economic and social welfare policy.[21] Ironically, the regime of the liberty of contract continued to flourish almost contemporaneously with the acceleration of the process of selective incorporation via the due process clause (Fourteenth Amendment) of the specific rights of the First Amendment.[22]

In writing this book, I have found it very useful to interact with Professor Akhil Reed Amar's interesting and intellectually challenging book, *The Bill of Rights: Creation and Reconstruction,*[23] in which he addresses the question of whether and how the Fourteenth Amendment incorporates individual rights secured in the Bill of Rights. Amar maintains that the privileges or immunities clause incorporates all these rights, but does so in such a nuanced fashion that the process has filtered out, as it were, extraneous elements in each relevant constitutional provision pertaining to states' or collective rights, or federal-state jurisdictional aspects. So the reader should be aware that Amar's use of the term *incorporates* differs from the conventional usage in that he would insist that a specific right in the Bill of Rights can be said to be *incorporated,* even if only some, but not all, of its components are protected by the privileges or immunities clause. Contrary to his usage, I follow the standard usage and speak of a right specified in the Bill of Rights as being *incorporated* if and only if each and every component right is equally secured and protected by the Fourteenth Amendment.

Those (including me) who favor a selective-incorporation theory of the privileges or immunities clause, those (such as Michael Kent Curtis) who adhere to the total-incorporation theory, and even those (such as Amar) who maintain a refined-incorporation model, have much more in common than what divides us. First and foremost, we share the conviction that it is the privileges or immunities clause, rather than the due process clause, of the Fourteenth Amendment that should be deemed as the vehicle of incorporation of the freedoms of the First Amendment. Another shared conviction is that the privileges or immunities clause embraces some rights secured against abridgment by the United States by the Constitution, other than the First Amendment freedoms. Areas of disagreement chiefly pertain to the identity of these other rights incorporated by the privileges or immunities clause.

I had initially delayed completing this book because otherwise, during development or shortly before or after the publication of this book, the Supreme Court would have decided a very important case.[24] I refer to *District of Columbia* v. *Heller,* No. 07-290 (*cert. granted,* November 30, 2007 and argued on March 18, 2008). The issue to be decided in *Heller* was whether District of Columbia legislation violates the Second Amendment rights of individuals who are not affiliated with any state-regulated militia, but who wish to keep handguns and other firearms for private use in their homes. The United States Court of Appeals for the District of Columbia Circuit had ruled in this case (*sub. nom., Parker* v. *District of Columbia,* 478 F.3d 370 (March 9, 2007)) that the Second Amendment protects an individual civil right to possess handguns in homes for private use and that the District of Columbia legislation unreasonably regulated that right by totally banning such possession (with certain exceptions) of handguns in private homes for private use. The ruling by the circuit court of appeal broke with the virtually solid position taken by the federal courts of appeal that had accepted the collective-rights model of the Second Amendment, according to which the right to keep and bear arms is predicable of only individuals in direct affiliation with a well-organized, state-supported militia.

The eagerly awaited decision in *Heller* appeared on June 26, 2008. In a five-to-four decision, the Court, in an opinion delivered by Justice Scalia, ruled that the Second Amendment protects an individual right to possess a firearm for personal purposes and is thus unconnected with militia service. The Court held that the Second Amendment was violated by the District of Columbia's total ban on handguns, as well by its requirement that firearms in the home be kept nonfunctional even when necessary for self-defense. In my opinion, the Second Amendment right is not incorporated by either the privileges or immunities clause or the due process clause of the Fourteenth Amendment. I address this issue in Chapter D of Part I.

The book, as the reader will readily and perhaps sadly discover, is very heavily end noted. Although there are many serious writers who think the fewer and shorter notes the better, I think my book (given its comprehensive subject matter and purpose) calls for it to be heavily end noted for the benefit of many readers who may be interested in the supplemental matter contained in the notes. Some readers might nevertheless object, perhaps borrowing the words of Holy Roman Emperor Joseph II to Wolfgang Amadeus Mozart in the film *Amadeus* (about the composer's opera "Die Entfurung aus dem Serail ["The Abduction from the Seraglio"]), that "[t]here are too many notes." To this objection, I reply (as Mozart did to the emperor): "There are just as many notes ... as are required. Neither more nor less." [25] Nevertheless, some readers may perhaps prefer to read through the entire text of this book without regularly consulting the endnotes. Despite the numerous endnotes, and the gaffes and glitches that the alert and learned reader may notice, I nevertheless hope that my book will not fall "stillborn from the press"—unlike the first printing of David Hume's *Treatise on Human Nature.*

I also hope that readers, even those who sharply disagree with some of the opinions expressed, will not fail to be charitable in interpreting what I have to say and avoid either rashly seeing what is not there or not seeing what is there. As James Madison justly remarked: "[N]o language is so copious as to supply words and phrases for every complex idea, or so correct as not to include many equivocally different ideas."[26] As Alexis de Tocqueville so well explained in his celebrated *De la Démocratie en Amérique,* "The expression is the exterior form, but if I may express myself in this way, the body of the thought, but it is not the thought itself."[27]

In writing this book, I am deeply aware of my indebtedness to named jurists and writers whose views I accept, as well as to those whose views I criticize. If I am now reasonably sure of the soundness of the fundamentals of the general theory of constitutional rights of the American people that I expound and advocate in this book, it is because I have exposed myself and taken very seriously and respectfully the views of such able scholars as Akhil Reed Amar and Michael Kent Curtis, as well as others, with whom I have come to disagree upon crucial matters. This book does not explicitly consider the important writings of some important jurists and scholars concerning the constitutional rights of the American people. However, I think that sometimes, it is more useful to focus on a few writers to sharpen the issues and better develop and expound one's own position than to canvas the views of many others.

In reading this book, again bear in mind that it presents the essentials of a theory about how the Constitution should be judicially interpreted. I am quite aware that it is unlikely that the Court will explicitly revise its general theory of constitutional rights. Nevertheless, it is important for citizens to express their considered opinions about what the constitutional law should be with the hope that publication of their views may have some impact on the way constitutional law may be shaped in the future. Moreover, it may be helpful to those who are, or will be, in the executive, legislative, and judicial branches of government in exercising their governmental powers. In the end, there is always the real possibility, however remote, that the Court will change its mind after a realization that the general theory of constitutional rights now extant is radically defective. Moreover, I feel that I must satisfy my need to complain about how badly, in some very important respects, the Court has gone about the task of interpreting the Constitution as a charter of the rights, privileges, and immunities of the American people.

Last, but not least, I should like to express my profound gratitude to my wife, Annegret, who has constantly encouraged me to fulfill my destiny. I especially appreciate her support because, unlike me, she chose to be an American citizen (having emigrated here from Bremen, Germany) and thus became entitled to all the constitutional rights, privileges, and immunities of the American people. In the same vein, I feel grateful that my grandparents, Józefa (z domu Typerówna) and Jacób Gumiński, and Stanisława (z domu Ciesielska) and Jan Radziwon, chose to immigrate to the United States in the late nineteenth century from then so-called Austrian Poland (Józefa from Przesław, Jacób from Kolbuszowa) and so-called Russian Poland (Stanisława from Słupce, Jan from Ciechanowiec), and eventually became American citizens. Similarly, I feel grateful to my deceased parents, Thaddeus and Tessie Guminski, who supported and encouraged my education through law school—thus enabling me to equip myself to better discover what it means to be an American citizen and a free person. It still moves me when I remember that Annegret and my mother, with David (my older brother) and Leiko (his Japanese-born wife and naturalized American citizen), were present both times when I, the grandson of Polish immigrants, argued before the United States Supreme Court in 1987 and 1989.

Arnold T. Guminski

November 5, 2008

Boulder, Colorado

Endnotes to Preface

1. At all times (unless otherwise stated), I mean to refer only to the rights secured or granted by the United States Constitution. However, we should not fail to recall that there are rights secured against violations by the constitutions of the individual states. Hence, in speaking of constitutional rights and other legal rights, in all cases, unless otherwise indicated, I am speaking of rights held only as against the State and not as against private persons.

2. The Fourteenth Amendment was adopted in 1868, but it was not until 1925 that the Court, in Gitlow v. New York, 268 U.S. 652, acknowledged (albeit by obiter dictum) that the Fourteenth Amendment due process clause protected the First Amendment freedoms. In 1896 the Court adopted the infamous separate-but-equal doctrine in Plessy v. Ferguson, 163 U.S. 537. But already, in Pace v Alabama, 106 U.S. 583 (1893), the Court had ruled that a statute that banned adultery, fornication, and interracial marriage did not violate the equal protection clause as applied to a white-black couple living in adultery or fornication because it imposed penalties more severe upon an interracial couple than to parties both of the same race. The process of purging the separate-but-equal doctrine from the corpus of constitutional law was not begun in earnest until 1954, when the Court decided Brown v. Board of Education, 347 U.S. 483.

3. "Government by Injunction," 15 Nat. Corp. Rep. 849 (1898).

4. Some jurists and writers refer to amendments I–X as the Bill of Rights. Amendment IX (unenumerated rights provision), according to some jurists and commentators is just a rule of construction. (This is my view.) But others maintain that it has an independent function in safeguarding rights. Amendment X (reserved powers provision) pertains only to the reserved powers of the states or of the people. Hence, it does not pertain to individual rights.

5. I shall assume that the reader is sufficiently familiar with American history, or can conveniently refresh his memory, so that I need not burden this book with background historical information, especially about the reconstruction era following the Civil War. However, it may be useful to have easy access to the background information; and this is readily available online at http://en.wikipedia.org/wiki/Reconstruction_era_of_ the_United_States. Reconstruction: America's Unfinished Revolution 1863–1877 (New York: Harper & Row, 1988) by Eric Foner is a very good, comprehensive political and social history of the reconstruction era.

6. But the Court has explained in Hampton v. Mow Sun Wong, 426 U.S. 88, 100n17 (1976): "Since the Due Process Clause appears in both the Fifth and Fourteenth Amendments, whereas the Equal Protection Clause

does not, it is quite clear that the primary office of the latter differs from, and is additive to, the protection guaranteed by the former." However, as was explained in the text: "there may be overriding national interests that justify selective federal legislation that would be unacceptable for an individual State. On the other hand, when a federal rule is applicable to only a limited territory, such as the District of Columbia, or an insular possession, and when there is no special national interest involved, the Due Process Clause has been construed as having the same significance as the Equal Protection Clause." Ibid., 100.

7. See Employment Division v. Smith, 494 U.S. 872, 881–82 (1990); City of Boerne v. Flores, 521 U.S. 507, 513–14 (1997).

8. There is another, very important, sense of the term natural rights that pertains to rights grounded upon the exigencies of human dignity rather than upon some social-compact theory of the origins of the State, and of the scope and limits of its sovereign powers. There is much overlap between the domains of the two notions of natural rights. I shall ordinarily use the term natural rights as pertaining to rights proximately (i.e., closely) grounded upon the exigencies of human dignity rather than the social-compact notion.

9. Annals of Congress (J. Gales ed. 1789), 1: 453.

10. U.S. CONST. art. III, § 1.

11. Ibid., art. I, § 9, cl. 2.

12. Ibid., art. I, § 9, cl.. 3, and § 10, cl. 1.

13. Ibid., amend. XV, § 1 (adopted 1865).

14. Ibid., amend. XIX (adopted 1920).

15. Ibid., amend. XXIV, § 1 (adopted 1964).

16. Ibid., amend. XXVI, § 1 (adopted 1971).

17. Joseph Story, Commentaries on the Constitution of the United States; With a Preliminary Review of the Constitutional History of the United States before the Adoption of the Constitution (Boston: Hilliard, Gray, 1833), 1: §451. Joseph Story (1779–1845) was associate justice of the Supreme Court from 1811 to 1845. His treatise on the Constitution (first published in 1833) was regarded as a work of profound learning and remained a standard treatise on the subject for many decades.

18. Ibid.

19. 83 U.S. (16 Wall.) 36.

20. Arnold T. Guminski, "The Rights, Privileges, and Immunities of the American People: A Disjunctive Theory of Selective Incorporation of the Bill of Rights." 7 Whittier L. Rev. 765–826 (1985).

21. The so-called liberty of contract, which seriously inhibited the enactment or enforcement of rational legislation in the domain of economic

and social welfare policy, was inaugurated in 1896 in the case of Allgeyer v. Louisiana, 165 U.S. 578, but judicially defanged in 1937 by the Court's decision in West Coast Hotel Co. v. Parrish, 300 U.S. 379.

22. See Gitlow v. New York, supra (1925); Fiske v. Kansas, 274 U.S. 380 (1927); Grosjean v. American Press Co., 297 U.S. 233 (1936); DeJonge v. Oregon, 295 U.S. 353 (1937).

23. (New Haven: Yale University Press, 1998). Professor Amar also has also discussed the constitutional rights of the American people in his more recently published book America's Constitution; A Biography (New York: Random House Trade Paperbacks, 2006), and in numerous articles.

24. I had further delayed submission to the publisher in order to await the outcome of the 2008 presidential elections.

25. See www.toomanynotes.com/Amadeus.htm.

26. The Federalist (ed. Jacob E. Cooke) (Cleveland: Meridian Books, 1961), No. 37, p. 236.

27. (ed. J.-P. Mayer) (Éditions Gallimard, 1961), 1: 186: "L'expression est la forme extérieure et, si je puis m'exprimer ainsi, le corps de la pensée, mais elle n'est pas la pensée elle-même."

Part I

THE PRIVILEGES OR IMMUNITIES CLAUSE AS A VEHICLE OF SELECTIVE INCORPORATION OF THE BILL OF RIGHTS

Introduction: Summary of the Court's Current Doctrine on Selective Incorporation

The provisions of the Bill of Rights (amendments I–VIII; adopted 1791) of the Constitution of the United States as such apply to and limit only the United States.[1] It was in 1868, with the adoption of the Fourteenth Amendment, that some rights specified in the Bill of Rights became as fully protected against violations by the states as they are against violations by the United States.[2] According to the United States Supreme Court, it is the due process clause, rather than the privileges or immunities clause, of the Fourteenth Amendment that incorporates the First Amendment freedoms and most of the specific rights of the remaining provisions of the Bill of Rights.[3]

This is so notwithstanding the presence of a due process clause in the Fifth Amendment. According to the Court's current doctrine, the privileges or immunities clause is incapable of incorporating any right specified in the Bill of Rights because it embraces only such rights possessed by American citizens that arise out of the nature and essential character of the national government, and are granted or secured by the Constitution to such citizens.[4] The only rights specified in the Bill of Rights that the Court holds to be incorporated by the due process clause of the Fourteenth Amendment are those that are fundamental.[5] A fundamental right, in the sense intended, is one that "cannot be denied without violating those 'fundamental principles of liberty and justice which lie at the base of all our civil and political institutions.'"[6]

The Supreme Court currently holds, or strongly indicates, that the Fourteenth Amendment due process clause incorporates the following specific rights: the rights specified in the First,[7] Fourth,[8] Fifth (except that of the grand jury clause),[9] Sixth,[10] and Eighth[11] Amendments. The Fifth Amendment grand-jury right[12] and the Seventh Amendment civil-jury right[13] have been held to be unincorporated. The specific right of the Third Amendment is surely one that should be deemed incorporated by the Fourteenth Amendment due process clause, but the Court has not had occasion thus far to definitively consider the issue.[14] The Court has never ruled on whether the Second Amendment right (SAR) is incorporated by the Fourteenth Amendment due process clause.

The reader should be aware that it is only a *façon de parler* (that is, a manner of speaking) whenever some jurists and writers talk about a state law violating a First Amendment freedom or some other incorporated specific right of the Bill of Rights. The practice is a very bad one since it misleads many persons into thinking that, for example, the First Amendment free speech provision itself now applies to the states. However, a state law abridging freedom of speech does not actually violate the First Amendment. Rather, it violates the Fourteenth Amendment due process clause, because, according to the Court, that clause incorporates the First Amendment freedom of speech.

Chapter A. Professor Amar's Refined Incorporation Theory

In his important book, *The Bill of Rights: Creation and Reconstruction,*[15] Professor Akhil Reed Amar presents a theory of (what he calls) *refined* incorporation of the Bill of Rights by the privileges or immunities clause. Essentially, he holds that the privileges or immunities clause incorporates every personal civil right that is explicitly or implicitly secured in the Bill of Rights, as well as elsewhere in the Constitution. According to Amar, the privileges or immunities clause does not incorporate the rights of states, nor does it incorporate collective rights (i.e., those of the public at large or those of the people, considered as a collectivity), or individual political rights (e.g., the right to vote, hold public office, serve on the jury or in the militia).[16] Nevertheless, Amar rightly observes, "To view an entitlement as a private right is not to deny that it may have public or political significance but only to recognize that it is a right vested in discrete individuals."[17]

What Amar repudiates is a notion of what he calls *mechanical* incorporation, by virtue of which every component of a specific right in the Bill of Rights deemed incorporated by the privileges or immunities clause is itself incorporated by that clause.[18] Hence, Amar's refined incorporation model is not to be confused with the total incorporation model of such scholars as Michael Kent Curtis[19] or the selective incorporation model proposed in this book. According to Amar's esoteric and misleading usage, the privileges or immunities clause could incorporate some but not all components of a particular right specified in the Bill of Rights. Amar thinks so because he maintains that not every component of a specific right is necessarily a civil right of an individual.[20] The reader should be aware, therefore, that Amar does not hold that a specific right is *incorporated* in the sense that all its components are as well secured by the privileges or immunities clause as those components are secured by the specifying provision in the Bill of Rights. Thus, Amar's model radically differs from other theories of total or selective incorporation of the Bill of Rights that use the term *incorporation* in a straightforward sense established by common usage among jurists and scholars.

What is especially appealing about Amar's book is his exposition of the notion that a constitutional right is redefined when a constitutional amendment occurs. Thus, for example, it may be properly said that the privileges or immunities clause incorporates each freedom of the First Amendment. However, we should understand each freedom as it was understood contemporaneously with the founding of the Fourteenth Amendment (1866–68), rather than simply limiting ourselves to its original understanding at the time of the founding of the Bill of Rights (1789–91). As Amar felicitously puts it, "[T]he very meaning of freedom of speech, press, petition, and assembly was subtly redefined in the process of being incorporated."[21] Moreover, according to Amar, "the Fourteenth Amendment has a doctrinal 'feedback effect' against the federal government, despite the amendment's clear textual limitation to state action[.]"[22] Therefore, the doctrine that the same standards apply to the United States, and to the several states with respect to First Amendment freedoms,[23] should be applied not only in the light of the original understanding of these freedoms, but also in light of the original understanding of the founders of the Fourteenth Amendment.[24] The original understanding of each incorporated specific right in the Bill of Rights has been enriched, augmented, or enhanced by the more democratic and liberal understanding of those who founded the Fourteenth Amendment. Professor Amar deserves much praise for so articulately pointing out, in a most persuasive way, that the process of incorporation legitimizes the redefinitions of the various incorporated rights. The concept of redefinition of a federal constitutional right by the process of incorporation is one that may prove to be very fecund—despite Amar's yoking this promising notion with that of refined incorporation.

But Amar also holds that an individual right can be *mutated*— for example, from a political right to a civil right.[25] Amar's use of the term "mutate" (or its derivatives) appears to be limited to instances involving a radical transformation, such as when a provision originally understood as securing a collective or political right, and thus as not pertaining to an individual civil right as such, is now to be considered as one that pertains to a civil right of individuals. Thus, he maintains that the First Amendment right of assembly and petition,[26] and the Second Amendment right to keep and bear arms,[27] were, according to the original understanding of some founders, core political rights that, nevertheless, had been mutated to be understood as being core civil rights at the founding of the Fourteenth Amendment. I reject Amar's notion, because the mutation of a political right into a civil right appears to me to be utterly radical in nature and effect, whereas the changes in the judicial or popular understanding of a civil right concerning what are or are not among its components may well be due to the evolution of constitutional doctrines because of the unfolding from within of the underlying or indwelling fundamental principles of the right in question. It seems to me that, at the very least, a rather heavy burden of persuasion should rest upon those who think that a core political right (as so considered at the founding of the right) could be properly held to have mutated into a core civil right (as so considered at the founding of the Fourteenth Amendment).

As to the assembly-petition right, at most Amar only succeeds in showing that *one* original understanding of the assembly-petition clause was to the effect that some, if not all, components of its specific right constituted a political rather than a civil right. But, he is, I think, conflating the civil right of the people, considered *distributively*, to assemble for political purposes with the political right of the people, considered *collectively*, to alter or abolish their government. When ordinary citizens, who may or may not exercise the suffrage, peaceably assemble to petition the government or to engage in other political activities, they are not exercising a political right in the same sense as the rights to vote, hold office, serve on juries, or even serve in the militia are said to be political rights. However, when the voters as such, pursuant to law, assemble to formally *instruct* their representatives, this activity plausibly appears to be the exercise of a political right, provided such instruction is legally binding. The probably dominant, original understanding of the assembly-petition right of the people was that it is a civil individual right to assemble with respect to the communication of ideas and facts concerning matters of public concern.[28] The assembly-petition right was, from the beginning, not only an individual civil right but also a freedom-right, and hence (according to the theory of this book), incorporated by the privileges or immunities clause. Whether the Second Amendment right was, according to the original understanding, a political rather than civil right is the subject of controversy today. But, assuming it was a civil right from the beginning, then the nature of this right becomes a critical issue with respect to whether it is incorporated by the Fourteenth Amendment—a matter I discuss in Chapter D of this part.

Professor Amar concludes that the privileges or immunities clause refinedly incorporates (and, thus, subtly redefines) not only First Amendment freedoms but also all other individual rights (whether specified or not) secured in the Bill of Rights and elsewhere in the Constitution against abridgment by the United States. According to Amar, these incorporated rights (as redefined in the process of incorporation) include as *individual civil rights*: the right not to be subject to a noncoercive establishment of religion;[29] the freedoms of religion, speech, press, assembly, and the right to petition (fully considered as individual civil rights);[30] the Second Amendment right to keep and bear arms (as strangely mutated into a core civil right);[31] the Third Amendment right concerning quartering of soldiers; the Fourth Amendment right against unreasonable searches and seizures;[32] and the Fifth Amendment right to just compensation.[33] According to Amar, "rather easy candidates for incorporation [by the privileges or immunities clause include the] "[p]rotections against double jeopardy and compelled self-incrimination, as well as the rights of confrontation, compulsory process, counsel, bail, and the like" (i.e., the rights against excessive fines and cruel and unusual punishment, in the Eighth Amendment).[34] Amar's treatment of the grand, petit, and civil jury clauses in the Fifth, Sixth, and Seventh Amendments, respectively, is much more nuanced. Suffice it to say, Amar maintains that only core components of each such specific right may be embraced by the privileges or immunities clause. Some components are not incorporated because they specify certain aspects peculiar only to proceedings in the federal courts.[35] Amar also insists that the privileges or immunities clause embraces rights found elsewhere in the Constitution, not just in the Bill of Rights (e.g., the privilege of the writ of habeas corpus).[36]

I shall now undertake to show why I think that Amar's doctrine of *refined* incorporation of all individual civil rights, whether or not specified in the Bill of Rights, is basically unsound—as is also any theory of total incorporation (such as that held by Curtis), according to which every right specified in the Bill of Rights is incorporated by the Fourteenth Amendment.

Chapter B. A Critique of Amar's Theory of the Privileges or Immunities Clause as a Vehicle of Selective Incorporation

Section 1. Amar's neglect of the citizenship clause

Amar starts with a textual analysis of the privileges or immunities clause. However, this is indeed starting on the wrong foot. His failure to initially consider the citizenship clause seriously affects his analysis of the privileges or immunities clause.[37]

The citizenship clause provides that, "All persons born or naturalized in the United States and subject to the jurisdiction thereof, are citizens of the United States and of the State wherein they reside." It would be odd if the term "persons" in the citizenship clause did not to have the same meaning as the term "person" as used in the due process and equal protection clauses in the same amendment. Hence, it is obvious that not all persons, as that term is used in section 1 of the Fourteenth Amendment, are citizens of the United States. Moreover, both the due process clauses of the Fifth and Fourteenth Amendments, respectively, forbid the United States and the individual states from depriving any person of life, liberty, and property without due process of law. Amar rightly observes, in another context, that "[i]t would be odd to think that the words *due process* in the Fourteenth Amendment were intended to mean something very different that they did in the Fifth."[38] It would be equally odd to think that the word "person" in the Fourteenth Amendment was understood to mean something very different than it meant in the Fifth. It is altogether evident that "person" is used in the Fourteenth Amendment as denoting every natural person, subject to the jurisdiction of the United States, including noncitizens. By virtue also of the *feedback effect* mechanism triggered by the adoption of the Fourteenth Amendment, the word "person" in both due process clauses must be deemed equivalent in meaning. But, that meaning is that of "person" in the due process clause of the Fourteenth Amendment. So, it follows that the term "person" in the Fifth Amendment due process clause must denote every natural person subject to the jurisdiction of the United States—including aliens and noncitizen nationals.[39]

Every person of whatever legal status (e.g., as an American citizen, noncitizen American national, resident alien, lawfully admitted nonresident alien, or illegal alien) is entitled to the benefit of *some* bundle of rights proper to that status, which rights are among the components of the specific right of either due process clause.[40] Amar correctly maintains that noncitizens, including aliens, are entitled to the benefit of the due process clause of the Fourteenth Amendment according to its original understanding.[41] Given his notion of the *feedback effect*, Amar should, therefore, have considered himself as estopped from claiming that the term "person" in the Fifth Amendment means something different from the same term in the Fourteenth Amendment. But, as a matter of fact, Amar astonishingly holds that the adoption of the Fourteenth Amendment did not itself overrule what he alleges to have been a doctrine of the Supreme Court in *Scott* v. *Standford*,[42] that only American citizens were then entitled (and, thus, entitled before the adoption of the Fourteenth Amendment) to the benefit of the rights specified in the Bill of Rights or elsewhere in the Constitution.[43]

Section 2. Amar and "No State shall"

Having already started on the wrong foot, Amar next considers the privileges or immunities clause in the following fashion. He parses the text of the clause first by treating the words "No State shall ..." He notes the identity between this term and that "phrase in Article I, section 10, imposing various limitations on states, including several key rights designed principally for the benefit of in-state residents."[44] The choice of the opening words of the privileges or immunities clause presupposes the doctrine of *Barron* v. *Baltimore*: that the provisions of the Bill of Rights apply only to the United States. Amar rightly comments that "had the framers of the original Bill of Rights meant to impose its rules on states, they would have used the Article I, section 10 phrase 'No State shall' or some reasonable facsimile."[45] As Amar so well puts it: "The Supreme Court Justices in *Barron* asked for 'Simon Says' language, and that's exactly what the Fourteenth Amendment gave them."[46]

Section 3. Amar and "make or enforce any law which shall abridge"

He then addresses the phrase "make or enforce any law which shall abridge." As he puts it: "As the key sentence rolls on, the incorporation reading gains steam. Various critical words of the next phrase—*make, any, law,* and *abridge*—call to mind the precisely parallel language in parallel sequence of the First Amendment—*make, no, law,* and *abridging.*"[47] But Amar does not here also specifically refer to the religion clauses (i.e., "Congress shall make no law respecting an establishment of religion, or prohibiting the free exercise thereof"). Although he does not specifically address here the question whether "prohibiting" is to be understood as meaning the same as "abridging," his view is that the two terms are equivalent because he holds that the privileges or immunities clause incorporates the specific right of the free-exercise clause. Moreover, elsewhere in his book, he remarks that the First Amendment provisions protecting freedoms "asymmetrically guarded against federal action *restricting*—'prohibit[ing] and abridg[ing]'—rights."[48]

Amar next considers three significant differences. "First, the Fourteenth Amendment imposes a prohibition on the states, whereas the First explicitly limits Congress. But, this is, of course exactly the point of incorporation. And what better way to make clear than even rights and freedoms in the original Bill of Rights that explicitly limited Congress should hereafter apply against states than by cloning the language of the First Amendment?"[49] He parenthetically observes that "[t]he word *abridge* in the Fourteenth Amendment is especially revealing, for nowhere outside the First Amendment had this word appeared in the Constitution before 1866."[50]

He then remarks, as a second point of difference, that "the Fourteenth Amendment uses the word *any* where the First uses *no,* but here again, there is an obvious reason. Following the 'Simon Says' rules of *Barron* 'to the letter,' the Fourteenth uses negative phrasing ('No State shall …') whereas the First uses affirmative

11

('Congress shall …'). The substitution of *any* for *no* simply balances the initial inversion."[51]

So far so good. However, Amar has a remaining point of difference to evaluate. He writes:

> Finally, the Fourteenth Amendment speaks of law "enforce[ment]" as well as lawmaking. Once again, this makes perfect sense if its purpose was to incorporate the rights and freedoms of the original Bill. Many of the Bill's provisions, especially those in Amendments V–VIII, dealt centrally with the enforcement of laws by executive and judicial officers.[52]

But the First Amendment does not include the phrase "or enforcing" precisely because Congress, before the adoption of the Bill of Rights, had not previously made (and, indeed, lacked the authority under the Articles of Confederation to enact) any law abridging any freedom subsequently secured by the First Amendment.[53] On the other hand, before the adoption of the Fourteenth Amendment, the slave states notoriously had both made and/or enforced laws that had abridged such freedoms.[54] Were the privileges or immunities clause to only prohibit the states from making laws abridging First Amendment freedoms, they would then not have been expressly precluded from enforcing such laws that predated the adoption of the Fourteenth Amendment. Therefore, it appears that Amar misunderstands the import of the words "or enforces" in the privileges or immunities clause.

He compounds the error by immediately adding: "However suggestive the tracking of the First Amendment may be, there is no suggestion thus far that only the First Amendment is to be incorporated."[55] First, I take it that Amar would admit the theoretical possibility that if the First Amendment freedoms are the only rights specified in the Bill of Rights incorporated by privileges or immunities clause, then there might well be other rights secured (explicitly or implicitly) elsewhere in the Constitution against abridgments by the United States that are also embraced by the privileges or immunities clause because they are privileges and immunities of American citizens (e.g., the freedom of travel or migration throughout the United States). Hence, I read Amar to actually mean to say that there is no suggestion thus far that, of all the specific rights in the Bill of Rights, only the First Amendment freedoms are incorporated by the privileges or immunities clause. But, so understood, his reliance upon the clause's prohibition of "law 'enforce[ment]'" as well as lawmaking," in support of the claim that "there is no suggestion thus far that [of the specific rights in the Bill of Rights] only the First Amendment is to be incorporated," appears to be unwarranted.

More importantly, Amar's claim as amended is unjustified for the additional reason that the use of the cloning language (i.e., "No State shall make or enforce any law which shall abridge") indeed signals that, thus far, the First Amendment freedoms are the only rights specified in the Bill of Rights that are incorporated by the privileges or immunities clause. For Amar had already adverted to the phrase "make or enforce any law which shall abridge" as providing no "better way to make clear that even the rights and freedoms in the original Bill of Rights that explicitly limited Congress should hereafter apply against states than by cloning the language of the First Amendment."[56] However, the only "rights and freedoms in the original Bill of Rights that explicitly limited Congress" in the general form of the First Amendment are the freedoms of the First Amendment. That the First Amendment freedoms, not counting the Second Amendment right (hereinafter SAR) for the time being, are the only specific rights of the Bill of Rights incorporated by the privileges or immunities clause appears to be also confirmed by the fact that "[m]any of the Bill [of Rights]'s provisions, especially those in Amendments V [read IV]–VIII, dealt centrally with the enforcement of laws by executive and judicial officers," given the copresence of a due process clause in the Fifth and Fourteenth Amendments.

The very sweeping operative terms of the First Amendment (i.e., "Congress shall make no law") and of the privileges or immunities clause ("No State shall make or enforce any law") appear to indicate that very few rights are within the scope of the descriptive term of the privileges or immunities clause. To pursue the question of the paradigmatic incorporation of First Amendment freedoms by the privileges or immunities clause, one must return to the matter of the structural similitude between the two classes of rights secured respectively by the First Amendment and those secured by the privileges or immunities clause. The privileges or immunities clause self-consciously (as it were) tracks the text of the First Amendment. The significance of such tracking, or cloning, cannot justly be minimized.

As Congressman James Wilson, chairman of the House Judiciary Committee and sponsor of the Civil Rights Act of 1866, eloquently remarked:

> The great [First Amendment] rights here enumerated were regarded by the people as too sacred and too essential to the preservation of their liberties to be trusted with no firmer defense than the rule that "Congress can exercise no power which is not delegated to it." Around this negative protection was erected the positive barrier of absolute prohibition. Freedom of religious opinion, freedom of speech and the press, and the right of assemblage for the purpose of petition belong to every American citizen, high or low, rich or poor, wherever he may be within the jurisdiction of the United States. With these rights no State may interfere without breach of the bond which holds the Union together.[57]

It is quite clear that Amar believes that the First Amendment freedoms, according to the dominant original understanding of the founders of the Fourteenth Amendment, only pertain to individual civil (as opposed to political) rights. However, he thinks it might be otherwise with respect to what was the dominant original understanding of the founders of the Bill of Rights. It is fairly arguable, according to Amar, that the First Amendment's sweeping language manifests one original understanding that the First Amendment include components that sound, as it were, only in the notion of federalism.[58]

This is very arguably the case with respect to the establishment clause. However, it cannot be denied that another original understanding of the founders of the Bill of Rights was to the effect that the First Amendment provisions (including the establishment clause) were enacted with the background assumption, whether actually or hypothetically entertained, that the provision for the enumerated powers of the federal government did not necessarily preclude all abridgments of First Amendment freedoms or laws respecting an establishment of religion. To be sure, there are no express enumerated powers with respect to speech, the press, or religion. However, the powers to legislate concerning them are arguably found in the necessary and proper execution of the enumerated powers. This is especially true where the federal government is empowered to act directly upon individuals in the exercise of its exclusive jurisdiction, that is, in the District of Columbia, federal territories and possessions, and the military.[59] In simple confirmation of this original understanding, it suffices to notice that the House of Representatives referred (on August 24, 1789) to the Senate its proposed amendments. These included:

> Art. III. Congress shall make no law establishing religion, or prohibiting the free exercise thereof; nor shall the rights of conscience be infringed.

> Art. IV. The freedom of speech, and of the press, and the right of the people peaceably to assemble, and consult for the common good, and to apply to the government for a redress of grievances, shall not be infringed....

> Art. XIV. No State shall infringe the right of trial by jury in criminal cases, nor the rights of conscience, nor the freedom of speech, or of the press.[60]

It is thus evident, given the text of the proposed (and eventually rejected) Article 14, that the ultimate choice of the sweeping words ("Congress shall make no law") is fully consistent with the most probable dominant original understanding that the First Amendment freedoms were solely considered as individual rights, and their absolute protection had nothing to do with federal-state relations—unlike the establishment clause. This is not to say, however, that the establishment clause does not serve other purposes, such as to create a buffer zone as a prophylactic measure to better secure individual rights pertaining to religion. Arguably, the sweeping words of limitation ("Congress shall, make no law") may well have been chosen for reasons of style, since the rights of free speech, free press, assembly, and petition are cognate to religious freedom—all being domains of freedom. However, the primary reason, it seems to me, may have been to indicate the nature of the sweeping limitations upon the legislative powers of Congress respecting the establishment of religion and those freedoms embodied in the First Amendment, and concomitantly emphasizing the breadth of those freedoms.

The reference to "Congress," without mention of the other branches of government, is easily explained. The First Amendment presupposes that the executive and judicial branches of the federal government are already without any constitutional authority (independently of legislative authorization) to abridge First Amendment freedoms. Hence, any abridgment of First Amendment freedoms by the executive or judicial branches would necessarily be *ultra vires* (in other words, beyond their scope or authority) and therefore unconstitutional.[61] This thesis is independently confirmed, by virtue of the now familiar *feedback effect* of the adoption of the privileges or immunities clause, given that First Amendment freedoms are privileges of American citizens, and accordingly secured against abridgment by any branch of government of the United States.

The the sweeping words of the privileges or immunities clause, cloning as they do those in the First Amendment, disclose that it is likely that the specific constitutional rights embraced by the privileges or immunities clause are relatively few in number. This is confirmed by comparing the First Amendment with the provisions in amendments III–VIII, which variously secure the numerous rights, which are variously considered: as the rights of those suspected, accused, or convicted of public offenses, or of litigants in civil cases; or as the procedural, remedial, or claim rights of all persons; or which provide protection for their security and that of their property and other judicially cognizable interests.[62]

Section 4. Amar and "the privileges or immunities"

Amar next proceeds to discuss the phrase "the privileges or immunities." He asserts: "Of course, my last sentence was a bit of a cheat; there is no suggestion 'thus far' that only the First Amendment is to be incorporated because it is not yet clear what rights shall not be 'abridge[d]' by the states."[63] Alas! Amar has already forgotten his acknowledgment on the immediately preceding page precisely that there was no "better way to make clear that even rights and freedoms in the original Bill of Rights that explicitly limited Congress should hereafter apply against states than by cloning the language of the First Amendment." As he elsewhere put it: "[A]s a matter of constitutional text and structure, these freedoms [referring expressly to those of speech, press, petition, and assembly] are indeed easy cases for full application against states via the Fourteenth Amendment."[64] Elsewhere, he parenthetically notes that the "text, history, and logic [of the free exercise clause] make it a paradigmatic case for incorporation."[65] Amar had previously remarked:

> Textually, the argument for applying these rights [rights of free speech, free press, free assembly, and petition] against the states via the Fourteenth Amendment is wonderfully straightforward. The First Amendment explicitly speaks of "right[s]" and "freedom[s]" (entitlements also known as "privileges" and "immunities"); and after the Civil War and Emancipation, it would be extraordinarily perverse to refuse to incorporate (in a refined way) clauses whose explicit battle cry is "freedom." What's more, the First Amendment's words that these freedoms and rights "shall" not be "abridg[ed] by "law" perfectly harmonize with their echoes in the key sentence of section I [of the Fourteenth Amendment].[66]

Based upon textual considerations alone, it is quite probable that the privileges or immunities clause incorporates, of the rights specified in the Bill of Rights, only the First Amendment freedoms. That is to say, given the ease with which one sees that the privileges or immunities clause incorporates First Amendment freedoms, it is not immediately obvious what other specific rights in the Bill of Rights are equally incorporated given the inapplicability to them of the sweeping words "Congress shall make no law ... prohibiting ... abridging."

Nevertheless, Amar proceeds to present evidences of how the terms "privileges" and "immunities," as well as "rights" and "liberties," are "roughly synonymous" and "seem to have been used interchangeably [in the eighteenth and nineteenth centuries]."[67] This can readily be conceded. However, I am afraid that Professor Amar, in his zeal to avoid the vice of *mechanical* incorporation, has failed to avoid that of *magical* incorporation worked by way of his *légerdeparole* (to coin a word).

In the first place, the terms "rights," "privileges," "liberties," and "immunities" are indeed ambiguous, and so each term bears several possible definitions. So, it is possible that these words as used in a particular writing are not necessarily synonymous or interchangeable. During the reconstruction era, some persons actually asserted that the terms "rights," "privileges," and "immunities" should not be supposed to be synonymous[68] or that these terms can be abusively used as if they were synonymous.[69] One legitimate definition of the term "privilege" is that of a legal freedom (i.e., the absence of a legal duty to do or not do such-and-such in a particular domain).[70] Hence, if it is true that the only specific rights in the Bill of Rights incorporated by the privileges or immunities clause are the First Amendment freedoms, then what better way (to paraphrase Professor Amar) is there to refer to such freedoms than to do so with the term "privileges"? What is the meaning of "immunities" if the term "privileges" in the privileges or immunities clause denotes legal freedoms? One hypothesis is that the terms "privileges" and "immunities" as used in the privileges or immunities clause are indeed synonymous. However, further inquiry discloses that this is not the case. My position is that the immunities of American citizens, within the meaning of the privileges or immunities clause, do not include any of the specific rights of amendments II–VIII. On the other hand, I contend that the phrase "immunities of American citizens" very aptly refers to those several constitutionally required exemptions from certain kinds of burdens and disadvantages (e.g., freedom from governmental racial or ethnic discrimination with respect to civil rights).

The *privileges* of American citizens encompass First Amendment freedoms.[71] Now, there is nothing more like a First Amendment freedom than another freedom. The only other specific right in the Bill of Rights that could possibly be a freedom is the specific right of the Second Amendment. Assuming, for the sake of argument, that the SAR is neither a collective nor a quasi-collective right, the first critical question then is whether that right is civil or political in nature, since Amar rightly holds that the privileges or immunities clause incorporates only the civil rights of individuals.[72] However, given that the Court has recently ruled that it is an individual civil right to keep and bear arms for personal purposes, I submit nevertheless that it is not a legal freedom as is each First Amendment freedom. Rather, as I shall argue in Chapter D of this part, the SAR is in the nature of a quasi-liberty; that is, a conditional liberty in that A, a proper holder of the SAR, has a constitutional right to keep and bear certain arms or not to do so in the absence of an otherwise lawful statute that requires him to keep and bear arms (of certain kinds as statutorily defined) for public purposes, even when he is not in the actual service of his country. Therefore, the SAR, because of its inferior quality, is not incorporated by the Fourteenth Amendment via the privileges or immunities clause (or, for that matter, via the due process clause according to current doctrine of the Court).

An even much less likely candidate to be a privilege in the requisite sense is the specific right of the Fourth Amendment: that is, the right to be free from unreasonable searches and seizures. The purported freedom-from right of the Fourth Amendment is not a legal freedom in the same sense as a First Amendment freedom. Moreover, the right in question, even if considered as a freedom-from right, is very qualified. That is to say, asserting that the right to be free from unreasonable and seizures shall not be violated is equivalent to asserting that the right to be free from searches and seizures shall not be unreasonably violated.[73] Thus, it is not a full freedom-from right in the sense applicable, as I argue in Part II, to the individual right not to be invidiously discriminated upon the basis of race or color is entailed by the notion of national citizenship because of its incompatibility with an inferior and degraded status based upon race or color.

Nevertheless, given that, all too frequently, the words "rights," "privileges," and "immunities" are used synonymously or interchangeably in legal documents, as well as in popular and even learned writings, it is quite understandable why something more should be evident before definitively concluding that the descriptive term of the privileges or immunities clause does not denote any specific rights in the Bill of Rights except those of the First Amendment.

Section 5. Amar and "of citizens of the United States"

Professor Amar next takes up the phrase "citizens of the United States." Here, Amar affirms "that the Bill's 'rights' and 'freedoms' are truly privileges and immunities of 'citizens of the United States.'"[74] He is, of course, quite right in asserting that "[i]n ordinary, everyday language we often speak of the United States Constitution and Bill of Rights as declaring and defining rights of Americans as Americans," even though a particular right may also be the right of persons who are not American citizens.[75] On the other hand, he asserts that the framers of the Fourteenth Amendment were entitled to rely, and did so rely, upon the alleged doctrine of *Dred Scott* (i.e., that only American citizens were entitled to the benefit of the specific rights of the Bill of Rights).[76] Thus, according to Amar, the descriptive term of the privileges or immunities clause is one of both description and limitation. But, on the contrary, the clause is open to either construction, that is, the descriptive term is one of description only, or that it is one of both description and limitation. And we have already shown why Amar is very off base with his claim that, notwithstanding the adoption of the Fourteenth Amendment, the term "person" as it appears in the Fifth Amendment is to be taken as denoting only American citizens until and unless the alleged doctrine of *Dred Scott* is judicially overruled. It seems to me that the alleged doctrine in question is merely an ad hoc attempt to explain away the ostensible redundancy of the copresence of a due process clause in the Bill of Rights and the Fourteenth Amendment.

Amar, having started on the wrong foot by not first considering the citizenship clause, also failed to keep in step in the course of his constitutional exegesis because he separately parsed the expressions "privileges or immunities" and "of citizens of the United States." What was necessary was to have parsed the expression "the privileges or immunities of citizens of the United States" as one unit. Had he done so, perhaps he would have avoided rushing down the primrose path to error. What Amar also failed to do was to have sufficiently reflected upon his acknowledgment that important components of the specific rights of the Bill of Rights are among the constitutional rights (i.e., rights, privileges, and immunities) of American citizens. For, putting the alleged (and, I say, fictitious) doctrine of *Dred Scott* aside, he admits that it is legitimate to say, for example, that freedom of speech or of the press are privileges of the American people even if some but not all non-American citizens are per se or derivatively entitled to these freedoms. And, I maintain, that if such is the case, in failing to parse as one unit the expression "the privileges or immunities of the citizens of the United States," Amar does not sufficiently show that the privileges or immunities clause presupposes that only American citizens had privileges and immunities that the United States could not constitutionally abridge even before the adoption of the Fourteenth Amendment. Moreover, taking the expression in question as one unit, the significance of the sweeping and comprehensive limitation upon the power of the states ("shall make or enforce any law") signals that the constitutional privileges and immunities of American citizens (in the requisite sense) are relatively few.

In making my case, I wish to make two more important points. First, the class of rights denoted by the descriptive term ("all Privileges and Immunities of Citizens in the several States") of the comity clause (art. IV, § 2, cl. 1) is not identical with that class of rights denoted by the descriptive term of the privileges or immunities clause ("the privileges or immunities of Citizens of the United States").[77] Second, that what should be deemed as the true origin of the descriptive term of the privileges or immunities clause is not that of the comity clause, but is rather to be found in a series of federal treaty and statutory provisions. These documents provide compelling evidence that some rights specified in the Bill of Rights are privileges or immunities of American citizens in the sense of the privileges or immunities clause.

I first turn to consider the comity clause. It is frequently asserted that the privileges or immunities clause is based upon, or derived from, the comity clause. However, it is difficult to see why this contention is made. The former provision pertains to the "privileges or immunities of citizens of the United States," whereas the latter does so with respect to the privileges and immunities of citizens in the several states. Moreover, the comity clause not only describes a class of rights, but also expressly specifies who is entitled to their benefit: "[t]he Citizens of each State." The privileges or immunities clause does not itself expressly provide that none but American citizens are entitled to the class of rights described as the "privileges or immunities of citizens of the United States." This difference shows that the descriptive term may very well be one only of description and thus not one of limitation. To say it is one of description does not determine what kinds of persons, other than American citizens, are respectively entitled to the benefit of the various rights that are the "privileges [and] immunities of citizens of the United States."

John Bingham, the leading framer of the Fourteenth Amendment (and so very much admired by Professor Amar), declared on March 31, 1871:[78]

[The Bill of Rights] secured ... all the rights dear to the American citizen. And yet it was decided, and rightfully, that these amendments, defining and protecting the rights of men and citizens, were only limitations on the power of Congress, not on the power of States.... These eight articles I have shown never were limitations upon the power of the States, until made so by the [F]ourteenth [A]mendment.... In that case [*Corfield v. Corywll.*[79]] the court only held that in civil rights the State could not refuse to extend to citizens of other States the same general rights secured to its own.... Is it not clear that other and different privileges and immunities than those to which a citizen of a State was entitled [by the comity clause] are secured by the provisions of the [F]ourteenth [[A]mendment], that no State shall abridge the privileges and immunities of citizens of the United States, which are defined in the eight articles of amendment, and which were not limitations on the power of the States before the [F]ourteenth [A]mendment made them limitations?[80]

On March 31, 1871, Bingham claimed that it was because he understood that the Bill of Rights does not apply to the states that he drafted what is now the first section of the Fourteenth Amendment less the citizenship clause, realizing when he did so that the comity clause forbade a host state to discriminate against visiting citizens of other states with respect to any rights denoted by the descriptive term of the comity clause.[81] He was emphatic, during an exchange with Congressman (later President) James A. Garfield on a later occasion, when he asserted that the comity clause was "always interpreted … to mean only privileges and immunities of citizens of the States, not of the United States."[82] But, as Garfield remarked (but as to another issue), in the course of his extensive remarks about Bingham's account of the framing of section 1 of the Fourteenth Amendment: "My colleague [Bingham] can make but he cannot remake history."[83] Because the fact of the matter is that, for many years, Bingham had consistently held that the comity clause should be understood to read that the citizens of each state (being ipso facto citizens of the United States) should be entitled to all the privileges and immunities of citizens of the United States in the several states, and not those rights grounded upon state law.[84] According to Bingham (before his enlightenment), the comity clause "is of the privileges and immunities of citizens of the United States in, not of, the several States."[85]

The history that Bingham made may be summarized as follows. On February 3, 1866, Bingham moved the Joint Committee on Reconstruction to accept as a proposed constitutional amendment: "Congress shall have power to make all laws which shall be necessary and proper to secure to citizens of each State all privileges and immunities of citizens in the several States (Art. 4, Sec. 2); and to all persons in the several States equal protection in the rights of life, liberty and property (5th Amendment)[.]" The proposed measure (less the parenthesized references most likely included by Bingham) was accepted by the Joint Committee and thereafter reported to both houses of Congress on February 13.[86]

On February 26th, Bingham explained the proposed amendment to the House:

[T]he proposed amendment stands in the very words of the Constitution of the United States as it came to us from the hands of its illustrious framers. Every word of the proposed amendment is today in the Constitution of our country, save the words conferring the express grant of power upon the Congress of the United States. The residue of the resolution ... is the language of the second section of the fourth article [i.e., the comity clause]. And a portion of the [F]ifth [A]mendment[.]

Moreover, Bingham said, the proposed amendment was designed to supply "an express grant of power ... to enable the whole people of every State, by congressional enactment, to enforce obedience to these requirements of the Constitution"—indicating his then (and long held) erroneous opinion that the Fifth Amendment due process clause applies to the states.[87] After considerable discussion of the proposed amendment, the House agreed to a motion to postpone further consideration on February 28.[88]

The Joint Committee thereafter developed another proposed constitutional amendment, one that would eventually became the Fourteenth Amendment. On April 21, 1866, Bingham first proposed a provision to the Joint Committee on Reconstruction that is now section 1 of the Fourteenth Amendment, less the citizenship clause.[89] Eventually, on April 28, the Joint Committee approved a proposed amendment that included what is now section 1 of the Fourteenth Amendment less the citizenship clause.[90] For our purposes, it suffices to note that the privileges or immunities clause of the proposed amendment did not expressly state (unlike the prototype amendment also authored by Bingham) that only American citizens are its beneficiaries. But, did Bingham believe, before his March 31, 1871 speech to the House, that the descriptive terms of the comity clause and the privileges or immunities clause of the proposed amendment are identical? That was precisely his position until approximately March 31, 1871. The following appears in the Report of the Committee on the Judiciary, purportedly made by Bingham on behalf of that committee on January 30, 1871: "The [privileges or immunities] clause of the[F]ourteenth [A]mendment ... does not, in the opinion of the committee, refer to privileges and immunities of citizens of the United States, other than those embraced in the original text of the Constitution, article 4, section 2 [i.e., the comity clause]."[91]

Given the foregoing, we readily see that Bingham was deceiving himself and others when he declared in his address of March 21, 1871, that before he had proposed (what eventually became) section 1 of the Fourteenth Amendment less the citizenship clause, he had already discerned that the class of rights denoted by comity clause and that of the privileges or immunities clause are not identical.

Indeed, not only is the descriptive term of the privileges or immunities clause analytically different from that of the comity clause, the former has its own ancestral line found in a series of federal treaties and statutes and thus quite different from that of the comity clause.[92] For example, article III of the Louisiana Purchase Treaty of 1803 with France provided:

> The inhabitants of the ceded territory shall be incorporated in the Union of the United States, and admitted as soon as possible, according to the principles of the Federal constitution, to the enjoyment of all the rights, advantages and immunities of citizens of the United States; and in the mean time they shall be maintained and protected in the free enjoyment of their liberty, property, and the religion which they profess.[93]

Amar states, with very good reason, that "[t]hough the precise verbal formulas [of the federal treaties and statutes in question] varied, they all were understood to encompass, among other things, the protections of the federal Bill of Rights."[94] This thesis is certainly true because, for example, President Thomas Jefferson, in a letter dated July 14, 1804 to James Madison, wrote of article III as follows:

> It is that the inhabitants shall be admitted as soon as possible, according to the principles of our Const., to the enjoyment of all the rights of citizens, and, in the mean time, en attendant, shall be maintained in their liberty,

property, and religion. That is that they shall continue under the protection of the treaty, until the principles of our constitution can be extended to them, when the protection of the treaty is to cease, and that of our own principles to take its place.[95]

Attorney General Benjamin F. Butler, in an official opinion issued in 1835 concerning the Arkansas Territory (which was part of the territory acquired by the Louisiana Purchase of 1803), referred to article III of the treaty of 1803. He advised that the citizens of Arkansas Territory could not lawfully take steps towards forming a state government in the absence of congressional authorization. However, he declared:

They undoubtedly possess the ordinary privileges and immunities of citizens of the United States. Among these is the right of the people "peaceably to assemble and to petition the government for a redress of grievances." In the exercise of this right, the inhabitants of Arkansas may peaceably meet together in primary assemblies, or in conventions chosen by such assemblies, for the purpose of petitioning Congress to abrogate the Territorial government and to admit them into the Union as an independent State.[96]

It is significant, I think, that Senator Trumball, author of the Civil Rights Act of 1866, noted and quoted relevant portions of the treaties of cession with France, Spain, and with Mexico, and the statute pertaining to the Stockbridge Indians, on April 4, 1866.[97] So, it is somewhat noteworthy that on April 21, 1866, only a few days after Trumball's remarks, Congressman Bingham first proposed to the Joint Committee on Reconstruction what is now Section 1 of the Fourteenth Amendment, save for the citizenship clause.[98] It is a remarkable coincidence that Bingham authored the privileges or immunities clause during a time that he was completely ignorant of what I call the true ancestral line of the clause found in public documents reciting treaties and statutes of the United States. Yet this appears to be the case.

Unfortunately, the frequently (and erroneously) held view, that the true precursor of the privileges or immunities clause is the comity clause, is a secular counterpart of the doctrine of original sin—a very poisoned tree bearing very poisoned fruit in the orchard of constitutional theory. It is erroneous to suppose that the terms "[p]rivileges and "[i]mmunities" in the comity clause are used in the same senses as their corresponding terms in the privileges or immunities clause. The former clause has it own proper functions and purposes that govern how the terms in question are to be construed. The comity clause, the Supreme Court has traditionally held, is included in the Constitution so that a citizen of state A, while temporarily present in state B, is equally entitled to the benefit of those rights denoted by the descriptive term of the comity clause as are the citizens of state B according to the law of state B.[99] Thus, the comity clause's essential function and purpose is antidiscriminatory. On the other hand, since the true precursors of the privileges or immunities clause are those federal treaties and statutes that referred to the "rights" and "privileges" (or "advantages") and "immunities" of citizens of the United States, these terms are to be understood globally as including some if not all individual civil rights specified in the Bill of Rights and the original Constitution.

Well before the adoption of the Fourteenth Amendment, the Court had already implicitly (but, nevertheless, definitively) rejected the idea that the original Constitution prohibits violations of religious freedom by a state with respect to its own citizens. The Court was called upon in *Permoli v. New Orleans*[100] to review a judgment fining Permoli, a Catholic priest, for having violated a New Orleans ordinance that prohibited (as a public health measure) the exposure of a corpse in any Catholic church. In the trial court, Permoli asserted that his conduct "was warranted by the Constitution and laws of the United States, which prevent the enactment of any law prohibiting the free exercise of any religion."[101] Before the Supreme Court, Permoli's counsel necessarily addressed the question whether the Court had "jurisdiction over cases of infringement of the religious liberty, of citizens of Louisiana by the municipal authorities of that State." However, counsel wisely chose not to base his jurisdictional argument before the Court on the ground that Permoli's First Amendment religious freedom-right had been violated. What he instead argued was that the protection of religious liberty due to federal treaty and statutory provisions applicable to Louisiana (prior to its statehood) remained in force after the adoption of the state constitution and the admission of Louisiana into the Union.[102] Counsel for New Orleans replied, rather extensively, to the nonconstitutional grounds presented by Permoli's counsel, but he also tersely stated that, "There is no repugnancy to the Constitution, because no provision thereof forbids its enactment of law or ordinance, under State authority, in reference to religion. The limitation of power in the [F]irst [A]mendment of the Constitution is upon Congress, and not the States."[103]

In addressing the jurisdictional issue, the Supreme Court declared, "The Constitution makes no provision for protecting the citizens of the respective states in their religious liberties; this is left to the state constitutions and laws: nor is there any inhibition imposed by the Constitution of the United States in this respect on the states."[104] This statement is broad enough to encompass any substantive religious liberty claim grounded upon the First Amendment, or the comity clause, or any other provision in the Constitution. The Court then considered and rejected Permoli's jurisdictional argument based upon nonconstitutional grounds. The declaration in *Permoli* concerning "religious liberties" applies *à fortiorari* to the freedoms of speech, press, and assembly.

We should now consider whether it is legally significant that the word "rights" is omitted from the descriptive term of the privileges or immunities clause. What if the clause read: "No State shall make or enforce any law which shall abridge the rights, privileges, or immunities of citizens of the United States"? What if, in addition, the due process clause had been omitted, but the equal protection clause had been retained? In such a case, I would have to concede that *this* section 1 would *prima facie* incorporate every individual civil right of American citizens specified in the Bill of Rights, as well as elsewhere in the original Constitution. However, the privileges or immunities clause does not actually include the term "rights," and it is, in fact, copresent with the due process and equal protection clauses.

I contend that the omission of the term "rights" is legally significant. The term "rights" bears several meanings; among them is one that has the most general sense as when we speak of First Amendment freedoms as rights and of the privilege of the writ of habeas corpus as a right. However, "right" can conceivably be used in a more limited sense such that every constitutional right (used in a generic sense) is either a right (in some limited sense), or a privilege (in some limited sense), or an immunity (in some limited sense); such that these terms are not synonymous or interchangeable in the particular context in question. Accordingly, when one notices how the operative term of the privileges or immunities clause (i.e., "shall make or enforce any law which shall abridge") clones an operative term of the First Amendment and of not other amendment in the Bill of Rights then the omission of the term "rights" from the descriptive term of the privileges or immunities clause serves to confirm the thesis that no specific right of the Bill of Rights is incorporated by the clause other than the freedoms of the First Amendment (except, perhaps, the SAR). So the probability that the privileges of American citizens, within the meaning of the privileges or immunities clause, are their freedoms and only their freedoms is somewhat increased given the fact that a due process clause appears in both the Fifth and Fourteenth Amendments. However, it is not necessarily the case that the only privileges of American citizens are their First Amendment freedoms (ignoring, for the time being, the SAR). On the other hand, the immunities of the American citizens, within the meaning of that clause, are something other than their privileges, and something other than the rights specified in amendments III through VIII (again ignoring the SAR).

Section 6. Amar and "nor shall any State deprive any person of life, liberty, or property, without due process of law"

Amar proceeds with his analysis of the Fifth Amendment due process clause in the following fashion: First, he again sets forth the alleged *Dred Scott* doctrine (that only American citizens are entitled to the benefits of the Bill of Rights)—despite "ordinary, everyday language" suggesting the contrary. Based on that, he explains: "By incorporating the rights of the Fifth Amendment, the privileges-or-immunities clause, under the precedent of *Dred Scott,* would have prevented states from depriving 'citizens' of due process."[105] However, according to Amar, the framers of the Fourteenth Amendment were anxious to "[extend] the benefits of state due process to aliens[, b]ut for this, a special clause—speaking not of 'citizens' but of 'persons'—was needed."[106] The net result of Amar's view is that, until the Court shall have overruled the alleged *Dred Scott* doctrine in question, the word "person" in the Fifth Amendment due process clause (and elsewhere in the Bill of Rights) denotes American citizens only. However, the same word in the Fourteenth Amendment due process clause includes all persons subject to the jurisdiction of the United States, including but not limited to American citizens. Surely, this is a very weird, counterintuitive thesis for Amar to maintain.

Section 7. An overview of the argument for selective incorporation by the privileges or immunities clause

According to the current doctrine of the Court, only natural persons who are American citizens can claim the benefit of the privileges or immunities clause.[107] This is a grossly erroneous ruling if, as I contend, the descriptive term of the privileges or immunities clause is not also one of limitation. To say that the descriptive term of the privileges or immunities clause is one of description but not of limitation is to define a class of rights rather than limit the class of right-holders. That a constitutional right is termed a *privilege* or *immunity of American citizens* signifies the importance of the right in question rather than identify its beneficiaries.[108] It does not follow, however, that with respect to any given incorporated right that the class of beneficiaries includes every noncitizen subject to the jurisdiction of the United States.[109]

One must, of course, examine the purposes and functions of each particular constitutional privilege or immunity to determine whether it is per se predicable of only American citizens. The same inquiry must be made as to whether a particular privilege or immunity is per se predicable of some artificial persons, corporate or not, depending upon their characteristics. For example, the constitutional privileges of freedom of speech and freedom of the press are fully predicable of a domestic artificial person that predominantly engages in publishing or other communicative activities within the scope of the free-speech and free-press clauses. On the other hand, a domestic artificial person insofar as it engages in the production or distribution of industrial, agricultural, or noncultural consumer goods has only derivative rights in those situations where a constitutional privilege or immunity of American citizens would otherwise be subject to abridgment.

Before the adoption of the Fourteenth Amendment, there was a series of federal treaties and statutes that referred to the rights, privileges (or advantages) and immunities of citizens of the United States, and this expression was understood as referring to the constitutional civil rights of American citizens in the Bill of Rights and elsewhere in the original Constitution. Some of these rights, before the notorious *Dred Scott* decision, were commonly well understood as *belonging* to (at least) all free white persons, whether American citizens or not. Hence, the term "privileges or immunities of citizens of the United States" for yet another reason should be considered as words of description only.

Well, we have seen that Amar is unwarranted in thinking that the alleged (and I claim fictitious) *Dred Scott* doctrine had not been overruled not later than with the adoption of the Fourteenth Amendment. Moreover, we have seen that if the descriptive term of the privileges or immunities clause is also one of limitation, it is then impossible for the privileges or immunities clause to incorporate most rights in the Bill of Rights. And, finally, if indeed all the specific individual rights of the Bill of Rights are privileges or immunities of American citizens, and the term "person" in both due process clauses has the same meaning, then it does follow that the Fourteenth Amendment due process clause is indeed superfluous.

We should look at the Bill of Rights as a whole. By synoptically viewing the text of the Bill of Rights side by side with that of section 1 of the Fourteenth Amendment, we may discern what is a truly remarkable structure of similarities and dissimilarities. The First Amendment has language (i.e., "Congress shall make no Law") (as Amar notes) that is tracked by the privileges or immunities clause ("No State shall make or enforce any law"). The only specific right expressly common to both the Bill of Rights and the Fourteenth Amendment is that of a due process clause.

Amar undermines his thesis that the privileges or immunities clause *refinedly* incorporates all the individual rights that are components of the rights specified in the Bill of Rights by his candid acknowledgement that "as a matter of constitutional right and structure, these freedoms and rights [of speech, press, petition, and assembly] are indeed easy cases for full application against the states via the Fourteenth Amendment.... During the Thirty-eighth and Thirty-ninth Congresses, Republicans invoked speech, press, petition, and assembly rights over and over—more frequently than any other right, with the possible exception of due process.... [T]he centrality of these rights was not an idea limited to a few leading lawyers or theorists but was widely understood by the polity." [110]

The individual rights embodied in the First Amendment, other than freedom-from rights entailed by the establishment clause, are legal freedoms (i.e., right to be free to do or not do such-and-such in a particular domain). No right specified in amendments III–VIII is even arguably a freedom in the sense that every component is itself a freedom (or liberty); although it may very well have a liberty-right as a component. Each of the other rights specified in the Bill of Rights and section 1 of the Fourteenth Amendment is facially either a procedural or remedial right, or another kind of claim-right, or a passive right pertaining to privacy or property, or a right of someone suspected, accused, convicted of a public offense—except the SAR. Both due process clauses of the fifth and Fourteenth Amendments (which are essentially equivalent in meaning) can easily be regarded as embracing some other rights specified in the Constitution, or some components of some of these specified rights.[111] Thus, for example, although the equal protection right fully applies only to the states, both due process clauses may legitimately be construed as having so-called equal protection components.[112]

It is that very copresence of a due process clause in both the Bill of Rights and in section 1 of the Fourteenth Amendment, together with the tracking of the First Amendment by the privileges or immunities clause, which indicates (speaking now only of the Bill of Rights) that the privileges or immunities clause incorporates only the First Amendment freedoms and, as I shall argue, the freedom and freedom-from individual rights entailed by the establishment clause. Let us assume that the descriptive term of the privileges or immunities clause is one of description only. If the privileges or immunities clause embraces all the specific individual rights in the Bill of Rights, the presence of the due process clause is superfluous because, given the citizenship clause, it is clear that the term "person" in the Fifth and Fourteenth Amendments are equivalent in meaning. If, on the other hand, the only specific rights denoted by the descriptive term of the privileges or immunities clause are the First Amendment freedoms (and the freedom-from right entailed by the establishment clause), the Fourteenth Amendment due process clause is not superfluous. And, each due process clause embodies some other specific rights, or some components of yet other specific rights, in amendments II–VIII. This type of intrinsic quasi-incorporation by both due process clauses of other specific rights coheres with their equivalence in meaning, and obtains by virtue of their intrinsic meaning.[113]

To assert that there are constitutional rights, privileges, and immunities of citizens of the United States is to implicitly assert that the United States shall not make or enforce any law that shall abridge them. However, this assertion does not necessarily entail that the states are constitutionally precluded from making or enforcing any law that shall abridge them.[114]

The privileges or immunities clause presupposes preexisting constitutional privileges or immunities of citizens of the United States, secured against abridgment by the United States. It does not purport to add to such privileges and immunities "one iota."[115] It does, however, add another security device for them since the clause prohibits the states from making or enforcing laws that shall abridge them. On the other hand, the privileges or immunities clause does not of itself prohibit states from making or enforcing any law that shall abridge the rights of American citizens other than their privileges and immunities (understood in the requisite sense).

The foregoing suggests the following question to me: Why are the freedoms of speech and the press, for example, so aptly called privileges of American citizens? It is because the Constitution secures for them their freedoms of speech and the press against all abridgments by the United States. The same may be said *mutatis mutandis* (i.e., the necessary changes having been made) about the immunities and other privileges of American citizens. Each First Amendment freedom is secured against some abridgments because some of their components are proximately (i.e., closely but not necessarily immediately) grounded upon the dignity of free persons as rational, social, and moral beings. However, these freedoms are secured against *all* abridgments because of public policy reasons founded in the fundamental constitutional principles underlying or embodied in our political and civil institutions besides those sounding in human dignity.

For example, the constitutional ban on all abridgments by the United States (and now by the states) of the freedoms of speech and the press obtains because: (1) The power to abridge these freedoms is especially liable to be egregiously and systemically misused or abused, as history well attests. (2) The freedoms of speech and the press have a checking value on the abuses and misuses of power. (3) These freedoms provide indispensible and expeditious means by which citizens obtain information about matters that may be relevant to make judgments about political and other issues of public concern. (4) That one is free in all appropriate domains to disagree with government, vested interests, and the current dominant public opinion as to fundamental matters in religion, philosophy, science, politics, et al., serves as a de facto check on the egregious or systematic abuse or misuse of power since authority does not like to be opposed, challenged, or criticized. (4) Repression in any domain, form or channel of the public expression of dissenting views by speech or writing on matters of general interest tends to excite widespread suspicion that the truth is being suppressed by governments—all too frequently with bad motives and for unjustifiable ends. (5) Given a fully protected freedom of speech and the press, everyone is at least free in all appropriate forms and channels of public communication to profess and maintain true principles, doctrines, and facts concerning matters of general interest. (6) The regime of fully protected freedom of speech and of the press is consistent with the Government noncoercively promoting (the actual or supposed) truth, and using its police power to constitutionally regulate uncommunicative action in ways that influence the formation of public opinion.

Chapter C: Amar and the Alleged Doctrine of *Dred Scott* that All Constitutional Rights of American Citizens Are Their Exclusive Rights

Every free American citizen is fully entitled to every constitutional freedom. It is possible that some but not necessarily all free persons who are not American citizens are also per se fully entitled to a particular freedom.[116] Thus, it is appropriate for First Amendment freedoms to be expressly termed as privileges of American citizens since every free American citizen, but not necessarily every free noncitizen, is per se entitled to them. Thus the term "privileges" in the privileges or immunities clause may perhaps be used both in the sense of denoting freedoms that per se are either applicable exclusively to American citizens, or are necessarily applicable not only as to them but as well as to some but not all persons who are not American citizens—all other things being equal. So it is possible that the term "privileges [and] immunities of citizens of the United States" is aptly expressed to indicate certain rights of American citizens that are necessarily theirs, although some but not all other persons may also be entitled to their benefit. But this is not the view of Amar since he holds that the descriptive term of the privileges or immunities clause pertains to the exclusive rights of American citizens because of the alleged doctrine of the notorious case of *Dred Scott Case* (1857)[117] that only American citizens are entitled to the benefit of constitutional rights held against the United States—until this doctrine is overruled by the Supreme Court.[118]

Because of his idée fixée that all civil rights explicitly or implicitly protected in the Bill of Rights are incorporated by the privileges or immunities clause, Amar must rely upon the alleged *Dred Scott* doctrine because otherwise he cannot overcome the serious objection that the Fourteenth Amendment due process clause is an embarrassing redundancy. Alas! He can only overcome the objection by counterintuitively positing that the term "person" has different meanings respectively in the fifth and fourteenth Amendments—until and unless the Supreme Court shall have overruled the alleged *Dred Scott* doctrine.

Although I believe Amar's view that the alleged doctrine of *Dred Scott* (assuming for argument's sake its existence) was overruled (at the latest) with the adoption of the Fourteenth Amendment, it is nevertheless important to discuss in greater detail this alleged doctrine because the opinion of Amar and other distinguished scholars[119] deserves further serious consideration.

At the outset, I simply deny that *Dred Scott* should even be understood as having declared that every antebellum noncitizen was not entitled to any right specified in the Bill of Rights. A careful reading of Chief Justice Taney's opinion for the Court would disclose that when he described the Bill of Rights as securing the rights of citizens he was not saying that every specified right has been secured for *only* American citizens. In support of his position, Amar cites the fact that "*Dred Scott* declared the rights in the Bill [of Rights] to be not simply privileges, but 'privileges *of the citizen.*'"[120] However, it seems to me that *Dred Scott* may pertain to certain rights that all citizens have but not necessarily exclusively so. But, when it refers, for example, to "all the rights, and privileges, and immunities, guaranteed by [the Constitution] *to the citizen*,"[121] or "the personal rights and privileges guarantied *to citizens*,"[122] the opinion appears to mean only such "rights and privileges" to which only American citizens are entitled. To be sure, the *Dred Scott* opinion is itself the cause of confusion because it is more likely than not that it is ambiguously uses the relevant terms. However, the *Dred Scott* opinion is quite clear when it asserts: "The question with which we are now dealing is, whether a person of the African race can be a citizen of the United States, and become thereby entitled to a special privilege, by virtue to his title to that character, and which, under the Constitution, no one but a citizen can claim."[123] Thus to refer to a certain right as a *privilege* of American citizens does not necessarily mean that it is their *special privilege*.

These *special* constitutional rights and privileges of American citizens, according to the doctrine of *Dred Scott*, include the right as a citizen to sue in a federal court in a diversity action between citizens of different states and the specific right of the comity clause. The Court, however, did not indicate which other constitutional rights were also the *special* rights and privileges of American citizens, although it is very likely that "the rights of man and rights of the people" were regarded as such *special* rights and privileges.[124] What needs to be emphasized is that the Court in *Dred Scott* never declared, expressly or impliedly, that nonblack aliens or noncitizen nationals were not entitled to some benefits of the due process clause of the Fifth Amendment, or of some other provisions in the Bill of Rights; albeit the opinion refers to "the rights and privileges of citizens [as] regulated and plainly defined by the Constitution itself."[125]

To be sure, the *Dred Scott* Court *appears* to have declared that blacks, whether free or slave, were not entitled per se to any right specified in the Bill of Rights, or elsewhere in the Constitution.[126] There can be no doubt that the Court's opinion *actually* declared that native-born blacks were not entitled to the *special* rights of American citizens, or to "the rights of man and the rights of the people."[127] Nevertheless, I do not think that *Dred Scott* is clearly teaching that free-and-native-born blacks were then not entitled to any right specified in the Bill of Rights (or elsewhere in the Constitution).[128] Rather, it is because such blacks were not (at the time) entitled by the law of the land to "the rights of man and the rights of the people," because of their inferior and degraded status associated with the institution of African slavery, that it must be concluded that they could not possibly be regarded as American citizens and hence were not entitled to the special rights of American citizens under the diversity and comity clauses, or to the rights of man and of the people. According to *Dred Scott*, if they were American citizens, then they would then be entitled to enjoy these special rights of citizens, as well as the rights of man and of the people, upon an equal basis with whites.

Amar urges that "[s]urely the framers of the Fourteenth Amendment were entitled to rely ... and did so rely" upon the alleged *Dred Scott* doctrine. He cites in support of his thesis that Congressman John Bingham "not only cited *Dred Scott* in a speech before the House in early 1866 but quoted, as also did Senator John Henderson, the passage from the Court's opinion: "The words 'people of the United States' and 'citizen' are synonymous terms."[129] However, what Amar offers as evidence is patently unwarranted since an examination of the referenced sources discloses that neither Bingham nor Henderson cited *Dred Scott* in support the alleged doctrine that only American citizens have the benefit of the Bill of Rights. In his more recent book, Amar claims that "[t]he citizen/person distinction [between the privileges or immunities and the due process clauses in the Fourteenth Amendment] took on particular significance because Taney's *Dred Scott* opinion had insisted that the Bill of Rights protected only 'citizens' and that free blacks, as noncitizens, had no rights under the Bill."[130] Amar makes this contention in support his rejection of the redundancy objection to the inclusion of the due process clause in the Fourteenth Amendment. According to Amar: "As Bingham and Howard both explained, the privileges-or-immunities clause would protect only *citizens* from oppressive state action. A separate due-process clause was thus needed to make clear that all 'persons'—even aliens—were entitled to basic rights of procedural fairness."[131] Speaking now only of Bingham, Amar's note 81 to the just-quoted text cites Bingham's speeches of February 28 and March 9, 1866, as evidence that Bingham had explained why "the privileges or immunities clause would protect only *citizens* from oppressive state action." However, it is absurd for Amar to make the claim in question since these two speeches were *not* about the privileges or immunities clause, which was only first proposed by Bingham to the Joint Committee on Reconstruction on April 21, 1866. The so-called "privileges or immunities clause" referred to by Amar in his anachronistic account pertains to the prototype of the privileges or immunities clause: viz., "The Congress shall have power to make all laws which shall be necessary and proper to secure to citizens of each State all privileges and immunities of citizens in the several States[.]"[132] However, in his speech of May 10, 1866, Bingham's initial explanation to the House of the privileges or immunities clause of the proposed Fourteenth Amendment (i.e., the clause in its present form) appears to still reflect his earlier opinion that the *privileges and immunities of American citizens* are those denoted by the descriptive term of the comity clause, which rights were insufficiently protected by that clause.[133]

Turning now to Senator Howard. Amar refers to Senator Howard's discussion of the privileges or immunities clause during the Senate debates on the Fourteenth Amendment. Amar claims that Howard "made plain that the language chosen was in response to *Dred Scott.*"[134] Amar then provides the following quotation from Howard's address: "[I]t is a fact well worthy of attention that the course of decision in our courts and the present settled doctrine is, that all these immunities, privileges, rights thus guarantied ... or recognized by [the first eight amendments to the Constitution] are secured to the citizen solely as a citizen of the United States."[135] The long and the short of it is that I must concede that Howard's address to the Senate, during which he presented the proposed Fourteenth Amendment (less the citizenship clause) on behalf of the Joint Committee on Reconstruction, can reasonably be read as Amar claims. But I believe that Howard's exposition of the privileges or immunities clause is remarkably confused and confusing. Moreover, it is inconsistent with his account of the clause that he later gave on February 8, 1869:[136]

The occasion of introducing the first section of the [F]ourteenth ... [A]mendment into that amendment grew out of the fact that there was nothing in the whole Constitution to secure absolutely the citizens of the United States in the various States against an infringement of their rights and privileges under the second section of the fourth article of the old Constitution [i.e., the comity clause].... The immediate object of [the privileges or immunities clause] was to prohibit for the future all hostile legislation on the part of the recently rebel States in reference to the colored citizens of the United States who had become emancipated, and who finally were declared to be citizens by the civil rights bill passed by Congress. It was to secure these against any infringement or violation of their rights by those southern Legislatures. That is the whole history of it.

So much for Congressman Bingham and Senator Howard as reliable expositors of the privileges or immunities clause! Bingham initially read that clause as a remake of the comity clause and later read it as incorporating all the rights specified in the Bill of Rights but not those protected by the comity clause. Howard initially read the descriptive term of the clause as including the rights denoted by the descriptive term of the comity clause and the rights specified in the Bill of Rights. He later read the clause as denoting only the rights denoted by the descriptive term of the comity clause.

Amar stresses that Bingham was the author of the privileges or immunities clause, and that Howard was a member of the Joint Reconstruction Committee. Both gave explanations of the newly proposed Fourteenth Amendment. Amar remarks: "And not a single person in either house spoke up to deny these men's interpretations of section I. Surely, if the words of section I meant something different, this was the time to stand up and say so."[137] Just so! But even Amar acknowledges that the relative paucity of debate in both houses of the Congress has a ready explanation. As he puts it:

> In 1866 the Thirty-ninth Congress … shroud[ed] early deliberations in the secrecy of the Joint Committee on Reconstruction.… [P]eople in 1866 impatiently looked for white smoke to emerge from the mysterious Joint Committee conclave. When official proposals did finally issue, their public exposition by leading architects like Bingham, Howard, and Stevens received special attention. But … partisanship impoverished deliberation. Many of the key discussions in Washington "were carried on not in the legal Senate of the United States, but in a party meeting" from which Democrats were excluded.[138]

Elsewhere Amar attempts to bolster his case that *Dred Scott* limited the protection of the Fifth Amendment to only American citizens by asserting: "But Bingham also said that *Dred Scott* had gone too far, limiting certain rights, such as due process, that under both natural law and constitutional text extended to all persons, whether citizens or not."[139] According to Amar, "Bingham once again quoted from *Dred Scott* on constitutional rights of 'citizens' as 'citizens,' yet repeated his claim that *Dred Scott* was too stingy in refusing certain due-process protections to 'persons, whether citizens or strangers.'"[140] Alas! A close inspection of the passages from Bingham's speeches cited by Amar in support of these contentions discloses that Amar's attribution to Bingham of the opinion, that *Dred Scott* had indeed declared (expressly or impliedly) that the Fifth Amendment due process clause protected only American citizens, is utterly unwarranted.

What Bingham had asserted was that the comity clause protects all and only American citizens, and that free-and-native-born blacks were such citizens since the abolition of slavery. Bingham believed that the absence of federal power to enforce the Bill of Rights and the comity clause against the states had been due to the existence of slavery "for although slaves might not have been admitted to be citizens they must have been admitted to be persons." But he acknowledged that: "As slaves were not protected by the Constitution, there might be some color of excuse for the slave States in their disregard for the requirement of the bill of rights as to slaves and refusing them protection in life and property[.]"[141] Such expressions are hardly the views of someone who thought that *Dred Scott* maintained that *all* noncitizens, and not just slaves, were not entitled to the benefit of any specific right in the Bill of Rights. Amar refers to Bingham's "position that no state could violate the Constitution's wise and beneficient guarantees of political rights to the citizens of the United States, as such, and of natural rights to all persons, whether citizens or strangers."[142] Amar then remarks: "These views, expressed in 1859, track almost perfectly the natural meaning of the words Bingham drafted in 1866 as section I of the Fourteenth Amendment."[143] This comment shows how Amar so grossly misunderstands Bingham; for Bingham was distinguishing between political rights of citizens (i.e., the right to vote, hold office) and the natural rights of all persons. However, the privileges or immunities clause does not, as Amar himself has elsewhere acknowledged, concern itself with political rights.[144]

Even assuming, for the sake of argument, that *Dred* Scott had declared that every specific right in the Bill of Rights applies only to American citizens, this doctrine and that companion doctrine asserting the inapplicability of any such right to free blacks, must be regarded as without binding force before the adoption of the Fourteenth Amendment.

First, this alleged doctrine should be regarded only as obiter dicta, made in the course of a long argument purporting to resolve the jurisdictional issue as to whether Dred Scott could sue in the federal court. The Court's holding was that Dred Scott could not sue in the federal court because free-and-native-born blacks were not and could not be American citizens, and hence, not "entitled to a *special* privilege, by virtue of his title to that character [i.e., being a citizen of the United States], and which, under the Constitution, no one but a citizen can claim."[145]

Second, Republicans almost universally regarded as obiter dicta everything in the opinion, except they expressly or impliedly acknowledged as authoritative the ruling concerning the incapacity of native-born blacks for American citizenship.[146]

Third, the orthodox Republican Party doctrine, as propounded in its 1856 and 1860 party platforms, asserted that the Fifth Amendment due process clause precluded slavery within federal territories.[147]

Fourth, Congress abolished slavery in the District of Columbia and the federal territories in 1862, well before the abolition of slavery in 1865 with the adoption of the thirteen amendment, thereby confirming the fact of presidential and congressional repudiation of *Dred Scott*.[148]

Fifth, Congressman John Bingham (the principal framer of the Fourteenth Amendment) had over the course of years repeatedly asserted that the Fifth Amendment due process clause applied per se to noncitizens, including aliens and native-born blacks, as well as to American citizens.[149]

Sixth, the abolition of slavery by the Thirteenth Amendment (adopted in 1865) itself utterly nullified that principle of *Dred Scott* to the effect that blacks were not entitled to any constitutional rights incompatible with their inferior and degraded status simply based upon the institution of African slavery.[150]

Seventh, *Dred Scott* was not generally understood as nullifying the original understanding that "person" as used in the Fifth Amendment applied to persons other than American citizens.[151]

Eighth, the opinion in *Dred Scott* on citizenship, although never formally overruled by the Court prior to the adoption of the Fourteenth Amendment, was widely considered as having been disregarded by every department of the government. For example, passports were granted to free men of color; Congress declared them to be American citizens, and the Supreme Court admitted them to the bar.[152]

Ninth, the alleged doctrine in *Dred Scott*, since it asserts that only natural persons who are American citizens are entitled to the benefit of any constitutional right, must be taken to understand that even domestic artificial persons, incorporated or otherwise recognized by the law of the United States or some state, are not entitled to the benefit of any constitutional right—before that happy date when the doctrine is overruled. But this corollary of the alleged *Dred Scott* doctrine is refuted by the fact that before and after the *Dred Scott* decision in 1857, the Supreme Court had ruled in *Louisville, Cincinnati, and Charleston Railway Co.* v. *Letson* (1844)[153] that in diversity-of-citizenship cases, despite the constitutional provision defining the "judicial Power [of federal courts] shall extend ... to Controversies ... between Citizens of different States,"[154] that "a corporation created by and doing business in a particular State, is to be deemed to all intents and purposes as a person, although an artificial person, an inhabitant of the same State, for the purposes of its incorporation, capable of being treated as a citizen of that State, as much as a natural person."[155] Interestingly, the Court in *Letson* overruled the doctrine of *Bank of United States* v. *Deveaux* (1809):[156] viz., "That invisible, intangible, and artificial being, that mere legal entity, a corporation aggregate, is certainly not a 'citizen' and consequently cannot sue or be sued in the courts of the United States, unless the rights of the members, in this respect, can be exercised in their corporate name." *Deveaux* is interesting because it suggests for us how, without resorting to a fiction, the privileges or immunities clause may be regarded as per se predicable of some corporations by virtue of their purposes and functions because "the rights of [American citizens and perhaps other natural persons] can be exercised in their corporate name." In 1877, the Court in *Muller* v. *Dows*[157] declared that a corporation is a citizen of the state in which it is chartered by virtue of the conclusive presumption that all the stockholders are citizens of the state that created the corporation.

Tenth, in the *Sinking Fund Cases*, decided in 1878, the Supreme Court for the first time expressly declared that the United States "equally with the States … are prohibited from depriving persons or corporations of property without due process of law."[158] There is no mention in the Court's opinion that its members were at all even cognizant of the alleged *Dred Scott* doctrine that only American citizens are entitled to the benefit of the Bill of Rights.

From all the foregoing, I submit that Amar's explanation of the presence of the due process clause in the Fourteenth Amendment is but a singularly unpersuasive fanciful construct besides being very counterintuitive. Amar, however, is not in error because he believes that the specific civil rights of the Bill of Rights and the original Constitution are aptly called the rights, privileges, and immunities of American citizens. His error consists in having failed to understand that the copresence of the due process clause in the Bill of Rights and the Fourteenth Amendment shows that not all specific rights in the Bill of Rights are privileges and immunities of American citizens—in the sense of the privileges or immunities clause. The copresence of the due process clauses, granted their virtual equivalence in meaning, is compatible with the view that the specific right of each due process clause can be said to include as components some but not all of the other rights specified in amendments III–VIII, or some components of unincorporated specific rights.

Chapter D: The Second Amendment Right and the States

I have deferred until now an extended discussion of the status of the right specified in the Second Amendment (SAR). To thoroughly discuss this highly controversial matter would require a very detailed analysis, given the explosion of judicial opinions and scholarly writings about its meaning during the last two decades—culminating in the recently decided *District of Columbia* v. *Heller*. [159] However, I need not do so here because that would be unnecessary for my purposes. I do not need to here expound and advocate the *true* meaning of the Second Amendment. All that I need do is to assume for argument's sake that the SAR is indeed, as the Court declares in its five-to-four decision in *Heller*, an individual civil right (unconnected to militia service) to keep and bear arms, and then proceed to consider whether or not it is incorporated by the privileges or immunities clause. Of course, were the *true* meaning of the Second Amendment such that it specifies a collective right or an individual right necessarily connected with militia service then that right would indeed not be incorporated by the privileges or immunities clause.[160] Therefore, what I hope to do is to explain why the SAR, understood to be an individual civil right unconnected to militia service, is neither incorporated by the privileges or immunities clause nor even by the Fourteenth Amendment due process clause (assuming the viability of the current Court doctrine).[161]

Suppose we would have to choose between a theory of selective incorporation whereby the privileges of American citizens include the First Amendment freedoms *and* the SAR (considered as an individual civil right unconnected to militia service), and one in which all these rights are not among the privileges of American citizens? For me, there would be no question but that I would choose the former alternative. But, as it so happens, I reject both alternatives. Instead, my position is that the SAR is not incorporated by the privileges or immunities clause precisely because it is neither a privilege nor an immunity in the sense of that provision. That is to say that the SAR is neither a freedom-right nor a freedom-from right. Moreover, the

SAR should also not be deemed an incorporated fundamental right according to the Court's current theory of selective incorporation via the Fourteenth Amendment due process clause.

So, since *Heller* deems the SAR to be an individual civil right, what are its chief characteristics? According to the *Heller* Court:

> We start ... with a strong presumption that the Second Amendment right is exercised individually and belongs to all Americans.[162]

> [T]he Second Amendment extends, prima facie, to all instruments that constitute bearable arms, even those that were not in existence at the time of the founding.

> [T]he most natural reading of "keep Arms" in the Second Amendment is to "have weapons."[163]

> "Keep arms' was simply a common way of referring to possessing arms, for militiamen *and everyone else.*[164]

> At the time of the founding, as now, to "bear" meant to "carry."[165]

> "[B]ear arms" was not limited to the carrying of arms in a militia.[166]

> [T]he Second Amendment conferred an individual right to keep and bear arms.[167]

> [T]he Second Amendment's prefatory clause announces the purpose for which the right was codified: to prevent elimination of the militia. The prefatory clause does not suggest that preserving the militia was the only reason American valued the ancient right; most undoubtedly thought it even more important for self-defense and hunting. But the threat that the new Federal Government would destroy the citizens' militia by taking away their arms was the reason that right—unlike other English rights—was codified in a written Constitution.... [T]he prologue [i.e., the prefatory clause] ... can only show that

self-defense had little to do with the right's *codification*; it was the *central component* of the right itself.[168]

[T]he inherent right of self-defense has been central to the Second Amendment right.[169]

[T]he Second Amendment does not protect those weapons not typically possessed by law-abiding citizens for lawful purposes.[170]...

[T]he right secured by the Second Amendment is not unlimited.... [T]he right was not a right to keep and carry any weapon whatsoever in any manner and for whatever purpose.[171]

[N]othing in our opinion should be taken to cast doubt on longstanding prohibitions on the possession of firearms by felons and the mentally ill, or laws forbidding the carrying of firearms in sensitive places such as schools and government buildings, or laws imposing conditions and qualifications on the commercial sale of arms.[172]

[T]he sorts of weapons protected were those "in common use at the time." ... We think that limitation is fairly supported by the historical tradition of prohibiting the carrying of "dangerous and unusual weapons."[173]

It may well be true today that a militia, to be as effective as the militias in the 18th century, would require sophisticated arms that are highly unusual in society at large.... But the fact that modern developments have limited the degree of fit between the prefatory clause and the protected right cannot change our interpretation of the right.[174]

The opinion [in *United States* v. *Cruikshank* (1876)] explained ... "[that t]he Second Amendment ... means no more than that it shall not be infringed by Congress." ... States, we said, were free to restrict or protect the right under their police powers.[175]

> With respect to *Cruikshank*'s continuing validity on incorporation, a question not presented by this case, we note that *Cruikshank* also said the First Amendment did not apply to the States and did not engage in the sort of Fourteenth Amendment inquiry required by our later cases.[176]

So, according to the Court in *Heller*, the SAR is an individual civil right, unconnected to militia service, to keep and bear arms, and that the Second Amendment prohibits its infringement by the United States. It is an open question for the Court about whether the SAR is incorporated by the Fourteenth Amendment. We now explore this question—bearing in mind that the same reasons I propose for holding that the SAR is not a constitutional privilege or immunity of the American people also apply to whether the SAR is a fundamental right incorporated by the Fourteenth Amendment due process clause.

It is very important to have a correct understanding of the relationship between the Second Amendment's prefatory clause (i.e., that a well-regulated militia is necessary for the security of a free state) and its operative clause (i.e., that the right of the people to keep and bear arms shall not be infringed). First, recall that the First Amendment freedoms and the SAR are secured against any infringement. But the reason why the SAR is secured against any infringement is expressed in the Second Amendment itself, namely, that a well-regulated militia is necessary for the security of a free state. The judiciary should deem itself estopped from eroding, as it were, the operative clause in the event it appears that the prefatory clause no longer has factual warrant. Bear in mind, however, that the Second Amendment codifies an individual right to keep and bear arms to which self-defense is central. However, had a well organized militia not been deemed by the founders as essential to the security of a free state, it is very probable that they would not have approved a constitutional provision that bars any infringement of the SAR. Instead, they might have well supported a provision that read, "The right of the people to keep and bear arms shall not be unreasonably infringed."

The Second Amendment thus precludes the argument: (a) if a well-regulated militia is necessary for the security of a free state then the right to keep and bear arms shall not be infringed; (b) but a well regulated militia is no longer (factually) necessary for the security of a free state; (c) therefore, it is no longer (legally) necessary that the right to keep and bear arms shall not be infringed. Notwithstanding the foregoing, the Second Amendment, properly read, necessarily presupposes that its command that its specified right shall not be infringed is legally necessary as a matter of political principle because a well-regulated militia is asserted as necessary for the security of a free state. Hence if one determines that it is no longer (if it ever was) the case that a well-regulated militia is necessary for the security of a free state, then it is no longer (if it ever was) the case that the SAR is not to be not be infringed as a matter of political principle—albeit that the constitutional bar to such infringement obtains until such time as the prohibition is repealed or modified.

It bears repeating: what the Second Amendment presupposes is not that the SAR be not infringed as a matter of political principle whether or not the prefatory clause lacks warrant. Instead, the Second Amendment presupposes that the reason why the SAR is not to be infringed at all is that a well-regulated militia is necessary for the security of the free state. This appears to me to be the case because it would have been so easy for the framers of the Second Amendment to have made it read: "The right of the people to keep and bear arms, being necessary for the security of a free state, shall not be infringed."[177] Were the Second Amendment to have so read than it would appear that the command in its operative clause would be necessary as a matter of political principle even were it come to pass that a well-regulated militia was no longer necessary for the security of a free state. It seems to me that the right to keep and bear arms should not be regarded as a fundamental right if only because the present prefatory clause explains why the right shall not be infringed.

That the framers of the Bill of Rights regarded the First Amendment freedoms quite differently from the SAR is evidenced by the House of Representatives referring (on August 24, 1789) to the

Senate an ultimately rejected proposed amendment that: "No State shall infringe the right of trial by jury in criminal cases, nor the rights of conscience, nor the freedom of speech, or of the press"—without any mention of the right to keep and bear arms.[178]

Neither any First Amendment freedom nor the SAR encompasses all logically possible rights pertaining to religion, speech, press, assembly, and the keeping and bearing of arms, respectively. However, every First Amendment freedom is absolute in the sense that the First Amendment bars every abridgment—whether reasonable or not. The SAR is also ostensibly absolute in the same sense because the Second Amendment bars every infringement of the right to keep and bear arms (within the meaning of the Second Amendment). Therefore, the SAR is quite unlike the Fourth Amendment right to be free from unreasonable searches and seizures.[179] That is to say, the Second Amendment secures a particular right that is to be free from any infringement—whether reasonable or not. However, even this does not entail that all reasonable regulations of arms keeping and bearing are infringements of the SAR, any more than the First Amendment bars every reasonable regulation of speech or of the press. However, as I now propose to show, any First Amendment freedom and the SAR are radically different in that the latter but not the former is a conditional liberty-right with respect to its core components.

What does it mean to say that the Second Amendment right is (or is not) a freedom in the same sense that any First Amendment right is a freedom? Religious freedom is a freedom in the following sense: I have, for example, the legal right to go [or not go] to some church on Sunday even though I have no present legal duty to do [or not do] so. More importantly, I have a legal right to go [or not go] to any church since it is constitutionally impossible for me to have the legal duty for me to go [or not go] to any particular church. Or, to take another example, I have a legal right to advocate polytheism even though I have no present legal duty to do [or not do] so.[180] Again, I have a legal right to advocate polytheism or not to do so because a legal duty for me to do or not do so is constitutionally impossible. When we speak of a constitutional freedom, we mean more than a domain in which I am free to do [or not do] x where there is not an extant constitutionally permissible legal duty obliging me to do [or not do] x. A constitutional freedom pertains to a domain in which it is legally impossible for there to be a legal duty on my part to do [or not do] x. I would not be constitutionally free to do [or not do] x if it is constitutionally possible for there to be a legal requirement for me to do [or not do] x, albeit by legislative grace there is no legal duty currently in force. Hence, generally speaking, the First Amendment freedoms pertain principally to domains of freedom in which it is constitutionally impossible for there to be legal duties to compel one to do or not do x.[181] In short, I cannot properly be said to be *free* to do or not do x unless it is legally impossible for me to be obliged to do or not do x.

According to the adherents of a strong reading of the Second Amendment, the principal reasons why it secures an individual right against any infringement are: first and foremost because the citizenry should be generally armed so as to provide a sufficiently large, self-armed population-base for a well-regulated militia for the several states. Second, the existence of a well-armed citizenry provides an additional security against tyranny and oppression (especially by the federal government). Third, well-armed and able-bodied citizens may be legally required to aid in law enforcement or crime prevention. Given the underlying theory, it appears obvious why the Second Amendment does not foreclose the possibility of a rather large body of constitutionally possible legal duties relating to arms keeping or bearing. For example, the underlying policy of the prefatory clause of the Second Amendment could conceivably be served by requiring citizens to procure their own suitable weapons at their own expense and to train with them. Thus, the SAR is not a freedom because it encompasses domains in which it is constitutionally possible for there to be legal duties to acquire, keep, and bear private arms. To be sure, where there is no relevant obligation to acquire, keep, and bear private arms, the right holder is constitutionally free to keep and bear private arms, or not to do so. The right holder, we can say, is constitutionally *entitled* to do what he may be constitutionally *obliged* to do by statute. Thus the right to be free to keep and bear private arms or not to do so, in the absence of a legal obligation to do so, does not entail that there cannot constitutionally be a legal obligation to do so.

The original states (and even as colonies), up to and for some time after the adoption of the Bill of Rights, generally required militia members to procure weapons at their own expense. Indeed, some statutes of the colonies and the early states even required the keeping of firearms by households, whether or not a household included a militia member. Some statutes required the carrying of firearms by citizens when going about in the course of just being private citizens. This fact is candidly acknowledged by adherants of the individual-rights theory of the Second Amendment. For example, Don B. Kates, Jr.[182] noted that colonial statutes imposed "a duty to keep arms and to muster occasionally for drill upon virtually every able-bodied white man [within certain age ranges]. Moreover, the duty to keep arms applied to *every* household, not just to those containing persons subject to military service. Thus, the over-aged and seamen, who were exempt from militia service, were required to keep arms for law enforcement and for the defense of their homes from criminals or foreign enemies."[183] He noted that one colonial statute (Georgia 1770) "actually required men to carry a rifle or pistol every time they attended church."[184] One advantage of a citizenry legally compelled to own and maintain arms was that it provided a population base not only for a well-organized militia, but also for the *posse comitatus,* slave patrols, and such police activities as watch at night and ward at day. The Supreme Court itself noted in *United States* v. *Miller*:

> The signification attributed to the term Militia appears from the debates in the Convention, the history and legislation of Colonies and States, and the writings of approved commentators. These show plainly enough that the Militia comprised all males physically capable of acting in concert for the common defense. "A body of citizens enrolled for military discipline." And further, that ordinarily when called for service these men were expected to appear bearing arms supplied by themselves and the kind in common use at the time.[185]

It is especially significant that the Congress enacted in 1792 the first militia statute. This statute provided in part:

> [E]ach and every free able-bodied white male citizen of the respective states, resident therein, who is or shall be of the age of eighteen years, and under the age of forty-five years (except as is herein after excepted) shall severally and respectively be enrolled in the militia.... [E]very citizen so enrolled and notified, shall, within six months thereafter, provide himself with a good musket or firelock, a sufficient bayonet and belt, two spare flints, and a knapsack, a pouch with a box therein to contain not less than twenty-four cartridges, suited to the bore of his musket or firelock, each cartridge to contain a proper quantity of powder and ball; or with a good rifle, knapsack, shot-pouch and powder-horn, twenty balls suited to the bore of his rifle, and a quarter of a pound of powder; and shall appear, so armed, accoutered and provided, when called out to exercise, or into service, except, that when called out on company days to exercise only, he may appear without a knapsack. That the commissioned officers shall severally be armed with a sword or hanger [a short, usually slightly curbed sword] and espontroon [a kind of half-pike], and that from and after five years from the passing of this act, all muskets for arming the militia as herein required, shall be of bores sufficient for balls of the eighteenth part of a pound....[186]

For well over a century, until the enactment of the Dick Act in 1903,[187] the 1792 militia statute was officially in force. According to one writer, the provisions of the 1792 act "were unworkable when they were adopted; they were worthless; and for generations prior to their repeal, in 1903, they were ... no more than 'an interesting cabinet of antiquities.'"[188] As another writer put it: "[The 1792 militia act] listed categories of men who were exempt from service, and it authorized the states to expand their lists of exemptions farther."[189] Moreover, "it contained no penalties, either upon states or individuals, for failure to comply. All in all, it had the weight not of a law but of a recommendation to the states."[190]

Despite these minimizing assessments, the states nevertheless had already in force or proceeded to enact statutes calculated to implement and to conform to the 1792 Militia Act. These state statutes can be summarized as follows:[191]

> Every member of the militia was required to attend militia drills and parades with all the necessary arms and equipment which he had to furnish at his own expense....
>
> Service in the militia was obligatory. Absence from a militia muster or appearing without the specified arms and equipment imposed the penalty of a fine. This fine was the crucial point in the militia system for it was the means used to enforce compulsory military service. If the fine was not paid, the militiaman's property was seized, just as in the case of distraint for debt; and, if he did not have sufficient property to cover the fine, he was sent to jail, just as he would be for inability to pay a debt....

Well before the Civil War, the obligatory militia system based upon the 1792 experienced a gradual, and then accelerating, demise during the 1820s through the 1850s.[192] Following the Civil War, Wiener writes: "[T]he armies were dissolved. The Militia contemplated by the Act of 1792, that is, the whole body of the people, virtually ceased to exist, and the States relied more and more upon select bodies of men, trained after a fashion and without uniform supervision, who, became known as National Guards."[193]

Don B. Kates, Jr., referring to the 1792 Militia Act, has rightly observed that "[l]egislation by Congress immediately following adoption of an amendment is entitled to great weight in the construction thereof."[194] Accordingly, he comments thus: "Since one can scarcely argue that the First Militia Act violated the amendment, it is difficult to see that it would be unconstitutional for Congress even today to require every member of the present militia to possess a firearm and regularly present it for inspection to assure that it is being maintained in good working order."[195] In this statement, his intuition is prescient. In *Perpich* v. *Department of Defense*,[196] the Court commented:

The second Militia Clause enhances federal power in three additional ways. First, it authorizes Congress to provide for "organizing, arming and disciplining the Militia." It is by congressional choice that the available pool of citizens has been formed into organized units. *Over the years, Congress has exercised this power in various ways, but its current choice of a dual enlistment system is just as permissible as the 1792 choice to have the members of the militia arm themselves.*[197]

So the hoary doctrine that general militia members may be legally obliged to arm themselves at their own expense is still very much with us—according to the United States Supreme Court. Thus, the SAR, although it has been according to *Heller* an individual civil right unconnected to militia service from the beginning, is not a freedom given the dictum of the Court in *Perpich.*[198]

As one writer, a supporter of a strong, individual rights reading of the Second Amendment, has put it, "Presumably the framers of that amendment considered that tradition [i.e., "militiamen were still required by state law to possess and furnish their own arms"] when they wrote the guarantee of 'the right of the people to keep and bear arms.'"[199] Referring to the 1792 militia act, this writer explained:

> Since the existence of a duty implies the right to perform the duty, and since it was the duty of each such individual citizen to keep and bear arms, it is clear that every individual citizen was to have the corresponding right to keep and bear arms.... Certainly the Militia Act of 1792 enacted by many of the same men who framed the Second Amendment throws definitive illumination upon the meaning of that amendment, particularly since it was enacted to carry into effect the militia clause of the Constitution immediately after the Second Amendment was adopted.[200]

Even so hearty an advocate of a strong individual civil right model as Stephen S. Halbrook, in a commentary on *United States v. Miller,* added emphasis to the words, "these men [i.e., general militia members] were expected to appear bearing arms supplied by themselves," appearing in the Court's opinion.[201] Thus, he appears to have agreed about the constitutionality of legal duties to personally own and carry arms, when he remarked: "The Supreme Court's historical analysis [in *Miller*] demonstrates that the 'well regulated militia' referred to in the Second Amendment meant the whole people armed and not a select group, that each private individual had the right and duty to keep and bear arms, and that the people were to provide their own armed protection[.]"[202]

In an article written in 1991, Halbrook noted, "Congress enacted legislation mandating that every man be armed."[203] He also remarked: "From the earliest interpretations of the Constitution to the present, it has been consistently held that the states have a concurrent power over the militia with the United States and that each state may require its able-bodied citizens to provide themselves with and keep firearms, especially militia weapons."[204] Moreover, "[t]he states passed militia laws in support of and to enforce the 1792 Act of Congress"—Halbrook noting a Massachusetts statute that "required that every citizen 'constantly keep himself furnished and provided with arms and equipments required by the laws of the United States[.]'"[205] He asserted, "Congress has no power to prohibit possession of such militia arms as the states are entitled to require that its citizens or a part thereof furnish themselves with and keep in their homes. The States' concurrent power to organize and provide for arming their militias is a reserved power which federal legislation may not contradict."[206] It would seem that Halbrook admitted that the right to keep and bear arms does not entail the absence of legal obligations to own arms, furnished at one's own expense, and to bear them for militia and other public purposes.

Halbrook, however, seems of two minds on the subject. In his 1991 article, he referred to the Senate deleting the religious scruples phrase (i.e., "no person religiously scrupulous shall be compelled to bear arms") from the proposed amendment submitted by the House. He explained this deletion as follows:

> [P]erhaps because the amendment depicts the keeping and bearing of arms as an individual "right" (and not as a

duty) for both public and private purposes, and perhaps to preclude any constitutional authority of the government to "compel" individuals (even those without religious scruples) to bear arms for any purpose. Deletion of the clause also addressed Congressman Gerry's argument in the House that "this clause would give an opportunity to the people in power to destroy the constitution itself. They can declare who are those religiously scrupulous, and prevent them from bearing arms."[207]

In his book, *That Every Man Be Armed*, Halbrook similarly referred to the eventual deletion from the proposed Second Amendment of the religious scruples clause. But Halbrook suggests in his book that its "purpose ... was to guarantee the individual 'right' to keep and bear arms rather than to create a 'duty' to do so. Arguably, this deletion was meant to preclude any constitutional power of the government to compel any person to bear arms rather than to exempt only the religiously scrupulous"; noting approvingly an article asserting that compulsory military service is confined to the militia.[208] The point, however, is not that the Second Amendment creates a duty to keep and bear arms. Rather, the point is whether what is purportedly a freedom-right to keep and bear arms can coexist with a legal duty to keep and bear arms. At worst, Halbrook has been evasive and disingenuous. At best, Halbrook has been of two minds upon the question whether militia members can be legally obliged to provide and maintain their weapons at their own expense.

Surely, the Second Amendment itself does not impose upon general militia members any legal duty to keep and bear arms. Also, given that citizens generally have legal civil and/or political obligations, the legal duty of members of the armed forces, and militia members, to be on active duty or otherwise to perform public service duties, would be consistent with the SAR considered as a freedom. Similarly, a legal duty for militia members to keep and bear government-provided arms when performing militia duties would be similarly consistent with the supposed freedom. However, if the right to keep and bear arms is a true freedom, a legal duty imposed on general militia members to procure specified firearms, and ammunition, bayonets, and related equipment, at their own expense, is a violation of the supposed freedom in question. Similarly, a legal duty imposed upon general militia members to carry privately owned, militia-type weapons when not performing actual militia duties would violate the purported freedom of arms bearing. Nevertheless, these hypothetical legal duties are not violations of the SAR since it is not a freedom. What the Second Amendment is supposed to insure, according to the strong view, is that general militia members are free within rather broad limits to keep and bear appropriate arms in the absence, or in excess of, what of legally required of them. This liberty, in excess of what is legally required, would be a benefit for relatively few members of the general militia, given the rather limited financial resources of most militia members were they required to procure legally prescribed arms and related items at their own expense.

Arguably, unreasonably unequal burdens with respect to obliging citizens to obtain their own arms at their own expense and train with them might violate a constitutional right other than the SAR. Even so, the SAR is not infringed by imposing legal obligations upon the citizenry to procure prescribed weapons at their own expense since the members of Congress that enacted the 1792 militia act were very well aware of the possible burdens on the poor.[209]

To properly judge whether the SAR is incorporated by the privileges or immunities clause as a freedom, consideration should be given to the dominant opinion of the founders of the Fourteenth Amendment. What is the evidence that it was then considered a violation of the right to keep and bear arms if enrolled general militia members, at least those financially able, were legally obliged to provide arms and equip themselves at their own expense? Was it the dominant opinion, at the founding of the Fourteenth Amendment, that it was unconstitutional to require general militia members to provide their own arms and equip themselves at their own expense rather than being unjust, unwise, or inexpedient for public policy reasons? Such evidence would be difficult to come by since legal obligations for militia members to provide their own weapons had either generally been eliminated or had fallen in desuetude.

However, it is noteworthy that the same Congress, which had submitted to the states of the proposed Fourteenth Amendment for ratification, enacted a statute that provided:

That the act entitled "An act more effectually to provide for the national defence by establishing an uniform militia throughout the United States," approved May eight, seventeen hundred and ninety-two, and the several acts amendatory thereof, be, and they are hereby, amended by striking out the word "white."[210]

So, it does not appear that the founders of the Fourteenth Amendment in Congress held that the right to keep and bear arms is inconsistent with the imposition of legal duties on enrolled militia members to procure and maintain arms at their own expense.

From the time of the enactment of the 1792 Militia Act until its virtual demise, I venture to predict that you will look in vain for any published evidences that any member of Congress protested against the imposition of legal duties to keep and bear private arms at the citizens' expense upon the grounds that the SAR was violated by such requirements.[211] Indeed, those who favored the government providing firearms for militia members, or at least for those financially unable to procure them, did not urge Second Amendment grounds against legally obliging those financially able to procure weapons to do so.[212] There were, on the other hand, many outside of Congress who throughout the years expressed objections to these legal obligations upon grounds of justice and expediency, or of religious scruples. Thus, "the existing compulsory militia [was attacked] as wasteful, useless, a burden on the poor, and a cause of vice," and "'of course unjust' for the heaviest burden falls upon the poor."[213] The system of militia fines was condemned "on two main grounds. In the first place, they were unjust because they imposed the same burden upon poor and rich alike; secondly, those who were too poor to pay them were punished by imprisonment."[214] From 1830 to 1860, the dominant trend was for the states to altogether eliminate or drastically reduce legal duties to keep and bear arms at one's own expense.[215] Additionally, some states amended their constitutions or statutes in order to preclude imprisonment for debt for failure to pay militia fines in time of peace.[216] Significantly, state constitutions that included a provision eliminating imprisonment for failure to pay militia fines bracketed it with that forbidding imprisonment for debt rather than any provision pertaining to the militia or to the securing of the right to keep and bear arms.[217]

Amar astutely asserts: "It is a well-regulated militia, and not an army of conscripts, that is *'necessary* to the security of a free state'; the Second Amendment estops Congress from claiming otherwise."[218] However, the amendment's prefatory clause should also estop the Supreme Court from claiming otherwise when it construes the Second Amendment. If such an estoppel precludes the watering down of the legal rights of the people under the Second Amendment, it also should preclude the watering down of their potential legal obligations—even though some of their rights and duties are supposedly outmoded because the prefatory clause of the Second Amendment is outmoded. If the SAR was indeed mutated into a freedom, then its supposed incorporation by the Fourteenth Amendment deprived Congress and the states of their erstwhile constitutional authority to require their able-bodied citizens to provide themselves with standard military arms at their own expense. Thus, the very existence of the prefatory clause in the Second Amendment provides an additional ground for concluding that the SAR cannot properly be mutated into a freedom with the adoption of the Fourteenth Amendment.[219] Amar's *feedback effect* doctrine confronts a limiting case given the Second Amendment's prefatory clause.

Admittedly, we are flying in a rather rarefied atmosphere, but then we have been compelled to do so given the polemics of the controversy concerning the Second Amendment. Returning by the force of gravity to terra firma, it is patently the case that the institution of the general militia as providing the basis of a well-regulated militia was in very bad trouble well before Civil War.[220] Justice Joseph Story, as early as 1833, in discussing the Second Amendment, lamented:

[I]t cannot be disguised, that among the American people, there is a growing indifference to any system of militia discipline, and a strong disposition, from a sense of its burdens, to be rid of all regulations. How is it practicable to keep the people duly armed without some organization, it is difficult to see. There is certainly no small danger that indifference may lead to disgust, and disgust to contempt; and thus gradually undermine all the protections intended by this clause of our national bill of rights.[221]

Given the foregoing, we may well inquire whether it is expedient and wise to insist that what (according to the original understanding of the founders of the Bill of Rights) was not a freedom should now be deemed to have been mutated into a freedom because of the adoption of the Fourteenth Amendment—especially in the absence of strong evidence that a significant body of opinion at the time of the founding of the Fourteenth Amendment regarded the imposition of legal duties to keep and bear firearms at one's own expense for militia and public purposes as not infringing upon the SAR.

Stephen P. Halbrook misses the point when he rightly (from one point of view) insists that denying the necessity for a free state to have a well-regulated militia does not entail denial of the proposition that the right to keep and bear arms shall not be infringed.[222] But my point is that since (arguendo, at least) the virtual obsolescence of a well-regulated, general militia had become rather obvious before the adoption of the Fourteenth Amendment, then there is every good practical reason that the SAR should not be judged as having been somehow mutated from a non-freedom into a freedom, thus enabling its incorporation by the privileges or immunities clause. The very point that the Second Amendment prohibits any infringement by the United States of the right to keep and bear arms should make us very leery of imposing the same limitation upon the states given that the preamble has been falsified by changing circumstances—unless, of course, you, the reader, have no objection to a watering down of the meaning of the Second Amendment.

Here is perhaps the best place to take notice of what Halbrook considers a very important fact bearing upon the issue of the incorporation of the SAR.[223] He has urged, "The same two-thirds of Congress that passed the Fourteenth Amendment to the United States Constitution also adopted the Freedmen's Bureau Act, which protected the 'full and equal benefit of all laws and proceedings concerning personal liberty, personal security, and … estate …, including the constitutional right to bear arms.'" Halbrook makes much of this statutory provision. But he did not advert sufficiently to the statute having been applicable only in not-yet-fully-reconstructed ex-Confederate states and as safeguarding that the "right … to have full and equal benefit of all laws and proceedings concerning personal liberty, personal security, and the acquisition, enjoyment, and disposition of estate …, including the constitutional right to bear arms, shall be secured to and enjoyed by all the citizens of such State or district without respect to race or color or previous condition of slavery." The Freedmen's Bureau Act may be reasonably understood to have provisionally secured to otherwise qualified persons within affected states entitlement against infringement by the affected states of the constitutional right to bear arms without respect to race, color, or previous condition of slavery. Thus, section 14 of the Act applies the SAR to the affected states and requires that entitlement to the right not be conditioned on race, color, or previous condition of slavery. However, this *statutory*, but not *constitutionally required*, incorporation of the SAR was territorially limited to only not-yet-fully-reconstructed ex-Confederate states and was of only temporary application pending the full reconstruction of an affected state. The congressional application of the SAR to the affected states, without respect to race, color, or previous condition of slavery, was much needed because the unarmed (and frequently disarmed) freedmen and women were subject to very great peril. Nevertheless, in any event, section 14 of the Freedmen's Bureau Act is not declaratory of any constitutional law that the SAR per se applies to the states. Nor does it support the view that the SAR is one of the rights denoted by the descriptive term of the privileges or immunities clause of the Fourteenth Amendment—any more than the "the right[s] to make and enforce contracts, to sue, be parties, and give evidence, to inherit, purchase, lease, sell, hold, and convey real and personal property."[224]

There is yet one more reason that shows that the SAR is not a constitutional freedom. Not only is it a conditional liberty-right. It is also predicable of only a subset (admittedly quite large) of those who are entitled to the full exercise of constitutional freedoms. For example, free persons (who are therefore not on parole or probation) are not entitled to the SAR if they have been previously convicted of a felony.

The Supreme Court has held that the Fourteenth Amendment incorporates First Amendment freedoms. The Court's theory is that the Fourteenth Amendment due-process clause is the vehicle of such incorporation. The Court's explanation is in error, but not the concrete legal fact to be explained. Were the Court to hold, as it should hold, that it is the privileges or immunities clause that incorporates the First Amendment freedoms, such a holding would not itself entail any radical change in the doctrines of the Court as to the nature, purposes, and functions of each of these freedoms. On the other hand, were the Court to hold that the SAR is incorporated by the privileges or immunities clause, it would necessarily involve a radical change in the doctrine of the Court concerning the right to keep and bear arms, elevating it to a constitutional right equal in dignity to a First Amendment freedom.

The Court has maintained that the privileges or immunities clause does not incorporate the SAR, and has never indicated otherwise.[225] It has never held that the Fourteenth Amendment due process clause incorporates the SAR. The very fact that the privileges or immunities clause tracks the First Amendment is a very good indication, as I have already suggested, that it should not be read as embodying any other right specified in the Bill of Rights, given the copresence of a due-process clause in both the Bill of Rights and section 1 of the Fourteenth Amendment, other than First Amendment freedoms. That the SAR is not a freedom (according to the original understanding) supplies a very good indeed compelling reason for positing that only the freedoms of American citizens are their privileges—within the meaning of the privileges or immunities clause.[226]

On the other hand, a federal or state law that would discriminate on the basis of race or color with respect to the keeping or carrying of arms would abridge (what I contend is) the constitutional immunity of American citizens to be free of invidious discrimination based upon race or color. One of the striking characteristics of Black Codes was to ensure that blacks would be disarmed, although the white citizens were generally permitted by the law of former slave states to own and carry arms. If, as I contend, the privileges or immunities clause forbids such racial discrimination, the incorporation of the SAR, considered as an individual civil right, is unnecessary to obviate this glaring inequality between whites and blacks with respect to arms keeping and bearing.

The Fourteenth Amendment, in my opinion, does not incorporate the SAR. Nevertheless, it would be very plausible for the Court to recognize that the substantive aspects of the due process clause encompass some fundamental rights with respect to arms indispensably needed for the defense of one's home or place of business. The states would be constitutionally free within the substantive limits provided by the due process clause to enact and enforce color-blind, reasonable limitations on the keeping and carrying of firearms in the interests of public health, peace, and safety. Although the rational basis test applies to many components of the right in question, it does not necessarily apply to every component of the right insofar as it is fundamental. The due process clauses arguably require the application of much more stringent standards with respect to such gun control legislation as comes closest to home. Clearly, there is a great difference between laws that regulate the carrying of firearms outside the premises of one's one home or place of business and within those premises. Similarly, there is a great difference between carrying a firearm (ready for immediate use) upon one's person on a public street (or within an easily accessible place within one's motor vehicle) and carrying it, unloaded or otherwise temporarily inoperative, within a secured trunk or box within the vehicle. However, a determination that there are fundamental rights pertaining to firearms by virtue of the due process clause would not assume that the states are constitutionally barred from any infringement of the SAR.

Part II

THE PARAMOUNTCY AND SUPERIORITY OF NATIONAL CITIZENSHIP, AND THE IMPLIED CONSTITUTIONAL PRIVILEGES AND IMMUNITIES OF AMERICAN CITIZENS

Introduction

The issues that Amar addresses in his book pertain to the specific rights in the Bill of Rights. Amar candidly acknowledges that his book "gestures toward, but fails to offer a systematic account of, many of the liberty-bearing provisions of our Constitution outside the Bill of Rights."[227] I, too, have made gestures in Part I of this book concerning what constitutional rights other than First Amendment freedoms are embraced by the privileges or immunities clause. Such rights include freedom of travel and migration throughout the United States; exemption from discrimination based upon an inferior or degraded status because of race, color, ethnicity, or caste; and the individual freedom-from rights entailed by the establishment clause. However, a satisfactory discussion of these matters ultimately depends upon determining the nature of citizenship of the United States before the adoption of the Fourteenth Amendment. I have undertaken this task in this part.[228]

We must first address the issue of the antecedent paramountcy of national citizenship, that is, whether, before the adoption of the Fourteenth Amendment (assuming arguendo the invalidity of the citizenship clause of the 1866 Civil Rights Act[229]) such citizenship was necessarily independent of, and thus not derived from, state citizenship. Before the adoption of the Fourteenth Amendment,[230] were native-born nationals, born in the District of Columbia or in an incorporated federal territory, citizens of the United States—even though they were not citizens of any state? I think that most informed readers believe that national citizenship was paramount before the adoption of the Fourteenth Amendment. Given *Dred Scott*, it would seem strange that before the Fourteenth Amendment's adoption, there was a class of white American nationals, born within the United States, who nevertheless were not American citizens just because they were not then or had never been citizens of states. It would seem strange to maintain that the preexisting law did not embody the paramountcy of national citizenship, if it were true (as Amar claims) that *Dred Scott* had maintained that only American citizens were entitled to the rights specified in the Bill of Rights; so that not only white aliens, but white, native-born, noncitizen nationals (according to this thesis) were also not entitled to some of the specific rights of the Bill of Rights.

Paramount and superior national citizenship entails certain *intrinsic* rights, privileges, and immunities of free American citizens—such as the freedoms of travel and migration throughout the United States, and exemption for discrimination due to an inferior and degraded status based upon a caste principle. *Intrinsic* privileges and immunities of American citizens are necessarily theirs because these rights are constitutive of paramount and superior national citizenship. However, it does not follow that all noncitizens of the United States are excluded from their benefits. Thus, for example,

68

resident aliens or resident noncitizen nationals within the United States should be deemed as per se entitled to a particular freedom in the event it would be unjust to withhold such entitlement, given that they live, work, play, and pray with American citizens.[231]

There are other privileges and immunities of free American citizens that are not *intrinsic*, but which are secured by the Constitution because they are paradigmatically the badges and incidents of their national citizenship (e.g., religious freedom, freedoms of speech and of the press, political freedom) based upon public policy considerations that justify securing them against any abridgment. These are *extrinsic* privileges and immunities of American citizens. Again, it is not necessary to suppose that these extrinsic privileges and immunities are exclusively for free American citizens. American noncitizen nationals and resident aliens could also be entitled to the benefit of some particular privilege or immunity of American citizens. An artificial person (such as a corporation, society or association, whether incorporated or not) is per se entitled to the religious freedom, political freedom, and freedoms of speech and of the press, only insofar as it predominantly functions as an instrumentality or vehicle by which American citizens exercise their rights.

In this part, I discuss religious freedom as a constitutional privilege of the American people. I do so because, in my opinion, religious freedom consists of not only the components of the specific right of the free exercise clause, but also those freedom-rights entailed by the establishment clause, besides such freedom-rights in matters religious that are components of the specific rights of the free speech, press, and assembly-petition clauses. I also explain why I hold that there is a constitutional immunity of the American people that consists of all the freedom-from rights that are entailed by the establishment clause. Part II closes with a chapter setting forth a federalist-accomodationist model of the establishment clause.

Chapter A. The Antecedent Paramountcy of National Citizenship

L et us consider whether the citizenship clause of the Fourteenth Amendment is actually declaratory of the law preexisting its enactment, or at least, should be conclusively deemed to be so thanks to the *feedback effect* mechanism explained by Amar.[232]

The citizenship clause of the Fourteenth Amendment provides, "All persons born or naturalized in the United States, and subject to the jurisdiction thereof, are citizens of the United States, and of the State wherein they reside." This provision was added as the first clause of the otherwise final version of Section 1. Professor Amar did not particularly address in his *The Bill of Rights* the issue whether, in addition to overruling *Dred Scott* concerning the incapacity of native-born blacks to be American citizens, the citizenship clause is to be understood as being declaratory of preexisting law with respect to the paramountcy of national citizenship.[233] In his more recently published *America's Constitution*, it is not at all clear what Amar means when he writes:

> These words [of the citizenship clause] codified a profound nationalization of American identity. Lacking any explicit definition of American citizenship, the Founders' Constitution was widely read in the antebellum era as making national citizenship derivative of state citizenship, except in cases involving the naturalization of immigrants and the regulation of federal territories. The Fourteenth Amendment made clear that all Americans were in fact citizens of the nation first and foremost, with a status and set of birthrights explicitly affirmed in a national Constitution.[234]

Thus, I cannot infer from the foregoing that Amar holds that national citizenship must be deemed to have been paramount before the adoption of the Fourteenth Amendment, and hence, declaratory of preexisting law.

70

Let us now consider the Supreme Court's opinion in the *Slaughter-House Cases* (1873) upon the issue in question. The opinion declared:

> The 1st section of the 14th article ... opens with a definition of citizenship—not only citizenship of the United States, but citizenship of the states. No such definition was previously found in the Constitution, nor had any attempt been made to define it by act of Congress. It has been the occasion of much discussion in the courts, by the executive departments and in the public journals. It has been said by eminent judges that no man was a citizen of the United States except as he was a citizen of one of the states composing the Union. Those, therefore, who had been born and resided always in the District of Columbia, or in the territories, though within the United States, were not citizens. Whether this proposition was sound or not had never been judicially decided. But it had been held by this court, in the celebrated *Dred Scott Case*, only a few years before the outbreak of the Civil War, that a man of African descent, whether slave or not, was not and could not be a citizen of the United States. This decision, while it met the condemnation of some of the ablest statesmen and constitutional lawyers of the country, had never been overruled; and, if it was to be accepted as a constitutional limitation of the right of citizenship, then all the negro race who had recently been made freemen were still, not only not citizens, but incapable of becoming so by anything short of an amendment to the Constitution.[235]

> [The citizenship clause] puts at rest both the questions which we stated to have been the subject of differences of opinion. It declares that persons may be citizens of the United States without regard to their citizenship of a particular state, and it overturns the *Dred Scott* decision by making all persons born within the United States and subject to its jurisdiction citizens of the United States.

That its main purpose was to establish the citizenship of the negro can admit of no doubt.[236]

The Court, it should be noted, does not expressly say that the citizenship clause is declaratory of preexisting law concerning the paramountcy of national citizenship. On the other hand, neither does it expressly indicate the contrary. It is curious that Court's opinion ignores the citizenship clause of the Civil Rights Act of 1866.[237] Moreover, it is also especially curious that the opinion makes the antecedent paramountcy of national citizenship appear to be so very doubtful, and thus, so very open to reasonable dispute—as if the Civil War had never occurred, and the indissoluble nature of the Union had not been so definitively confirmed on the battlefield so as to estop those claiming otherwise.

Thus, the Court's opinion soft-pedals the issue of whether the citizenship clause is declaratory of preexisting law. The reason, perhaps, is that to have asserted that such was the case would have undermined the Court's sterile doctrine that the privileges or immunities clause embraces only such rights "which owe their existence to the Federal government, its national character, its Constitution or its laws."[238] This suspicion is confirmed by the fact that the opinion refers to the right of the American citizen, as defined in *Crandall* v. *Nevada,*[239] to go to the seat of government for matters pertaining to the federal government and to enjoy free access to its seaports, through which all operations of foreign commerce are conducted, to the sub-treasuries, land offices, and courts of justice in the several states.[240]

The Court's opinion concerning *Crandall* is excessively minimalistic. The Court in *Crandall* held that a Nevada tax levying a tax upon railroad or state coach passengers leaving or passing through the state was unconstitutional. This decision is not totally explained by the purported right of the American citizen to travel for purposes pertaining to federal matters, as described in the *Slaughter-House Cases.* Moreover, the Court in the *Slaughter-House Cases* failed to fully quote from the most pertinent portion of the *Crandall* opinion.[241] In *Crandall*, the Court described the dissenting opinion by Chief Justice Taney in the *Passenger Cases,*[242] as stating "[t]hose principles [that] must govern the present one."[243] Now the relevant passage from Taney's dissenting opinion in the *Passenger Cases* as quoted in *Crandall* is as follows:

> Living as we do under a common government, charged with the great concerns of the whole Union, every citizen of the United States, from the most remote states or territories, is entitled to free access, not only to the principal departments established at Washington, but also to its judicial tribunals and public offices in every state in the Union.... *For all the great purposes for which the Federal government was formed, we are one people, with one common country. We are all citizens of the United States*; and as members of the same community, must have the right to pass and repass through every part of it without interruption, as freely as in our own states. And a tax imposed by a state, for entering its territories or harbors, is inconsistent with the rights which belong to citizens of other states as members of the Union, and with the objects which the Union was intended to attain. Such a power in the states could produce nothing but discord and mutual irritation, and they very clearly do not possess it.[244]

It is immediately evident Chief Justice Taney had distinguished between the American citizen's right of free access to federal establishments and the freedom of American citizens to travel throughout the United States for any lawful purpose. The former right is but a component of the second, which is best understood as being a privilege grounded upon the paramountcy of national citizenship. This freedom is implicitly secured by the Constitution against abridgments by the United States. It was also secured, at least as to some components, against abridgments by the states, prior to the adoption of the Fourteenth Amendment.[245] Not to be overlooked is that the freedom of all American citizens to interstate travel throughout the United States, even for purposes unrelated to the federal government, as declared by Taney, is one that may not constitutionally be abridged by a state with respect to its own citizens. However, this freedom cannot possibly be, according to the majority in the *Slaughter-House Cases*, within the scope of the privileges or immunities clause.

Although Chief Justice Taney's extreme racism is justly subject to the most severe censure, it was not necessarily unreasonable for Taney (prescinding from the issue of the national citizenship of native-born blacks) to maintain that native-and-free-born persons in the United States could not be properly deemed to be citizens of the United States if they were not legally free, under the Constitution, to leave the state in which they resided and to enter or pass through every other state. What he had concluded in *Dred Scott* was that native-and-free-born persons of color could not be American citizens because the institution of African slavery was recognized by the Constitution, and that free persons of color in slave states (or federal slave territorial jurisdictions, such as the District of Columbia) were subject to very stringent police regulations assigning them to an inferior and degraded legal status because of their race or color. The doctrine of *Dred Scott*, concerning the incapacity for national citizenship for native-born blacks, was but the corrupted fruit of yet another, but even more, poisoned tree—the constitutionalized institution of African slavery and radical racism.[246]

Unfortunately, the Court in the *Slaughter-House Cases* and some later cases disingenuously downplayed Taney's doctrine so approvingly quoted in *Crandall* because otherwise the rule that the privileges or immunities clause is limited to only those rights as are created by the Constitution and other federal law would seem much less plausible.[247] We confront an amazing fact when we pass on to the dissenting opinions in the *Slaughter-House Cases*. The fact is that all four dissenting justices (Chief Justice Chase, and Justices Field, Swayne, and Bradley) agreed that the dissenting opinion by Justice Curtis in *Dred Scott* provided what "has been generally accepted by the profession of the country as the one containing the soundest views of constitutional law. And he held that, under the Constitution, citizenship of the United States in reference to natives was dependent upon citizenship in the several states, under their constitutions and laws." [248] Justice Field's dissenting opinion, however, described the

Dred Scott opinion as maintaining that the descendants of the people of the several states as parties to the Constitution, their descendents, and persons naturalized were the only persons who could be citizens of the United States.[249] Justice Field's opinion proceeded to declare:

> The first clause of the [F]ourteenth Amendment changes this whole subject, and removes it from the region of discussion and doubt. It recognizes in express terms, if it does not create, citizens of the United States, and it makes their citizenship dependent upon the place of their birth, or the fact of their adoption, and not upon the Constitution or laws of any state or the condition of their ancestry. A citizen of a state is now only a citizen of the United States residing in that state.[250]

The fact that this dissenting opinion declined to assert that the citizenship clause is declaratory of preexisting law is explained by the fact that the doctrine common to all four dissenting justices is that the descriptive term of the privileges or immunities clause (i.e., "the privileges or immunities of citizens of the United States") denotes the same rights as are denoted by the descriptive term of the comity clause (i.e., "all Privileges and Immunities of Citizens of the several States"). Thus, Justice Field characterized Justice Washington's explanation in *Corfield* v. *Coryell*[251] of the rights embraced by the comity clause as what appears to be a "sound construction," and that "[t]he privileges and immunities designated are those which of right belong to the citizens of all free governments."[252] Hence, "[t]he fundamental rights, privileges, and immunities which belong to [a citizen of a state] as a free man and a free citizen, now belong to him as a citizen of the United States, and are not dependent upon his citizenship of any state."[253] According to the dissenting justices, these numerous so-called fundamental rights, privileges, and immunities are "the natural and inalienable rights which belong to all citizens."[254] Thus, it is a remarkable coincidence that all justices in the *Slaughter-House Cases* declined to affirm that the citizenship clause is declaratory of preexisting law, for were these justices to have done so, they would have thereby confirmed the preexisting nature of national citizenship as paramount and independent of state citizenship. Had they explicitly affirmed the antecedent paramountcy of national citizenship, the majority and dissenting justices would have weakened the plausibility of their respective theories concerning what rights are denoted by the descriptive term of the privileges or immunities clause.

This tradition (as one might call it), originating in the *Slaughter-House Cases*, has found expression in some succeeding cases— notably the *Selective Draft Law Cases*[255] and *Colgate* v. *Harvey*,[256] in which latter case the Court declared: "[W]hile the Fourteenth Amendment does not *create* a national citizenship, it has the effect of making that citizenship 'paramount and dominant' instead of 'derivative and dependent' upon state citizenship."[257] However, these pronouncements in the cases are mere obiter dicta.

Fortunately, the doctrine of *Colgate* v. *Harvey* is contradicted by other but more authoritative cases. In 1875, the Court rightly held in *Minor* v. *Happersett*[258] that the right of suffrage is not embraced by the descriptive term of the privileges or immunities clause. The Court had occasion to declare: "There is no doubt that women may be citizens.... [I]n our opinion, it did not need [the Fourteenth] Amendment to give them that position" [i.e., to be citizens of the United States and of the state wherein they reside if born or naturalized in the United States and subject to their jurisdiction]."[259] It explained that, prior to the adoption of the Constitution, the citizens of the United States were the citizens of the several states.[260] The Court proceeded to declare:

> Whoever, then, was one of the people of either of these States when the Constitution of the United States was adopted, became *ipso facto* a citizen—a member of the nation created by the adoption. He was one of the persons associating together to form the nation, and was, consequently, one of its original citizens. As to this there has never been a doubt. Disputes have arisen as to whether or not certain persons or certain classes of persons were part of the people at the time, but never as to their citizenship if they were.[261]

Birth, the Court stated, was one of the ways in which "[a]dditions might always be made to the citizenship of the United States." According to the Court, resort must be made to the common law to determine who are the natural-born citizens of the United States. The Court put the matter as follows:

> [I]t was never doubted that all children born in a country of parents who were its citizens became themselves, upon their birth, citizens also. These were natives, or natural-born citizens, as distinguished from aliens or foreigners. Some authorities go further and include as citizens children born within its jurisdiction, without reference to the citizenship of their parents. As to this class there have been doubts, but never as to the first. For the purposes of this case it is not necessary to solve these doubts. It is sufficient for everything we have now to consider that all children born of citizen parents within the jurisdiction are themselves citizens.[262]

Thus less than two years after the *Slaughter-House Cases* had been decided, the Court unanimously declared that, independently of the Fourteenth Amendment, (at least white) persons born within the United States, and within their jurisdiction, were citizens thereof if they were the descendants of the citizens of the several states at the adoption of the Constitution or of American citizens by birth or naturalization. This is surely quite inconsistent with the widespread antebellum opinion that a native-born national is an American citizen if and only if he is a citizen of one of the states, as determined by its constitution and laws. Thus we see that the Court, having erected its building (i.e., its neutering interpretation of the privileges or immunities clause) in the *Slaughter-House Cases*, no longer had any further need of the scaffolding (i.e., its uncertainty about the paramountcy of national citizenship before the adoption of the Fourteenth Amendment).[263]

The unresolved doubt in *Minor*, concerning the acquisition of national citizenship of children born of foreign parents within the United States, was definitively settled in *United States* v. *Wong Kim*

Ark.[264] In this case, the Court held that a child born in the United States is a citizen thereof, even though his parents were at his birth still subjects of the Emperor of China, although domiciled in the United States and not employed in any diplomatic or official capacity under the Chinese emperor, and that later the parents returned to China with their child. The case turned on the question whether Wong Kim Ark was born in the United States and subject to their jurisdiction within the meaning of the citizenship clause. Hence, the Court felt itself required to determine what was a natural-born American citizen by resorting to common law doctrines. The Court declared:

> Passing by questions once earnestly controverted, but finally put at rest by the Fourteenth Amendment of the Constitution, it is beyond doubt that, before the enactment of the Civil Rights Act of 1866, or the adoption of the Constitutional Amendment, all white persons, at least, born within the sovereignty of the United States, whether children of citizens or of foreigners, excepting only children of ambassadors or public ministers of a foreign government, were native born citizens of the United States.… In the forefront, both of the Fourteenth Amendment of the Constitution, and of the Civil Rights Act of 1866, the fundamental principle of citizenship by birth within the dominion was reaffirmed in the most explicit and comprehensive terms.[265]

> As appears from the face of the amendment, as well as from the history of the times, this was not intended to impose any new restrictions upon citizenship, or to prevent any persons from becoming citizens by the fact of birth within the United States, who would thereby have become citizens according to the law existing before its adoption. It is declaratory in form and enabling and extending in effect. Its main purpose doubtless was, as has been often recognized by this court, to establish the citizenship of free negroes, which had been denied in the opinion of the court delivered by Chief Justice Taney in

Dred Scott v. *Standford* [citation omitted], and to put it beyond doubt that all blacks, as well as whites, born or naturalized within the jurisdiction of the United States, are citizens of the United States.[266]

Clearly, the Court was asserting the doctrine that national citizenship was paramount before the adoption of the Fourteenth Amendment, and that its citizenship clause is declaratory of such preexisting law.[267] Unfortunately, this declaration was ignored in the *Selective Draft Cases* and *Colgate* v. *Harvey.*

Indeed, it would be very strange were the constitutional law that obtained before the adoption of the Fourteenth Amendment such that it did not include the doctrine of the paramountcy of national citizenship since not later than the adoption of the Constitution. This is because of the nature of the "more perfect Union" formed by the Constitution.

In *Texas* v. *White* (1869),[268] the Court had occasion to emphatically define the nature of the Union as follows:

The Union of the States never was a purely artificial and arbitrary relation. It began among the Colonies, and grew out of common origin, mutual sympathies, kindred principles, similar interests, and geographical relations. It was confirmed and strengthened by the necessities of war, and received definite form, and character, and sanction from the Articles of Confederation. By these the Union was solemnly declared to "be perpetual." And when these articles were found to be inadequate to the exigencies of the country, the Constitution was ordained "to form a more perfect Union." It is difficult to convey the idea of indissoluble unity more clearly than by those words. What can be indissoluble if a perpetual Union, made more perfect, is not?[269]

Thus, according to the Court, "The Constitution, in all its provisions, looks to an indestructible Union, composed of indestructible States."[270] The notion of national citizenship as paramount is implicit in the doctrine as stated by the Court, "It is the union of such States, under a common constitution, which forms the distinct and greater political unit which that Constitution designates as the United States, and makes of the people and States which compose it one people and one country."[271]

Although the original Constitution uses the terms "citizen of the United States," it does not define it although it indicates that there were such citizens for at least nine years prior to the adoption of the Constitution.[272] Before the adoption of the Constitution, whereby the Union was made "more perfect," "citizen of the United States" arguably meant the same as "citizen of one of the United States," such that a citizen of the United States was necessarily a citizen of a state.[273] Such, however, could not have been the case with the adoption of the Constitution, because the United States became "an indestructible Union, composed of indestructible States," in the words of *Texas* v. *White.*

The doctrine of the antecedent paramountcy of national citizenship, so authoritatively set forth in *Minor* and *Wong Kim Ark*, is fully in accord with the nature of the Union as explicated in such cases as *Texas* v. *White* and *Crandall* v. *Nevada.*[274] The *feedback effect*, so well expounded by Amar, should not be thought of as just being limited to incorporation of individual rights. It applies just as well to the citizenship clause, since the dominant original understanding was that the clause is declaratory of preexisting law insofar as it had asserted the paramountcy of national citizenship.

The antecedent paramountcy of national citizenship embraces more than the notion that such citizenship is dominant; that is, it is not derivative or dependent upon state citizenship. It embraces the idea that national citizenship is also supreme. It is supreme because an American citizen's first allegiance is to the United States, rather than to the state of which he is a citizen, and he may not even be a citizen of any state. It would be quite remarkable if such national citizenship were not supreme, because the United States is an indestructible union of indestructible states, with the Constitution being the supreme law of the land.

Chapter B: The Superiority of National Citizenship and the Implied Privileges and Immunities of American Citizens

Section 1. The superiority of national citizenship

Before the adoption of the Fourteenth Amendment, some jurists and writers maintained that every American national not a slave was an American citizen. Therefore, every native-born African-American not a slave was an American citizen. Nevertheless, according to what appears to have been the dominant version of this theory, such citizenship was compatible with an inferior and degraded legal status based upon race or color. This particular version was expounded, for example, in Justice McClean's dissenting opinion in *Dred Scott*[275] and Attorney General Bates' 1862 opinion.[276] According to this viewpoint, entitlement of free, black Americans to the right of free interstate ingress and regress was not entailed by national citizenship but had to rely upon an interpretation of the comity clause for its justification. It is therefore important to keep in mind that the notion that every native-born American national is an American citizen often went hand-in-hand with the view that what was considered the fundamental rights of American citizens as such did not exclude racially discriminatory statutes affecting important civil constitutional rights (not to speak of political rights).

Therefore, the antecedent paramountcy of national citizenship takes us only so far. For before the adoption of the Fourteenth Amendment, there was a sharp difference of opinion as to whether, and to what extent, national citizenship was also intrinsically superior (as I shall term it). National citizenship is intrinsically superior if its notion entails a status superior to that of American noncitizen nationals—all other things being equal.[277]

The nature of the antecedent paramountcy of national citizenship is understandably neglected in Professor Amar's book because he intentionally focuses on the specific rights in the Bill of Rights and in the original Constitution. And it may be conceded that this matter does not immediately appear to be relevant in considering which of the rights specified in the Bill of Rights are incorporated by the privileges or immunities clause. However, resolution of this matter is necessary to determine what rights (other than those expressly secured by the First Amendment) are secured by the privileges or immunities clause. But in order to do this, we must first address in detail the issue of whether national citizenship is not only paramount but also superior to that of being a free noncitizen national.

Section 2. The freedom of travel and migration throughout the United States[278]

I maintain that national citizenship is intrinsically superior because if it has at least one key characteristic by which an American citizen is to be distinguished from such free American nationals as are not citizens. The one key characteristic I have in mind is per se (or intrinsic) entitlement to the freedoms of travel and migration throughout the United States as a constitutional privilege of American citizens by virtue of their national citizenship. If some noncitizens, present within the United States, are also constitutionally entitled to this freedom, this entitlement is contingent upon the fact that American citizens are per se so entitled, or it is independently grounded upon some justice-based reasons.[279]

As the Court declared in *United State* v. *Wheeler*,[280] "In all the states, from the beginning down to the adoption of the Articles of Confederation, the citizens thereof possessed the fundamental right, inherent in citizens of all free governments, peacefully to dwell within the limits of their respective states, to move at will from place to place therein, and to have free ingress thereto and egress therefrom[.]"[281] *Wheeler,* despite its doctrine (since disapproved[282]) that the constitutional privilege of national citizens with respect to travel throughout the United States is limited to only such rights as grow out of the governmental functions of the United States, is nevertheless of great heuristic value in that it considers the freedoms of travel and migration within a state as inherent in state citizenship— reminding one of the Roman law that a citizen is not simply a freeman (i.e., a person not a slave or otherwise in involuntary servitude) or a freedman, but a person who has, by fundamental right, the freedom of the city. Similarly, the citizen of an individual state is one who has by fundamental right the freedom of that state. Now, if I as a citizen of the State of Colorado necessarily have, by virtue of my state citizenship, the freedom of travel and migration throughout Colorado, then *à fortiori* I as a citizen of the United States must have, by virtue of my paramount national citizenship, the plenary freedom of travel and migration throughout the entire nation. This privilege necessarily obtains as to American citizens because their national citizenship is not only paramount but also because it is intrinsically superior to the status of free noncitizen nationals. Thus, the very nature of national citizenship implicitly excludes the power of the United States to abridge the freedoms of travel and migration of American citizens throughout the United States.

What about the states? Before the adoption of the Constitution, the right of American citizens to free interstate ingress and egress as citizens of one state with respect to other states was a matter of comity expressly provided for by article IV of the Articles of Confederation.[283] But the comity clause of the Constitution does not expressly provide for the right of free *interstate* ingress and regress, against infringements by the states, for the citizens of the several states. But why should it since it is presupposed by the entitlement of the citizens of each state to the privileges and immunities of citizens in the several states in a "more perfect Union"? The original Constitution also precludes the states from violating those rights of travel and migration of citizens as are entailed by the performance by the United States of its governmental functions. Although the freedom of travel and migration throughout the United States is an implicit constitutional privilege of the American people, the original Constitution otherwise fell far short of securing the freedoms of travel and migration against all abridgments by the states.[284] However, with the adoption of the Fourteenth Amendment these freedoms of American citizens were completely secured against abridgments by the states. Therefore, the constitutional basis of these freedoms, these privileges of American citizens, should not be regarded as somehow mysterious.[285]

Justice Robert Jackson, in his eloquent concurring opinion in *Edwards* v. *California*,[286] urged that the Court recognize the freedom of interstate travel and migration as a privilege of national citizenship. But, his argument was marred by two crucial mistakes. The first was that he believed: "[The citizenship clause] was adopted to make United States citizenship the dominant and paramount allegiance among us."[287] The second error was to suppose that the rights of free interstate travel and migration are in their totality the sole privilege of national citizenship pertaining to travel and migration.[288] However, Justice Jackson was quite right in urging:

> This Court should, however, hold squarely that it is a privilege of citizenship of the United States, protected from state abridgment, to enter any state of the Union, either for temporary sojourn or for the establishment of permanent residence therein and for gaining resultant citizenship thereof. *If national citizenship means less than this, it means nothing.*[289]

Justice Douglas's concurring opinion in *Edwards*[290] is also noteworthy for its hits and misses. His opinion rightly opined that "the dictum in [*United States* v. *Wheeler*] which attempts to limit the Crandall Case to a holding that the statute in question directly burdened 'the performance of the United States of its governmental functions' and limited the 'rights of the citizens growing out of such functions,' does not bear analysis."[291] However, he erroneously believed that the Court in the *Slaughter-House Cases* had stated that the freedom of interstate travel is a privilege of national citizenship.[292] For the fact is that the opinion recognized the privilege only insofar as it pertains to governmental functions and operations, and their complementary rights of citizens.[293] On the other hand, Douglas appears to indicate that the privilege of national citizenship pertaining to travel is one extending to "the free movement of persons throughout this nation."[294] Finally, Douglas remarked that the California statute under review

> would also introduce a caste system utterly incompatible with the spirit of our system of government. It would permit those who were stigmatized by a State as indigents, paupers, or vagabonds to be relegated to an inferior class of citizenship. It would prevent a citizen because he was poor from seeking new horizons in other States. It might thus withhold from large segments of our people that mobility which is basis to any guarantee of freedom of opportunity. The result would be a substantial dilution of

the rights of *national* citizenship, a serious impairment of the principles of equality. Since the state statute here challenged involves such consequences, it runs afoul of the privileges and immunities clause of the Fourteenth Amendment.[295]

Douglas, therefore, rightly perceived that national citizenship entailed such equality of rights as is inconsistent with "a caste system [whereby] indigents, paupers, or vagabonds [are] related to an inferior class of citizenship." This insight, in my view, is profound because the national citizenship embodied in the citizenship cause, considered as declaratory of preexisting law, is such that it is incompatible with free American nationals being stigmatized as belonging to an inferior and degraded legal status based upon some caste principle.

Here we must return to *Dred Scott*. The Court in that case concludes that native-and-free-born blacks were not and could not become citizens of the United States. Had they been citizens of the United States, they would then have been entitled to the freedoms of travel and migration throughout the United States,[296] to the benefits of the comity clause, and immunity from the enforcement of laws that stigmatized them as belonging to an inferior and degraded class[297]— so inferior and degraded that intermarriage between whites with free persons of color was stringently forbidden.[298] Some free states, before the Civil War and even well before the *Dred Scott* decision (March 6, 1857), had legislation prohibiting or restricting the immigration of free persons of color. Illinois, Indiana, and Oregon had, during the antebellum period, such anti-immigration provisions in their constitutions. These provisions were defended at the constitutional conventions in these free states upon the basis that free persons of color were not then citizens of the United States.[299] Indeed, the legitimacy of such provisions was extensively defended in Congress upon the same basis.[300] On the other hand, others denounced such state constitutional provisions upon the ground that free, native-born blacks are American citizens and entitled to freedom of travel throughout the United States.[301]

Section 3. The freedom from the badges and incidents of an inferior and degraded caste status based upon race or color[302]

National citizenship is intrinsically superior for another reason besides that pertaining to freedom of travel and migration throughout the United States. I contend that the intrinsic superiority of national citizenship in part consists of its incompatibility with a stigmatized inferior and degraded legal status based upon a caste principle—as was the case of free, native-born persons of color before the abolition of slavery. The doctrine of *Dred Scott*, by which native-born blacks were deemed incapable of national citizenship, was necessarily based upon the notion of national citizenship as entailing such equality of rights as precludes a stigmatized inferior and degraded caste status based upon race or color. Persons of color in slave jurisdictions were (nonconclusively) presumed to be slaves, and free persons of color in slave jurisdictions were subjected to stringent police regulations. Every free person of color, in a slave state, could be potentially be reduced to slavery for cause (and often, very little of the same), including but not limited to punishment for serious crime or failure to leave a slave state after a prescribed period of time following his emancipation, depending upon the law of the jurisdiction in question.[303] Even with the abolition of slavery by the Thirteenth Amendment, it was still widely believed that free persons of color remained members of a stigmatized inferior and degraded caste status as determined by law—such as, for example, by the black codes in the former slave states.

Let me state most emphatically: the institution of African slavery was a grossly immoral abomination, and so is any constitutional system insofar as it assigns persons to an inferior and degraded status based upon a caste principle—such as race or color, ethnic origin or place of birth. One must nevertheless prescind from one's own moral abhorrence of slavery and racism to truly appreciate what is at stake here. First, the notion of the intrinsic superiority of national citizenship does not itself entail a constitutional system of racial supremacy. For example, the native-born inhabitants of territory ceded to or otherwise acquired by the United States, until such territory is *incorporated,* are *nationals* but not *citizens* of the United States—unless by treaty or statute it is stipulated that their nationality may be retained if they so choose. Their status as nationals does not per se constitutionally entitle them to a right to migrate to the United States. Moreover, noncitizen nationals who lawfully acquire permanent residence in the United States do not necessarily retain their status as noncitizen nationals.[304] Hence, the notion of national citizenship as being intrinsically superior as well as paramount should not be rejected simply because of historical accident it had been yoked to the pernicious institution of African slavery and white supremacy.

Nevertheless, it cannot be denied that *this* notion of superior national citizenship is that upon which depended the *Dred Scott* holding that native-and-free-black nationals were incapable of such citizenship. It is *this* notion of superior national citizenship, widely held even by many opponents of slavery, upon which necessarily depended the doctrine that free blacks were not constitutionally entitled to the freedoms of travel and migration throughout the United States. It is *this* notion of superior national citizenship that was maintained by those abolitionists who rejected the doctrine that the law of the land should assign to free persons of color an inferior and degraded legal status because of their race or color. The citizenship clause is declaratory of *this* notion of superior national citizenship— otherwise, the enactment of that clause would not have been a boon for African Americans. The competing view of paramount national citizenship, which deemed every free American national (even a former slave) to be an American citizen, did not exclude an inferior and degraded legal status based upon some caste principle.[305] The citizenship clause should have been a boon for native-born blacks because the intrinsic superiority of paramount national citizenship includes immunity from such discriminations with respect to civil rights that were the badges and incidents of an inferior and degraded status because of race or color.

The notion of national citizenship as being paramount and superior is linked to the doctrine so well expressed in *McCulloch*

v. *Maryland*:[306] "The [federal] government proceeds directly from the people; is 'ordained and established' in the name of the people; and is declared to be ordained "in order to form a more perfect union, establish justice, insure domestic tranquillity, and secure the blessings of liberty to themselves and to their posterity." The Court thus emphasized that "[t]he government of the Union ... is, emphatically, and truly a government of the people. In form and in substance it emanates from them, its powers are granted by them, and are to be exercised directly on them, and for their benefit."[307]

The *Dred Scott* opinion simply confirmed this doctrine in somewhat different words when it declared:

The words "people of the United States" and "citizens" are synonymous terms, and mean the same thing. They both describe the political body, who, according to our republican institutions, form the sovereignty, and who hold the power and conduct the government through their representatives. They are what we familiarly call the "sovereign people," and every citizen is one of this people, and a constituent member of this sovereignty[.][308]

Professor Amar recognizes the importance of the doctrine of popular sovereignty. He noted, "The Preamble's dramatic opening words ... trumpeted the Constitution's underlying theory of popular sovereignty. Those words and that theory implied a right of 'the People' ... to alter or abolish their government whenever they deemed proper: what the 'People' had 'ordain[ed] and establish[ed]' ... they or their 'posterity' could disestablish at will[.]"[309] He explains: "We the People, acting collectively, have delegated some powers to the federal government, have allowed others to be exercised by state governments, and have withheld some things from all governments. The Preamble and the Tenth Amendment are perfect bookends, fittingly the alpha and omega of the Founders' (revised) Constitution."[310] Amar states that "[t]he central meaning and logic of the [*Dred Scott*] opinion, which took pains to stress the words of the Preamble, was that the Constitution and the Bill of Rights were ordained and established by citizens of the United States, and for their benefit only"[311] Thus there is an ostensibly objective dignity of American citizens, considered as individuals, that obtains by virtue of their sovereignty, when considered collectively. And, this in part explains why national citizenship is both paramount *and* superior. Some people regard the principle of popular sovereignty as philosophical nonsense-upon-stilts. However, this principle, so firmly rooted in our jurisprudence, informs the Constitution as a fundamental charter of governmental powers and personal rights. As such, this political principle (even if it is deemed but a theoretical construct or a legal fiction) is juridically binding upon us when interpreting the Constitution.

The notion of national citizenship as paramount and superior, understood in terms of the doctrine of popular sovereignty, is impossible to reconcile with the opinion that there can be free American citizens who belong to an inferior and degraded status based upon race, color, ethnic origin, or similar caste basis. This antebellum constitutional doctrine is not, I should emphasize, what was egregiously wrong. What was wrong was the pernicious institution of African slavery and the extreme racism that warranted (given the premises of the argument) the inferior and degraded legal status of free persons of color. The conclusion, however, is inescapable: if antebellum native-and-free-born black nationals were citizens of the United States, then they would have been necessarily exempt for invidious racial discrimination, including miscegenation laws.

The enactment of the citizenship clause turned *Dred Scott* on its head, thus overturning not only its holding (i.e., Dred Scott was not a citizen and therefore could not sue in a federal diversity case) but also the justifying doctrine (i.e., because of their inferior and degraded legal status, antebellum free-and-native-born blacks were not, and could not become, American citizens). The Court, in the *Slaughter-House Cases*, described the holding in *Dred Scott* as one that "had never been overruled; and, if it was to be accepted as a constitutional limitation of the right of citizenship, then all the negro race who had recently been made freemen were still, not only not citizens, but were incapable of becoming so by anything short of an amendment to the Constitution."[312]

A disappointing feature of Amar's book is its rather lame, and surely confusing, consideration of freedom from racial discrimination. His position is that one may use the *feedback effect* of *reverse* incorporation against federal actors.[313] As I understand him, his argument is as follows: the Ninth Amendment provision for unenumerated rights came to be understood during the reconstruction era as embodying individual rights. Thus, Amar explains, "[a]ll Americans, black and white alike, [are] citizens of the United States," and all such are entitled to "certain privileges and immunities—against all governments, state and federal.[314] Amar says:

> The entire spirit of the Fourteenth Amendment was to affirm rights against all governments and insist that state and federal governments be held to the same standard. Thus we should not be surprised by the first Justice Harlan's linkage of incorporation and reverse incorporation in a couple of his greatest dissents. In *Plessy* v. *Ferguson*, for example, Harlan affirmed "the clear, distinct, unconditional recognition of our governments, *National and State*, of every right that inheres in civil freedom [that is, incorporation], and of the equality before the law of all citizens of the United States without regard to race [that is, reverse incorporation]."[315] Similarly, in his dissent in the *Civil Rights Cases*, Harlan proclaimed that citizenship itself entailed various "rights, privileges, or immunities," one of which was "exemption from race discrimination in respect to any civil right belonging to citizens of the white race."[316] In 1896 he put the point even more simply: "All citizens are equal before the law."[317]

The second and third of Amar's sentences in the passage just quoted defy comprehension. That he describes as "incorporation" Harlan's affirmation of universal governmental recognition of every right that inheres in civil freedom is utterly misleading in the context of the controversy of total *refined* incorporation as opposed to total or to selective incorporation. Here Amar engages in *légerdeparole* since the rights inhering in civil freedom may be described as "incorporated" only in the sense of being its constituent parts, or its essential badges and incidents.

Justice Harlan had a two-prong basis for asserting that the Constitution prohibits all discrimination as to civil rights upon the ground of race. The first was that the universal personal freedom established by the Thirteenth Amendment "necessarily involved immunity from, and protection against, all discrimination against [blacks] because of their race, in respect to such civil rights as belong to freemen of other races.[318] This ground makes entirely senseless any talk of incorporation or reverse incorporation since per Harlan exemption from racial discrimination is necessarily entailed by that universal freedom established by the Thirteenth Amendment. Harlan's second prong was that the citizenship clause secured to colored citizens of the United States by the national grant of state citizenship "exemption from race discrimination in respect of any civil right belonging to citizens of the white race in the same State."[319] He definitively affirmed that such exemption is fundamental to state citizenship and that blacks as American citizens became entitled to the benefits of the comity clause.[320] This is just a skip-and-a-hop away from saying that such exemption is essential in *national* citizenship. And this is what Harlan actually maintained when he also declared, "It cannot be that the [right to exemption from racial discrimination with respect to the suffrage] is an attribute of national citizenship, while [the right to exemption from race discrimination as to civil rights] is not essential to national citizenship, or fundamental in state citizenship."[321] This is hardly a surprising affirmation since Harlan had earlier explained that the citizenship clause "introduced all of [the black] race, whose ancestors had been imported and sold as slaves at once into the political community known as the 'People of the United States.' They became, instantly, citizens of the United States, *and* of their respective States."[322]

Amar's characterization of Harlan's assertion of the equality before the law of all citizens of the United States without regard to race as "reverse incorporation" is utterly mysterious since the citizenship clause must, per Harlan, directly secure exemption for African-Americans from racial discrimination as to civil rights by the United States, and indirectly via the comity clause by the states. That is, this immunity obtains (according to Harlan) because the citizenship clause made African-Americans citizens of the United States and of their respective states, and brought them within the ambit of the comity clause.[323] Thus, Harlan's theory provides no support whatsoever for Amar's hypothesis of reverse incorporation with respect to exemption from racial discrimination.

Amar invites us "[t]o see the point one final way." The right not to be denied equal protection of the laws is secured by section 1 of the Fourteenth Amendment against the states. The equal-protection-right includes freedom from racial discrimination. The Fifth Amendment prohibits the United States from denying any person of life, liberty, or property of due process of law. According to the Court, that clause has an equal-protection component; but "a quick look at the Fourteenth Amendment may make us skeptical." However, according to Amar, "on a declaratory view [the due process and equal protection clauses of the Fourteenth Amendment] were not so much separate ideas as connected ones, two sides of the same coin." He adds, "Both [clauses] affirmed the rights of persons as contradistinguished from the rights of citizens. And due process *of law* connoted a suitably general, evenhanded law." Ergo, the modern Court is right in reading the Fifth Amendment's due process clause as a ban on invidious race discrimination due to the mechanism of a reserve incorporation.[324]

There must have been a lot of cooking in Amar's kitchen to have enabled him to come up with this tasty dish. It is so much at odds with that thesis of textualism that Amar professes. First, the equal protection clause is expressly focused upon the equal protection of the laws, rather than requiring laws providing for equality of rights or benefits.[325] Second, the failure of the Constitution, as amended by the Fourteenth Amendment, to expressly provide the denial by the United States of equal protection of the laws either presupposes that the United States was already prohibited from violating freedom of racial discrimination—or that it was not. However, the first alternative is not possible except upon the hypothesis that, since the abolition of slavery by the Thirteenth Amendment or the adoption of the citizenship clause (if not earlier with the 1866 Civil Rights Act), native-born blacks are constitutionally entitled to exemption from racial discrimination as to civil rights as against the United States. In this case, there is no need for reverse incorporation since the immunity (i.e., the right to exemption from racial discrimination) was already a constitutional immunity of American citizens, or because the establishment of universal freedom (by the Thirteenth Amendment) entails such exemption. As to the second alternative, Amar's argument for "reverse incorporation" is plausible only if it is posited that the due-process clauses of the fifth and Fourteenth Amendments are equivalent. However, Amar had denied this equivalence when he affirmed that *person* in both clauses has different meanings, given his alleged *Dred Scott* doctrine that the Bill of Rights secures rights only for American citizens—until this doctrine is judicially overruled.[326] If the adoption of the Fourteenth Amendment did not ipso facto overrule the alleged doctrine of *Dred Scott*, it is difficult to see why or how it nevertheless overruled the doctrine of *Dred Scott* that the Fifth Amendment due process clause is consistent with free, African Americans having an inferior and degraded legal status because of their race.

Now it is surely the case that from virtually the "very beginning" the Fourteenth Amendment was judicially understood as prohibiting invidious racial discrimination by the states with respect to civil rights, thereby establishing equality of right of black with white citizens.[327] Moreover, the dominant original understanding of the Fourteenth Amendment is that it had at least constitutionalized the Civil Rights Act of 1866, and that it indeed had secured for blacks equality with white citizens with respect to those rights mentioned in the Act and all others denoted by the descriptive term of the comity clause (i.e., the so-called fundamental rights of citizens of all free governments).[328] My position is that an immunity of American citizens, within the meaning of the privileges or immunities clause, is the right of free citizens to be exempt from all such inequalities of civil rights as are the badges and incidents of an inferior and degraded legal status based upon a caste principle, these inequalities being incompatible with the dignity of being a citizen of the United States, a member of that political community in which the sovereignty ultimately reposes.[329] Because of their inferior and degraded legal status, antebellum-free persons of color were not American citizens according to *Dred Scott.* One badge and incident of this status was the ban on racial intermarriage. Since intermarriage between blacks and whites was forbidden because of the inferior and degraded status of antebellum-free persons of color, this prohibition was nullified ipso facto with the adoption of the Fourteenth Amendment by virtue of its citizenship clause. But, according to the current doctrine of the Court as announced in *Loving* v. *Virginia,*[330] the constitutional ban against prohibition of interracial marriages in Virginia is grounded upon the equal protection and due process clauses of the Fourteenth Amendment, without any consideration of the privileges or immunities clause.

It is most interesting that, after the approval of the Fourteenth Amendment by Congress for submission to the states for ratification, some opponents of that amendment made some rather candid (one might also say unguarded) comments about the meaning of national citizenship. According to these comments, antebellum-free-and-native-born, black Americans, had they been American citizens, would have been indeed entitled to exemption from the badges and incidents of an inferior and degraded legal status based upon race or color, including but not limited to the ban on racial intermarriage.

A few days after the House had approved the final version of the Fourteenth Amendment, Congressman William E. Niblack (Dem., Ind.) presented to the House his exposition of the reasons supporting the Indiana legislation forbidding immigration of free blacks into that state. He did so quite evidently because he was concerned about the honor of his state and because he wanted to demonstrate the reasonableness and wisdom, as he saw it, of the Indiana policy.[331] Niblack actually opposed slavery, but he was certainly a racist—acknowledging however "[t]hat all human beings, however low in the scale of humanity, have certain rights which ought not to be, and cannot be with impunity, disregarded."[332] Niblack, who had voted against both the Civil Rights Act of 1866 and the Fourteenth Amendment, stated:

This subject has a renewed interest in the people of our State on account of the action of the present Congress, which in many respects changes, or at least attempts to change very materially the *status* of the negro race everywhere in the United States, and which, if sustained by the courts and people of the country, will override all State laws and State regulations in regard to that class of persons, and practically annul all that the people of Indiana or any other State may have done to separate the white and black races within its territorial limits.[333]

Niblack discussed at length the provision of the Indiana Constitution, adopted in 1851, which prohibited the immigration of blacks. He explained:

[The Indiana constitutional convention] acted upon the theory that negroes and mulattos were not citizens of the United States, were not parties to the political compact which formed the Constitution and Government of the United States, and were not entitled to become citizens of the United States under the then existing law of Congress and without a radical change of policy on the part of the General Government.[334]

Niblack had denied the validity of the Civil Rights Act of 1866 insofar as it purported to naturalize native-born blacks and regulate racial matters within the states. He insisted that a constitutional amendment was necessary to make native-born blacks citizens of United States.[335]

In 1870, the qualifications of Senator-elect Hiram R. Revels (Rep., Miss.) were considered by the Senate, objection having been made that Revels, an African-American, had not been an American citizen for the required nine years.[336] Senator Garrett Davis (Dem., Ky.) argued that Revels had not been a citizen for the requisite time, relying upon *Dred Scott*. He contended that free, native-born blacks could not have been American citizens before the adoption of the Fourteenth Amendment because otherwise they would have been entitled to the benefit of the comity clause.[337] Davis explained that, had antebellum free, native-born blacks been American citizens, then any such person

> by this provision [the comity clause] had a right to go into any slave State and address a free white woman, and if she would consent, to marry her. That is one of the privileges that is guaranteed under this clause of the Constitution to those whom it was intended to embrace. Do you say that a free negro might go into a slave State and erect a printing office, and publish his essays against the existence of the institution of slavery, collect together the people of his race and everybody who would come and hear him, and denounce the institution, and tell his race that it was an institution cruel and inhuman, and ought to be overthrown? Do you say that a free negro could have gone to any slave State, gone into a hotel, claimed the right to sit in its parlor and its best chambers and sit down among its white guests and partake of all its fare, precisely as the white people of the vicinage or locality, and the white people of any other State could?[338]

Not to be outdone, Senator George Vickers (Dem., Md.) undertook to show why Revels could not have been an American citizen for the requisite number of years in order to qualify to be a senator. Similarly relying on *Dred Scott*, Vickers insisted that native-born blacks became American citizens by virtue of the adoption of the Fourteenth Amendment, and not before, and denied that the amendment had a retroactive effect.[339] In an exceptionally revealing expression of his view of the nature of American citizenship, Vickers identified "some of the rights which one citizen enjoys as a citizen of the United States, according to the constitutional term [that] he enjoy[s] when he goes into another State." [340] According to Vickers, they include: "1. To travel into and sojourn in it. 2. To purchase and hold real estate. 3. To enter into trade and commerce. 4. To exercise the freedom of speech and the freedom of the press. 5. To give testimony in court. 6. To intermarry with white persons. 7. To enter public hotels, churches, steamboats, and other public places with white people. 8. To be exempt from all degrading punishments."[341]

Vickers in effect denied that black Americans "could ... have enjoyed any of these privileges which [he had just] enumerated before the adoption of the civil rights bill or the fourteenth constitutional amendment."[342]

Also instructive are the remarks of then-Congressman (later Senator) James B. Beck (Dem., Ken.), who first entered Congress in 1867. Beck's professed principle was to support equal civil rights for African Americans, but to deny them the suffrage. On January 28, 1869, during his address on the issue of suffrage for black Americans, Beck declared that "[p]rior to the adoption of [the fourteenth] amendment negroes were not citizens of the United States" and, therefore, were unable to have the benefit of the access to the federal courts under article 3, section 2 of the Constitution, or of the comity clause [referring to South Carolina law that prohibited free negroes from other States from landing on her soil]." In speaking of the Fourteenth Amendment (which he assumed for argument's sake to have been adopted), he explained that "negroes, as well as Indians, Gipsies, Chinese, and all the Mongolian races born in the United States, men and women, young and old, can now sue and be sued in the courts of the United States. They ... can move from State to State, locate in any State, acquire, hold, and enjoy property under the protection of the laws of the State upon the same terms as white citizens going there from other States can; they are entitled to the privileges and immunities of citizens of the United States."[343]

Prior to the adoption of the Fourteenth Amendment, Congress had enacted the Civil Rights Act of 1866, against invidious discrimination on account of race, color, or previous condition of servitude with respect to the rights specified in the statute.[344] Some founders of the Fourteenth Amendment intended that the privileges or immunities clause constitutionalize the protections of the statute in question in view of the naturalization of native-born African Americans.[345] But the privileges or immunities clause and the due process clause of the Fourteenth Amendment apply only to the states. So what about the United States? The adoption of two provisions did not constitutionalize section 1 of the statute with respect to the United States. Such constitutionalization was possible only if there was an already extant immunity of American citizens exempting them from racial discrimination with respect to civil rights (at least those enumerated in the 1866 Civil Rights Act). And how is this possible with respect to the United States unless the possession of this immunity is entailed by American citizenship such that the adoption of the citizenship clause was a great boon to African Americans?

It is pleasing to note that in Amar's more recent book (unlike his *The Bill of Rights*) he starts on the right foot by discussing the citizenship clause before talking about the privileges or immunities clause.[346] Amar explained his position thus:[347]

Though the word "equal" did not explicitly appear in the Fourteenth Amendment's first sentence, the concept was strongly implicit. All persons born under the flag were citizens, and thus *equal* citizens. The companion Civil Rights Act had spoken of the right of all citizens to enjoy "full and equal' civil rights, and a later Supreme Court case glossed the citizenship clause as follows: "All citizens are equal before the law."

Amar thus discloses his understanding that the status of national citizenship is incompatible with an inferior and degraded status based upon a caste principle of race or color. The view he professes in his second book is that, "Read alongside Article I's prohibitions on both state and federal titles of nobility, the citizenship clause thus proclaimed an ideal of republican equality binding on state and federal governments alike."[348] But, this position is plausible only if Amar also holds that the doctrine of *Dred Scott* that national citizenship is incompatible with an inferior and degraded status based upon a caste principle of race or color continued to be in force notwithstanding the adoption of the Fourteenth Amendment.

To agree that national citizenship entails the freedom of travel and migration throughout the United States as a constitutional privilege and its incompatibility with an inferior and degraded status based upon race or color serves to confirm that the privileges and immunities of the American people are necessarily predicable of American citizens (but not necessarily only them).

Section 4. The freedom from invidious gender and other similar kinds of discrimination as to civil rights based upon birth status

Amar commendably perceives that the citizenship clause has an underlying principle that generalizes from the freedom from racial discrimination with respect to civil rights to a broader freedom: the right to be free from invidious discrimination with respect to civil rights based upon birth status. Amar felicitously puts it this way In his *America's Constitution*: "The amendment's text [referring to the citizenship clause, "and in particular to its key word; 'born'"] summoned up a provocative vision of birthright citizenship: Government could properly regulate its citizens' behavior—their conduct and choices—but should never degrade or penalize a citizen or treat that citizen as globally inferior to others simply because of his or her [(I'm sure Amar means) allegedly] low birth status."[349]

Thus, the freedom from racial and ethnic discrimination is but one of a family of immunities of American citizens that are in the nature of rights to equalities that the adoption of the Fourteenth Amendment, by virtue of its privileges or immunities clause, constitutionalized with respect to the states. Accordingly, there is another very important immunity of American citizens: viz., exemption from invidious discrimination as to civil rights based upon gender. This freedom-from right is very much like the exemption from invidious discrimination based upon race, color, ethnicity, or place of birth. Moreover, this immunity is very arguably presupposed by the Nineteenth Amendment (adopted 1919), which prohibits denial or abridgment by the United States or the states of the right to vote on account of sex. Thus, the immunity in question precludes any kind of invidious discrimination as to civil rights by government that constitutes a badge or incident of an inferior or degraded legal status based upon a gender, because such a status is incompatible with the dignity of paramount national citizenship.[350] On the other hand, freedom from discrimination based upon sexual orientation (as manifested in some people's "behavior—their conduct and choices") does not credibly constitute a constitutional immunity (within the meaning of the privileges or immunities clause) because the justifying principle for such discrimination is not predicated upon caste or similar birth status. Whatever constitutional limitations obtain with respect to discrimination based upon sexual orientation would have to be justified upon some other basis.

Section 5. The freedom from invidious discrimination as to civil rights based upon civil or political status otherwise incompatible with the nature of the Union and the equality of states

The Court declared in *United States* v. *Cruikshank*,[351] "The equality of rights of citizens is a principle of republicanism." Thus, for example and as Amar in effect notes, freedom from discrimination based upon the principle of nobility is a right to an equality constitutionalized in sections 9 and 10 of article I of the Constitution.[352] Another immunity of American citizens is exemption from invidious discrimination based upon how national citizenship has been acquired.[353] Another important constitutional immunity is freedom from invidious discrimination, with respect to any of the rights denoted by the comity clause, upon the basis of an American citizen's present or former residence or citizenship of a state, district, territory, possession, or commonwealth,[354] of the United States.[355] This constitutional immunity of American citizens is complementary to his constitutional freedom of travel and migration throughout the United States. Absent the Fourteenth Amendment, only American citizens who are citizens of other states while sojourning within the host state are entitled to the benefits of the comity clause. But with the privileges or immunities clause, each state is precluded from abridging the constitutional immunity in question with respect to even its own citizens upon the basis of a present or past place-of-birth status.[356] The constitutional immunity of American citizens with respect to the rights denoted by the comity clause exempting them from discrimination based upon present or former citizenship or residence, or the mode by which national citizenship was acquired, is grounded upon the indestructibility of the union of states equal in dignity. To abridge this immunity would subvert the paramountcy and superiority of national citizenship generated by the establishment of a more perfect (but nevertheless federal) union with the adoption of the Constitution.

Section 6. Political freedom as entailed by our republican institutions and popular sovereignty[357]

A nother privilege of American citizens, is *political freedom*—a term to be understood to refer only to a freedom-right pertaining to expression and publication as to political and cognate matters, as distinguished from political rights (e.g., the right to vote, hold office, serve on juries or in the militia). This freedom necessarily shares components in common with freedoms of speech and press but chiefly with freedom of assembly. However, the republican form of government established for the United States and required for the states by the Constitution[358] entails political freedom independently of the First Amendment and includes some components that are not those of First Amendment freedoms.

The Fifteenth Amendment (adopted 1870) denies the United States and to the states the power to abridge or deny the right of American citizens to vote on account of race, color, or previous condition of servitude. The Nineteenth Amendment (adopted 1920) does so with respect to sex. The Twenty-sixth Amendment (adopted 1970) does so with respect to the age of eighteen years or older. These amendments necessarily presuppose that political freedom is a privilege of American citizens. Since virtually universal suffrage obtains on national, state, and local levels, political freedom should be very encompassing.

As the Supreme Court declared in *United States* v. *Cruikshank*:

> The right of the people peaceably to assemble for the purpose of petitioning Congress for a redress of grievances, or for any thing else connected with the powers or the duties of the national government, is an attribute of national citizenship, and, as such, under the protection of, and guaranteed by, the United States. *The very idea of a government, republican in form, implies a right on the part of its citizens to meet peaceably for*

> *consultation in respect to public affairs and to petition for a redress of grievances.*[359]

However, matters of state and local concern are as much a matter of legitimate concern to American citizens everywhere as are matters of national concern because all Americans are members of one and the same political community that is national, perpetual, and indissoluble. As the Court also explained in *Stromberg* v. *California:*[360] "The maintenance of the opportunity for free political discussion to the end that government may be responsive to the will of the people and that changes may be obtained by lawful means, an opportunity essential to the security of the Republic, is a fundamental principle of our constitutional system." The Court stated in *Knauer* v. *United States*,[361] "citizenship obtained through naturalization [or birth] carries with it the privilege of full participation in the affairs of our society, including the right to speak freely, to criticize officials and administrators, and to promote changes in our laws, including the very Charter of our Government." Furthermore, to quote from *DeJonge* v. *Oregon:*[362]

> The greater the importance of safeguarding the community from incitements to the overthrow of our institutions by force and violence, the more imperative is the need to preserve inviolate the constitutional rights of free speech, free press and free assembly in order to maintain the opportunity for free political discussion, to the end that government may be responsive to the will of the people and that changes, if desired, may be obtained by peaceful means. Therein lies the security of the Republic, the very foundation of constitutional government.

It would appear that the *DeJonge* opinion appears to presuppose that all the components of what I term *political freedom* are among the components of the First Amendment rights of free speech, free press, and free assembly. But on the contrary, the specific right of the free assembly clause is itself a component of the broader right of political freedom because the components of the specific rights of the First Amendment are not congruent with all components of the right of political freedom.

Political freedom includes among its components the specific right of the assembly-petition clause of the First Amendment. This provision reads: "Congress shall make no law ... abridging ... the right of the people peaceably to assemble, and to petition the Government for a redress of grievances." According to one view, this clause took the right of petition as the primary right and the right peaceably to assemble as a subordinate and instrumental right. However, the Court has broadly construed the clause to apply to assemblies gathered for political purposes other than to petition for a redress of grievances. Hence, the specific right of the assembly-petition clause of the First Amendment as judicially construed turns out to be a component of political freedom, because the former right is itself implied by the republican form of our governments and the principle of popular sovereignty. Moreover, it is significant that, of the thirty-seven states in the Union in 1868, "[a] full thirty-four states, or more than three-quarters of the total, protected the right of citizens to peaceably assemble for their common good and to petition the government.... Typical state constitutional language used to protect these rights read: 'The people shall have the right freely to assemble together, to consult for the common good, to instruct their representatives, and to petition the legislature for redress of grievances.'"[363]

As Amar so well puts it: "The Preamble's dramatic opening words ... trumpeted the Constitution's underlying theory of popular sovereignty."[364] According to the principle of popular sovereignty, all power is vested in, and consequently derived from the people. Therefore, the people of the United States have the collective right to reform, alter, or abolish their governments. Those who hold public office are the trustees and servants of the people, and are accountable to them. The collective right of the people of the United States to reform, alter, and abolish their governments entails in turn an individual right of any free American citizen (whether or not he has the political rights to vote and hold office) to freely express his political opinions and to otherwise freely engage in political and cognate activities pertaining to public affairs in all appropriate forms and channels of communication or expression—so that those citizens with the right to vote may wisely exercise their suffrage, and government officers (whether executive, legislative, or judicial) may responsibly discharge their official duties.

The political freedom includes as a component a broad journalistic freedom involving all appropriate forms or channels of public communication in order that American citizens are provided with relevant information about matters of public concern. Thus, political freedom (and journalistic freedom insofar as it is a component of political freedom) might conceivably have some components specific to predominantly visual mass electronic media that are not shared with the freedoms of speech, press, and assembly. Political freedom might be broader in scope than freedom of speech or the press with respect to the more robust forms or channels of communication or expression—such as billboards, picketing or patrolling on sidewalks with posters, parades, mass meetings or demonstrations in public places ordinarily used for vehicular or pedestrian traffic (e.g., public streets, alleys, and squares), picketing— forms of public communication more likely than the traditional media to involve semi-captive and perhaps even captive auditors or spectators. Moreover, the right of political freedom involves, in my view, rights of access to public buildings or other structures (such as public school auditoriums or stadiums) not ordinarily available as appropriate forums for the exercise of free speech rights.

That political freedom might have components that the First Amendment freedoms lack raises the possibility that the First Amendment freedoms are subject to being improvidently construed by the Court. I hesitate to say much more about political freedom as a constitutional privilege of the American people because this would require a very detailed account of what are its components as well as those of freedom of speech and the press in political matters. However, there are possible difference between political and the First Amendment freedoms. I think that certain viewpoint-and-content-neutral time, place, and manner regulations governing speech and the press do not abridge First Amendment freedoms; but they could abridge political freedom.

One example readily comes to mind. Unsolicited live or recorded telephonic propaganda involves intrusions on privacy interests that are very much more intrusive and annoying than the delivery of unsolicited printed matter (including CDs, DVDs, videos, and audio tapes). A carefully crafted, viewpoint-and-content neutral law that forbids all robocall or other unsolicited live or recorded telephonic messages (other than authorized public service messages) devoted to propaganda or educational matter (whether or not political) would not, in my opinion, violate freedom of speech. It would, however, violate political freedom as applied to predominantly political speech, especially when made in the course of political campaigns incident to elections for candidates for office or ballot measures. Registered voters may be presumed to have consented to, or to have taken the risk of, receiving otherwise unwelcome or annoying calls—unless the prospective recipient has manifested a contrary intent such as by placing himself on some official or authorized no-call registry.

The right of political freedom pertains to expression that is predominantly devoted to political matters and public affairs. However, the freedoms of speech and the press also pertain to the interest of the public as to that information that they should have in order to be responsibly exercise political rights. Freedom of speech and the press also provide the means by which abuses and misuses of power may be exposed and the risk of such exposure has a corresponding checking value with respect to the exercise of power. But the rights of free speech and free press pertain to other than political matters or public affairs. Thus, unlike political freedom, the rights of free speech and free press also pertain to speeches and writings that may be predominantly nonpolitical in purpose and effect, such as writings concerning philosophy, religion, the natural or social sciences, history, technology, the literary arts, and so forth. In addition, this proposition is fully in accord with the dominant original understanding of the founders of the Bill of Rights and the Fourteenth Amendment.[365]

Section 7. Religious freedom as consisting of all those freedom-rights in matters of religion that are secured against abridgments by the First Amendment

The reader will recall that I do not propose to discuss whatever is the special theory of any particular constitutional right except insofar as it may be necessary to adequately set forth my general theory of the constitutional rights of the American people; and also just to indicate in fairness to the reader my basic philosophy concerning personal rights. But it is necessary, for my purposes, to discuss religious freedom in greater detail in order to better explain how religious freedom, as protected by the First Amendment, is a constitutional privilege of the American people; and how there is a complementary freedom-from right in religious matters that is entailed by the establishment clause and is thus a constitutional immunity of American citizens.

At the outset, again bear in mind that a constitutional privilege of the American people is per se a freedom-right and not a freedom-from right. So let us assume (for argument's sake only) that the establishment clause entails a personal freedom-from right of American citizens that a government not expend monies from general tax funds, to which as taxpayers they have contributed, to give financial support to one or more religious institutions to be spent for religious purposes. Such a scenario would not pertain to a constitutional privilege of the American people in matters of religion, but rather to a constitutional immunity (i.e., a freedom-from right) in matters of religion. In short, the scenario in question does not involve the issue of religious freedom as such but something quite different.

According to one plausible special theory of the religious freedom secured against abridgments by the First Amendment (let's call it STRF-A), religious freedom is identical with the specific right of the free exercise clause. STRF-A does not exclude the legal fact that the establishment clause entails freedom-rights in matters of religion, or that the free speech, free press, and assembly-petition specific rights each have some components that are also freedom-rights in matters religious. That there is no freedom-right in matters religious secured by the First Amendment that is not a component of the specific right of the free exercise clause is the central feature of STRF-A.

Another, more plausible, special theory of religious freedom (STRF-B) is that its components are the components of the specific right of the free exercise clause and freedom-rights entailed by the establishment clause—the two clusters of freedom-rights not being congruent.

Another, and an even more plausible, special theory (STRF-C) asserts that religious freedom is not identical with the specific right of the free exercise clause and that the components of religious freedom include freedom-rights entailed by the establishment clause and freedom-rights in matters religious that are themselves components of the specific rights of the free speech and free press clauses.[366] Thus, STRF-C also affirms that religious freedom, as a constitutional privilege of the American people, consists of all those freedom-rights in matters of religion secured against abridgments by the First Amendment. I accept STRF-C partly because it makes the best fit with the general theory proposed in this book. Its acceptance obviates some plausible worries about whether the establishment and free exercise clauses protect all those freedom-rights that should be components of that *religious freedom* that is secured against all abridgments by the First Amendment. Moreover, it is obvious in any case that the freedoms of speech, press, and assembly must have some components that are freedom-rights in matters of religion.

Religious freedom, in the requisite sense, is a *civil freedom within necessary limits in matters of religion*. Admittedly *within necessary limits* is vague. Suffice it to say that the term *necessary limits* pertains to such limits to freedom in matters of religion that are necessary (and thus not just reasonably appropriate) to efficaciously provide for the indispensible secular needs of civil society pertaining to peace and good order, public health, safety, morals, and decency, and the security of person and property. Further precision is possible, but need not be pursued here since we are focused upon a general theory of constitutional rights of which religious freedom is but one.

Religious freedom has some component freedom-rights as markers, as it were, of its scope and limits. And these markers pertain to rights to be legally free (within necessary limits) to do or not do **x** in matters of religion—the **x** including but not limited to: whether or not to believe, profess, advocate, or criticize any proposition in matters of religion such as whether God exists, whether God created the world in time, whether Jesus Christ was the incarnation of the eternal Son of God (the second person of the Trinity), whether the promised messiah is yet to come or not, whether Mohammed is the true prophet of Allah (God), and so on. And, religious freedom in the requisite sense includes rights to freely (whether individually or in association with others) privately or publicly propagate beliefs or opinions in matters religious, or to freely engage in the exercise of some particular religion or not at all—with corresponding rights to not join or to disassociate oneself from any society organized for purposes pertaining to matters of religion. The right to be legally free to do or not do **x** also includes but is not limited to: giving or not giving tithes or other donations to such-and-such church, denomination, sect, or other religious association, or an association devoted to promoting religious or irreligious doctrines and principles; attending or not attending a religious service, and so forth. Religious freedom, just as every other constitutional freedom, has necessary derivative or auxiliary freedom-from rights that are entailed by the constitutional prohibition of all abridgments of that freedom, including but not limited to freedom from governmental invidious discrimination in matters of religion with respect to eligibility for public welfare benefits or equality of civil rights.

In my article, I made the following statement about religious freedom as a constitutional privilege of American citizens:

> The general practice of using the term "religious freedom" as meaning more than just the right specified in the free exercise clause of the [F]irst [A]mendment is followed in this article. Religious freedom also includes

among its components those individual rights concerning religion which are entailed by the absence of a religion established by law. As Judge Thomas M. Cooley put it: "There is not complete religious liberty where one sect is favored by the State and given an advantage by law over other sects."[367]

I should like to retract this statement in part as not having been providentially made. In the first place, I do not hold that "[t]here is not complete religious liberty where one sect is favored by the State and given an advantage by law over other sects."[368] I maintain that the establishment clause is violated but that religious freedom is not abridged where a government gives grants-in-aid to a particular church or denomination (say, to build and maintain public houses of worship) appropriated from general tax funds, and which money grant the church or denomination is free to decline. Adherents of either the nonpreferentialist, accomodationist, or separationist theory of the establishment clause may consistently hold this opinion.[369] There are some persons who hold that the right of religious freedom is abridged by the government making expenditures or appropriations from general tax funds to propagate doctrines in religious matters that they hold false. But I do not agree with this proposition anymore than I do with the proposition that the freedoms of speech and the press are abridged whenever the government makes expenditures or appropriations from general tax funds to propagate certain principles and beliefs in nonreligious matters.

The famous Virginia statute on religious freedom of 1786 should not be read to be inconsistent with the foregoing merely because its preamble so emphatically affirms:

[T]hat to compel a man to furnish contributions of money for the propagation of opinions which he disbelieves, is sinful and tyrannical; that even forcing him to support this or that teacher of his own religious persuasion, is depriving him of the comfortable liberty of giving his contributions to the particular pastor, whose morals he would make his pattern, and whose powers he feels most persuasive to righteousness, and is withdrawing from the ministry those temporal rewards, which proceeding from an approbation of their personal conduct, are an additional incitement to earnest and unremitting labours for the instruction of mankind[.][370]

Yes, I agree with this statement if understood to only apply to a situation where a person is legally compelled to pay tithes (or its equivalent), or where a tax is imposed on him that is specifically assessed or otherwise definitively earmarked for expenditures in violation of the establishment clause.[371] Were the taxpayer to seek judicial relief, he would have his tax liability proportionally reduced, or be entitled to a refund of the money if already paid. But if the reader holds that religious freedom is necessarily violated by the expenditure of public tax funds (generated by general taxes) to financially support a particular church or denomination for religious purposes based upon a broad reading of the above-quoted passage, then he should also hold that religious freedom is necessarily violated by the expenditure of public funds to financially support the teaching of the theory of the evolution of species in public schools or popular educational programs because the theory of evolution is contrary to special creationist doctrines firmly believed by many to be divinely revealed. Similarly, governmentally-owned public educational institutions that teach that the universe is several billions years old is contrary to those creationists who adhere to a young earth doctrine as being divinely revealed. For any such person would be "compel[led] ... to furnish contributions of money for the propagation of opinions which he disbelieves," such compulsion being "sinful and tyrannical." Many other scenarios could easily be formulated and presented to the reader to the same effect. My bottom line is that nobody has a personal right, considered as a component of religious freedom, that the government not expend monies drawn from public funds (generated by general revenues to which his tax payments have contributed) for projects and programs in violations of the establishment clause. In such a case, he is not being *compelled*, in the sense of that term as used in the Virginia statute of religious freedom, "to furnish contributions of money for the propagation of opinions which he disbelieves."

The quoted passage from my article is also defective in that I failed to adequately explain why the term *religious freedom* should not be understood as being identical to the specific right of the free exercise clause (i.e., STRF-A). Some people might plausibly argue that although a person (whether or not a believer) cannot be constitutionally compelled to attend church services, profess an article of faith established by law, or to belong to some religious entity, the specific right of the free exercise clause does not per se encompass rights to organize anti-religious associations, and/ or to engage in public anti-religious propaganda because the free exercise clause only pertains to the *free exercise of religion*—which then does not include the *free exercise of irreligion* as a component. Some persons might conceivably hold that whatever rights there are to propagate anti-religious propaganda that obtain by virtue of the free exercise clause are derivative or auxiliary rather than being per se in nature. That is, such rights are necessary in order that the free exercise of religion not to be abridged but are not themselves constitutive of what is meant by the *free exercise of religion*. However, in my view, religious freedom includes as a per se component that "all men shall be free to profess, and by argument to maintain, their opinions in matters of religion, and the same shall in no wise affect, diminish or enlarge their civil capacities"[372]—even when exercised by those with antireligious opinions.[373] And this would clearly be the case were it agreed that the freedom-rights in matters religious that are components of freedom of speech and of the press include the component in question[374]—even though it is very arguable that this component is not a per se component of the specific right of the free exercise clause.[375]

I should here note another mistake in the quoted passage from my article that I now notice and recant. I wrote, "Religious freedom also includes among its components those individual rights concerning religion which are entailed by the absence of a religion established by law." But, religious freedom is a freedom; so each per se component of which is also a freedom (i.e., a right to be free to do or not do **x**). Religious freedom, as such, is not a freedom-from right; each per se component of which is also a freedom-from right (i.e., a right to be free from being burdened or incapacitated in certain ways). Now, in my view, the establishment clause entails both per se freedom-rights and per se freedom-from rights. The former are components of religious freedom; the latter are not. So the quoted passage from my article is defective in that I imply that the freedom-from rights entailed by the establishment clause are per se components of religious freedom.

The establishment clause, whether understood according to the more likely versions of the nonpreferentialist, accomodationist, or separationist models, entails freedom-rights in religious matters, whether or not they are also components of the specific right of the free exercise clause. And these entailed freedom-rights are components of that religious freedom that is fully secured by the First Amendment against all abridgments.[376] The case of *Watson* v. *Jones*,[377] decided in 1872, is of significant value in serving to confirm this view because it was decided after the adoption of the Fourteenth Amendment in 1868 but before the neutering of the privileges or immunities clause in the *Slaughter-House Cases* in 1873. The underlying litigation in this federal diversity-of-citizenship case involved a dispute between proslavery and antislavery factions of a Presbyterian church in postbellum Louisville, Kentucky, which resulted in the members of the church dividing into two bodies, each claiming the exclusive property right to the church building. *Watson* is very important because it is the only case involving religious freedom decided by the Court after the founding of the Fourteenth Amendment. However, the decision was not based upon either the First or the Fourteenth Amendment as such, but rather pursuant to the then (but no longer) extant rule that federal common law principles apply to the adjudication of diversity civil cases litigated in federal courts. Hence, the Court used the religious freedom principles realized in the First Amendment to determine the case before its construction of the Fourteenth Amendment in the *Slaughter-House Cases*.[378]

Justice Miller, speaking for the Court, noted the doctrine of the English courts concerning intra-ecclesiastical legal disputes was not to be followed in federal courts. This determination was made not only because the Church of England was established by law; but also because it was subject to the authority of "the Lord Chancellor of England, who is, in his office, in a large sense, the head and representative of the Established Church, who controls very largely the church patronage, and whose judicial decision may be, and not infrequently is, invoked in cases of heresy and ecclesiastical contumacy[.]"[379] Justice Miller declared:

> The dissenting church in England is not a free church in the sense in which we apply the term in this country, and it was much less free in Lord Eldon's time [circa, 1801–27] than now. Laws then existed upon the statute-book hampering the free exercise of religious belief and worship in many most oppressive forms, and though Protestant dissenters were less burdened than Catholics and Jews, there did not exist that full, entire, and practical freedom for all forms of religious belief and practice which lies at the foundation of our political principles....

> In this country, the full and free right to entertain any religious belief, to practice any religious principle, and to teach any religious doctrine which does not violate the laws of morality and property, and which does not infringe personal rights, is conceded to all. The law knows no heresy, and is committed to the support of no dogma, the establishment of no sect. The right to organize voluntary religious associations to assist in the expression and dissemination of any religious doctrine, and to create tribunals for the decision of controverted questions of faith within the association, and for the ecclesiastical government of all the individual members, congregations, and officers within the general association, is unquestioned. All who unite themselves to such a body do so with an implied consent to this government, and are bound to submit to it. But it would be a vain consent and would lead to the total subversion of such religious bodies, if any one aggrieved by one of their decisions could appeal to the secular courts and have them reversed.

It is of the essence of these religious unions, and of their right to establish tribunals for the decision of questions arising among themselves, that those decisions should be binding in all cases of ecclesiastical cognizance, subject only to such appeals as the organism itself provides for.[380]

The foregoing declaration in *Watson* can be studiously parsed and scrutinized in detail. However, it appears quite evident that the Court necessarily discerned that the "full, entire, and practical freedom for all forms of religious belief and practice which lies at the foundation of our political principles" are those that obtain by virtue of the establishment and free exercise clauses of the first amendment—these provisions providing the requisite basis for the application of that "general law" that was at the time applicable to federal diversity cases. That "[t]he law knows no heresy, and is committed to the support of no dogma, the establishment of no sect" entails *freedom*-rights in religious matters. A person's freedom in matters religious (within necessary limits) cannot be constitutionally limited by legislation obliging him to remain in or join a particular church, denomination or sect; or profess its doctrines; to not publicly express and argue for heterodox or officially disapproved opinions upon religious matters; to pay tithes or tax assessments for the support of the established church. For one mode by which an establishment of religion obtains is where the government explicitly or implicitly specifies such doctrines that are juridically deemed desirable as worthy of being generally believed or disbelieved, as the case may be, and to prohibit, at least in some forms or channels of public communication, the propagation of dissenting views. Moreover, complete religious freedom entails that no church, denomination, or sect may be established by law and given special rights and duties without its continuing free and autonomous consent because otherwise it would not be free.

I do not propose to set forth a detailed account of how the Supreme Court's doctrine pertaining to freedom in religious matters has evolved since the incorporation by the Fourteenth Amendment of religious freedom in 1940 and that of the establishment clause in 1947.[381] We should, however, pay attention to what is the current doctrine of the Court relevant to the instant inquiry. That doctrine is found in *Employment Division* v. *Smith.*[382] In *Smith,* the Court held that the free exercise clause (as applied to the states by the Fourteenth Amendment) does not preclude a state from including religiously motivated peyote use incident to participation in religious ceremonies within the scope of its general criminal prohibition of use of that drug, and hence it is not foreclosed from denying unemployment benefits to individuals dismissed from their jobs because of such religiously motivated use. The Court's decision was based upon the doctrine that "the right of free exercise does not relieve an individual of the obligation to comply with a 'valid and neutral law of general applicability on the ground that the law proscribes (or prescribes) conduct that his religion prescribes (or proscribes).'"[383]

Pertinent to our inquiry is the declaration by Justice Scalia (speaking for the Court) that gives us the Court's explanation of how religious freedom is purportedly protected by the First and Fourteenth Amendments:

> The only decisions in which we have held that the First Amendment bars application of a neutral, generally applicable law to religiously motivated action have involved not the Free Exercise Clause alone, but the Free Exercise Clause in conjunction with other constitutional protections, such as freedom of speech and of the press [case citations and summaries], or the right of parents ... [citation], to direct the education of their children [case citation and holding].

> Some of our cases prohibiting compelled expression, decided exclusively upon free speech grounds, have also involved freedom of religion [case citations and holdings]. And it is easy to envision a case in which a challenge on freedom of association grounds would likewise be reinforced by Free Exercise Clause concerns. [Case citation and quotation.]

The present case does not present such a hybrid situation, but a free exercise claim unconnected with any communicative activity or parental right....[384]

I agree with the Court's decision in *Smith* that peyote use incident to a bona fide participation in religious ceremonies is not protected by the free exercise clause, and that there is no constitutional duty to apply a balancing test according to which governmental actions substantially burdening a religious practice must be justified by a compelling governmental interest. But what I find to be extremely objectionable is that the Court in the *Smith* opinion appears to hold that neither the free exercise nor the establishment clauses independently or in conjunction entail important freedom-rights in matters religious pertaining to communicative or organizational activity in matters of religion notwithstanding there being neutral, generally applicable laws in that domain.[385]

Section 8. Freedom-from rights entailed by the establishment clause as collectively constituting a constitutional immunity of American citizens

The thesis of this section is that important freedom-from rights are entailed by the establishment clause. These rights collectively constitute a constitutional immunity of the American people. Hence, the privileges or immunities clause secures this immunity from abridgments by the states. However, what may seem anomalous or disquieting to some readers is that I do not hold that every one of the prohibitions (and I do not count those involving federal-state relations), constitutive of the establishment clause, entails a corresponding freedom or freedom-from right. Therefore, the privileges or immunities clause does not fully apply the establishment clause-prohibitions to the states other than the freedom and freedom-from rights entailed by them. On the other hand, the establishment clause embodies other prohibitions on the exercise of power by Congress with very important functions other than entailing freedom and freedom-from rights.[386]

I suspect that the one thing that some readers will heartily dislike about the general theory expounded in this book it is that the theory does not include the doctrine that the Fourteenth Amendment somehow fully 'incorporates' the establishment clause in cases where religious freedom is not at issue. But the general theory of this book cannot admit that all the prohibitions of the establishment clause (not counting those strictly sounding in federal-state relations) somehow fully apply to the states by the privileges or immunities clause—given, according to this book's general theory, that only personal freedoms and freedom-from rights are denoted by the descriptive term of the privileges or immunities clause. Even if it could plausibly be argued that the establishment clause entails a freedom from establishment as the right of the people, it is nevertheless a long way to Tipperary because one must show that the right of the people in question is an individual rather than a collective right. And, by hypothesis, neither the privileges or immunities clause nor the due process clause of the Fourteenth Amendment incorporates collective rights.

I am not alone in finding it quite bizarre that the Court holds that the Fourteenth Amendment due process clause incorporates all the prohibitions of the establishment clause.[387] The chief ground for this view is that it is so wildly implausible to claim that any person is necessarily deprived of life, liberty, or property without due process of law where a state expends monies from its general tax revenues to noncoercively endorse and support a particular religion or religion in general, or even some form of irreligion. And, moreover, it appears strange and ironical that so important a constitutional provision adopted in order to (among other things) vindicate states' rights in the domain of religion was abolished without an audible whimper. But among the present members of the Court, Justice Clarence Thomas appears to be quite alone in maintaining that the establishment clause should not be held as being incorporated by the Fourteenth Amendment.[388]

Both the Fifth and the Fourteenth Amendments have a due process clause. Those who participated in the founding of the Fourteenth Amendment can be reasonably presumed to have understood that both clauses are essentially equivalent in meaning. There is no substantial evidence to show that the Fifth Amendment due process clause was understood by founders of the Fourteenth Amendment to have substantive aspects so comprehensive as to include all the personal rights entailed by the prohibitions of the establishment clause. Moreover, the only substantial evidence available that shows that some founders of the Fourteenth Amendment who believed that religious freedom is incorporated by the Fourteenth Amendment also shows that they thought that the privileges or immunities clause is the vehicle of such incorporation.

It was not until 1947 that the Supreme Court definitively ruled in *Everson* v. *Board of Education*, that the Fourteenth Amendment fully applies the First Amendment's prohibition against any law respecting an establishment of religion to the states. The Court, having made reference to its "decisions concerning an individual's religious freedom since the Fourteenth Amendment was interpreted to make the prohibitions of the First applicable to state action abridging religious freedom, immediately proceeded to announce that "[t]here is every reason to give the same application and broad interpretation to the 'establishment of religion' clause."[389] From this declaration, one can infer that the establishment clause embodies prohibitions on the power of United States to legislate in religious matters in addition to securing against abridgment all the freedom-rights that are the components of religious freedom and the freedom-from rights entailed by the clause. In the course of its opinion, the Court declared:

> The "establishment of religion" clause of the First Amendment means at least this: neither a state nor the Federal Government can set up a church. Neither can pass laws which aid one religion, aid all religions, or prefer one religion over another. Neither can force nor influence a person to go to or to remain away from church against his will or force him to profess a belief or disbelief in any religion. No person can be punished for entertaining or professing religious beliefs or disbeliefs, for church attendance or non-attendance. No tax in any amount, large or small, can be levied to support any religious activities or institutions, whatever they may be called, or whatever form they may adopt to teach or practice religion. Neither a state nor the Federal Government can, openly or secretly, participate in the affairs of any religious organizations or groups and vice versa. In the words of Jefferson, the clause against establishment of religion by law was intended to erect "a wall of separation between church and State."[390]

> [The First Amendment] requires the state to be neutral in its relation with groups of religious believers and non-believers; it does not require the state to be their adversary. State power is no more to be used so as to handicap religions than it is to favor them.[391]

According to the *Everson* Court, the establishment clause precludes the power to "set up a church, pass laws which aid one religion, aid all religions, or prefer one religion over another." The Court specified that the establishment clause forbids a state from "contribute[ing] tax-raised funds to the support of an institution which teaches the tenets and faith of any church."[392] But the exercise of these forbidden powers may or may not, depending on the particular case, involve the issue of an abridgment of religious freedom.

An actual or threatened violation of a person's right to religious freedom will necessarily ground a claim that the litigant has suffered some direct, substantial injury (or, in some cases, is immediately in danger of sustaining some such injury as a result of the alleged violation); which claim presents a justiciable issue that can be redressed if found meritorious. In federal cases, the judicial power of the United States is limited by Article III of the Constitution to the resolution of "Cases" and "Controversies." Therefore, the litigant in the federal court must have the requisite standing to assert a claim based upon constitutional grounds. This requirement can be readily satisfied in cases involving alleged violations of religious freedom. But how the standing requirement is satisfied in cases involving claims of violation of the establishment clause presents different issues. Suffice it to say, as the Court declared in *Abington School District v. Schempp* (1963), "the requirements for standing to challenge state action under the Establishment Clause, unlike those relating to the Free Exercise Clause, do not include proof that particular religious freedoms are infringed."[393]

Frothingham v. *Mellon*[394] (decided in 1923) announced the general standing rule in federal courts to the effect that a federal taxpayer does not have standing to challenge the constitutionality of a federal statute involving the expenditure of funds extracted from general revenues to which his tax payments contributed. However, in *Flast* v. *Cohen*[395] (decided in 1968) the Court qualified the *Frothingham* standing rule. This case involved income tax payments of a federal taxpayer included in the general revenues from which funds were extracted that financed a congressional program claimed to be in violation of the establishment clause. The *Flast*

Court held that the federal taxpayer, who alleges and shows that he has contributed tax monies to the general revenues from which expenditures have been appropriated allegedly in violation of the establishment clause, has standing to secure judicial review of the expenditure of federal funds pursuant to congressional legislation authorizing the program enacted pursuant to its taxing and spending power authorized by article I, section 8 of the Constitution. The Court, however, has steadfastly declined to extend the *Flast* rule to scenarios other than those involving the establishment clause.[396] According to the Court, the federal taxpayer lacks the requisite standing to assert that his right to religious freedom as such has been violated because the unconstitutional expenditure of funds drawn from general tax revenues does not involve coercion.[397] If his establishment clause claim is found to have merit, the only relief to which the aggrieved taxpayer would be entitled is that the government would be enjoined from enforcing the law in the future.

So the bottom line is that some abridgments of religious freedom by the United States are violations of the establishment clause, but that a violation of the establishment clause is not necessarily an abridgment of religious freedom. But abridgments of per se freedom-from rights entailed by the establishment clause would be sufficient to establish a requisite standing according to pre-*Flast* standards.

What are the per se freedom-from rights entailed by the establishment clause? Now, again, it is not my purpose in this book to definitively choose a special theory of a constitutional right except insofar as it is necessary to develop the general theory of constitutional rights. But it suffices for me to cite some examples of freedom-from rights entailed by the establishment clause to make my case that such freedom-from rights collectively constitute a constitutional immunity of American citizens within the meaning of the privileges or immunities clause. For the sake of convenience, let us call this immunity the *No-Establishment Immunity* (NEI). Because there are some readers who are disturbed by the idea that the Fourteenth Amendment does not incorporate the establishment clause, I should like to point out that there is a special theory of the NEI that might find favor with them. Before briefly describing this special theory, I should immediately say that I do not agree with it because, although somewhat plausible, it is not sufficiently persuasive for reasons set forth after my summary of this special theory.

The somewhat plausible special theory of the no-establishment immunity that I have in mind (let's call it ST-NEI-A) involves three very important features: (1) that the establishment clause generally prohibits (but not necessarily without exception) the government from using its taxing and spending power to acquire public funds by taxation and make an expenditure from such public funds that financially supports religious or irreligious institutions or operations as such; (2) that this particular prohibition entails a corresponding personal right of any taxpayer whose monies are included in the public funds from which the unlawful expenditure is made; (3) that the corresponding personal right of the taxpayer is for him not to have to suffer an added tax burden (however minute) occasioned by an expenditure of public funds in violation of the establishment clause. Unless a violation of religious freedom itself is in question, the tax itself is not per se unconstitutional but rather it is only the expenditure that is. However, the taxpayer has been *indirectly* taxed, it is said, because he has made tax payments that are included in public funds from which unlawful expenditures have been made. Thus essential to the ST-NEI-A is the claim that there is personal right of the taxpayer not to suffer a financial tax burden (however minute) occasioned by the expenditure of public monies or the disposition of public property in violation of the establishment clause.

ST-NEI-A (with perhaps some qualifications) is what I believe to be maintained by four sitting justices of the Supreme Court, as expressed in the dissenting opinion by Justice Souter (with Stevens, Ginsburg, and Breyer concurring) in *Hein* v. *Freedom From Religion Foundation*,[398] and in the dissenting opinion by Justice Brennan (Marshall, Blackmun concurring) in *Valley Forge College* v. *Americans United for Separation of Church and State, Inc.*[399]

But how plausible is the ST-NEI-A? Doubtless for some readers, the ST-NEI-A would have considerable appeal because it asserts that among freedom-from rights entailed by the establishment clause are those pertaining to governmental expenditures of tax raised funds in violation of the that clause. So, in this regard, it is approximately equivalent in effect to that of the proposition that prohibitions of the establishment clause generate *Flast*-type standing. Moreover, four sitting justices, as I have already noted, essentially adhere to ST-NEI-A as evidenced in the dissenting opinion in *Hein*. However, the ST-NEI-A does have a serious problem: it is not the current doctrine of the Court. There was nothing in the Court's opinion in *Flast* that suggests that its standing doctrine as to expenditures from tax-raised funds in violation of the establishment clause implies or is implied by the doctrine that there is a complementary freedom-from personal right. It is noteworthy that Justice Stewart found it necessary to expressly assert that "every taxpayer can claim a personal constitutional right not to be taxed for the support of a religious institution," but only after remarking: "I join the judgment and opinion of the Court, which I understand to hold only that a federal taxpayer has standing to assert that a specific expenditure of federal funds violates the Establishment Clause of the First Amendment."[400] And the very fact that the Court has declined to extend the *Flast* standing rule to cases in involving expenditures of federal funds allegedly to aid a religion or religion by the executive branch of the government, as evidenced by its holdings in *Valley Forge* and *Hein*, should be sufficient to warrant the conclusion that the ST-NEI-A is not a part of the Court's current doctrine. And, it does seem odd and far-fetched to affirm that there is a constitutional personal right entailed by the establishment clause even in a case where the claimed added financial burden to the individual taxpayer occasioned by the expenditure of funds or the disposition of property in putative violation of that clause is infinitesimal.

The dissenting justices in *Valley Forge* and *Hein*, respectively, based their doctrine upon a reading of Madison's "Memorial and Remonstrance Against Religious Assessments" and the Virginia statute of religious freedom.[401] But their reading uncritically assumes that the "Memorial" or the Virginia statute asserts that a person is *coerced* to financially support a religion whenever he is legally obliged to pay taxes that are included in a public fund from which monies are expended to aid a particular religious institution or religion in general.[402] No, these documents pertain only to scenarios where a person is legally obliged to pay tithes to a religious institution or to pay a tax specifically assessed to support a religion or religion in general.[403] Finally, the opinion of the dissenting justices in *Hein* about this matter is inconsistent with their having agreed with the plurality opinion that the *Flast* standing rule does not apply to cases involving the free exercise of religion. And that can only be if there is indeed no compulsion in a *Flast*-type scenario.

Although the *Flast*-type standing rule still holds, the majority of sitting justices does not agree with the dissenting justices in *Hein* that there is a personal constitutional right of a taxpayer that the government not expend funds (in which his tax payments, as well as those of others, are included) in violation of the establishment clause. Assume, if you will, that there is no such constitutional right and, further, that the *Flast*-type standing rule is reversed. There is, as Justice Harlan so well pointed out in his dissenting opinion, no reason why "individual litigants [should not] have standing to represent the public interest, despite their lack of economic or other personal interests, if Congress enacts legislation to authorize such suits."[404]

There is a special theory of the NEI (let's call this theory ST-NEI-B) that affirms that there is a constitutional immunity of American citizens pertaining to freedom-from rights entailed by the establishment clause; but its components do not include the right of a *Flast*-type taxpayer not to have an added tax burden (however minute) due to the expenditure of monies taken from a public fund (or the disposition of public property) in violation of the establishment clause. Quite obviously, the ST-NEI-B will necessarily postulate fewer components of the constitutional NEI than the ST-NEI-A.

Here are some, but certainly not all, doctrines of one version of the ST-NEI-B that I find very plausible (and that I find quite acceptable):

(1) The right to be free from being legally subject to the authority of any ecclesiastical person or entity exercising governmental or quasi-governmental powers or functions, as to religious or nonreligious

matters. A very good example of this kind of per se freedom-from right in nonreligious matter entailed by the establishment clause is provided in *Larkin* v. *Grendel's Den, Inc.*[405] In this case the Court reviewed a Massachusetts statute prohibiting the issuance of a liquor license to any premises within five hundred feet of a church or school if either makes a written objection to the issuance of the license. The Court held that the statute violates the establishment clause (as applied to the states via the Fourteenth Amendment) because a delegation of a standardless veto power to churches enmeshes them "in the exercise of substantial governmental powers."[406] Similarly, "a State may not delegate its civic authority to a group chosen according to a religious criterion."[407] The republican form of national government established by the Constitution for the United States is also secular (but not secularist). No ecclesiastical entity is directly or indirectly vested by the Constitution with governmental executive, legislative, or judicial powers. The original Constitution signals the secular nature of our republican institutions established for the United States by providing that "no religious Test shall ever be required as a Qualification to any Office or public Trust under the United States."[408] Thus, according to the Constitution, the government of the United States cannot be the secular arm of the Church; and the Church cannot be the sacral arm of the federal government. The importance of the freedom-from right entailed by the establishment clause cannot be minimized given the need to avoid the serious danger arising from the formation of enclaves that are de facto theocratic mini-states, which likely have *no-go zones* for infidels (relative to the religion in question), and in which the rules of the particular religious institution in question may be coercively enforced with penalties characteristic of civil society.

(2) The right to be free from the enforcement of a law that facially or as applied violates the establishment clause (but does not abridge religious freedom), the proper enforcement of which would very likely result in direct, serious injury or detriment to judicially cognizable property or other interests of natural or artificial persons. What immediately comes to my mind are the Sunday closing laws reviewed in *McGowan* v. *Maryland*,[409] *Two Guys From Harrison-Allentown* v. *McGinley*,[410] *Braunfeld* v. *Brown*,[411] and *Gallager* v. *Crown Kosher Super Market*.[412] Of significance to us is the *McGowan*

Court's declaration that: (1) the defendant store employees lacked standing to assert free exercise grounds because they alleged only economic injury as a result of the enforcement of the Sunday closing law without also alleging a violation of the their own religious freedom interests or those of the store's present or prospective patrons,[413] and (2) because "[the defendant store employees] here concededly have suffered direct economic injury, alleged due to the imposition on them of the tenets of the Christian religion ... [they] have standing to complain that the statutes are laws respecting an establishment of religion."[414] Clearly, these cases implicitly affirm that there is a freedom-from right—assuming arguendo (contrary to legal fact) that the Sunday closing law in question constitutes an establishment of religion.

To take another example, assume that there is a District of Columbia Sunday closing law that, besides including provisions typical of such closing laws in secular states, has as its predominant or primary purpose the indirect facilitating and promoting of religious observances by severely limiting the kinds of secular recreational and cultural activities permitted on Sunday. Such a law, in my opinion, would seriously violate the establishment clause. The statute, in my view, also violates a freedom-from right entailed by the establishment clause because it would, if properly enforced, cause "direct and particular economic detriment,"[415] thereby engaging the freedom-from right in question. Such a statute would also cause direct and particular noneconomic detriment to many people who would be deprived of many liberties in nonreligious matters that they would otherwise have absent the statute. Moreover, our hypothetical District of Columbia statute would also violate the freedom-from right, entailed by the establishment clause, not to be subject to criminal or civil penalties pursuant to a law that constitutes an establishment of religion that, if enforced, would result in indirectly but seriously burdening the lawful exercise of one or more particular religions.

(3) The several public school cases decided by the Supreme Court involve scenarios that serve to suggest the existence, or nonexistence, of freedom-from rights entailed by the establishment clause. I do not propose an extensive survey of the cases since this

would unduly broaden the scope of my inquiry. Moreover, any analysis is complicated because there are several competing special theories of the establishment clause that entail somewhat different freedom and freedom-from rights. The three principle special theories, each of which comes in different versions, are the nonprefentialist, the accomodationist, and separationist models.[416]

Let us assume the separationist model for the sake of argument. Suppose there is a District of Columbia statute that requires, at the commencement of the first class each day in the first through the sixth grades in all public schools, the teacher in charge of the room in which each such class is held to announce a period of silence, not to exceed one minute in duration; during which time the students are told that they may, if they wish, pray silently while they remain silent while seated, but engage in no distracting activities. Moreover, this hypothetical statute prohibits the teacher from expressly or impliedly recommending to the students whether or not to pray.[417] Further, let us stipulate (for argument's sake) that this statute would indeed violate the establishment clause—and indeed this would be in accord with the present doctrine of the Court. The question that arises is whether the statute if properly enforced violates any freedom-from right entailed by the establishment clause. And, in my opinion, it does not for this statute, if properly enforced, pertains to a scenario in which neither teacher nor student need engage in vocal prayer, the student remains seated and silent during the period during which the silent praying takes place, and the teacher is forbidden to make any recommendation as to whether the students should or should not pray. It follows, therefore, that according to ST-NEI-B that there is no freedom-from right pertaining to the scenario in question that is a component of a constitutional immunity of the American people.

Let us now consider, on the other hand, a hypothetical District of Columbia statute[418] that requires the reading without comment at the opening of each school day of verses from the Bible and the recitation of the Lord's Prayer in unison. These exercises are prescribed as part of the curricular activities of students legally required to attend school and held in school buildings under the supervision and participation of teachers employed in those public schools. The reading of the biblical verses and the Lord's Prayer is be done by students and broadcast into each classroom through an intercommunications system; but the students in each classroom are also to be asked to stand and join in the recitation of the Lord's Prayer. In schools without an intercommunications system, the Bible reading is to be conducted by the teacher or by students under the teacher's supervision. This is to be followed by a standing recitation of the Lord's Prayer in unison. No prefatory statements are to be made, no questions asked or solicited, no comments, explanations, interpretations to given at or during the exercises. Students and their parents are to be advised that the student may absent himself from the classroom or, should he elect to remain, may choose not to participate in the exercise. The religious exercise is to be followed with the flag salute.

I hold that this hypothetical statute violates the establishment clause—and this is in accord with the Court's doctrine. In this scenario, unlike the preceding one, the enforcement of the statute very seriously subverts the legitimate interest of parents having children attending public schools not to have their children subject to daily, school prescribed religious exercises under circumstances that make them virtually captive or semi-captive audiences (i.e., audiences the members of which cannot easily avoid pressure to participate in the religious exercises without serious detriment albeit they have a formal right to be legally free to opt out of being present or being required to stand or participate during the exercises). And, not to be overlooked, there would be tremendous pressure upon teachers to participate in the religious exercise—assuming they too have a formal legal right to opt out. Because the religious exercise is to be conducted every school day and is otherwise intensive and pervasive, the paramount interest of parents to freely determine, within due limits, the kind of indoctrination or education in matters of religion that their children are to receive would be seriously burdened by the District of Columbia statute were it properly enforced and implemented. For all the reasons given, I submit that the NEI has among its components the right of parents not to have their paramount right (within due limits) to determine what indoctrination and education their children receive in religious matters severely compromised or subverted by the type of pervasive and intensive religious exercises instantiated in foregoing scenario.[419]

(4) Last, but not least, mention should be made of freedom-from rights involving exemption from governmental discrimination based upon religious grounds as to civil and political rights and benefits. Some such freedom-from rights, although not components of religious freedom as such, are nevertheless derivative or necessary auxiliary rights as their denial would constitute abridgments of religious freedom. But, quite independently of the foregoing, freedom-from rights pertaining to governmental discrimination as to civil and political rights and benefits based upon religious grounds are entailed by the establishment clause.

The freedom-from rights entailed by the establishment clause are quite diverse. I do not propose to include here a treatise on the NEI, and so I shall not present any more scenarios that suggest other freedom-from rights entailed by the establishment clause since it would be necessary to first determine what special theory of that clause should be adopted by the Court and how it should be applied to close or hard cases. However, in determining whether there is a particular freedom-from right entailed by the establishment clause as to a particular factual scenario, it would be necessary to demand more than the very attenuated factual grounds that the litigant must allege and prove in order to satisfy the present Court's de facto minimal standing requirements in establishment clause cases not involving religious freedom claims. Thus the aggrieved litigant should be required to satisfy the ordinary standing requirement that he allege and show that he has suffered or is about to suffer a concrete, individualized injury-in-fact, which has a but-for causal relation to the putative constitutional violation and is legally and judicially cognizable.[420]

Incident to a rigorous exposition of the special theory of the no-establishment immunity (ST-NEI-B) presented in this section, great care must be taken as to each significant freedom-from right entailed by the establishment clause so that it is phrased without mention of the establishment clause as such. Consider, for example, the freedom-from right exempting persons from the imposition of serious indirect burdens on the otherwise lawful exercise of a religion as a result of the enforcement of a Sunday closing law enacted by a state that would violate the establishment clause were it a federal statute. It would be more exact to say that the privileges or immunities clause prohibits the abridgment of the right to be exempt from the duty to obey a civil or criminal law that *constitutes an establishment of religion* rather than to say *constitutes a violation of the establishment clause.* The establishment clause also prohibits the Congress from enacting laws that endorse or purposively promote, or have the primary effect of promoting, irreligion. Therefore, in the interest of economy of expression, the term *No-Establishment Immunity* should be understood to encompass all freedom-from rights entailed by the establishment clause's prohibitions as applied to the states by the privileges or immunities clause.

Chapter C: A Federalist-Accomodationist Theory of the Establishment Clause

A decent respect for the opinions of mankind compels me to discuss the functions of the establishment clause prescinding from its role as entailing freedom and freedom-from rights.[421] I had initially hoped not to have further burdened this book with extensively setting forth the essentials of what I conceive to be the sound special theory of the establishment clause beyond its entailment of freedom and freedom-rights. However, I now see the need to further discuss the establishment clause because I think that not adequately accounting for that provision does not adequately address the concerns of some readers who might otherwise be inclined to accept the general theory of this book. The best way to address these concerns, it seems to me, is to forthrightly state some theses about the establishment clause and comment about each in turn. Now here are my theses about the establishment clause:

Thesis A. The unitary separationist model of the establishment clause should be abandoned by the Court.

The unitary separationist model affirms that the Congress is prohibited generally by the establishment clause from making any law the evident purpose or effect of which is to endorse or appear to endorse (as determinable by some objective standard) religion (or one or more particular religions) or irreligion (or one or more particular irreligions). The model precludes any law lacking a predominantly secular legislative purpose, or that either primarily advances or inhibits religion or irreligion, or fosters an excessive entanglement with religion or irreligion as its primary effect. Despite some hard-to-reconcile decisions on concrete issues due to shifting majorities and pluralities in the Court, it is nevertheless safe to say that the unitary separationist model, or something fairly close to it, is the Court's standing theory of the establishment clause.[422]

Let us prescind from federal-state considerations for the time being in order to better understand the unitary separationist model since this model has been judicially developed concurrently with the Court ruling that the Fourteenth Amendment due process clause incorporates all the prohibitions of the establishment clause other than those sounding in federal-state relations. There are, as I see it, three principal reasons that have been plausibly advanced to support the unitary separationist model.

The first is that the model best approximates the essentials of what appears to have been the dominant original understanding of the framers of the original Constitution and the Bill of Rights: that the Congress has no authority whatsoever to legislate with respect to matters of religion as such. The Constitution, according to this view, neither expressly nor impliedly endows the Congress with any power to legislate in matters of religion. Indeed, the very lack of this power has been advanced to support the argument that a constitutional amendment pertaining to religion was unnecessary and, indeed, unwise since a constitutional prohibition in this matter would be taken by some to imply (as a *negative pregnant*) that the Congress does have a constitutional power to "intermeddle with religion" (to use Madison's words) save as it is limited by a constitutional amendment. Thus, the religion clauses of the First Amendment are best understood as expressly confirming the original understanding of the framers that Congress lacks constitutional authority to legislate as to matters religious as such.[423] And the unitary separationist model, according to what appears to be the received opinion of scholars and commentators, was the position maintained by James Madison and Thomas Jefferson. This model eventually became canonical in the watershed case of *Everson v. Board of Education* when the Court declared, "In the words of Jefferson, the clause against establishment of religion by law was intended to erect 'a wall of separation between Church and State.'"[424]

Leonard W. Levy, in support of the unitary separationist model, has claimed: "The fundamental defect of the non-preferential interpretation is that it results in the unhistorical contention that the First Amendment augmented a non-existent power to legislate in the field of religion.[425] This assertion is unsound because, whatever the dominant understanding of the *framers* of the Constitution and the

Bill of Rights, the powers delegated to the Congress together with the necessary-and-proper clause are easily understood as implicitly attributing some power in Congress to legislate in matters of religion even though the power to legislate in such matters is not explicitly mentioned—especially as to places where the Congress has exclusive jurisdiction to legislate with all the sovereign powers of a state. It simply is not textually sound to claim "that religion as a subject of legislation was reserved exclusively to the states,"[426] even in places where the states completely lack jurisdiction. Interestingly, Levy affirmed: "The nonpreferential interpretation seems persuasive if one can ignore the fact that the First Amendment, no matter how parsed or logically analyzed, was framed to deny power, not to vest it."[427] But neither the nonpreferentialist nor the accomodationist models, properly formulated, need make any such outlandish assertion. Moreover, the establishment clause itself does not provide that Congress shall make no law respecting religion; rather it provides that no law shall be made respecting an establishment of religion.

Madison apparently did not belong to the *framers' intent* school of interpretation of constitutional text because, in a letter to Henry Lee (June 25, 1824), he wrote: "I entirely concur in the propriety of resorting to the sense in which the Constitution was accepted and ratified by the nation."[428] Thus, for Madison, what was controlling is the *founders'* intent, which necessarily includes the understanding of those who participated in the ratification of the constitutional provision in question. But even with this *originalist* notion of constitutional interpretation in mind, it surely was the case that one very warranted original understanding of the original Constitution and of the First Amendment must have been that, absent the First Amendment, Congress would have some authority within the scope of its delegated powers to make laws respecting an establishment of religion or prohibiting the free exercise thereof. Otherwise, why should the establishment clause have been proposed to the states for their ratification and ratified by them? Indeed, it does seem strange were it the case that there was no such original understanding—given that a textualist analysis of the relevant constitutional text compels the conclusion that the Congress, absent the First Amendment, necessarily has some power to legislate directly in matters of religion.

In the first place, the Constitution expressly vests the Congress with the power to legislate with respect to the armed forces of the United States.[429] The District of Columbia[430] and federal enclaves within the territorial limits of states,[431] and also other federal territories and possessions[432]—which powers are at least as coextensive as that of any state. The Congress, as the federal legislature, is also delegated the power by article I, section 8, "[t]o lay and collect Taxes, Duties, Imposts and Excises"; "[t]o regulate Commerce ... among the several States"; "[t]o establish Post Offices and post Roads"; to enact copyright legislation. Moreover, article I, section 8 of the Constitution endows the Congress with the power "[t]o make all Laws which shall be necessary and proper for carrying into execution the foregoing Powers, and all other Powers vested by this Constitution in the Government of the United States, or in any Department or Officer thereof." That, absent the First Amendment, at least some congressional delegated powers were understood by the First Congress to encompass direct legislation with respect to religious matters is amply evidenced by the re-enactment on August 7, 1789 of the Northwest Ordinance;[433] of which article III provided in part: "Religion, morality, and knowledge, being necessary to good government and the happiness of mankind, schools and the means of education shall forever be encouraged[.]" Similarly, the First Congress in a statute enacted March 3, 1791, authorized the appointment of, and compensation for, a chaplain for the military establishment of the United States.[434]

The second reason that appears to plausibly support the unitary separationist model is the doctrine announced by Chief Justice Burger, speaking for the Court, declared in *Lemon* v. *Kurtzman* (1971):

> The language of the Religion Clauses of the First Amendment is at best opaque, particularly when compared with other portions of the Amendment. Its authors did not simply prohibit the establishment of a state church or a state religion, an area history shows they regarded as very important and fraught with great dangers. Instead they commanded that there should be "no law *respecting* an establishment of religion." A law may be one

"respecting" the forbidden objective while falling short of its total realization. A law "'respecting" the proscribed result, that is, the establishment of religion, is not easily identifiable as one violative of the Clause. A given law might not *establish* a state religion but nevertheless be one "respecting" that end in the sense of being a step that could lead to such establishment and thus offend the First Amendment.[435]

This rationale is egregiously disingenuous because absent from the Court's opinion is any mention that the words *shall make no law respecting an establishment of religion* were included in the establishment clause in order to insure that Congress not limit in any way the authority of the states to make laws establishing or disestablishing a religion.[436] What is significant about *Lemon* it that it also confirmed the rule that in order for a statute to survive a claim that it violates the establishment clause (as applied to the states via the Fourteenth Amendment): "First, the statute must have a secular legislative purpose; second, its principal or primary effect must be one that neither advances nor inhibits religion [citations], [and] finally, the statute must not foster 'an excessive government entanglement with religion."[437] That the Court followed its announcement of its construction of the term *make no law respecting* in the establishment clause with a statement of what is called the *Lemon* test discloses what upon what shaky grounds rests the Court's present adherence to the unitary separationist model.

The third reason, it seems to me, is that according to the unitary separationist model the establishment clause equally protects religion and irreligion, and likewise particular religious and irreligious institutions or societies, against being hindered, disfavored, or burdened by the government. However, the clause does not textually lend itself to support this doctrine, especially if federal-state relations are ignored. Recall again that the First Amendment fully protects religious freedom, and freedom-from rights entailed by the establishment clause, against any abridgments. So what concerns me is why the Court maintains that the establishment clause entirely prohibits the government from endorsing irreligion in general, or some particular form of irreligion, in the same way that the clause, according to unitary separationist model, entirely prohibits the government from endorsing religion in general or some particular form of religion. For example, quite clearly the establishment clause prohibits Congress from enacting a statute requiring that public schools in the District of Columbia offer an optional religious studies course that endorses and promotes some positive religion (e.g., the characteristic doctrines of theologically conservative generic Christianity). But what is there about the language of the establishment clause that supports the unitary separationist model insofar as it means that Congress is also prohibited from enacting a statute requiring District of Columbia public schools to offer an optional religious studies course that endorses and promotes one or more forms of irreligion (atheism, agnosticism, metaphysical naturalism)? The only arguments that appear plausible would be those somehow based upon the first and second reasons for the model discussed in the preceding paragraphs, or upon the patently implausible ground that *irreligion* in its various forms is a subset of *religion.*

The term "religion" as used in the religion clauses of the First Amendment pertains to the notion of the existence of one and only one supreme being, the creator of the universe, to whom there are duties pertaining to prayer and worship, and of obedience to norms imposed and/or sanctioned by him. But the term "religion" should not be assigned only a monotheistic interpretation. "Religion" should instead be understood to encompass beliefs that necessarily include the affirmation of the existence of at least one supernatural personal being, having great power and knowledge, who is the proper object of worship and prayer—which notion is compatible with both monotheism and polytheism. Recent opinions of the Court distinguish between religion (and its particular forms) and irreligion (and their particular forms). But if irreligion is, at bottom, just a different kind of religion (e.g., the so-called religion of secular humanism), then it is just nonsense for the Court to have declared, for example, that the establishment clause requires that a statute have "a secular legislative purpose and a primary effect that neither advances nor inhibits religion"[438] unless there is a difference between what constitutes a religion and what does not.[439]

Thesis B. The nonpreferentialist model should not be adopted by the Court.

Congress, according to nonpreferentialist model, would be constitutionally free in the exercise of its delegated powers to purposively but nondiscriminately aid (understood to include endorsing or promoting) all legitimate religions or religion in general—without being limited to certain kinds of aid within the scope of historically sanctioned practices that do not involve coercion, proselytism, or exploitation. Moreover, Congress would not be forbidden by the establishment clause to enact laws that (without violating freedom-from rights entailed by the clause or religious freedom) disfavor or burden irreligion in its various forms.[440] (A *legitimate religion* is one insofar as it does not include any particular exercise of religion not within the ambit of religious freedom.)

But, on the contrary, the establishment clause does not only prohibit the Congress from purposively aiding one or more, but not all, particular religions. Rather, the clause should be understood to prohibit the Congress, in the exercise of its otherwise lawful powers, from purposively and nondiscriminately aiding all particular religions, or religion in general—with the exception of certain historically sanctioned practices not involving coercion, proselytism, or exploitation. According to some scholars, the nonpreferentialist model is seriously flawed on historical grounds.[441] But what has most probative value for me is the following. The ratifying conventions of Virginia, New York, and North Carolina each proposed an amendment to the Constitution that would have incorporated the nonpreferentialist model; and the Senate considered and ultimately rejected motions that would have incorporated the nonpreferentialist model into what eventually became the First Amendment.[442] It is evident that these proposed provisions distinguish *an establishment of religion* from *an establishment of one religion in preference to others*. Moreover, there is both a great difference between saying the establishment of *one* as opposed to *only one* religion in preference to others—the use of one being consistent with a multiple establishment of some but not all religions. Hence, I conclude that the better view is that the adoption of the establishment clause constitutes a rejection of the nonpreferentialist model since a constitutional ban on any establishment of religion entails a ban on an establishment of only one particular religion.

Some commentators, such as Robert L. Cord[443] have assigned as evidence in support of the nonpreferentialist model the fact that Congress provided direct financial support to build churches and for other supposed religious needs of Indians, or for religious schools and religious training, for Indian tribes and/or Indian country from 1803 to 1897; and that it also appropriated land in the Northwest Territory for religious purposes both before and after adoption of the Bill of Rights. However, in the first place, such aid and support was anything but nonpreferential. But, more significantly, Cord gratuitiously assumed that the provisions of the First Amendment fully applied *ex proprio vigore* [i.e., by their own force] to relations with the Indian tribes or country, and to the territories and possessions of the United States.[444]

Thesis C. The accomodationist model (according to which not all governmental acts of endorsement of religion constitute an establishment of religion) should be adopted by the Court.

Although frequently the terms "nonpreferentialist" and "accomodationist" are used synonymously, I propose that two very different terms should denote two very different notions instead of just one, such that the nonpreferentialist model is not a subset of the accomodationist model. I shall use the term "accomodationist model" to refer to the model that includes the doctrines: (1) the establishment clause prohibits the Congress from making a law that establishes only one, some, or all religions, or religion in general; (2) governmental endorsement, recognition, or aid in religious matters of the kind that are historically sanctioned and free of coercion, exploitation, or proselytizing, does not constitute an establishment of religion in the requisite sense; (3) the establishment clause presupposes and its adoption confirms that the Congress lacks the power to enact laws of which the dominant purpose or the primary effect is to favor, promote, or advance irreligion, in general or in any of its particular forms; and (4) the failure of Congress to endorse, recognize, or otherwise aid religion in a constitutionally permissible way does not per se constitute aiding, favoring, or promoting irreligion.[445]

There is an establishment of religion whenever, with certain very limited and historically sanctioned exceptions (e.g., military chaplains and chapels on military installations, as well as legislative and institutional chaplains), legislation authorizes the expenditure of public funds to endow or otherwise financially support any legitimate religious institutions or programs as such (e.g., to build and maintain churches, temples, and other places of public worship, to give grants-in-aid to any legitimate religious institutions to propagate or indoctrinate its theological doctrines, or to give financial support to its clergy as such). An establishment of religion also obtains, for example, where the government itself organizes and operates a religious institution for the purpose of providing places of public worship according to officially approved rites and to propagate officially approved doctrines in religious and moral matters. A law that would have the predominant purpose or primary effect of hindering, disfavoring, or burdening irreligion in general or some particular forms of irreligion would not per se constitute an establishment of religion according to the nonpreferentialist model. However, it would violate the establishment clause according to accomodationist model unless such a law was itself an instance of a historically sanctioned exception of very narrow scope.[446]

Arguing that not every endorsement of one or more particular religions or religion in general constitutes an establishment of religion in the requisite sense is not an exercise in légerdeparole. And I think I shall have sufficiently made my case were I to show that something similar takes place elsewhere in constitutional law. For an example, let us turn to the Thirteenth Amendment, section 1 of which provides: "Neither slavery nor involuntary servitude, except as a punishment for crime whereof the party shall have been duly convicted, shall exist within the United States, or any place subject to their jurisdiction." Notwithstanding the breadth of its terms, the Court has explained[447]

[T]he amendment was not intended to introduce any novel doctrine with respect to certain descriptions of service which have always been treated as exceptional, such as military and naval enlistments, or to disturb the right of parents and guardians to the custody of their minor children or wards. The amendment, however, makes no distinction between a public and a private service. To say that persons engaged in a public service are not within the amendment is to admit that there are exceptions to its general language, and the further question is at once presented, where shall the line be drawn? We know of no better answer to make than to say that services which have from time immemorial been treated as exceptional shall not be regarded as within its purview.

Among those exceptional services, mentioned by the Court, are the contracts of seamen, military service by recruits, enforced military service pursuant to draft laws, jury service, work-or-fight laws during wartime applicable to conscientious objectors, and even (now obsolete but nevertheless questionable) laws for enforced labor by able-bodied men for a reasonable time on public roads near their residences without direct compensation.

Certain historically sanctioned practices, including ceremonial and symbolic exercises or displays, not involving coercion, proselytizing, undue pressue, or similar exploitation of captive or semi-captive auditors that officially endorse or recognize (the) popular religion(s), do not constitute an establishment of religion. As Lord James Bryce observed in his epic work about America published in 1888:

[I]t never occurs to the average American that there is any reason why State churches should exist....

Just because these questions have been long since disposed of, and excite no present passion, and perhaps also because the Americans are more practically easy-going than pedantically exact, the national Government and the State governments do give to Christianity a species of recognition inconsistent with the view that civil government should be absolutely neutral in religious matters. [448]

Similar sentiments by Justice Thomas M. Cooley are found in his celebrated treatise on constitutional law published in 1868.[449] Cooley explained:

> But while thus careful to establish, protect, and defend religious freedom and equality, the American constitutions contain no provisions which prohibit the authorities from such solemn recognition of a superintending Providence in public transactions and exercises as the general religious sentiment of mankind inspires, and as seems meet and proper in finite and dependent beings. Whatever may be the shades of religious belief, all must acknowledge the fitness recognizing in important human affairs the superintending care and control of the great Governor of the Universe, and of acknowledging with thanksgiving his boundless favors, of bowing in contrition when visited with the penalties of his broken laws. No principle of constitutional law is violated when thanksgiving or fast days are appointed; when chaplains are designated for the army and navy; when legislative sessions are opened with prayer or the reading of the Scriptures, or when religious teaching is encouraged by a general exemption of the houses of religious worship from taxation for the support of State government. Undoubtedly the spirit of the constitution will require, in all these cases, that care be taken to avoid discrimination in favor of or against any one religious denomination or sect; but the power to do any of these things does not become unconstitutional simply because of its susceptibility to abuse. [450]

But Cooley very pointedly advises: "Whatever deference the constitution or the laws may require to the paid in some cases to the conscientious scruples or religious convictions of the majority, the general policy always is, to avoid with care any compulsion which infringes on the religious scruples of any, however little reason may seem to others to underlie them."[451] Following this wise counsel, it seems to me, is imperative with respect to such cases as those involving daily participation in open prayer and the flag salute in public schools, because children are required to attend school and are, given their immaturity and vulnerability, a virtually captive audience notwithstanding the presence of a provision for a formal legal right to excuse oneself from participating or even being excused from being present at the exercise in question.

That a popular religion is recognized officially does not necessarily mean that it is being endorsed as true. To affirm that historically sanctioned practices (including ceremonial and symbolic exercises or displays, not involving coercion, proselytizing, undue pressure, or similar invidious exploitation) that officially recognize one or more popular religions) do not constitute an establishment of religion is not to affirm that changing conditions do not require changes as a matter of public policy as determined by the legislative branch of government.

Those who founded the Constitution, the Bill of Rights, and the Fourteenth Amendment, whatever their beliefs and opinion in matters of religion, were very well aware that in the standard Judeo-Christian theological and philosophical traditions there is a profound difference between those doctrines that a person believes independently of God's special (i.e., supernatural) revelation and those that he believes true solely or chiefly because they have been divinely revealed. It was commonplace for people engaged in theological and philosophical discussion to distinguish between the *truths of natural religion* and *supernaturally revealed truths*, and thus between *natural theology* and *dogmatic* (or *systemic*) *theology*. Deists and other theistic freethinkers of the eighteenth and nineteenth centuries, who denied that there are any supernaturally revealed truths, nevertheless believed there were important truths of natural religion integrally related to morality. Hence, according to the accomodationist model, no establishment of religion necessarily obtains in the cases of governmentally sponsored prayers used in public assemblies acknowledging God's existence and providence, and our duties to him, free from sectarian or denominational references reflecting beliefs about what has been supernaturally revealed. There would, however, be an establishment of religion if the government in public document were to officially declare *articles of faith* (i.e., doctrines that should be believed as a matter of intellectual and moral duty because they have been supernaturally revealed). There would be an establishment of religion were the government itself (going far beyond merely acknowledging God's existence and providence and invoking his blessing) to engage in or to financially support the systematic propagation through the mass media or through public education of religious doctrines in order to proselytize since such governmental enterprises would constitute an establishment of religion.

I adhere to the accomodationist model because, among other things, virtually all the founders of the Constitution, the Bill of Rights, and the Fourteenth Amendment, professed to believe that it is to the public political, social and moral good that belief in God, his providence, and our duties to him, should be as widespread as possible; provided, of course, that any additional particular religious beliefs are substantially consistent with the exigencies of public peace and order, morals and decency, and health and safety. It is for this reason that some historically sanctioned governmental practices aiding religion, and particularly monotheism, until the regime inaugurated with the *Everson* decision in 1947, had been generally thought not to constitute an establishment of religion. Indeed, this very rationale for not equating every endorsement or recognition of religion with an establishment of religion constitutes one ground for affirming that the establishment clause presupposes and by its adoption confirms that the Congress is without power to endorse or purposively promote irreligion or any particular form of irreligion even in cases where there is no violation of religious freedom or any freedom-from right entailed by the establishment clause.[452] Moreover, for Congress to endorse or purposively promote irreligion in any of its particular forms would constitute a "law respecting an establishment of religion" because the same would subvert the policies of such states that have established a religion or have undertaken to do so.

145

I say all the foregoing despite the fact that I do not believe in any doctrine in religious matters upon the ground that it has been supernaturally revealed. Moreover, I do not even believe that God or some other supernatural being exists. Indeed, I think it is much more antecedently probable than not that supernatural personal beings do not exist. Hence, my reason for adhering to the accomodationist model is not based upon some theological commitment, but instead, includes a commitment to what I conceive to be the constitutional order required for our very pluralist society and a recognition that most Americans have been, are, and will be monotheists for the reasonably foreseeable future. It is not necessary for me to agree in fact with the theological presuppositions of the original founders of the Constitution, the Bill of Rights, and the Fourteenth Amendment with respect to religion.

Thesis D. The establishment clause continues to prohibit Congress and the federal courts from interfering with state constitutional and statutory policies regarding the promotion or hindering of religion or irreligion, or any particular form of either, in cases not involving violations of religious freedom or freedom-from rights entailed by the establishment clause.

The Court, in my opinion, undermines confidence in the constitutional order when it is widely perceived as pulling a fast one on the American people with the unitary separationist model; a model so obviously inconsistent with the course of our pre-*Everson* constitutional history; which history had for so many decades disclosed that an equilibrium had been established (to be sure always in need of some adjustment) between the general but not exceptionless rule that precludes purposive governmental promotion of religion by methods not involving coercion, invidious exploitation, or proselytizing, and the vindication of generally acceptable, historically sanctioned practices favorable to religion. It may be, however, that the Court might someday decisively move away from the unitary separationist model and toward the accomodationist model. But that would not be the end of our problems given the doctrine that the Fourteenth Amendment due process clause incorporates the establishment clause prohibitions (prescinding from those sounding in federal-state relations).

The overwhelming majority of church-and-state cases adjudicated in federal courts involve claims of violations of the establishment clause by the states. I do not believe that the common political good of the American people is served by that act of will rather than of judgment by the Supreme Court when it ruled, and persists in that ruling, that the Fourteenth Amendment fully applies to the states all the prohibitions constitutive of the establishment clause—not counting those strictly sounding in federal-state relations. This erroneous doctrine of the Supreme Court tends, and has tended, to radically subvert the principles of the separation of powers, republicanism, and of federalism, and also judicial self-restraint in a domain in which mandatory national uniformity of constitutional policy is not needed or even desirable for our common political, social, and moral good. The prejudicial impact of this doctrine is compounded by the Court having neutered the privileges or immunities clause of the Fourteenth Amendment as the vehicle of selective incorporation of the Bill of Rights and its unwarranted preference for the due process clause as an instrument of incorporation of First Amendment and kindred rights.

The establishment clause insures that the Congress lacks the power to require the states to disestablish a religion or keep it from doing so, or otherwise interfering with an establishment of religion by a state. Amar rightly asserts, "the nature of the states' establishment-clause right against federal disestablishment makes it quite awkward to mechanically 'incorporate' the clause against the states via the Fourteenth Amendment."[453] And there is another very good reason why it is quite awkward to incorporate the prohibitions of the establishment clause, other than those that entail freedom or freedom-from rights, or that strictly sound in federal-state relations. This reason should be especially important for Amar given his doctrine of the *feedback effect* of redefinition. Of the thirty-seven states in the Union in 1868, ten did not have constitutional provisions that were analogs of the establishment clause. Seven state constitutions had provisions that disallowed preference for any religious institution and/or mode of worship as well as compelling support of a place of worship and/or ministry. Seven other state constitutions simply disallowed preference for any religious institution and/or mode of worship.[454] So it appears that the majority of the state constitutions in force in 1868 either did not have an establishment clause analog or had one that embodied the nonpreferentialist model. Since this is the case, a person holding either the separationist or accomodationist model of the establishment clause has an added reason for rejecting the thesis that the Fourteenth Amendment somehow incorporated those prohibitions of the establishment clause not strictly sounding in federal-state relations or entailing freedoms or freedom-from rights.

Amar claims that "[t]he original establishment clause, on a close reading, is not antiestablishment but pro-states' rights; it is agnostic on the substantive issue of establishment versus nonestablishment and simply calls for the issue to be decided locally."[455] But the founders of the Bill of Rights approved of the First Amendment's ban of an establishment of religion by Congress for different but overlapping sets of reasons. One set of reasons pertains to the need to more fully protect religious freedom rather than just relying on a free-exercise clause. The lessons of history had taught them that the establishment of one or more religious institutions, by providing financial support to such institutions from tax-raised funds and giving special civil privileges and immunities to the clergy, had frequently led to the corruption of the clergy. There is so much merit to the argument that historically the formal establishment of religion by a union of Church and State has been good neither for religion nor civil society, and that religion flourishes best in the absence of any establishment of religion provided that religious freedom is fully protected against abridgments and that no legislation is calculated to hinder or burden any particular religion or religion in general because of the real or supposed truth-value of their doctrines in matters of religion. Establishment of a religious institution tends to frequently lead to the ultimately fatal identification of Throne with Altar, and breeds the twin evils of arrogant clericalism and abrasive anticlericalism. The foregoing considerations have nothing to do with federal-state relations. Indeed, some supporters of the First Amendment could very well have advocated the preservation of the establishment of religion in their own states. There are other reasons pertaining to the strong sense of states' sovereignty and states' rights in the fledgling nation such that while they might have strongly approved of the substantive prohibitions for their own states, they did not want to interfere with the public policy of other states in order to make possible a more perfect Union that will be perpetual and indissoluble.

A very broad religious pluralism obtained before and during the founding of the Bill of Rights, together with the great diversity of the policies followed by the several states respecting religion. Hence, the general realization that a national consensus approving any constitutional public policy other than that eventually embodied in the religion clauses made it virtually impossible as a practical matter to have anything other in the Bill of Rights than those clauses. Thus, the preservation of that more perfect Union established by the Constitution required the religion clauses for public policy reasons in addition to those sounding in human dignity. Well before the founding of the Fourteenth Amendment in 1866–68, the even more diverse religious pluralism of the American people was a very obvious nation-wide phenomenon, as was also the very widespread travel and migration by American citizens throughout the United States. The Civil War definitively settled on the battlefield the issue whether the United States is a perpetual and indissoluble union of indestructible states; and that "[f]or all the great purposes for which the Federal government was formed, we are one people, with one common country. We are all citizens of the United States, and as members of the same community, must have the right to pass and repass through every part of it without interruption, as freely as in our own states."[456] And since the Civil War, religious pluralism (i.e., pluralism in matters of religion) has significantly broadened to substantially encompass religions and quasi-religions that are not monotheistic; such pluralism also encompasses the various forms of irreligion. These factors serve to show how religious freedom and the freedom-from rights entailed by the establishment clause serve to promote the common political and social good of the American people. On the other hand, the common good of the American people is not served by applying all the prohibitions of the establishment clause (prescinding from those pertaining to federal-state relations) to the states via the Fourteenth Amendment—albeit it may be to the common political, social, moral and religious good of a particular state that its own state constitutional and statutory disallow any establishment of religion. On a state or local level, it is preferable for the people of a particular state to learn by trial and error that a public policy constituting an establishment of religion is mistaken rather than to submit the matter for decision by a majority of sitting justices on the Court.[457]

By now, it should be clear to the reader what I regard as the principal justifying *common denominator* ground for concluding that the establishment clause, by prohibiting an establishment of religion for the United States and precluding Congress from interfering with the policies of the several states with respect to establishments of religion. The First Amendment, prescinding from all grounds sounding in human dignity, was needed in order to make possible the flourishing of a federal union of sovereign states, its population characterized by pluralism in religious matters and the diversity of the policies of the several states concerning religion. Moreover, this public policy embodied in the establishment clause can be discerned as helping to preserve the republican form of government for the United States and of the several states. As time went on, there emerged a general consensus that the establishment clause was not only good national policy as the only practically feasible constitutional provision, but also because national unity was thereby promoted and that the several popular religions flourished. Accordingly, state constitutions and statutory policies have tended to implement the nonpreferentialist or accomodationist models.[458] Vital, however, to the proper understanding of the First Amendment's religion clauses is the principle that the ban against Congress making any law respecting an establishment of religion must always be understood as being subordinate to the constitutional ban against making any law, whether on the federal or state level, abridging religious freedom or any freedom-from personal rights entailed by the establishment clause. Since we constitute one people with one common country, it is imperative that the Constitution should prohibit the states from abridging the constitutional privileges and immunities of American citizens in matters of religion. I do not see the same imperative need for a constitutional provision making applicable to the states all the prohibitions constitutive of the establishment clause.

As a personal matter, I am adamantly opposed to any establishment of religion by any state. My opposition is grounded, in the first place, upon reasons that hold whether or not I am a theist, or whether or not (were I a theist) an adherent of some positive religion (i.e., a religion that embodies claims of supernaturally revealed truths)—assuming, of course, that the positive religion does not itself include components requiring an adherent to reject religious freedom or to favor an establishment of that particular religion. And I am further opposed to any establishment of religion, whether by the United States or the State of Colorado, simply because I do not believe that supernatural beings exist. As to historically sanctioned accommodations of religion that do not constitute an establishment of religion, my opinion concerning whether or not they should be undertaken as a public policy matter would need to be decided on a case-by-case basis.

The great majority of Americans professedly adhere to and will continue to adhere to some positive religion or another. In the interest of our common political, social and moral good, no constitutional policy should be followed by the courts and other branches of government that tends to needlessly alienate deeply religious people (particularly those who are theologically conservative) from our civil and political institutions if the policy embodies the principle that any endorsement of religion constitutes an establishment of religion. Any strident, aggressive secularist ideology and any particular theonomistically, or theocratically, driven political theology are equally offensive and equally dangerous in principle to our national interest.

Part III

TOWARD A THEORY OF THE PROCEDURAL AND SUBSTANTIVE
ASPECTS OF THE DUE PROCESS CLAUSES OF THE FIFTH AND FOURTEENTH
AMENDMENTS

Chapter A. Some Considerations Applicable to the Substantive and Procedural Aspects of the Due Process Clauses

I shall now examine the substantive and procedural aspects of the due process clauses and how these aspects fit into the general theory of this book. However, the following discussion of the substantive aspects of the due process clauses presupposes that the reader assumes for argument's sake that the privileges or immunities clause incorporates the First Amendment freedoms and other constitutional freedom and freedom-from rights as expounded in Parts I and II.

(1) The due process clauses are virtually equivalent in meaning, so judicial cases about one clause are fungible with those of the other clause—appropriate changes having been made. Thus what constitutes a violation by the United States of the Fifth Amendment due process clause would be a violation of the Fourteenth Amendment due process clause were the governmental action that of a state, and vice versa. With this in mind, we may simply speak of the *specific right of the due process clause* unless there is a special need to distinguish between the two clauses.

(2) From (1) it follows that no right specified in the Bill of Rights is a component of the specific right of the Fourteenth Amendment due process clause unless it is also a specific right of the Fifth Amendment due process clause; and vice versa. But although a particular right specified in amendments I though VIII is not a component of the specific right of the due process clause, it does not then follow that no component of the former right is a component of the specific right of the due process clause. Since we are not writing on a clean slate, the doctrine of *stare decisis* should be given due consideration in resolving whether-this-or-that specific right should be deemed a component of the specific right of the due process clause. Incident to this process, it is necessary to consider whether affirming that a particular specific right is a component of the specific right of the due process clause constitutes an otherwise questionable inflation or deflation (the "watering up" or the "watering down") of the particular specific right in question.

(3) The due process clause has substantive as well as procedural aspects. Although there is and has been much disagreement about what should be the identity, scope, and limits of the substantive aspects of the due process clause, the imputation of such aspects to these clauses is prescriptively sanctioned and supported by an overwhelming consensus of jurists, commentators, and of the informed public. Indeed, the Court has continuously maintained that the due process clauses have substantive aspects of one kind of another since not later than 1884 when the Court declared by way of obiter dicta in *Hurtado* v. *California*:[459]

> In the Fourteenth Amendment, by parity of reason, [the due process clause] refers to that law of the land in each State which derives its authority from the inherent and reserved powers of the State, exerted within the limits of those fundamental principles of liberty and justice which lie at the base of all our civil and political institutions, and the greatest security for which resides in the right of the people to make their own laws, and alter them at their pleasure. [460]

Indeed, the first time, after the adoption of the Fourteenth Amendment, that the Court definitively ruled that the due process clause has substantive aspects was in 1897 when it decided *Allgeyer* v. *Louisiana*.[461] With *Allgeyer*, the Court inaugurated the forty-year long reign of the liberty of contract as the preferred constitutional substantive right.[462]

However, the Court even during the reign of liberty of contract also ruled or affirmed that the due process clause has other substantive aspects in such cases as: *Williams* v. *Fears*,[463] which declared that "[u]ndoubtedly the right of locomotion, the right to remove from one place to another according to inclination, is an attribute of personal liberty, and the right, ordinarily, of free transit from or through the territory of any state is a right secured by the Fourteenth Amendment and by other provisions of the Constitution"; *Buchanan* v. *Warley*,[464] which held that the due process clause is violated by a city ordinance prohibiting colored persons to occupy houses in blocks in which the great number of houses are occupied by white persons, and vice versa; *Meyer* v. *Nebraska*,[465] in which the Court ruled that a statute prohibiting the teaching in school of any language other than English until the pupil has passed the eighth grade violates the due process clause in time of peace and domestic tranquility; *Pierce* v. *Society of Sisters*;[466] which held invalid a statute requiring nearly every parent to send a child between the age of eight and sixteen to public school; *Gitlow* v. *New York*,[467] which stated in its opinion that "[f]or present purposes we may and do assume that freedom of speech and of the press ... are among the fundamental personal rights and 'liberties' protected by the due process clause of the Fourteenth Amendment from impairment by the States."[468]

Despite the misgivings of some jurists and commentators, it is very doubtful whether we would for long feel comfortable were the Court to abolish the substantive aspects of the due process clause. Those who propose that the substantive aspects of the due process clause be eliminated would do well to reflect upon "the concluding lines of Mr. [Hilaire] Belloc's *Cautionary Tale* about the boy who ran away from his nurse in the Zoo and was eaten by a lion. 'Always keep hold of Nurse, for fear of finding Something Worse.'"[469] The problem is the difficulty in finding a thoroughly reliable Nurse who is also so benign that no child would be rashly tempted to run away and imprudently risk the companionship of Something Worse than Nurse. Indeed, at times the Court acts as if it were a parent whose child is out of control and who desperately needs a super nanny.

(4) The specific right of the due process clause should not be deemed to incorporate political freedom or any First Amendment freedom.[470] But it does have among its components some but not all the components of each such freedom. On the other hand, there could conceivably be some fundamental liberty-rights pertaining to religion, speech, and the press that are components of the specific right of the due process clause but not of any First Amendment freedom. There is ample evidence of one original understanding during the founding of the Fourteenth Amendment that supports the thesis that the privileges or immunities clause incorporates First Amendment freedoms. There is no substantial evidence whatsoever that there was an original understanding that the specific right of the due process clause incorporates any First Amendment freedom. Moreover it is strikingly counterintuitive that the Fifth Amendment due process clause (because of its supposed equivalence in meaning with that of the Fourteenth Amendment) incorporates the First Amendment freedoms, protected as they are by the sweeping limitations imposed on congressional power by that amendment. Indeed, that the specific right of the due process clause incorporates any First Amendment freedom presupposes a special theory of that clause that endows it,

the due-process clause, with a formidable potency for causing as much mischief as that of a loose gun on a frigate's deck.

(5) According to the Court's current special theory of the due process clause: (a) The ordinary test of validity of governmental action applicable to what are deemed nonfundamental rights is the rational basis test (i.e., that the governmental action in question is rationally related to a constitutionally legitimate objective). (b) The same constitutional standards equally apply to both the United States and the states with respect to whatever specific right is secured against any infringement by the United States and has been deemed fundamental by the Court.[471] (c) A governmental infringement of a fundamental personal right that is not specified in the Constitution (and not a component of one that is so specified) may be justified only by satisfying the *strict scrutiny* test (i.e., the governmental entity imposing the restriction on the liberty interest must demonstrate that the limitation is both necessary and narrowly tailored to serve a compelling interest). According to the Court's theory, a personal right is deemed *fundamental* because it has "been found to be implicit in the concept of ordered liberty"[472] or, more compendiously, because "the right is one that cannot be denied without violating those fundamental principles of liberty and justice which lie at the base of all civil and political institutions—principles which the Fourteenth Amendment embodies in the general terms of its due-process clause." [473] A specific right is not *fundamental* in the requisite sense simply because the constitutional provision specifying it provides that it cannot be abridged, infringed, or violated. For example, the specific right of the grand jury clause of the Fifth Amendment is held by the Court not to be incorporated by the Fourteenth Amendment due process clause because it is not a fundamental right in the requisite sense. Whether a specific right is *fundamental* or not (in the sense just explained), the constitutional ban on any abridgment or infringement of a specific right (e.g., freedom of speech) admits of (actually or virtually) no exception.[474]

(6) I quite agree that the Court should retain within its armamentarium the rational basis test to be ordinarily used to determine the constitutionality of governmental action claimed to

be in violation of substantive due process. For surely there have been, are, and will be bizarre misuses or egregious abuses of power that are so outrageously out-of-line with a broad consensus of the American people (and thus cutting across class, occupational, educational, ethnic, gender, regional, or most ideological lines) as to be intolerable and thus warrant judicial intervention based upon constitutional grounds. However, I reject the current Court's theory concerning unenumerated or unspecified fundamental rights to which the strict scrutiny test purportedly applies in part because it makes the due-process clause unduly restrictive of the legitimate powers of the State. The fatal flaw, in my opinion, lies in the practice if not the theory of the Court by which a certain complex of related substantive rights in a certain domain is deemed to constitute a *fundamental* right not specified in the Constitution; and it then falls upon the government to show that an infringement of the particular component under review satisfies the strict scrutiny test. This implicit presupposition is due to the rather facilely made assumption that every component of some particular substantive right judicially characterized as fundamental is actually so in the requisite sense. However, it should be axiomatic that no substantive right is fundamental (as to the due process clause) unless each per se component is fundamental in the requisite sense (i.e., the legitimate interest of the putative right-holder with respect to the right in question overrides or trumps the rational basis for the legitimate interest of the State in its repression).[475] This determination must be made before concluding that any particular substantive right is per se a component of a fundamental right in the requisite sense.

(7) The Court's official doctrine is that the due process clause encompasses personal rights entailed by those fundamental principles of liberty and justice that lie at the base of all our civil and political institutions. But the reality is that the Court treats some personal rights as fundamental because they are entailed by the fundamental principles of the civil and political institutions of the American commonwealth—as well as by what is required as national public policies by the common political, social, economic, and moral good of the nation. We must be very careful here. There may be an independent rationale for some if not all the components of any given constitutional freedom or freedom-from right of the

American people that sounds principally in human dignity, including the dignity of free persons as such. And, to be sure, the constitutional ban on any abridgment of other components of any such freedom serves to prophylactically protect those components of such-and-such freedom, which are proximately based upon grounds sounding in human dignity. My point, however, is that the rationale for the total ban on all abridgments of every constitutional privilege or immunity of the American people is to be found upon considerations chiefly based upon the fundamental principles of our civil and political institutions and the permanent exigencies of the common political, social, economic and moral good of the American people as a whole. For example, that freedom of speech and of the press should not be abridged is a political imperative in a federal civil society that is republican, with virtually universal suffrage, and demographically very pluralist. But these factors are rather irrelevant in determining what constitutes the components of a fundamental liberty of free persons as such with respect to expression by speech or the press.

(8) The fundamental principles of our civil and political constitutions include: (a) that the Constitution establishes for the United States and requires for each state a government republican in form with competitive elections; (b) an underlying basic political principle is that of popular sovereignty, realized by a virtually universal suffrage on a national, state, or local level; (c) the tripartite nature of the federal government with its legislative, executive, and judicial branches; (d) the independence of the federal judiciary and the doctrine of judicial review; (e) the federal system by which powers are exercised, some exclusively and others concurrently, by the United States and the states respectively; (f) that national citizenship is supreme and superior, and that the people of the United States constitute one nation; (g) that the form of government of the United States and that of the states is secular in that no government can be legally subordinate to the authority of any ecclesiastical entity; and (h) the basic equality of all citizens as excluding the order of nobility and any caste system based upon race or color, or other similar birth status.

(9) Everything that is needed to insure that all the constitutional rights of the American people, entailed by or which presuppose

the fundamental principles of our civil and political institutions, or which are required by the common temporal, social, economic, and moral good of the American people (in excess of what is needed to protect rights proximately grounded upon human dignity), are totally protected against all abridgments by the United States and the states by the Constitution without reliance upon the substantive aspects of the due process clause. With respect to the states, that total ban on all abridgments of the constitutional privileges and immunities of the American people is provided by the privileges or immunities clause of the Fourteenth Amendment—a clause that presupposes that the Constitution expressly or impliedly deprives the United States from abridging any right denoted by the descriptive term of the privileges or immunities clause.

(10) The specific right of the due process clause encompasses the right that no person, whether natural or artificial, shall be deprived of any substantive right absent (at least) a rational basis relating to a legitimate interest of the State. So what should be the substantive aspects of the due process clause other than those that involve just the application of the rational basis test of constitutional validity? My thesis is that the specific right of the due process clause also includes those essential liberty rights (i.e., privileges) and liberty-from rights (i.e., immunities) to which all free persons as such should be entitled by virtue of their dignity as rational, social, and moral beings. Therefore, these rights are not determined by consideration of the fundamental principles that govern our political and civil institutions. No component of any fundamental right, privilege or immunity of free persons as such can be constitutionally infringed absent exigent circumstances that warrant an overriding interest of the State because these rights are proximately (i.e., closely but not necessarily immediately so) grounded upon the dignity of free persons as rational, moral, and social beings. Artificial as well as natural persons have fundamental procedural and property rights under the due process clause. Nevertheless, fundamental liberty and liberty-from rights are predicable of artificial persons only insofar as such persons are the instrumentalities by which the fundamental liberty and liberty-from rights of natural persons are realized.

Chapter B. More on the Legitimacy of Imputing Substantive Aspects to the Due Process Clause

B ut is the imputation of substantive aspects to the due process clause legitimate? The dominant original understanding of the Fifth Amendment due process clause was that it has only procedural aspects. But even well before the adoption of the Fourteenth Amendment, something was very definitely in the air when Justice William Johnson, writing for the Court in *Bank of Columbia* v. *Okely* in 1819, stated by way of obiter dicta: "As to the words from Magna Charta ["No freeman ought to be taken or imprisoned, &c., or deprived of his life, liberty or property but by the judgment of his peers or by the law of the land"], incorporated into the Constitution of Maryland after volumes spoken and written with a view to their exposition, the good sense of mankind has at length settled down to this: that they were intended to secure the individual from the arbitrary exercise of the powers of government, unrestrained by the established principles of private rights and distributive justice."[476] In *Murray's Lessee* v. *Hoboken Land & Improvement Co.* (1856), the Court stated, "The words, 'due process of law' were undoubtedly intended to convey the same meaning as the words 'by the law of the land,' in Magna Charta."[477]

It has been frequently said that the expressions "substantive due process" and "procedural due process" are respectively oxymoronic and redundant; and it is further insinuated that these anomalous expressions somehow discredit the notion that the due process clause has substantive aspects. However, if we advert to the fact that (according to the Court) the terms "due process of law" and "law of the land" are synonymous, it is not oxymoronic to say "substantive law of the land" and it not redundant to say "procedural law of the land." Nevertheless, it seems to me, that it is convenient to persist in using the expressions "substantive due process" and "procedural due process."

As Edward S. Corwin (the great constitutional scholar) commented, "The absorptive powers of the law of the land clause, the precursor in the original State constitutions, of the due process clause, was foreshadowed as early as 1819 in the [above quoted] dictum by Justice William Johnson [in *Bank of Columbia* v. *Okely*].... Thirty-eight years later the prophecy of these words was realized in the famous Dred Scott case, in which Section 8 of the Missouri Compromise, whereby slavery was excluded from the territories, was held void under the fifth Amendment, not on the ground that the procedure for enforcing it was not due process of law, but because the Court regarded it as unjust to forbid people to take their slaves, or other property, into the territories, the common property of all the States."[478] But the ruling in *Dred Scott* in 1857, that in effect asserts a fundamental substantive right by virtue of the Fifth Amendment due process clause in favor of slaveholders, is concededly not a very pretty start for the Court's realization of the substantive aspects of the law of the land. However, just because the doctrine that the due-process clause has substantive aspects was conceived in original sin, it does not then follow that there could not have been any cleansing by the baptismal waters drawn from the wells of the Thirteenth and Fourteenth Amendments.

At this point, we may profitably switch our attention to Congressman John Bingham, whose deficient analytical ability I have criticized but certainly neither his high idealism nor his devotion to the cause of personal rights. Bingham, like the Court's opinion in *Dred* Scott, attributed substantive aspects to the Fifth Amendment due process clause. But, unlike the *Dred Scott* opinion, his principle of interpretation was based upon a strong notion of human rights rather than one that included the affirmation of special privileges of members of the master caste. On May 10, 1866, he addressed the House about a version of the proposed Fourteenth Amendment (of which its first section was identical to the final version less the citizenship clause). He spoke as follows:[479]

There was a want hitherto, and there remains a want now, in the Constitution of our country, which the proposed amendment will supply. What is that? It is the power in the people, the whole people of the United States, by express authority of the Constitution to do that by congressional enactment which hitherto they have not had the power to do, and have never even attempted to do; that is, to protect by national law the privileges and immunities of all the citizens of the Republic and the inborn rights of every person within its jurisdiction wherever the same shall be abridged or denied by the unconstitutional acts of any State.[480]

What did Bingham mean by "the inborn rights of every person"? Bingham represented a district in Ohio (and served 1855–1863 and 1865–73); a state that included in its constitution a provision about all men being born free and equal, have certain natural, essential, and inalienable rights. In 1859, he had occasion to speak of the meaning of the due process clause during a debate upon whether Oregon should be admitted to the Union despite the provision in its constitution that prohibited free blacks from entering into the state and residing there. He declared:

[N]atural or inherent rights, which belong to all men irrespective of all conventional regulations, are by this constitution guaranteed by the broad and comprehensive word "person," as contradistinguished from the limited term citizen—as in the fifth article of amendments, guarding those sacred rights which are as universal and indestructible as the human race, that "no person shall be deprived of life, liberty, or property but by due process of law, nor shall private property be taken without just compensation."[481]

A person's "natural rights; those rights common to all men, and to protect which, and not to confer, all good governments are instituted" include, according to Bingham, "[t]he equality of all to the right to live; to the right to know; to argue and to utter, according to conscience; to work and enjoy the product of their toil."[482] According to Bingham, "all men, before the law, are equal in respect of those rights of person which God gives and no man or State may rightfully take away, except as forfeiture for crime." Indeed, the Oregon exclusion of free persons of color from entry into the state was "a flagrant violation of the law of nature, as recognized by every civilized nation on the globe." "It is," Bingham explained, "the public law of the civilized world, that every free man is entitled to live in the land of his birth"—and Oregon was part of the land of the free native-black American.[483]

Bingham's opinion that the due process clause has substantive aspects was not unique during the founding of the Fourteenth Amendment. Thomas M. Cooley, whose opinions as a jurisprudentialist were very much esteemed at the time, stated in his supplementary chapter about the Fourteenth Amendment to his 1873 edition of Justice Joseph Story's *Commentaries on the Constitution of the United States*:[484]

> It should be observed of the terms life, liberty, and property, that they are representative terms, and are intended to cover every right to which a member of the body politic is entitled under the law. The limbs are equally protected with life; the right to the pursuit of happiness in any legitimate calling or occupation is as much guaranteed as the right to go at large and move from place to place. The word liberty here employed implies the opposite of all those things which, beside the deprivation of life and liberty, were forbidden by the Great Charter. In the charter as confirmed by Henry III, no freeman was to be seized, or imprisoned, or deprived of his liberties, or free customs, or outlawed or banished, or anyways destroyed, except by the law of the land. The rights thus guaranteed are something more than the mere privileges of locomotion; the guarantee is the negation of arbitrary power in every form which results in a deprivation of right. The word we employ to comprehend the whole is not, therefore, a mere shield to personal liberty, but to civil liberty, and to political liberty also so far as it has been conferred and is possessed.

Moreover, Cooley not only maintained that the *liberty* protected by procedural safeguards embodied in the due process clause includes among its components substantive rights besides that pertaining to locomotion. He also held that the clause imposes substantive limitations upon the power of government to eliminate or limit important liberty-rights denoted by the term *liberty* in the due process clause. He explained:[485]

> It would be absurd, for instance, to say that arbitrary arrests were forbidden, but that the freedom of speech, the freedom of religious worship, the right of self-defence against unlawful violence, the right freely to buy and sell as others may, or the right in the public schools, found no protection here; or that individuals might be selected out and by legislative act arbitrarily deprived of the benefit of exemption laws, pre-emption laws, or even of the elective franchise. The word, on the other hand, embraces all our liberties—personal, civil, and political. None of them are to be taken away, except in accordance with established principles; none can be forfeited, except upon the finding of legal cause, after due inquiry.[486]

Cooley expounded upon the substantive aspects of the due process clause by virtue of its own per se potency as follows:

> A popular form of government ... does not necessarily assure to the people an exemption from tyrannical legislation. On the contrary, the more popular the form, if there be no checks or guards, the greater, perhaps, may be the danger that excitement and passion will sway the public councils, and arbitrary and unreasonable laws be enacted. Nor are laws necessarily equal and just because professedly they act upon all alike. A general law may establish regulations upon subjects not properly falling within the province of government, and yet be desired and cheerfully submitted to by the majority, who might be included, under any circumstances, voluntarily to establish such regulations for themselves; while, on the other hand, the same law might to the minority be in the highest degree offensive, unjust, and tyrannical. Could

a law, for instance, for the compulsory attendance of all persons upon the church of the majority, or upon the political meetings of the majority, or upon sports which the majority favored but the minority believed demoralizing, be admissible merely because everybody was included in its command? Would not, on the contrary, its very universality constitute offensive discrimination, precisely because it would compel conformity where equality of right would demand liberty of choice? [487]

Wisely observing the maxim, *it is better to be vaguely right than exactly wrong,*[488] Cooley explained the due process clause in these terms: "[L]ife, liberty, and property are placed under the protection of known and established principles, which cannot be dispensed with either generally or specially; either by courts or executive officers, or by legislators themselves.... [D]ue process of law in each particular case means such an exertion of the powers of government as the settled maxims of law permit and sanction, and under such safeguards for the protection of individual rights as those maxims prescribe for the class of cases to which the one being dealt with belongs."[489] For those who demand greater precision, I gladly refer them to *Davidson v. New Orleans,* (1878) in which the Court stated: "[A]part from the imminent risk of a failure to give any definition which would be at once perspicuous, comprehensive, and satisfactory, there is wisdom, we think, in the ascertaining of the intent and application of such an important phrase in the Federal Constitution by the gradual process of judicial inclusion and exclusion, as the cases presented for decision shall require, with the reasoning on which such decisions may be founded."[490]

Unfortunately, the Court's opinion in the *Slaughter-House Cases* (1873) did not impute any substantive aspects to either due process clause, and the Court relied exclusively upon the equal protection clause as providing whatever constitutional protection was needed for African Americans against racial discrimination.[491] However, both Justices Bradley and Swayne in their dissenting opinions expressly attributed significant substantive aspects to the due process clause of the Fourteenth Amendment.[492] Despite the Court's apparent rejection of the notion that the due process clause has substantive aspects, the fact is that thereafter there was considerable, demonstrable waffling on the issue following the decision in the *Slaughter-House Cases.*

Let us trace this judicial waffling. Justice Miller, who authored the Court's opinion in the *Slaughter-House Cases* (1873), spoke for the Court in *Loan Association* v. *Topeka* (1875):

> It must be conceded that there are such rights in every free government beyond the control of the State. A government which recognized no such rights, which held the lives, the liberty, and the property of its citizens subject at all times to the absolute disposition and unlimited control of even the most democratic depository of power, is after all, but a despotism. It is true, it is a despotism of the many, of the majority, if you choose to call it so, but it is nevertheless a despotism. It may be doubted, if a man is to hold all that he is accustomed to call his own, all in which he has placed his happiness and the security of which is essential to that happiness, under the unlimited dominion of others, whether it is not wiser that this power should be exercised by one man than by many.

> The theory of our governments, state and national, is opposed to the deposit of unlimited power anywhere. The executive, the legislative, and the judicial branches of these governments are all of limited and defined powers.

> There are limitations on such power which grow out of the essential nature of all free governments. Implied reservations of individual rights, without which the social compact could not exist and which are respected by all governments entitled to the name....[493]

The next item in our review is *United States* v. *Cruikshank* (1876), in which the Court remarked by way of obiter dictum:

> The Fourteenth Amendment prohibits a State from depriving any person of life, liberty, or property, without due process of law; but this adds nothing to the rights

of one citizen as against another. It simply furnishes an additional guaranty against any encroachment by the States upon the fundamental rights which belong to every citizen of society. As was said by Mr. Justice Johnson, in *Bank of Columbia v. Okely* [citation], it secures "the individual from the arbitrary exercise of the powers of government, unrestrained by the established principles of private rights and distributive justice." [494]

Thus, the *Cruikshank* Court appears to affirm that the due process clause has substantive aspects. Significantly, Justice Miller joined in the opinion of the Court. As if to undo the damage wrought by the above quoted dictum in *Cruikshank*, Justice Miller authored the opinion for the Court in *Davidson* v. *New Orleans* (1878).[495] The opinion affirmed that the due process clause has only procedural aspects and explained that taking private property without just compensation "may possibly violate some of those principles of general constitutional law, of which we could take jurisdiction if we were sitting in review of a Circuit Court of the United States, as we were in *Loan Association* v *Topeka* [citation]. But however this may be, or under whatever other clause of the Federal Constitution we may review the case, it is not possible to hold that a party has, without due process of law, been deprived of his property when, as regards the issues affecting it, he has, by the laws of the State, a fair trial in a court of justice according to the modes of proceeding applicable to such a case."[496]

Finally, we come full circle with Justice Miller joining in the opinion in *Hurtado* v. *California* (1884)[497] that, in grounding its attribution of substantive aspects to the due process clause, favorably quoted Miller's declaration in *Loan Association.* And this the Court did despite *Loan Association* being a federal diversity civil case that applied the then controlling rule in *Swift* v. *Tyson* (1842) [498] (i.e., that when federal jurisdiction in a case the case depends solely on diversity, the federal court's holding it to be based on the general principles and doctrines of jurisprudence rather than law of the state). As Edward S. Corwin aptly put it: "Thus were the States put on notice that every species of state legislation, whether dealing with procedural or substantive rights, was subject to the scrutiny of the Court when the question of its essential justice was raised."[499]

Suppose the Court should continue to maintain the doctrine that the due process clause has substantive aspects. What should be the theory by which issues pertaining to the substantive aspects of the clause are to be determined? The *Hurtado* theory, insofar as it came to be used by the Court to exalt liberty rights in economic matters (particularly liberty of contract) as fundamental, has been rejected by the Court fairly continuously since 1937. The *Hurtado* theory insofar as it used to vindicate fundamental liberty rights in noneconomic matters is still in force. The theory is sufficiently potent to serve as the grounding principle by which the First Amendment freedoms and other specific rights deemed fundamental by the Court are held to have been incorporated by the Fourteenth Amendment due process clause. One reason for the excessive potency of the due process clause is that the Court's theory includes among those rights deemed fundamental such as are implied by the principles underlying our political and civil institutions.

According to current doctrine, rights not specified in the Constitution but deemed fundamental are protected against any particular infringement by the United States only if the infringement fails the strict scrutiny test. But this book rejects the current theory of the Court concerning *fundamental rights* jurisprudence as being analytically and historically flawed. What this book proposes is that there are fundamental liberty and liberty-from aspects of the due process clauses and these are proximately grounded upon the exigencies of human dignity: the dignity of all human persons and that of free persons as such in virtue of their being rational, moral, and social. But what is it that provides that necessary legitimacy to the principles just stated? Is it enough just to show that the notion that the due process clause of the Fifth Amendment has substantive aspects was one of several original understandings contemporary with the founding of the Fourteenth Amendment?—Or that, after a bad start with *Dred Scott* and a period of judicial waffling, our cause is secure because eventually the Court came to definitively hold and thereafter maintain that the due process clauses have substantive aspects? Well, this may not be enough because what is desperately needed are sound principles respecting the substantive aspects of the due process clause that are: (1) consistent with the doctrine that the privileges or immunities clause incorporates the First Amendment freedoms and several other constitutional privileges and immunities of the American people; and (2) that firmly ground the substantive aspects asserting fundamental liberty and liberty-from rights to the due process clauses upon considerations sounding in human dignity.

Chapter C: The Fundamental Rights, Privileges, and Immunities of Free Persons and the Establishment of Universal Civil Freedom with the Adoption of the Thirteenth Amendment

The adoption of the Thirteenth Amendment radically changed the fundamental law of the land. As the Court declared in the *Civil Rights Cases*:[500] "It is true that slavery cannot exist without law, any more than property in lands and goods can exist without law, and, therefore, *the Thirteenth Amendment* may be regarded as nullifying all State laws which establish or uphold slavery. But it *has a reflex character also, establishing and decreeing universal civil and political freedom throughout the United States*[.]" The adoption of the Thirteenth Amendment conclusively repudiated any theory of substantive rights based upon a social compact theory that concerned itself chiefly with the substantive rights of white persons instead of all free persons whatever their race or color.

With the adoption of the Thirteenth Amendment, the fundamental law of the land became informed by the principle that universal civil freedom is established and decreed throughout the United States. This principle in turn generates another: that there are fundamental substantive rights grounded in the first place upon the exigencies of the human dignity of all persons—such that every person is endowed with a bundle of rights appropriate to his status by virtue of his humanity. In the second place, there are fundamental substantive rights, liberties, and immunities that a free person should have by virtue of his complete civil freedom and the exigencies of human dignity as applied to free persons in this country. The equal protection clause, however, is not redundant since it prohibits the states from invidiously failing to provide for or enforce equal laws for the protection of life, liberty, and property upon the ground of race, color, ethnicity, or some other similarly arbitrary birth status; and it endows the Congress with the power to enforce this prohibition by appropriate legislation. But quite independently of the equal protection clause, both due process clauses have so-called equal-protection components.

The Fifth Amendment due process clause had been judicially assigned substantive aspects even before the adoption of the Thirteenth and Fourteenth Amendments. But the antebellum Court did not ground these aspects upon the notion of human dignity and its exigencies. How could this have been since *Dred Scott* was the only case decided before the adoption of the Thirteenth and Fourteenth Amendments that involved an authoritative ruling by the Court that presupposed that the due process clause has substantive aspects. And what was that? To wit: that Congress could not constitutionally forbid a slave-owner from bringing a slave into and keeping him as such in federal territory. Implicit in this ruling was that a free person of color, in the District of Columbia, or in any federal territory or possession, does not have a fundamental substantive right not to be reduced to slavery or involuntary servitude. We are here not speaking of the analog of the due process clause in the constitution of an antebellum free state. Rather, we are speaking of the due process clause of the Fifth Amendment before the establishment (with the adoption of the Thirteenth Amendment) of universal civil freedom throughout the United States.

Let us think about it. According to the doctrine of *Dred Scott*, there was a fundamental substantive right of white persons to own slaves (or be the master of persons in involuntary servitude) in places subject to the exclusive jurisdiction of the United States. So, the *Dred Scott* Court was not speaking of substantive personal rights grounded proximately upon the exigencies of human dignity. Rather, it was speaking of substantive personal rights that, before the adoption of the Thirteenth Amendment, had been chiefly grounded upon prescriptive rights predicable of only free white persons protected by the then extant fundamental *law of the land* of the United States. Even in the antebellum free states, the inferior and degraded status of persons of color could not be completely eliminated because every person of color was tainted, as it were, with the stigma of belonging to a race the members of which were slaves or subject to the possibility of being enslaved. Slaves who fled to the free states remained slaves subject to capture and return. In antebellum free states, federal fugitive slave statutes failed to adequately provide just procedural safeguards to protect the interests of free-born or emancipated black Americans against false charges.[501] And even in a free state, it depended upon the law of that state whether the mere entry of a slave in transit with his owner to another state did not necessarily serve to make him a free person. With respect to the District of Columbia or any federal territory, even if it is assumed (contrary to *Dred Scott*) that the Congress could have forbidden slavery in such places, Congress nevertheless would have had the power to repeal any statute forbidding slavery or involuntary servitude in a place subject to its exclusive jurisdiction, and thus reinstitute African slavery.

Now there were thirty-four states in the Union just before the start of the Civil War: nineteen free states and fifteen slave states. Of the latter group, four states (Delaware, Maryland, Kentucky, and Missouri) remained in the Union; the other eleven constituted the Confederate States of America. Fourteen states had constitutions each of which included a provision of which the following is typical:

> All men are born free and equal, and have certain natural, essential, and inalienable rights: among which may be reckoned the right of enjoying and defending their lives and liberties; that of acquiring, possessing, and protecting property; in fine, that of seeking and obtaining their safety and happiness.

Of this group, thirteen were free states;[502] and one was a slave state.[503] Significantly, Charles Cotesworth Pinckney, an important delegate to the constitutional convention of 1787, explained the absence of a bill of rights in the South Carolina Constitution of 1776 as follows: "Such bills generally begin with declaring that all men are by nature born free. Now, we would make this declaration with a very bad grace, when a large part of our property consists in men who are actually born slaves."[504] It should be no surprise to discover that at least twenty-four of the thirty-seven state constitutions in 1868 explicitly asserted the existence of essential and inalienable natural rights of all persons.[505]

With the adoption of the Thirteenth Amendment, the substantive aspects of the Fifth Amendment due process clause necessarily encompassed certain natural, essential, and inalienable rights to which all men are entitled by virtue of their being born free and equal. Among those natural, essential and inalienable rights "may be reckoned the right of enjoying and defending their lives and liberties; that of acquiring, possessing, and protecting property; in fine, that of seeking and obtaining their safety and happiness." Some essential and inalienable natural rights, which pertain to defending life and liberties and seeking and obtaining safety, are in principle sufficiently protected by the fundamental law of the land insofar as it embraces procedural aspects and those substantive rights the denial of which would constitute servitude or the badges or incidents of servitude, and the acquiring, possessing, and protecting of property. But what about those essential and inalienable natural rights pertaining to the enjoyment of life and liberties, and seeking and obtaining happiness?

In writing of the effect, following the adoption of the Thirteenth Amendment, of state constitutional provisions securing life, liberty, and property against deprivation without due process of law in former slave states, Justice Cooley commented:

> Yet, under the altered circumstances of the country, it was not now thought to be sufficient. The difficulty was, that certain classes of persons in some of the States had not been within its protection, either because held as property, and, as such, subject in great degree to the arbitrary dominion of masters, or because, belonging to a proscribed race, they occupied an anomalous position, and were conceded but an imperfect measure of right and privilege.[506]

Cooley evidently thought that the inclusion of the due process clause in the Fourteenth Amendment was needed to preclude the enactment or judicial approval of "legislation [by former slave states] … the actual purpose of which might be, whether avowed or not, or the effect even if not designed, to keep the colored race for a time at least in that condition of pupilage and dependence for which only, any many believed and declared, they were adapted either by nature or acquirements[.]"[507]

Notwithstanding the *one pervading purpose* of the adoption of the reconstruction amendments professed in the *Slaughter-House Cases*,[508] it would not be difficult to judge what appears to be the *one dominant purpose* of section 1 of the Fourteenth Amendment were this evaluation based solely upon the decisions of the Court from circa 1884 until 1923. That one dominant purpose appears to have been the promotion of the substantive aspects of the due process clause in the domain of economic liberty and commercial property interests. However, in 1923 the case of *Meyer v. Nebraska* was decided, which markedly accelerated the process by which the due process clauses were judicially endowed with significantly more important noneconomic liberty interests. *Meyer* held that due process of law was violated by a statute that forbade the teaching in any private or public school of any modern language other than English to any child who had not successfully passed the eighth grade. The Court declared:

> While this Court has not attempted to define with exactness the liberty thus guaranteed [by the due process clause], the term has received much consideration and some of the included things have been definitely stated. Without doubt, it denotes not merely freedom from bodily restraint, but also the right of the individual to contract, to engage in any of the common occupations of life, to acquire useful knowledge, to marry, establish a home and bring up children, to worship God according to the dictates of his own conscience, and generally to enjoy those privileges long recognized at common law as essential to the orderly pursuit of happiness by free men. [Citations.] The established doctrine is that this liberty may not be interfered with, under the guise of protecting the public interest, by legislative action which is arbitrary or without reasonable relation to some purpose within the competency of the State to effect. Determination by the legislature of what constitutes proper exercise of police power is not final or conclusive, but is subject to supervision by the courts.[509]

With the declaration that the *liberty* of the due process clause encompasses *those privileges long recognized at common law as essential to the orderly pursuit of happiness by free men*, we arrive at the inauguration of a new regime more in accord with the constitutional provisions of most antebellum free states, enlightened as it were by the adoption of the Thirteenth Amendment, that all men are born free and equal, and possess essential and unalienable natural rights. And among those essential and unalienable natural rights are entitlements by constitutional law to those civil liberties that free persons should have since they are "essential to the orderly pursuit of happiness."

In speaking of essential *natural rights* predicable of persons born free and equal, it is useful to notice the writings of Francis Lieber, a very gifted and very influential jurisprudentialist of the nineteenth century. The German-born Francis Lieber (1798–1872) immigrated to the United States in 1827, eventually becoming a professor of history and political economics at South Carolina College. Because of his Union sympathies, he moved to New York in 1856 where he taught at Columbia University. During the Civil War, he authored the very important *Code for the Government of Armies in the Field* (1863) (also known as the *Lieber Code*). His best-known works are his influential *Manual of Political Ethics* (1838) and his *Civil Liberty and Self-Government* (2d ed. 1859).

In his *Political Ethics* Lieber proclaimed "that the only axiom necessary to establish the science of natural law is this: 'I exist as a human being, *therefore* I have a right to exist as a human being.'"[510] And this dictum, simple yet so eloquent, expresses the deeply felt sentiment of all rational men and women of good will who value every human being because of his humanity. How often in common discourse and literature one notices such expressions as, "They treated us like cattle!"; "They didn't look upon us as human beings!"; "They behaved just like animals!"; and even, "They treated us as if were children." And, although I readily agree that humans have moral duties with respect to animals, there are some things quite special about humans such that we are especially worthy and have a unique moral status as such because of, among other things, our potential or actual rationality and moral agency.

As Lieber put it:

[T]he [natural] rights of man [are] derived from his nature, both physical and moral, for the latter is closely connected with the former; it inquires in *quid sit justum aut injustum* [what is just or unjust], not into *quid sit juris* (what is law or lawful). The word nature is a term used in so many various significations that it has led to great confusion of ideas in several branches; and it is not an uncommon mistake to believe that natural law is that law which existed in the erroneously supposed state of nature…. [T]he body of [natural] rights [are those] which we deduce from the essential nature of man.[511]

Lieber prefers to speak of natural rights as being *primordial*:

[T]hose which flow directly from the nature of man inasmuch as he is a social being, rights which are of primordial importance, and which present themselves the more distinctly to the human mind and are acted out the more definitely in reality, the more mankind advance in civilization. It is on this account that the word primordial has been preferred to indelible, indefeasible, or inherent rights[.][512]

But Lieber insists that "[p]roperly, there is but one original or primordial right, that of my personality, the right I have expressed already by way of axiom: 'I am a man, *therefore* I have a right to be a man.' By my existence I prove my imprescriptible right to my existence as man, physical, intellectual, moral—my right that humanity in me is not annihilated[.]"[513] This one primordial right is predicable of every human person.

The epistemological and ontological foundations of the natural morality and natural rights are the subject of much dispute. Fortunately, people of widely differing philosophical and religious backgrounds can reach theoretical and practical agreement upon many important moral issues. Rational men and women of good will are very likely to agree as to what characteristics a person should have in order to have an *ideal* human nature. The person of good will with an ideal human nature is someone with a power to effectively reason in theoretical and practical matters. The person of good will is one who values peace and tranquility as a necessary condition for optimal human flourishing both individually and in society. So what is the proverbial bottom line? It is that we are all human beings. So, therefore, let us treat ourselves and each other as human beings. We do so by conforming, as best we can, to such universally moral rules, precepts, and norms as are in harmony with those basic principles and ideals that necessarily characterize (or are commonly held by) rational men and women of good will in modern civilized society.

Although all human persons, free or not, have in common the original right to an existence as human, my primary interest here is to write about the fundamental rights of a free person as such. To facilitate our inquiry, I limit my exposition as to what are the fundamental substantive rights of free persons to American citizens and noncitizen nationals and to permanent resident aliens within the United States. This is because such persons, all other things being equal, have the maximal amount of substantive rights possible by virtue of the due process clause. The term *free person* for our purposes does not include someone during his minority since he is in the care and custody, and thus subject to the control, of his parent or guardian;[514] although, in the sense of the Thirteenth Amendment, a newborn child is born free since he is not born to be in slavery or involuntary servitude. However, in the sense that I use *free* in speaking of the fundamental rights of free persons, a person is not completely free until he reaches majority, unless he demonstrably has a serious mental defect or disease so disabling as to require that he remain in the care and custody of his parent or legal guardian for his good and that of others. Thus too, the term *free person* does not include someone in actual or constructive custody of the State because of being charged with or convicted of a crime. Nor does the term refer to someone while in active military service because he is subject to extensive military discipline. But, of course, each person who is not free in the sense just indicated has fundamental substantive rights appropriate to his status safeguarded by the due process clause (and other constitutional provisions). In making this inquiry, I assume, moreover, that the national, regional, or local state of affairs is such that neither a regime of martial law or its functional equivalent obtains nor a serious, widespread disaster, pestilence, civil disorder, or the like that calls forth for the exercise of extensive emergency powers of the State.

The principal natural rights applicable to free persons vis-à-vis the State are the complementaries of basic human goods valued by men and women of good will. These basic goods include, but are not limited to, the preservation of life, bodily integrity, and good health; social intercourse whether domestic or otherwise; play, sports, and other recreational activity; intellectual activity whether theoretical or practical; esthetic enterprise and appreciation; and the needs for self-respect, the respect of others, and to one's own sense of individuality. The principal natural rights in turn have corresponding clusters of rights, privileges and immunities vis-à-vis the State. Moreover, in evaluating what are the fundamental rights of free persons as such one must pay close attention to what are those rights deeply rooted in our history and tradition that are identified with being a free person not a member of an inferior or degraded caste defined by some caste principle during antebellum years. With this qualification, the reference in *Meyer* v. *Nebraska* to "those privileges long recognized at common law as essential to the orderly pursuit of happiness by free men" helpfully reminds us that some components of the fundamental rights of free persons as such are those that are essentially customary rights associated in our history and traditions with being the badges and incidents of free persons as such—and, to be blunt about it, I mean the badges and incidents of free white persons.

With the adoption of the Thirteenth and Fourteenth Amendments, these same badges and incidents of free white persons are predicable of all free persons of color. So it is not quite accurate to say that the fundamental rights of all free persons as such are limited to only those natural rights that are determined as the result of a philosophical inquiry to be applicable to any well-ordered civil society. Because we are concerned also with the fundamental rights of all free persons as such in the United States, we must necessarily take into account "those privileges long recognized at common law as essential to the orderly pursuit of happiness by free men." These privileges are the essential badges and incidents of civil freedom after we also take into account the establishment of universal civil freedom throughout the United States with the adoption of the Thirteenth Amendment. Among the fundamental rights of free persons in the United States are those, to borrow from Russell Kirk, that obtain because there is "a moral system applied to jurisprudence: a body of belief in certain rights long established by custom and prescription, and found by the test of time to accord with human nature and civil social nature."[515] So, in a manner of speaking, the fundamental rights of free persons as such are natural rights essential to the dignity of free persons by virtue of their freedom and as further realized in the fundamental common law of our nation.

Chapter D: Some Fundamental Rights of Free Persons as Components of the Specific Right of the Due Process Clause

Among those natural rights essential to the dignity of free persons are some pertaining to the basic good of being respected or esteemed by others based upon one's own personal merits and capabilities rather than upon some arbitrary classification such as race or color, ethnicity, place of birth or residence, or gender. To legally stigmatize a person as belonging to an inferior and degraded caste status because of race or color, or some other similar birth status, inevitably operates to seriously deprive such a person of entitlement to basic legal rights entailed by the essential natural rights of all free persons. It has taken us many years to recognize that miscegenation and separate-albeit-equal laws are actually grounded upon and perpetuate notions of the superiority and/or inferiority of individuals based simply upon their race or color. Such deeply rooted and widespread notions result in morally intolerable discrimination. These notions, being the relics of the pernicious institution of African slavery, had effects that long pervaded even the antebellum free states.

Even after the adoption of the Thirteenth Amendment, persisting notions of racial supremacy hooded by the separate-but-equal doctrine were the fruit of the poisoned tree. Hence, they were not generally perceived by most white Americans in even the antebellum free states as being incompatible with the establishment of universal civil freedom by the Thirteenth Amendment. And, unfortunately, these notions were reinforced and perpetuated throughout the nation with the Court's decisions in *Pace* v. *Alabama* (1883)[516] and *Plessy* v. *Louisiana* (1896),[517] which sanctioned, or were very widely taken to sanction the Jim Crow regime as constitutionally permissible. The lessons of history confirm that the separate-but-equal doctrine in theory resulted in a separate-and-unequal praxis in fact. Miscegenation laws and other Jim Crow laws were in fact popularly justified upon the ground that blacks are too inferior and degraded to permit lawful intimate association with them in any way that implied their social equality with whites.

Correcting decades of egregious error, the Court eventually ruled in *Loving v. Virginia* (1967) how "under our Constitution, the freedom to marry, or not marry, a person of another race resides with the individual and cannot be infringed by the State."[518] And this decision, in my opinion, strikingly confirms that the substantive aspects of the due process clauses obtain, given the establishment of universal civil freedom throughout the United States with the adoption of the Thirteenth Amendment. These aspects, to borrow words from Justice William Strong speaking for the Court in *Strauder* v. *West Virginia*, include "a positive immunity, or right, most valuable to the colored race—the right to exemption from unfriendly legislation against them distinctively as colored— exemption from legal discriminations, implying inferiority in civil society, lessening the security of their enjoyment of the rights which others enjoy, and discriminations which are steps towards reducing them to the condition of a subject race."[519] Justice Strong actually attributed the immunity from racial discrimination to section 1 of the Fourteenth Amendment as a whole. But the Court had previously neutered the privileges or immunities clause, and the equal protection clause applies only to the states. Hence it follows that Strong should have attributed to both due process clauses the function of prohibiting governmental discrimination based upon race or color.

Given its ostensibly narrow construction of the privileges or immunities and due process clauses, the Court in the *Slaughter-House Cases* was compelled to rely upon the equal protection clause as that imperatively needed constitutional text that would provide constitutional "protection of the newly made freemen and then citizen from the oppressions of those who had formerly exercised unlimited dominion over him." According to the Court: "The existence of laws in the states where the newly emancipated negroes resided, which discriminated with gross injustice and hardship against them as a class, was the evil to be remedied by [the equal protection] clause, and by it such laws are forbidden."[520] Oddly, there is no constitutional provision that expressly prohibits the denial of equal protection of the laws by the United States. Of course, there is the Fifth Amendment due process clause. But for anyone to concede that this clause prohibits racial discrimination by the government based upon race is to concede that the clause has substantive aspects, albeit we are now speaking of only liberty-from rights in this context. But even this is something that no self-respecting adherent of the *procedural-aspects-only* theory of the due process clause should ever want to concede. The comments of John Hart Ely are unexceptionably appropriate concerning the absence of an equal protection clause applicable to the United States. He wrote in his excellent *Democracy and Distrust: A Theory of Judicial Review*:[521]

> The Equal Protection Clause does not apply to the federal government. Nonetheless, in *Bolling* v. *Sharpe*—striking down segregation schooling in the District of Columbia the same day that *Brown* v. *Board of Education* struck it down in the states—the Court held, in essence, that the Due Process Clause of the Fifth Amendment incorporates the Equal Protection Clause of the Fourteenth Amendment. This is gibberish both syntactically and historically, and was explained by Chief Justice Warren in terms of a judicial unwillingness to hold the States to a higher constitutional standard than the federal government. "In view of our decision that the Constitution prohibits the states from maintaining racially segregated public schools, it would be unthinkable that the same Constitution would impose a lesser duty on the Federal Government."[522]

What can be easily overlooked is that there had been a desperate need by the Republican-controlled Thirty-ninth Congress to undertake the constitutionalization of the Civil Rights Act of 1866 as quickly as possible, since their control of the Congress could end with the next round of elections—especially if more former Confederate states were admitted to representation in Congress.[523] Such constitutionalization was necessary given the widespread opinion that the Civil Rights Act of 1866 was invalid in two ways: (1) Congress, given the *Dred Scott* decision, was without authority to naturalize native-born blacks; and (2) Congress lacked authority to enact civil rights legislation requiring governmental racial equality with respect to the states notwithstanding the adoption of the Thirteenth Amendment. But surely, one would suppose, that if the Fourteenth Amendment was needed to constitutionalize section 1 of the Civil Rights Act of 1866 with respect to the states then it would also have been needed to do the same work with respect to the United States—unless that Act was already constitutionalized with respect to the United States.

The equal protection clause, according to the received opinion, accomplished the constitutionalization of the Act with respect to the states. But what clause in section 1 of the Fourteenth Amendment served to accomplish the constitutionalization of the Act with respect to the United States?— assuming such constitutionalization was necessary. Surely, the founders of the Fourteenth Amendment must be deemed to have thought that there was a constitutional exemption from racial discrimination with respect to the United States that already obtained or that was secured with the adoption of the Fourteenth Amendment.

If the Fifth Amendment due process clause lacks substantive aspects, then it follows that among the constitutional immunities of American citizens there must have been a pre-existing constitutional immunity from racial discrimination for American citizens—a conclusion contrary to the Court's theory of the privileges or immunities clause in the *Slaughter-House Cases*. According to the foregoing scenario, the adoption of the Fourteenth Amendment was necessary to constitutionalize the Civil Rights Act of 1866 with respect to the United States because the amendment's citizenship clause was needed because that clause would overrule the *Dred Scott Case* as to the issue of the national citizenship of African Americans. But it then follows that the privileges or immunities clause incorporates the exemption from racial discrimination as a constitutional immunity of the American people.

If, on the other hand, one maintains that American citizens did not have a constitutional immunity against racial discrimination before the adoption of the Fourteenth Amendment, then the adoption of the citizenship clause of the Fourteenth Amendment was insufficient to constitutionalize the Civil Rights Act as to the United States. If, however, the Fifth Amendment due process clause already had an equal-protection component embracing antidiscriminatory-substantive aspects relating to race or color, then the Fourteenth Amendment presupposed that the Civil Rights Act of 1866 was already constitutionalized. But how could this have been possible? The theory that the Fifth Amendment due process clause was radically changed with the adoption of the Thirteenth Amendment supplies the necessary basis for explaining why, before the adoption of the Fourteenth Amendment, the Fifth Amendment due process clause by its own force prohibits any racially discriminating laws and governmental actions that rationally presuppose the inferior and degraded caste status of a person based upon race or color. And this hypothesis is probable only if the adoption of the Thirteenth Amendment radically changed the fundamental law of the land more than just by abolishing slavery and involuntary servitude and their badges and incidents. So in either case the Court in the *Slaughter-House Cases* erred in failing to hold that freedom from racial discrimination was a constitutional immunity of American citizens before the adoption of the Fourteenth Amendment and/or that the specific right of the Fifth Amendment due process clause already included as a component the right to be free from any infringement of the freedom from racial discrimination—provided it is agreed that the adoption of the Fourteenth Amendment either presupposed the constitutionalization of the Civil Rights Act of 1866 or was needed to accomplish the same.

My conclusion is that, with respect to the United States before the adoption of the Fourteenth Amendment, freedom from racial discrimination was: (1) a constitutional immunity of the American people that became predicable of all native-born persons of color by virtue of the citizenship clause of that amendment; and that (2) this freedom was also a fundamental liberty-right of all free persons of color, a component of the specific right of the Fifth Amendment due process clause, because of the establishment of universal civil freedom with the adoption of the Thirteenth Amendment. So, you see, you can have it both ways. You can have your cake and eat it too.

The now rejected thesis in *Washington* v. *Glucksberg,* teaching that the rights that should be regarded as fundamental are limited only to those rights deeply rooted in the nation's history and traditions, is flawed for three reasons.[524] First, the thesis pays insufficient attention to the radical change in the fundamental law of the law wrought by the adoption of the Thirteenth Amendment that established universal civil freedom. Hence, the changed fundamental law of the land must now embody principles by which substantive rights, privileges, and immunities are attributed to free persons as such by virtue of their common humanity and the dignity of their civil freedom. Some rights, prior to the abolition of slavery and involuntary servitude, were indeed deeply rooted in the nation's history and traditions but they were uprooted with the adoption of the Thirteenth Amendment. With the adoption of the Thirteenth Amendment certain rights were de novo deeply rooted but still needing the proper nutritive soul in which to grow and thrive. Second, the thesis fails to take into proper account that to determine what are *fundamental rights* one must pay close attention as to what are the *fundamental principles* governing whether such-and-such a putative right is fundamental in the requisite sense. In determining what are the essential fundamental rights of free persons, one must determine what are those rights as to zones of liberty and privacy that all free people should have by virtue of the dignity of their civil freedom. Third, the thesis fails because it does not sufficiently allow a true development of constitutional doctrine so that, although remaining true to those fundamental principles of liberty and justice pertaining to what rights are essentially worthy of free people, these principles will allow that some other rights, also deeply rooted in our history and traditions, may be eventually discerned by an enlightened judiciary to be incompatible with the fundamental principles in question. So, to consider one example, the specific right of the Fifth Amendment due process clause, yet uninformed by the establishment of universal civil freedom with the adoption of the Thirteenth Amendment, was not then understood as being inconsistent with a ban on miscegenation. But, given the establishment of universal civil freedom, the ban on miscegenation clearly appears violative of the fundamental rights and liberties of free persons as such because its warrant depends upon the existence of an inferior and degraded caste status for persons of color.

And here we may profitably return, as promised above, to *Lawrence* v. *Texas* and its ruling invalid, upon substantive due process grounds, a state statute making it a criminal offense for two adults of the same sex to consensually and privately engage in oral or anal intercourse. The opinion of the Court, by Justice Kennedy (Stevens, Souter, Ginsburg, and Breyer, concurring) is quite remarkable for its exercise in judicial chutzpa. For a close reading of the opinion discloses that the majority's rationale presupposes that homosexual intercourse (regardless of sexual orientation) in private is something morally good or indifferent—all other things being equal. Thus, the Court declared, "When sexuality finds overt expression in intimate contact with another person, the contact can be one element in a personal bond that is more enduring."[525] Moreover, according to the Court, "[t]he case does involve two adults who, with full and mutual consent from each other, engaged in sexual practices common to a homosexual lifestyle. The petitioners are entitled to respect for their private lives. The State cannot demean their existence or control their destiny by making their private sexual conduct a crime."[526] So the operative principle of liberty and justice, relied upon by the *Lawrence* Court, is that it is unconstitutional for the State to legislate upon the principle that homosexual intercourse (regardless of sexual orientation) is immoral and that the homosexual life style (particularly if widespread and notorious) is prejudicial to society and for individuals—even were a person adhering to this rejected principle to agree that there are zones of privacy wherein two adults of the same sex have a constitutional right to be legally free to consensually, privately, and noncommercially engage in homosexual intercourse.

Some readers might object that I err in interpreting the *Lawrence* Court. I think not. To take one example, one would not ordinarily say that persons engaged in homosexual intercourse "are entitled to respect in their private lives" unless such conduct is morally good or indifferent—all other things being equal. Similarly, one would not ordinarily say that persons, in their homes with like-minded guests, who engage in vilifying members of other races are entitled to respect in their private lives unless such conduct is morally good or indifferent. Yet, someone who believes that neither kind of private conduct is entitled to respect might nevertheless hold that the actors should be constitutionally free to do so in their homes because of overriding interests in preserving zones of liberty and privacy.

The Court acknowledged "that for centuries there have been powerful voices to condemn homosexual conduct as immoral ... [and that] [f]or many persons these are not trivial concerns but profound and deep convictions accepted as ethical and moral principles to which they aspire and which thus determine the course of their lives." But the Court assures us the "majority may [not] use the power of the State to enforce their views on the whole society through operation of the criminal law."[527] The Court also affirmed (approvingly quoting from Justice Stevens' dissenting opinion in *Bowers* v. *Hardwick*[528]): "[T]he fact that a governing majority in a State has traditionally viewed a particular practice as immoral is not a sufficient reason for upholding a law prohibiting the practice; neither history nor tradition could save a law prohibiting miscegenation from constitutional attack."[529] The Court concludes its analysis with the judgment: "The Texas statute furthers no legitimate interest which can justify its intrusion into the personal and private life of the individual."[530]

But, according to one view consistent with the general theory of this book, a statute criminalizing same-sex intercourse might be constitutionally applied to a different scenario with aggravating factors in the absence of another statute equally applicable to same or opposite-sex sexual partners. Thus, for example, there would be a scenario with aggravating factors where two consenting adults, in their residence, engage in same-sex intercourse incident to entertaining their guests, all consenting adults, during a private party, or where such conduct in engaged in incident to making a pornographic movie. But the Court's opinion does not expressly state that Texas statute is invalid as applied to the salient facts of the case but that it may be constitutionally applied in other contexts.[531] However, the ordinary rule in cases involving substantive due process, other than in a First Amendment freedom case not involving so-called commercial speech, is that the statute be judged as invalid as applied to the facts of the case rather than invalid on its face because of substantial overbreadth.[532]

The *Lawrence* Court's rationale for its holding is seriously flawed because it erroneously presupposes that the fundamental principles of liberty and justice by which the fundamental rights of free persons as such are determined precludes any legislation based upon the principle that same-sex oral and anal intercourse is immoral (i.e., contrary to natural and/or customary morality) and/or that the homosexual life-style (especially if widespread and notorious) is on the whole harmful to society and individuals. Implicit in the Court's rationale is that the state cannot even manifest popular moral disapproval of homosexual intercourse as such outside the zone of constitutionally protected privacy. There are great differences of opinion about this matter about reasonable men and women. However, I think it should be treated as essentially a public policy, and not a federal constitutional, issue whether the State should legislate within due limits according to the principle in question. It should also be a public policy and not a federal constitutional issue whether the State may legislate within due limits upon the principle that private homosexual intercourse is morally good or indifferent (all other things being equal), and that a homosexual life-style (even if widespread and openly manifested in some ways) is not socially harmful.

The widely held and traditional belief, whether or not erroneous, that homosexual intercourse is immoral and that the homosexual life style (especially if widespread and notorious) is socially harmful provides the rational basis for the opinion that even private homosexual intercourse should be criminalized. Indeed, the Court's opinion in the overruled *Bowers* case rightly affirmed that the "presumed belief of the majority of the electorate in Georgia that homosexual sodomy is immoral and unacceptable" provides the rational basis for the law whether or not the belief in question is erroneous.[533] But the *Lawrence* Court is correct, on the other hand, when it declared that the fact that a governing majority has traditionally viewed a particular practice as immoral is an insufficient reason for upholding a law prohibiting the practice wherever it takes place. The *Lawrence* Court is correct on this point because the power to legislate based upon the principle that a particular practice has been traditionally viewed as immoral must be confined within due limits imposed by the fundamental law of the land. Thus where the *Bowers* Court erred was in having failed to identify the nature of the fundamental right of free persons that provides due limits to the power of the State to legislate based upon the principle that homosexual intercourse is immoral and unacceptable. The rational basis for such legislation is overridden or trumped, as it were, by some fundamental liberty or liberty-from interests. So, more precisely, the cardinal issue is whether criminalization of private homosexual intercourse between two adults (with all the necessary qualifications being made) violates any fundamental right of free persons as such. It cannot by hypothesis be that private homosexual intercourse is morally good or indifferent if it is presupposed that it is a public policy and not a constitutional issue whether the State may legislate upon the principle within due limits that homosexual intercourse is morally wrong and/or that the homosexual life-style (especially if widespread and notorious) is socially harmful.

The relevant fundamental principles of liberty and justice are: (1) that two or more adults, whether or not of the same sex, are constitutionally free to be present in the same dwelling either as residents or visitors, subject to reasonable zoning and other regulations limiting the number of persons that can be present and prohibiting disorderly conduct affecting their neighbors;[534] and (2) that it would be unduly intrusive of the legitimate privacy interests of such individuals to subject them to the possibility of arrest and of searches of their persons or property just because they, as a matter of fact, consensually, privately, nonviolently, and noncommercially engaged in (what is believed to be) illicit sexual behavior (absent aggravating factors), or because there was probable cause to believe such was the case, or probable cause was thought to exist by the searching or arresting authority. For if arrests and/or searches may lawfully be made upon probable cause with respect to private consensual, nonviolent, and noncommercial sexual activity in a dwelling or its functional equivalent, then theoretically it is possible, given the probable cause standard, that at least as many innocent as guilty persons might be subject to lawfully conducted arrests or searches as the case may be. But it is patently unreasonable to subject innocent people to the risk of arrest or searches based upon the probable cause standard with respect to consensual, nonviolent, private, and noncommercial, intimate sexual activity involving one couple within a dwelling or its functional equivalent. And it is also patently unreasonable to subject people who engage in the activity in question to the possibility of arrest, searches, or prosecution with respect to that activity when committed in a zone of privacy because such activity, even assuming its immorality, amounts to a not uncommon and indeed a rather widespread personal vice. The vindication of the fundamental right in question has the merit of not seriously affecting the efficacious exercise of the police power because it is very rare that laws prohibiting anal or oral intercourse will as a matter of fact be applied to situations in which only two adults are discretely and intimately engaged and where the evidence of their conduct would then ordinarily depend upon the invasion of their privacy by third parties, whether by intention or mistake.

All that has been said above applies *mutatis mutandis* to opposite-gender anal or oral intercourse, fornication, and adultery (absent aggravating factors), but not to such utterly dehumanizing vices as bestiality or to violations of cross-cultural taboos relating to incestuous conduct with close relatives.

Some readers have strongly held views that it is outrageous that the State should be constitutionally entitled to enact legislation within due limits upon the principle that homosexual intercourse (even absent additional circumstances) is immoral or that the homosexual life style (on a widespread and notorious scale) is socially harmful. But the adoption of the Fourteenth Amendment did not enact John Stuart Mill's *On Liberty.* That the State may constitutionally legislate upon a certain principle does not mean that its power to do so is unlimited, or that the State should do so as a matter of constitutionally permissible public policy. Any system of laws limits liberty and liberty-from interests to some extent; and some legislation may even fail the rational basis test without violating a *fundamental* liberty and liberty-from interest.

Moreover, there is no fundamental substantive right, encompassed by the due process clause, that American people be wisely governed and not be subject to oppressive regulation. Otherwise, the Court would necessarily be a super-legislature deciding political, economic, or social issues upon which opinions may sharply differ.

I do not propose to review the several fundamental rights of free persons in detail since my chief purpose is to propound a general theory of the constitutional rights of the American people rather than to systematically review the special theories of these rights. However, I have already made two exceptions (i.e., regarding racial discrimination and same-sex intercourse); and so to further illustrate my general approach I shall make one more exception and that pertains to the substantive aspects of the due process clause with respect to expression by the spoken or written word.

The First Amendment freedom of speech and the press insofar as it pertains to verbal communication (FSP-VC) has an analog that is a fundamental right of free persons pertaining to expression by the spoken or written word. Let's call this the *fundamental liberty of verbal communication* (FLVC).[535] Every component of the FLVC is equally fundamental although perhaps some components are not as important or valuable as some other particular components. There are other liberty interests pertaining to verbal expression that are not fundamental. Hence there are nonfundamental rights that pertain to verbal expression; and the test of constitutional validity with respect to infringements of a nonfundamental right is the rational basis test. There is a master right, as it were, applicable to all nonfundamental rights pertaining to verbal expression. This master right is not itself a fundamental liberty. But it may be usefully considered as a *fundamental right* (*right* used in a stricter sense) in that it is necessarily a violation of substantive law of the land (i.e., substantive due process) for the State to deprive persons of any nonfundamental liberty right pertaining to verbal expression unless such deprivation satisfies the rational basis test.

In order to best understand the scope and limits of the FLVC, it may be desirable to prescind from considerations appropriate to the republican and secular form of government established for the United States and required for all the states by the Constitution. The FLVC does not presuppose the doctrine of popular sovereignty. It is consistent with an establishment of religion in which the State formally endorses and financially supports a particular religion or religious institution from general tax funds. And I say this because the FLVC relates to liberty interests concerning verbal communication that free persons should have in every well-ordered, modern civil society (whatever its form of government) that are proximately grounded upon their dignity of free persons as rational, moral, and social beings, as further augmented by those deeply rooted prescriptive rights (pertaining to verbal communication) of the American people that can be legitimately regarded as among the essential badges and incidents of free persons as such.

Even a civil society with a republican and secular form of government may flourish although it may not have a constitutional ban on all abridgments of FSP-VC. Suppose, for example, a constitutional provision (applicable to the United States and the states) were to read, "No law shall be made or enforced which shall unreasonably abridge freedom of speech or of the press." The applicable test of constitutional validity should then necessarily be much more than even a rather strong version of the rational basis test. In determining whether the making or enforcing of a law unreasonably abridges the FSP, the Court would consider whether the purported object of the abridgment had a legitimate and substantial objective. The legitimacy of the purported objective of an abridgment of FSP would involve a consideration of those fundamental principles that underlie the civil and political institutions of the nation. For example, an abridgment would have to be judicially deemed unreasonable were its objective the perpetuation of the ruling political party in office by shielding it from verbal defamation in any appropriate form or channel of communication. In our constitutional order, which now includes the rule that no person may be discriminated against because of some caste status based upon race or color, it would have to be judicially deemed per se unreasonable were some rogue state legislature to enact a statute forbidding defamation of white supremacist doctrines in any form or channel of public communication. On the other hand, careful consideration would be called for in order to determine whether a statute forbidding the advocacy of white supremacist doctrines through the mass media constitutes an unreasonable abridgment of the FSP-VC—assuming (as I in fact hold) that the FSP-VC itself includes as a component the right to freely advocate white supremacist doctrines in any appropriate form or channel of public communication. Here I parenthetically note that I use the term "any appropriate form or channel of public communication" to refer to such forms and channels of public communication not involving captive 'audiences' as are appropriate for the expression of matter not reasonably regarded as substantially indecent or injurious. Thus, I use the term "any appropriate form or channel of public communication" as a term of art to block the contention that such-and-such form or channel of public communication is inappropriate for the advocacy of white supremicist doctrines but very appropriate for the advocacy of racial equality. So, in my opinion, a statute that prohibits, in some specified appropriate channels or forms of public communication, the advocacy of white supremacist doctrines might not necessarily constitute an unreasonable abridgment of FSP-VC; but it would necessarily be an abridgment of FSP-VC.

Some people maintain that generally (but not necessarily exceptionlessly): (1) if A has a right, as a component of FSP-VC, to freely say **T** in some particular form or channel of public communication then A has a right to freely say **T** in all appropriate forms and channels of public communication; and (2) if A does not have a right, as a component of FSP, to freely say **T** in some particular form, or channel of public communication then A does not have a right, as a component to FSP, to freely say **T** in any other appropriate form or channel of public communication. And the position that I have just described is, as a matter of fact, a well-established doctrine of the Court—and one with which I agree with respect to FSP-VC.[536] One implication of this doctrine is rather obvious: if the FSP includes as a component the right to freely propagate white supremacist doctrines in all appropriate forms and channels of public communication, then it follows that however reasonable would be the prohibition of such propagation in some appropriate forms and channels the constitutional ban on all abridgments of FSP-VC would preclude such a prohibition.

Now if we assume arguendo (and contrary to legal fact) that the FSP-VC does not include as a component the right to freely propagate white supremacist doctrines in any appropriate form or channel of public communication,[537] does it then follow that there is not a fundamental right protected by the due process clause to be free to verbally propagate white supremacist doctrines in some but not all appropriate forms or channels of public communication? My view is that there is such a right, but it is a component of a fundamental liberty right protected by the due process clause. But it does not appear that this would be the position of the present Court because, according to current 'First Amendment' jurisprudence, if a particular expression in some forms and channels of public communication is unworthy of being protected by the 'First Amendment' then it is ipso facto worthy of application of only the rational basis test in determining whether the due process clause has been violated since there is no other fundamental right pertaining to verbal expression in the forms and channels of public communication recognized by the Court other than the FSP-VC, besides the those components specific right of the assembly-petition clause and religious freedom insofar as it pertains to public communication.[538]

The thoroughgoing application of the principle, that any expression in the forms and channels of public communication worthy of constitutional protection greater than its survival value vis-à-vis the rational basis test must necessarily be within the ambit of a First Amendment freedom, results in the generation of anomalous doctrines in the Court's jurisprudence. For example, the protection afforded by current *First Amendment* jurisprudence to so-called commercial speech or expression is, according to the Court's doctrine, much more limited in scope than the domain of constitutional liberty pertaining to noncommercial expression.[539] But the fact that the Court deems expression of certain kinds to be within the ambit of FSP, despite "its subordinate position in the scale of First Amendment values," nevertheless leads to an inflation or watering-up of the extent of the constitutional protection that the Court's doctrine allows. Consider, for example, private casino gambling. Some commercial advertising of such enterprises should be constitutionally protected in jurisdictions where the same is lawful. But the Court unanimously ruled in *Greater New Orleans Broadcasting Association* v. *United States*[540] that a federal statute that bans radio and television advertising of private casino gambling in states where such activity is lawful violates the First Amendment. This, in my view, is an unfortunate holding since widespread commercial speech promoting casino gambling is something that informed reasonable people might believe should not be legally permitted in all the forms and channels of public communication. Assuming that such gambling with some limited advertising should not be outlawed although strictly regulated, many people could reasonably hold that it is not to the public good that casino gambling should be promiscuously promoted via 'commercial speech.' Similarly, because the Court has canonized purely commercial expression and nonobscene pornography (as defined according to contemporary, highly-permissive judicial standards) as potentially within the ambit of 'First Amendment' protection, it is quite evident how difficult it is for the Court to credibly assert that it "do[es] not sit as a super-legislature to determine the wisdom, need, and propriety of laws that touch economic problems, business affairs, or social conditions.'"[541] Unfortunately, the Court's bringing so-called commercial speech and nonobscene pornography within the ambit of the 'First Amendment' undermines its high value in the constitutional order.

Unlike FSP-VC, the theory of the FLVC takes into account, in a commonsensible way, that there is no fundamental right of free persons as such to propagate some pernicious doctrines, such as the more extreme forms of racialist propaganda, in all appropriate forms or channels of public communication. The FLVC, however, affirms that there is a fundamental right to freely engage in such propaganda in some but not all forms or channels of public communication. For the purpose of determining the scope and limits of FLVC, every free person must be presumed to be capable of engaging in rational inquiry. The FLVC is a constitutional privilege of the wise, the unwise, and (to borrow John Stuart Mill's bemusing term) the otherwise. So there cannot be any secular counterpart of an ecclesiastical index of forbidden books and provisions in canon law requiring permission to read writings subversive of the true religion (whatever that may be) and good morals. Nevertheless, in determining what are those appropriate forms and channels of public communication that fall within the ambit of FLVC, the State is entitled to take into account (absent relevant constitutional provisions such as the First Amendment) that there are in fact many free persons who are habitually unwise or otherwise because of intellectual, emotional, or moral immaturity. Since we are concerned with a fundamental right proximately grounded upon the dignity of free persons as such, the determination of what forms and channels of public communication are within the ambit of FRVC will not be based upon arguments as to why FSP-VC should not be abridged upon public policy grounds.

The wise counsel of Ernst Freund, with respect to obscene or sexually indecent expression, may usefully be generalized to all expressional content fairly within the ambit of FRVC that, in principle, could be subject to repression in some but not all forms or channels of public communication. To paraphrase Freund: "The interest of public decency [or any other interest subject to the police power] demands that even in the legitimate pursuit of truth [and literature] the [forms and] channels selected for the spreading of truth [or error] [or of the literary arts] be those least harmful to the community[.]"[542] Again to paraphrase Freund: "Custom is the best criterion [of what are the most appropriate forms and channels of communication for such expressional content that is potentially subject to repression in some but not all forms and channels of communication] and in the absence of positive enactment established conventions should be regarded as part of the law."[543]

To correctly understand the scope of the protection afforded FSP by a constitutional provision prohibiting all abridgments of that right, let us consider the following scenario. Let us suppose that Congress enacts a statute that among other things generally (but not exceptionlessly) prohibits the solicited or unsolicited mailing (including via the internet) of propaganda promoting racialist doctrines and public policies—such as advocacy of a constitutional amendment establishing white supremacy and authorizing the enactment of racially discriminatory statutes.[544] Rational people of good will necessarily would condemn the willful promotion of racialist doctrines and public policies as grossly immoral. But would our hypothetical statute abridge FSP-VC? I am sure it would. And this is also the doctrine of the Court. Consider another scenario. Suppose a state statute generally (but not exceptionlessly) prohibits the practice of going house-to-house to deliver racialist propaganda to occupants of private residences or to leave such propaganda on the premises of the residences—whether or not the occupant had previously solicited delivery by the distributing agent but where the occupant has failed to post a conspicuous notice barring solicitations and the delivery or depositing of unsolicited matter. Again, this statute would violate the constitutional ban on abridgments of FSP-VC.

But would either hypothetical statute violate the FLVC? In my opinion, the mailing or delivery of the racialist verbal propaganda is within the scope of FLVC if it had been solicited or otherwise consented to by an adult recipient prior to the attempted mailing or delivery of the matter to the recipient. But the FLVC would not be violated were the State to require that verbal racialist matter be sealed or otherwise securely wrapped by the distributing agent against casual perusal by other persons prior to delivery by the postal service or a common carrier to the recipient or addressee.

Now to the extent that some components of the FLVC are identical to those of FSP-VC, the FLVC's potency is to that extent masked and fails to disclose that it has its own bite. However, it is possible for the FLVC to include as a component the right to freely advocate **T** in some particular but not all appropriate forms and channels of communication, but the FSP-VC lacks as a component the right to freely advocate **T** in all appropriate forms and channels of communication. Accordingly, there are some problem areas pertaining to public communication issues, which might arguably be more satisfactorily resolved if we bear in mind that there are some important fundamental liberty rights pertaining to expression that fall within the ambit of the due process clause but not FSP.

Let us quickly consider textual pornography—unaccompanied by pictorial matter deemed patently indecent were it to be displayed to minors or unconsenting adults. And let us stipulate, if only for argument's sake, that the textual pornography is text that is sexually explicit and patently offensive to decency and morality were it willfully exhibited or distributed to unconsenting adults or to minors without parental consent, and whether or not such text has serious value.[545] Suppose for argument's sake that the mailing or delivery to consenting adults by common carrier of a solicited, suitably wrapped book or other writing containing such pornographic textual matter, where the provider takes reasonable care to substantially minimize the incidence of delivery to minors, should be constitutionally protected by the due process clause. Such textually pornographic books might either be that notorious eighteenth-century pornographic classic, John Cleland's *Memoirs of a Woman of Pleasure* (commonly known as *Fanny Hill*)[546]— which arguably has some literary and historic value although it is pervasively sexually explicit; or it could be (let us assume) pure literary trash such as the the book *Suite 69*, which "has a plain cover and contains no pictures ... [and] is made up entirely of repetitive descriptions of physical, sexual conduct, 'clinically' explicit and offensive to the point of being nauseous; there is only the most tenuous 'plot.' Almost every conceivable variety of sexual contact, homosexual and heterosexual, is described. Whether one samples every 5th, 10th, or 20th page, beginning at any point or page at random, the content is unvarying."[547] In my opinion, whether or not *Fanny Hill* and *Suite 69* are deemed to have serious value, the publication of neither book falls within the ambit of FSP-VC since such textual pornography is essentially viewpoint neutral. And my reason for saying neither book falls within the ambit of FSP-VC is that I do not believe that there should be a constitutional right to publish these writings in all appropriate forms and channels of public communication. However, I affirm that the mailing or sending by common carrier of textually pornographic writings (whether with or without serious value) to consenting adults where reasonable care is taken to avoid delivery to, or acquisition by, minors should be deemed a component of the FLVC rather than of FSP-VC. Given the scope of the FLVC, any reasonable regulation of the publication of textual pornography in order to prevent distribution or minimize access to minors of such matter in some forms or channels of communication must not unduly limit the number of remaining forms or channels of communication available for consenting adults. In my opinion, there are overriding reasons why consenting adults should be constitutionally entitled to acquire textually pornographic writings where reasonable care is taken by the provider to prevent or substantially minimize the delivery or access of such writings to minors or unconsenting adults without having the liberty interest in question subject to judges and juries determining whether or not a textually pornographic writing is with or without any redeeming social value, or is with or without serious literary, artistic, political, or scientific value.[548]

I maintain that whatever substantive rights there are to publish pictorial pornography, whether hard or soft core (and even such with serious value), these rights are not per se components of FSP but rather derivative in nature, as in the case of a proscribing statute that is not viewpoint neutral. Any constitutional substantive rights to publish pictorial pornography obtain by virtue of the due process clause. To be sure, the constitutionally permissible power of the State to regulate the publication of pictorial pornography is much more broad than that allowable with respect to textual pornography. But this book is not the place to discuss in detail what should be the scope and limits of the constitutional power to regulate pictorial pornography consistent with the substantive aspects of the due process clause. Similarly, I do not discuss similar issues with respect to pictorial matter depicting or representing violence, which considered in its context, substantially offends the standard of decency of reasonable men and women were the matter so published as to be viewed by minors or unconsenting adults. But here too I would hold that the constitutional power to regulate the publication of such matter is rather broad but not unlimited. And I fully agree that just because a legislature is constitutionally empowered to enact laws that forbids such-and-such, it does not then follow that it would be wise or prudent for it to do so.

It would be remiss of me to fail to express my dismay as to how terribly the Court has fashioned its *First Amendment* jurisprudence in other ways. Contrary to the current official doctrine, I hold that FSP does not encompass live or visually transmitted live or recorded theatrical or other artistic performances and exhibitions such as plays and drama, operas, ballets, dances, musical comedies or shows, and the like. But, it should be recalled, the FSP encompasses motion picture films or other visually recorded or transmitted publications of debates, speeches, talks, sermons, conversations, and the like.[549] On the other hand, the specific right of the due process clause includes fundamental substantive rights pertaining to artistic performances and exhibitions consistent with the reasonable exercise of the police power in the interest of public peace and good order, public morals and decency, and public health and safety—but consistent with the fundamental principles of the republican and secular form of government for the United States and the states. Otherwise, the legislation would not be rationally related to a legitimate governmental interest. Moreover, political freedom, a constitutional privilege of the American people, precludes the exercise of the power of the State to regulate artistic performances and exhibitions for political or partisan purposes, such as to prevent or hinder the defamation of the government, its officers, and allied and supporting special interests. Again, to say that the State has the constitutional power to enact laws that prohibit such-and-such expression or communication does not mean that it would be to the public good to enact any such laws. Although I think that the constitutional power to regulate artistic performances and exhibitions is much broader than is allowed according to present doctrine, the state of public opinion is such (and is likely to remain so for the reasonably indefinite future) that the Congress and the states should target only the more egregiously offensive publications, performances, productions, or exhibitions that are seen as clearly within the constitutionally permissible scope of their legislative powers and only enact laws that is supported by a broad consensus of public opinion that cuts across partisan lines.

There are so many more scenarios concerning fundamental rights of free persons other than the FLVC—including but not limited to liberty-interests pertaining to religion, education, travel, migration, and to the so-called *right to privacy* interests relating to highly controversial issues concerning procreation, abortion, contraception, same-sex marriage, divorce, civil unions or domestic partnerships, cohabitation, consensual sexual conduct, and so on. But I need not do so in this book, having chosen to discuss substantive rights concerning racial discrimination, same-sex intercourse statutes, and the FLVC, so that the reader better understands my philosophy concerning how the essential fundamental rights of free persons are to be identified.

What I have done in this part of my book is to expound in general outline a special theory of the fundamental rights of free persons as such that necessarily belong to them as components of the specific right of the due process clause. Thus, the fundamental rights, privileges, and immunities of free persons as such are among the constitutional rights of the American people. In the exposition of what are the components of the fundamental rights, privileges and immunities of free persons as such, it is all-important for the Court to constantly adhere to the principle that it is not a super-legislature that reviews the wisdom, expediency, or prudence of ordinary legislation to which only the rational basis test applies. In any event, the constitutional text should not be manipulated by the Court to establish as constitutional law public policy proposals that should have been but are very unlikely ever to be legislatively enacted.

My theory of fundamental substantive rights is ultimately rooted in the premise that the adoption of the Thirteenth Amendment not only established universal civil freedom throughout the United States but that it also informed or infused the Fifth Amendment due process clause with the principle that all free persons as such have essential natural rights proximately based upon their human dignity as rational, moral, and social beings. These essential natural rights, together with judicially noticeable facts about humans and human societies in any well-ordered civil society, considered together with deeply rooted principles of liberty and justice concerning what should be the essential badges and incidents of free persons as such in this country, entail complementary fundamental rights, liberties, and immunities of free persons as such. Thus, for example, the essential natural right of free persons to not only believe but to know or reasonably believe the truth in matters of general interest together with the fact that there must be some particular forms and channels of public communication in which free and rational inquiry can take place in any well ordered society, regardless of the form of government, entails a complementary fundamental liberty interest that should be constitutionally protected. Another example I have stressed is that the essential natural right of free persons as such to flourish individually and in society requires that they be treated as presumptively entitled to self-respect and the respect of others based upon their own personal qualities. The fact is that treating people as belonging to an inferior and degraded case or quasi-caste because of their race, color, ethnicity, gender, or birth status seriously damages the prospects for the realization of that particular natural right. Hence, there is a complementary fundamental liberty-from interest that should be constitutionally protected.

To juridically treat free persons as such in harmony with their human dignity requires that there must be some constitutionally secured domains or zones of liberty and privacy in which they may act upon their own judgment—their own initiative and responsibility. The fundamental liberties and immunities of free persons as such are posited by constitutional law in response to the demand of all rational men and women of good will: I am a human being; therefore, treat me as a human being. And the essential fundamental liberties and immunities of free persons are among the components of the specific right of each due process clause. These liberties and immunities constitute a set, which can be considered as the complement of that set of rights denoted by the privileges or immunities clause of the Fourteenth Amendment. And the constitutional privileges and immunities of American citizens are predicated upon an strong notion of national citizenship that is paramount, supreme, and superior— such that every free American citizen might rightfully claim the benefit of these rights by virtue of their national citizenship somewhat in the same way as the Apostle Paul claimed the benefits to which he was entitled by virtue of his Roman citizenship when threatened with the scourge though not yet condemned.[550] Alas! The exalted notion of national citizenship, before the reconstruction amendments, coexisted with the institution of African slavery, just as the exalted notion of Roman citizenship coexisted with the institution of slavery. What is now called for is that any theory adhering to a strong notion of national citizenship must be compatible with a strong notion of essential natural rights common to all humanity.

Part IV

Chapter A. The Textualist Probability of the Theory

Professor Amar rightfully emphasizes the importance of a proper textual analysis of the Bill of Rights and the Fourteenth Amendment. He so well puts it: "[H]ere ... lies perhaps the strongest reason for offering an account of the Bill of Rights that takes text seriously. The American people—outside courtrooms, outside law offices—confront, and lay claim to, the Bill of Rights as a text. Its grand phrases ... define a basic vocabulary of liberty for ordinary citizens."[551] Amar contends: "The easy case for (nonmechanical) incorporation, then, rests on the plain meaning of the words of section

[1 of the Fourteenth Amendment] circa 1866."[552] On the contrary, the plain meaning of section 1, interpreted intertextually with other provisions of the Constitution, makes a patently much better case for this book's theory of selective incorporation of the Bill of Rights by the privileges or immunities clause.

First, the theory of this book more satisfactorily takes into account and in an integrated way: (a) the presence of the citizenship clause; (b) the tracking or cloning of the First Amendment by the privileges or immunities clause; (c) the copresence of the due process clauses in the Bill of Rights and section 1 of the Fourteenth Amendment; (d) the absence in section 1 of any other common specific right from amendments I–VIII; (e) the presence of an equal protection clause in section 1 the Fourteenth Amendment but its absence in the Bill of Rights; and (f) the failure of the Fourteenth Amendment to expressly apply the prohibitions of the establishment clause to the states. The result is that the Fourteenth Amendment due process clause is not superfluous. But then neither is the privileges or immunities clause. Each provision has therefore an "independent bite."[553]

Second, the theory of this book fits and best justifies the lower-level doctrines of the United States Supreme Court in cases involving claims of violations of constitutional rights secured against abridgments by the states. Thus, the privileges or immunities clause fully protects First Amendment freedoms, and the freedom and freedom-from rights entailed by the establishment clause, against abridgments by the states. The theory of this book also takes into account the doctrine that some other rights specified in the Bill of Rights are components of the specific right of the Fourteenth Amendment due process clause. We are not, therefore, writing on a clean slate. But this may not be so radical in effect because the Court in a de facto way has already ruled, due to shifting pluralities, such that some supposedly incorporated specific rights have more components with respect to the United States than with respect to the states.[554]

Third, the theory of this book rejects the notion that the Fourteenth Amendment incorporates any prohibitions constitutive of the establishment clause other than freedom and freedom-from rights entailed by the prohibitions of that provision—not counting those sounding in federal-state relations. The entailed freedom-rights are components of religious freedom, a constitutional privilege of the American people; the entailed freedom-from rights collectively constitute a constitutional immunity. If the establishment clause entails a freedom from establishment as a right of the people, the right in question is a collective right and, therefore, cannot be either incorporated by the privileges or immunities clause or be a component of the specific right of the due process clause.

Fourth, the theory of this book explains why exemptions from racial and similar kinds of invidious discrimination are equally secured against the United States and the states. This is first done by ultimately grounding these immunities upon the citizenship clause being declaratory of the antecedent paramountcy and superiority of national citizenship; which citizenship is incompatible with an inferior and degraded legal status based upon a caste or similar principle (such as race, color, or gender). The theory of this article fully takes into account that the adoption of the citizenship clause, not only overturned the holding of *Dred Scott* that free, native-born blacks were not (and were incapable of being) American citizens, but that it also implicitly confirms that such incapacity of African Americans for national citizenship obtained only because of their inferior and degraded legal status based upon their race or color. Thus, by an inverse operation due to the overturning of *Dred Scott*, the constitutional extension of national citizenship to African Americans immediately liberated them as to the United States, and mediately by the privileges or immunities clause as to the several states, from all the badges and incidents of an inferior and degraded legal status based upon race or color with respect to civil and cognate rights.

Fifth, as I argue in Chapter D of Part I, the theory of this book satisfactorily resolves any difficulty presented by the Second Amendment right to keep and bear arms. This individual civil right is not a freedom; but it is a rather a conditional liberty right since the right in question is one where the right holder is not prohibited from keeping and bearing suitable arms in the absence of a constitutionally possible legal obligation to do so at his own expense. The SAR is not, by the terms of the Second Amenment, necessary to the security of a free state. Rather, the ban on any infringement of the SAR is due to the stipulation that a well-regulated militia is necessary to the security of a free state.

Sixth, the theory of the book completely takes into account the essential equivalence of the Fifth and Fourteenth Amendments' due process clauses. The latter clause is not posited with the preposterous function of incorporating some rights specified in the Bill of Rights that are not already reasonably considered upon independent grounds as components of the specific right of the Fifth Amendment due process clause. Moreover, the copresence of a due process clause in the Bill of Rights and in section 1 of the Fourteenth Amendment signals that the amendment does not incorporate all rights specified in the Bill of Rights. The copresence of the term "person" in both due process clauses, and of "persons" in the citizenship clause, compels the conclusion that a *person* according to all three clauses denotes natural persons whether or not American citizens— thereby negating the alleged doctrine of *Dred Scott* that the specific rights of the Bill of Rights are predicable of only American citizens.

Seventh, the theory of this book offers a satisfactory explanation of whatever similarities it superficially has with the comity clause, and why the descriptive term of the privileges or immunities clause (i.e., "the privileges or immunities of citizens of the United States") is one of description and not of limitation. Although the comity clause has an operative term specifying who are exclusively its beneficiaries (i.e., "the Citizens of each State"), the privileges or immunities clause does not. However, the descriptive term of the latter clause is one of description only since we take it as given that each specific right of the Bill of Rights is very appropriately called a right (in a general sense) of American citizens, whether or not some persons other than American citizens are per se entitled to its benefits. This analytical argument is confirmed by the discovery that the true ancestral line of the descriptive term of the privileges or immunities clause is found in a series of federal treaties and statutes that use, in somewhat varying order, the three terms "rights," "privileges" (or "advantages"), and "immunities," and that refer to them as being those "of citizens of the United States." It was generally understood, that the phrase "rights, privileges [or "advantages"], and immunities of citizens of the United States" denotes, inter alia, the individual rights specified in the Bill of Rights.[555] Thus the presence of the term "rights" in the various relevant federal statutes and treaties and its absence in the privileges or immunities clause confirms the hypothesis that not all rights, in the generic sense, specified in the Bill of Rights are rights in a limited sense. Further confirmation is found in comparing how rights secured by the First Amendment (other than that some entailed by the establishment clause) are freedoms, whereas those in the other provisions of the Bill of Rights are not. Finally, although the descriptive term of the privileges or immunities clause is one of description only, it is nevertheless significant that there is a rough fit between those specific rights that are incorporated by the privileges or immunities clause and those explicit rights to which either only American citizens are per se constitutionally entitled or those to which American citizens are necessarily per se entitled but not all noncitizens—all other things being equal.

Eighth, the theory of this book takes into account the radical change in the fundamental law of the land whereby, with the adoption of the Thirteenth Amendment in 1865 not only was slavery and involuntary servitude (save as due punishment for crime) abolished but that universal civil freedom was thereby established throughout the United States. Instantly, the specific right of the Fifth Amendment due process clause was informed with the principle that it fully protects all the fundamental rights, privileges, and immunities of free persons as such because all persons are born (to be) free and equal, and to enjoy the essential natural rights of such persons as augmented and realized in the deeply rooted prescriptive rights of the American people that are the badges and incidents of their civil freedom. All free persons as such have basic substantive rights that are proximately grounded in their dignity as rational, moral, and social beings, which rights are components of the specific right of the due process clause. With the adoption of the Fourteenth Amendment in 1868, all free persons are protected by that amendment's due process clause with respect to exactly the same substantive and procedural rights that are protected by the Fifth Amendment due process clause. The equal protection clause not only requires that states enact laws that provide equal protection he laws with respect to the life, liberty, and property of each person subject to their jurisdiction. The clause also requires the states to enforce such laws. The equal protection clause may have other functions that we need not address in this book.

Ninth, the general theory of this book is rather open-textured in the sense that it is textually compatible with several different special theories of each constitutional right of the American people. I have expressed several opinions, for example, about freedom of speech and the press with respect to verbal communication and its analog, the fundamental liberty of verbal communication. Nevertheless, the general theory of this book is not formally inconsistent with adhering to the Court's special theory of FSP and its rejection of a fundamental right pertaining to verbal communication considered independently of the First Amendment. However, it would be better were the specific right of the due process clause construed so as to include, independently of the First Amendment freedoms, several fundamental rights pertaining to expression among its components. Thus the FSP need no longer be inflated or deflated in order to accommodate all public expression or communication that are deemed worthy of constitutional protection greater than that provided by the rational basis test. Hence, an advantage of the general theory of this book is that it allows but does not require developments in constitutional doctrine that are virtually impossible given the Court's current theory of fundamental rights.

Chapter B. The Nontextualist Probability of the Theory

The theory of this book is superior for nontextualistic reasons to the competing theories assigning the privileges or immunities clause with the function of a total incorporation of the specific rights in the Bill of Rights, or with the refined incorporation model of Professor Amar; as well as the current official theory of selective incorporation by the Fourteenth Amendment due process clause. There appears to be no substantial evidence that there was any original understanding by some founders of the Fourteenth Amendment that its due-process clause incorporates any other right specified in the Bill of Rights, besides those that upon independent grounds are already considered as being included as components of the specific right of the Fifth Amendment due process clause. On the other hand, there is substantial evidence of an original understanding among the founders that at least some specific rights of the Bill of Rights were incorporated by the privileges or immunities clause.[556]

Amar asks: "Is there anything in the legislative history of these words that contradicts this straightforward reading?"—that is, that the privileges or immunities clause incorporates all the individual rights specified in the Bill of Rights. He tersely answers, "On the contrary."[557] He then proceeds to a review of the evidences in support of his claim. Alas! There were several original understandings among those who participated in the founding (i.e., the framing *and* ratification) of the Fourteenth Amendment. And that is what is so exasperating!

Evidence that some founders of the Fourteenth Amendment adhered to a total-incorporation-by-the-privileges-or-immunities-clause-theory is not to be disregarded simply because it is concluded that the no total-incorporation theory should not be adopted by the Court. This conclusion fails because such founders who had accepted one or another version of it gave woefully insufficient consideration to the copresence of a due process clause in the Fifth and Fourteenth Amendments, and that the term "person" denotes persons whether or not American citizens. Had these founders been confronted with arguments similar to those presented in favor of the theory of this article, it is much more probable than not that they would have accepted a theory of selective incorporation as a fall-back position, rather than concluding that no specific right in the Bill of Rights is incorporated by the privileges or immunities clause. Their theme song would not have been "All or nothing at all."

Even Amar himself acknowledges that the Republicans in Thirty-eighth and Thirty-ninth Congresses, "invoked speech, press, petition, and assembly rights over and over—more frequently than any other right, with the possible exception of due process."[558] Amar candidly acknowledges: "[P]artisanship impoverished deliberation. Many of the key discussions in Washington 'were carried on not in the legal Senate of the United States, but in a party meeting' from which Democrats were excluded, And during the ratification debates, many Republicans again kept silent in public deliberations, content that they had the votes to pass the amendment and fearful that any statement might give Democrats political ammunition."[559] Thus, we are all now obliged to undertake what was so inadequately done during the founding of the Fourteenth Amendment. Perhaps, we may be able to transcend partisanship. The bottom line is that we should not be greedy, in the process of resurrecting the privileges or immunities clause, by extending incorporation to any but the most promising candidates.

Professor Curtis has justly observed, "In a real sense one can never prove that the amendment was designed to apply the Bill of Rights to the states. One can simply take the hypothesis and see how well it fits the evidence. The hypothesis [of total incorporation of individual rights by the privileges or immunities Clause] fits the evidence very well indeed."[560] Now I for one would not deny that this hypothesis fits some evidence. What I urge is that the theory of this book best fits the evidence and is more textually plausible. It does not overload the Fourteenth Amendment due process clause with the burden of incorporating First Amendment freedoms, when textually it makes more sense that the privileges or immunities clause has that function. It makes it possible for the substantive aspects of the due process clauses to survive—albeit with a more humble but yet honorable role to play on the stage of constitutional law.

Professor Amar shares in the sentiment that it is preposterous for the Court to persist in holding that the due process clause of the Fourteenth Amendment is the vehicle of selective incorporation of the Bill of Rights and especially of the First Amendment freedoms. One very good practical reason for resurrecting the privileges or immunities clause is the widespread opinion that the credibility of the Constitution as our fundamental charter of rights and liberties is undermined by judicial doctrines that are perceived, or are capable of being perceived, by the ordinary citizen as nonsense-upon-stilts.

The Court's theory as to how the Fourteenth Amendment due process clause incorporates some but not all of the rights specified in the Bill of Rights and as to how both due process clauses protect unenumerated fundamental rights is full of anomalies and mysteries. Indeed, it strikingly resembles the astronomical theory of Claudius Ptolemy (circa AD 85–165), which postulated that the Earth was the center of what is now known as the solar system and which required numerous epicycles and deferents to save the appearances. As I. Bernard Cohen told the story:[561]

> It is said that Alfonso X, King of León and Castile, called Alfonso the Wise, who sponsored a famous set of astronomical tables in the thirteenth century, could not believe the system of the universe to be that intricate. When first taught the Ptolemaic system, he commented, according to legend: "If the Lord Almighty had consulted me before embarking upon the creation, I should have recommended something simpler."

It is quite understandable why the process of constitutional interpretation tends to have a life of its own due to the quirks and accidents of history. The Court, having assigned the privileges or immunities clause to a secular counterpart of Limbo, eventually turned to the Fourteenth Amendment due process clause as the vehicle of providing substantive protection for First Amendment and other freedoms in the American republic. It could hardly have avoided doing so, having given such a broad sweep to the *liberty of contract* during its hegemony in the constitutional order.[562] The Court has since downgraded the hoary *liberty of contract* to very manageable (if not almost vanishing) limits, but it has also developed its particular theory of selective incorporation to fully safeguard First Amendment freedoms with respect to the states. Having done so, it could hardly fail to accord the same measure of protection to the other rights specified in the Bill of Rights. Stepping back, however, it is impossible not to regard the whole system as looking somewhat childish—so childish, that the time has come for the Court to "put away childish things."[563] We may hope with some confidence that some day the Court will re-evaluate its general theory of constitutional rights and replace it with one more credible—one that restores the privileges or immunities clause to its rightful place in our constitutional order.[564] Thus, the privileges or immunities clause would have rightly imputed to it a very important function such that it can no longer be said: "[I]t was a vain and idle enactment, which accomplished nothing, and most unnecessarily excited Congress and the people on its passage."[565]

There was another major way in which the judicial construction of the Fourteenth Amendment was seriously flawed. The Court neutered the citizenship and privileges or immunities clause in the *Slaughter-House Cases,* and deprived it of its potency to endow African Americans with a national citizenship of a kind incompatible with an inferior and degraded caste status based upon race and color. The Court looked upon the equal protection clause as being the instrument to secure equality of persons of color with their white compatriots with respect to civil rights. But for many years, the Court deceived itself with the separate-but-equal doctrine that in practice very imperfectly secured some civil rights for nonwhite Americans.[566] I look upon the independence of the judiciary and the principle of judicial review as indispensible elements in our constitutional order. Nevertheless, the wise counsel of the great Swedish statesman, Axel Oxenstierna (1583–1654) to his son ("Behold, my son, with how little wisdom the world is governed"[567]) unfortunately appears to apply just as frequently to justices and judges as to those who hold political office in the executive and legislative branches of government. Fortunately, the Court, since its decision in *Brown* v. *Board of Education* in 1954, has endeavored to develop constitutional law in such a way as to secure the right to racial equality and vindicate other constitutional rights of the American people.

Epilogue

Despite many false steps and setbacks, the evolution of American constitutional law has more recently progressed in a way such that the Court may now take the next step and explicitly adopt a more intellectually satisfactory general theory of the constitutional rights, privileges, and immunities of the American people—including the fundamental rights, privileges, and immunities of free persons as such in every place subject to the jurisdiction of the United States. This would not have been possible save as the eventual outcome of the Civil War, which preserved the Union; as well as wars since then in which American citizens, whether native-born or naturalized, and resident aliens, of whatever place of origin, have honorably and often courageously served in the armed forces with all too many of these men and women losing life or limb in doing so. Here, one cannot pass without mention those many members of the armed forces who were persons of color while the policy of segregation continued in full force until President Harry S. Truman boldly initiated its termination by executive order in 1948. Nor would the eventual laudable outcome of the Bill of Rights and the reconstruction amendments as a charter of our rights and liberties have been possible without the sacrifice of so many American men and women of every race and color, of every faith or no faith, and of every place of origin—Americans who toiled from time to time at their peril and who sometimes suffered the loss of their lives during the long struggles for the vindication of the new birth of freedom for all the American people.

I cannot conclude without special mention of President Abraham Lincoln, the Great Emancipator, and Dr. Martin Luther King, Jr. In his famous "I Have a Dream" speech, delivered on August 28, 1963 at the Lincoln Memorial in Washington, DC, Dr. King firmly and eloquently insisted that his dream be peacefully realized. So, at last, his dream has been dramatically realized in our time with the election of Senator Barack Obama as President of the United States of America. Were he with us today, how Dr. King would have joyfully exclaimed: "Free at last! Free at last! Thank God Almighty, we are free at last!"

So to thee, great festival of the past, and to thee, blood of Sacrifice, be praise, honor, and glory through all the ages[568]

November 5, 2008

Boulder, Colorado

218

Endnotes to Parts I–IV

Note references have been omitted in virtually all quoted matter. Emphasis in quoted matter is in the original unless otherwise noted. Bracketed matter, unless otherwise indicated, has been supplied by me.

1. *Barron* v. *Baltimore*, 32 U.S. (7 Pet.) 243 (1833); *Livingston* v. *Moore*, 32 U.S. (7 Pet.) 649 (1833); *Permoli* v. *New Orleans*, 44 U.S. (3 How.) 589 (1845). (Opinions of the United States Supreme Court are conveniently available online at http://supreme.justia.com/us/.) The Supreme Court is unquestionably correct on this issue. Thus, for example, see and compare sections 9 and 10 of article I of the Constitution, which provide, respectively, that "No Bill of Attainder or ex post facto Law shall be passed" and "No State shall ... pass any Bill of Attainder, ex post facto Law ..." The constitutional limitations in section 9 pertain to Congress; the constitutional limitations in section 10 pertain to the states.

2. Relevant constitutional provisions are set forth in the Appendix.

3. For my critique of the Court's selective incorporation theory, as well as some other total or selective incorporation models, see my article, "The Rights, Privileges, and Immunities of the American People: A Disjunctive Theory of Selective Incorporation of the Bill of Rights," 7 Whittier L. Rev. 765 (1985) (hereinafter Guminski). Corrigenda to my article are set forth below in the Addendum to the Select Bibliography with Endnote Citations.

4. The *Slaughter-House Cases*, 83 U.S. (16 Wall.) 36, 79 (1873): more broadly stated as those rights "which owe their existence to the Federal Government, its National character, its Constitution, or its laws"; *Maxwell* v. *Dow*, 176 U.S. 581, 593–94 (1900); *Twining* v. *New Jersey*, 211 U.S. 78, 97 (1908). The *Twining* Court declared that the privileges or immunities clause "[does] not forbid the states to abridge the personal rights enumerated in the first eight amendments, because these rights were not within the meaning of the clause 'privileges and immunities of citizens of the United States.'" 211 U.S. at 99.

5. See *Duncan* v. *Louisiana*, 391 U.S. 145, 148–49 (1968). It needs to be emphasized that a specific right is standardly said to be incorporated once it has been decided that the same constitutional standards equally apply to the United States and to the states with respect to that right. *Malloy* v. *Hogan,* 378 U.S. 1, 10 (1964); *Benton* v. *Maryland*, 395 U.S. 784, 794–95 (1969).

6. *Powell* v. *Alabama*, 287 U.S. 45, 67 (1932) (quoting *Hebert* v. *Louisiana*, 272 U.S. 312, 316 [1926]).

7. *Everson* v. *Board of Education*, 330 U.S. 1 (1947) (no establishment); *Cantwell* v. *Connecticut*, 310 U.S. 296 (1940) (free exercise);

Gitlow v. *New York*, 268 U.S. 652 (1925) and *Grosjean* v. *American Press Co.*, 297 U.S. 233 (1936) (free speech and free press); *DeJonge* v. *Oregon*, 299 U.S. 353 (1937) (free assembly); *Edwards* v. *South Carolina*, 372 U.S. 229, 235 (1963) (dictum as to right to petition considered separately).

8. *Mapp* v. *Ohio*, 367 U.S. 643 (1961); *Ker* v. *California*, 374 U.S. 23 (1963) (searches and seizures).

9. *Benton* v. *Maryland*, 395 U.S. 784 (1969) (double jeopardy); *Malloy* v. *Hogan*, 378 U.S. 1 (1964) (self-incrimination); *Chicago, Burglingon & Quincy Railroad Co.* v. *Chicago*, 166 U.S. 226 (1897) (just compensation).

10. *Klopfer* v. *North Carolina*, 386 U.S. 213 (1967) (speedy trial); *In re Oliver*, 333 U.S. 257 (1948) (public trial); *Duncan* v. *Louisiana*, 391 U.S. 145 (1968) (criminal jury trial); *Irvin* v. *Dowd*, 366 U.S. 717 (1961) (impartial jury); *Cole* v. *Arkansas*, 333 U.S. 196 (1948 (notice of charges); *Pointer* v. *Texas*, 380 U.S. 400 (1965) (confrontation); *Washington* v. *Texas*, 388 U.S. 14 (1967) (compulsory process); *Gideon* v. *Wainwright*, 372 U.S. 335 (1963) (right to counsel).

11. *Robinson* v. *California*, 370 U.S. 660 (1962) (cruel and unusual punishment); The Court has not squarely ruled that the excessive fines and bail rights apply to the states, but it would be surprising if it did not do so. (See dicta in *Schlib* v. *Kuebel*, 404 U.S. 357, 365 (1971) (excessive bail); *Browning-Ferris* v. *Kelco Disposal*, 492 U.S. 257, 262–63 (1989) (excessive fines)).

12. *Hurtado* v. *California*, 110 U.S. 516 (1884).

13. *Walker* v. *Sauvinet*, 92 U.S. 90 (1876).

14. See dictum in *Griswold* v. *Connecticut*, 381 U.S. 479, 484 (1965), which indicates that the specific right of the Third Amendment, prohibiting the quartering of soldiers, is an incorporated right. As Justice Miller wrote, "This amendment seems to have been thought necessary. It does not appear to have been the subject of judicial exposition; and it is so thoroughly in accord with all our ideas, that further comment is unnecessary." Samuel F. Miller, *Lectures on the Constitution of the United States* (1893), 646.

15. (New Haven: Yale University Press, 1998) (hereafter AMAR). In his more recently published book, *America's Constitution: A Biography* (New York: Random House, 2006) (hereafter Amar (2006), Amar discusses the reconstruction amendments in chapter 10 (349–401). In note* on page 386, in the section headed "'No State shall'" he remarks: "For much more discussion and documentation of the ideas summarized over the next several pages, the interested reader may wish to consult my earlier book, *The Bill of Rights: Creation and Reconstruction*, especially Chapters 7–12."

16.   AMAR, xiv–xv, 217–23. No constitutional provision creates, grants, or secures political rights (i.e., rights that pertain to the participation in the establishment or administration of government). The right to vote however "preservative of other basic civil and political rights" (*Reynolds v. Sims,* 377 U.S. 533, 562 (1964) *"per se,* is not a constitutionally protected right." (*San Antonio School District* v. *Rodriquez,* 411 U.S. 1, 35n78 (1973). However, the Constitution expressly protects the right to vote of American citizens from denial or abridgment by the United States or by any State on account of race, color, or previous condition of servitude (amend. XV), gender (amend. XIX), poll tax as to "any primary or other election for President or Vice President, for electors of President or Vice President, or for Senator or Representative in Congress" (amend. XXIV), or age as to those 18 years or older (amend. XXVI). The Supreme Court, however, has also construed the equal protection clause (and the equal-protection component of the Fifth Amendment due process clause) as possessing antidiscriminatory functions with respect to political rights. See *Strauder* v. *West Virginia,* 100 U.S. 303, 310 (1880) (jury service); *Harper* v. *Virginia State Board of Elections,* 383 U.S. 663 (1966) (poll tax). The reapportionment cases (i.e., *Baker* v. *Carr,* 369 U.S. 186 (1962), *Reynolds* v. *Sims,* 377 U.S. 533 (1964), and their progeny) are also other instances of the Court's use of the equal protection clause with respect to political rights. However, the Court has declared in *San Antonio School District* v. *Rodriquez,* 411 U.S. at 33: "It is not the province of the Court to create substantive constitutional rights in the name of guaranteeing equal protection of the laws." Strictly speaking, the Court should have used the words "constitutional freedoms or freedom-from rights" in lieu of "substantive constitutional rights" since a freedom-from right is a substantive right.

17.   AMAR, 221. I similarly maintained in my article that "neither the [F]ourteenth [A]mendment privileges or immunities clause nor its due process clause creates, grants or secures political rights, i.e., rights which pertain in the participation in the establishment or administration of government, such as the right to vote or hold public office." Guminski (supra note 3), at 816n171.

18.   AMAR, 174–75, 179–80.

19.   See his *No State Shall Abridge: The Fourteenth Amendment And The Bill Of Rights* (Durham, Duke University Press, 1986); "Resurrecting the Privileges or Immunities Clause and Revising the Slaughter-House Cases Without Exhuming Lochner: Individual Rights and the Fourteenth Amendment," 38 B. C. L. Rev.1 (1996); "Two Textual Adventures: Thoughts on Reading Jeffrey Rosen's Paper," 66 Geo. Wash. L. Rev.

1269 (1998); "Historical Linguistics, Inkblots, and Life after Death: The Privileges or Immunities Clause of the Fourteenth Amendment," 78 N.C.L. Rev. 1071 (2000); "John A. Bingham and the Story of American Liberty," 36 *U. Akron L. Rev.* 617 (2003). Although Part I of this book focuses on the views of Professor Amar, I shall also sometimes consider those of other important writers such as Professor Curtis. I have great regard for Professor Curtis's able scholarship and his contributions to the literature on what should be the general theory of constitutional rights of the American people. However, with all due respect to Professor Curtis, I believe that if my refutation of Professor Amar's refined incorporation theory is sound then (the reader shall see that) à fortiori Curtis's theory of total incorporation is also successfully refuted.

    20.   AMAR, 221–23, 225.

    21.   Ibid., 236; and see also 256–57 (since Amar should also have added religion to his inventory). Amar makes essentially the same points in his "The Bill of Rights and the Fourteenth Amendment," 101 Yale L. J. 1193, 1266, 1277 (1992); as does Curtis in Curtis (1998) (supra note 19), at 1282–83. It appears, according to Curtis, that the notion of constitutional redefinition was explicitly originated by Kurt Larsh who, in his "The Second Adoption of the Free Exercise Clause: Religious Exemptions Under the Fourteenth Amendment," 88 Nw. U. L. Rev. 1106, 1108–09 (1994), "suggest[ed] that the adoption of the Fourteenth Amendment altered and broadened the scope of religious freedoms granted by the First Amendment." Curtis (1998) (supra note 19), at 1283n97.

    22.   AMAR, 243.

    23.   *Malloy* v. *Hogan,* 378 U.S. at 10; *Benton* v. *Maryland*, 395 U.S. 784, 794–95 (1969).

    24.   For a very good, comprehensive treatment of the evolution of the understanding of the freedoms of speech and the press, see Michael Kent Curtis, *Free Speech, "The People's Darling Privilege": Struggles for Freedom of Expression in American History* (Durham: Duke University Press, 2000).

    25.   AMAR, 248–9 (establishment clause), 280–81 (Ninth Amendment unenumerated rights viewed as originally collective).

    26.   Ibid., 26–32, 244–46.

    27.   Ibid., 47–59.

    28.   Thus, for example, James Madison's initial draft (June 8, 1789) of the Bill of Rights in Congress included: "The people shall not be deprived or abridged of their right to speak, to write, or to publish their sentiments; and the freedom of the press, as one of the great bulwarks of liberty, shall be inviolable"; and "The people shall not be restrained from

peaceably assembling and consulting for their common good; nor from applying to the Legislature by petitions, or remonstraces, for redress of their grievances." *Annals of Congress* (J. Gales ed. 1789) (*The Debates and Proceedings in the Congress of the United States 1789–1824*), 1: 451. (The various volumes of the *Annals of Congress* are available online at http://lcweb2.loc.gov/ammem/amlaw/lwcg.html.)

29. AMAR, 251–54. According to Amar, this is "because even if we did not [incorporate the establishment clause], principles of religious liberty and equality could be vindicated via the free exercise clause (whose text, history, and logic make it a paradigmatic case for incorporation) and equal-protection clause (which frowns on state laws that unjustifiably single out some folks for special privileges and relate others to second-class status)." Ibid., 254. To him it appears that "[t]he original establishment clause, on a close reading, is not antiestablishment but pro-states' rights." Ibid., 34. Because of this, "the nature of the states' establishment clause right against federal disestablishment makes it awkward to mechanically 'incorporate' the clause against the states via the Fourteenth Amendment." Ibid., 33. Therefore, per Amar, refined incorporation is in order given that the establishment clause was sufficiently mutated by the time of the adoption of the Fourteenth Amendment.

30. Ibid., 231–46, 254–57.

31. Ibid., 217–18, 223, 257–67.

32. Ibid., 266–68.

33. Ibid., 268–69.

34. Ibid., 278. Amar also maintains that, given the Supreme Court's declaration in *Murray's Lessee* v. *Hoboken Land & Improvement Co.*, 59 U.S. (18 How) 272, 276–77 (1856), "procedural due process embodied—incorporated, if you will—all the other procedural rules laid down in 'the constitution itself.'" AMAR, 173; see also ibid., 278 (procedural rights specified in accompanying text "were in 1866 seen not only as fundamental 'privileges' and 'immunities' but also as components of 'due process'"). On the other hand, Amar states (Ibid., 202): "We need not even say definitively that due process in 1866 necessarily included a grand-jury requirement; it is enough to say that the argument was a very strong one indeed, supported by eminent legal authorities on both sides of the Atlantic."

35. AMAR, 269, 276–78. Amar does not seem altogether clear about the Seventh Amendment right. See ibid., 92, 222, 275–76.

36. Ibid. 175. Amar also appears to hold that the descriptive term of the privileges or immunities clause (i.e., "the privileges or immunities of citizens of the United States") includes common or state law rights

denoted by the comity clause; but that the former perhaps only secures them against discriminatory action. Ibid., 178–79. According to Amar, the rights retained by the people of the Ninth Amendment have been mutated from core collective rights into individual rights, but "add little to the privileges-or-immunities clause itself." Ibid., 280; see also 120, 124.

37.   I more fully discuss the citizenship clause in Part II of this book. Part I of this book (just as is Amar's book) is focused upon the question of the incorporation of some or all of the rights specified in the Bill of Rights. In his more recent book, Amar begins his analysis of the Fourteenth Amendment with an exposition of the citizenship clause that provides a substantially sound approach about the significance of that clause in relation to implicit constitutional rights of American citizens. Amar (2006) (supra note 15), 383–85. It suffices, however, for my purpose here to show that Amar's failure to initially analyze the citizenship clause in his *The Bill of Rights: Creation and Reconstruction* made possible his failure to acknowledge that that clause conclusively signals that "person" in the Bill of Rights is to be understood for all purposes in exactly the same sense as the same term in the Fourteenth Amendment.

38.   AMAR, 173.

39.   8 USC §1101 (a) (22) (2007): "The term 'national of the United States' means (A) a citizen of the United States, or (B) a person who, though not a citizen of the United States, owes permanent allegiance to the United States." It would include, for example, the native-born inhabitants of a territory, acquired by treaty or conquest, owing permanent allegiance to the United States, before the territory's incorporation into the United States. See 8 U.S.C. §1408 (2007) for the various modes by which a person acquires nationality but not citizenship at birth.

40.   See *Matthews* v. *Diaz*, 426 U.S. 67, 77–80 (1976). For example, a fully free American citizen (i.e., an adult, neither in actual or constructive custody, nor in actual military or quasi-military service) is constitutionally entitled to a bundle of rights that is very much greater than, say, an adult illegal or undocumented alien not in actual or constructive custody. Moreover, I do not wish to be understood as maintaining that American citizens on active duty in the military service are not entitled to per se or derivative components of any particular constitutional privilege or immunity of American citizens.

41.   AMAR, 172–73.

42.   60 U.S.(19 How.) 393 (1857). There has been much disagreement as to whether the so-called opinion of the Court in *Dred Scott* (written by Chief Justice Roger B. Taney) actually states the position of the majority of

the Court on every issue definitively discussed in that opinion. However, it has been well stated: "[T]here can be no doubt that Taney's opinion was accepted as the opinion of the Court by its critics as well as its defenders. In all branches of government and in popular thought, the 'Dred Scott decision' came to mean the opinion of the Chief Justice. The evidence of this linkage is overwhelming, and it includes the ultimate passage of the Fourteenth Amendment. As a matter of historical reality, the Court decided what Taney declared that it decided." Don E. Fehrenbacher, *The Dred Scott Case: Its Significance in American Law and Politics* (New York: Oxford University Press, 1978), 333–34

43.   AMAR, 170–72, 182, 364–65n42. We shall discuss below in greater detail whether the *Dred Scott* opinion actually taught this doctrine (hereinafter the alleged doctrine of *Dred Scott*); and if so, whether it could possibly have been in force before the adoption of the Fourteenth Amendment. Curtis also adheres to the alleged doctrine in question. See Curtis (1986) (supra note 19), 173: "As Crosskey has noted, *Dred Scott* had treated rights in the Bill of Rights and other privileges in the Constitution as belonging only to the class composed of citizens of the United States, a class that excluded all blacks, even those who might be citizens of a particular state"—citing W. W. Crosskey, "Charles Fairman, 'Legislative History,' and the Constitutional Limitations on State Authority," 22 U. Chi. L. Rev. 1, 1–10 (1954).

44.   AMAR, 163–64.

45.   Ibid., 164.

46.   Ibid.,

47.   Ibid., 165.

48.   Ibid., 250. It seems clear enough that the difference in terminology is essentially one of style. The free exercise clause forbids the making of any law prohibiting the free exercise of religion. It is fairly arguable the term *no law shall be made prohibiting the free exercise of religion* is equivalent to saying *no law shall be made abridging the free exercise of religion*. But, in any event, that religious freedom properly said to be secured against abridgment by the First Amendment includes components pertaining to freedom in religious matters protected by the First Amendment that are not components of the specific right of the free exercise clause—such as the freedom-rights entailed by the establishment clause as well as freedom-rights in matters of religion within the scope of the free speech and free press provisions.

49.   AMAR, 165.

50.   Ibid.

51.   Ibid., 165–66.

52.   Ibid., 166. Amar's omission of the Fourth Amendment as one concerning "enforcement of laws by executive and judicial officers" appears to be just a slip.

53.   The Supreme Court, very early on, ruled that a federal common law of crimes does not exist. *United States* v. *Hudson*, 11 U.S. (7 Cran.) 32 (1812).

54.   See Curtis (2000) (supra note 24), at 131–299, for an excellent account of this repression.

55.   AMAR, 166.

56.   Ibid., 165.

57.   *Cong. Globe*, 38th Cong., 1st Sess., 1202 (1864). Evidently, Wilson can be here read as either taking the erroneous *contrarian* view that the First Amendment as such applies to the states or that the states have a moral or political obligation not to abridge First Amendment freedoms. (The various volumes of the *Congressional Globe* are available online at htpp://1cweb2.loc.gov/amen/amlaw/lwcg.html.)

58.   AMAR at 35–42, 231–34.

59.   The accompanying text very loosely paraphrases Gerard V. Bradley, *Church-State Relationships in America* (New York: Greenwood Press, 1987), 144 (speaking of the religion clauses). James Madison, in his initial remarks about the proposed amendments, addressed the objection that Congress has only enumerated powers. He "admit[ted] that these arguments are not entirely without foundation, but they are not conclusive to the extent which has been supposed. It is true, the powers of the General Government are circumscribed, they are directed to particular objects; but even if Government keeps within these limits, it has certain discretionary powers with respect to the means, which admit of abuse to a certain extent ... because in the constitution of the United States, there is a clause granting to Congress the power the make all laws which shall be necessary and proper for carrying into execution all the powers vested in the Government of the United States, or in any department or officer thereof[.]" *Annals of Congress* (J. Gales ed. 1789), 1: 455.

60.   *Annals*, 1: 808–09; *Journal of the Senate of the United States* (1st Cong., 1st Sess., Aug. 25, 1789), I; 63–64. (The various volumes of the *Journal of the Senate* are available online at http://1cweb2.loc.gov/ammem/amlaw/lwsj.html.) James Madison opined (on August 17, 1789), during a discussion of his original draft of Article XIV, that "[he] conceives this to be the most valuable amendment in the whole list. If there were any reason to restrain the government of the United States from infringing upon these essential rights, it was equally necessary that they should be secured against the State Governments. He thought

that if they provided against one, it was as necessary to provide against the other, and it was satisfied that it would be equally grateful to the people." *Annals*, 1: 784. Earlier, on June 8, 1789, he had remarked: "[E]very Government should be disarmed of powers which trench upon these particular rights.... [I]t must be admitted, on all hands, that the state governments are as liable to attack these invaluable privileges as the general government is, and therefore ought to be as cautiously guarded against." Ibid., 1: 457.

61. I fully agree with Amar's remark: "To be sure, the amendment speaks only of 'Congress'; but any automatic inference that citizens therefore lack analogous rights against the president or federal judges ... flies in the face of the Ninth Amendment [unenumerated rights]." AMAR, 233. Moreover, it would violate the due process clause were a person deprived of his life, liberty, or property, by an ultra vires action of the judicial or executive branch of the government of the United States.

62. The SAR, in my opinion, is not embraced by the privileges or immunities clause for reasons advanced in Chapter D of this part.

63. AMAR, 166. The "last sentence" referred to is: "However suggestive the tracking of the First Amendment may be, there is no suggestion thus far that only the First Amendment is to be incorporated." Ibid. I take it that Amar is speaking of only the Bill of Rights.

64. Ibid., 234.

65. Ibid., 254.

66. Ibid., 231–32. Amar was equally, if not more, explicit in his article, "The Bill of Rights as a Constitution" (1991) (supra note 21), at 1149n85: "To recast the historical argument into a textual one, at the heart of the Fourteenth Amendment is the idea that no state shall 'abridge' the freedoms of free[d]men; it would be odd indeed to refuse to apply the one pair of clauses of the Bill of Rights whose explicit battle cry is 'freedom' and whose language prohibiting 'abridging' expressly tracks the 'abridg[ment]' language of the privileges or immunities clause." The "historical argument referred to by Amar is: "Indeed, incorporation of free speech and free press principles make especially strong sense in light of the free speech crusade that the (often unpopular) abolitionists had waged from the 1830's on, fighting discriminatory gag rules on abolitionist petitions in Congress, and censorship of abolitionist literature by both southern state governments and a Democrat-controlled federal postal service." Ibid.

67. AMAR, 166–67.

68. *Cong. Globe*, 42nd Cong., 1st Sess., App. 47 (1871) (remarks of Rep. Kerr).

227

69.   See Attorney General Edward Bates, 10 Op. Att'y Gen. 497 (Nov. 29, 1862); George W. Paschal, *The Constitution of the United States: Defined and Carefully Annotated* (Washington, DC: W.H. & O.H. Morrison, Law Booksellers, 1868), 225; *Cong. Globe*, 42nd Cong., 1st Sess., App. 313 (1871) (remarks of Rep. Blanchard); and *Lonas v. State*, 3 Tenn. (Heisk.) 287, 306–07 (1871).

70.   See: *Webster's Third New International Dictionary* (1993), 1805, defines "privilege" as, inter alia, "a condition of legal nonrestraint of natural powers either generally or in respect to a particular case—compare—LIBERTY"; Bryan A. Garner, *a Dictionary of Modern Legal Usage* (2d ed. 1955), 293: "privilege is a slippery legal word most commonly denoting a person's legal freedom to do or not to do a given act"; Wesley N. Hohfeld, *Fundamental Legal Conceptions As Applied In Judicial Reasoning And Other Legal Essays* (ed. W.W. Cook) (New Haven: Yale University Press, 1923), 47: "The closest synonym of legal 'privilege' seems to be legal 'liberty' or legal 'freedom.'[57a]" [Note 57a: "Compare the expression: 'Freedom of speech.'"]; Albert Kacourek, *Jural Relations* (Indianapolis: Bobs-Merrill Co., 2d ed. 1928), 8n2: "'[P]rivilege' ... has at least six well defined variations ... (5) it may mean "liberty" (e.g., the privilege of using or abusing one's land)"; John Salmond, *Jurisprudence* (G.L. Williams 10th ed.) (London: Street & Maxwell, 1947), 238: "Just as my legal rights (in the strict sense) are the benefits which I derive from legal duties imposed upon other persons, so my legal liberties (sometimes called licenses or privileges) are the benefits which I derive from the absence of legal duties imposed upon myself. They are the various forms assumed by the interest which I have in doing as I please. They are the things which I may do without being prevented by the law. The sphere of my legal liberty is that sphere of activity within which the law is content to leave me alone." Amar's drive to have the privileges or immunities clause incorporate every individual right guaranteed and protected in the Bill of Rights appears to rest upon his implicit insistence that the terms in question ("rights," "privileges," and "immunities") are to be understood as necessarily being synonymous or interchangeable. Yet, he himself refers to the fact that "[o]nly weeks before adopting the Fourteenth Amendment, Congress passed the Civil Rights Act of 1866.... In draft, the act spoke of 'civil rights and immunities,' leading its sponsor to play the role of law dictionary: 'What is an immunity? Simply 'freedom or exemption from obligation'" AMAR, 168–69 (internal quote marks modified). It appears to me that Amar seriously errs in failing to notice that the term "privileges or immunities" acquires more precision and content

when considered as part of the larger term "privileges or immunities of citizens of the United States."

71.   Such usage is exemplified in the Constitution of Maryland of 1867, which provided: "That the *liberty* of the press ought to be inviolably preserved; and that every citizen of the State ought to be allowed to speak write and publish his sentiments on all subjects, being responsible for the abuse of that *privilege*." MD. CONST. OF 1867, art. 40 (emphasis added). And the constitutions of Texas of 1845, 1866, and 1868 each provided: "Every citizen shall be at *liberty* to speak, write, or publish his opinions on any subject, being responsible for the abuse of that *privilege*; and no law shall ever be passed curtailing the liberty of speech or of the press." TEX, CONST. OF 1845, art. I, §5; TEX. CONST. OF 1866, art. I, §5; TEX. CONST. OF 1868, art. I, §5 (emphasis added). Relevant extant and superseded state constitutions or constitutional provisions are reprinted in Francis Newton Thorpe, *The Federal And State Constitutions, Colonial Charters, And Other Laws, of the States, Territories, and Colonies Now Or Heretofore Forming The United States Of America* (Washington: Government Printing Office, 1909).

72.   AMAR, 216–18.

73.   I make this point in my article; see Guminski (supra note 3), at 815. Cf. Curtis (1996) (supra note 19), at 21–22: "A correlative of the right to be free from unreasonable searches and seizures is the government's duty not to search and seize unreasonably." Of course, the Fourth Amendment right may be a component of the specific right of the due process clause; or, alternatively, some principal components of the former may be components of the latter right. The free speech provision is not that the-freedom-of-speech-subject-to-reasonable-regulations shall not be abridged. Nor is it that the right of freedom of speech shall not be reasonably abridged. It provides rather that the freedom of speech shall not be abridged. It is implicit, however, that the right of freedom of speech does not include among its components all logically possible rights pertaining to speech (e.g., the right to solicit murder).

74.   AMAR, 169–70.

75.   Ibid., 170. He also remarks: "[T]here was widespread support [among members of the Thirty-ninth Congress] for the idea that the Bill of Rights was paradigmatically, even if not exclusively, a catalogue of privileges and immunities of 'citizens.'" Ibid., 171.

76.   Ibid. 170–173. See also AMAR, 364–65n42: "These privileges [i.e., the specific rights of the Bill of Rights] were understood to be privileges only by citizens because of *Dred Scott*. But if this aspect of *Dred Scott* were later abolished vis-à-vis the federal government for any

privilege, perhaps we should read the Fourteenth Amendment, in the spirit of dynamic conformity, to incorporate the broader understanding of that privilege against states. As [John Hart] Ely rightly points out, the text [of the Fourteenth Amendment] can be read to include aliens; and the legislative history shows an intent to give aliens broader rights against states than they enjoyed against federal officials. Technical redundancy of the due process clause is also avoided because the clause would have independent bite until judges repudiated *Dred Scott* on the question of alien rights vis-à-vis the federal government." Amar also restates the alleged doctrine of *Dred Scott* in his *American Constitution*. Amar (2006) (supra note 15), at 388–89.

77. Amar himself does not fail to make this important distinction. However, he fails to remember that some framers of the Fourteenth Amendment (e.g., John Bingham) did so. See note 80 infra and accompanying text.

78. *Cong. Globe*, 42d Cong., 1st Sess., App. 84 (1871).

79. 6 F.Cas. 546 (No. 3230) (C.C.E.D. Pa. 1823) (Washington, Circuit J.).

80. Thus Bingham eventually came to repudiate the opinion, so long previously held by and so dear to him, that *Barron* and its progeny erroneously held that the Bill of Rights does not apply to the states, and the opinion that (to use my terminology) the descriptive terms of the comity and the privileges or immunities clauses completely denote the same rights. His repudiation of these doctrines did not take place until well after the adoption of the Fourteenth Amendment in 1868. See Guminski (supra note 3), at 780n45. Curtis eventually acknowledged Bingham's change of opinion when he affirmed: "By 1871, Bingham seems to have bowed to Supreme Court interpretation and to have abandoned his abolitionist reading of the original Privileges and Immunities Clause" (i.e., the comity clause). Curtis (1996) (supra note 19), at 62n220. Amar, on the other hand, appears to be unaware of the fundamental inconsistency between the Bingham's view before the 1866 drafting of the final version of the privileges or immunities clause and that after his 1871 declaration. AMAR, 181–84. What Amar seems to overlook is that Bingham, previous to and not later than 1871, held that the descriptive term of the comity clause embraces only those so-called *fundamental rights* as described by Justice Washington in *Corfield* v. *Corywell*. Bingham had initially believed that the comity clause protected all fundamental rights of American citizens, but only as to them because the comity clause expressly limits entitlement to only American citizens. Thus the reason why, in his view, only American citizens could claim federal constitutional protection as to

a discriminatory deprivation (based upon a disparity of state citizenship) by the states of life, liberty, or property, without due process of law, prior to the adoption of the Fourteenth Amendment, was because the antidiscriminatory comity clause only applies to American citizens, and the Fifth Amendment, according to *Barron*, and its progeny, could not be enforced against the states. Although I greatly admire his high idealism, his zeal for civil rights and liberties, and indeed his inspiring eloquence, I reluctantly share the view of some that Bingham was exasperatingly confused and confusing in his exposition of legal doctrine because of his impoverished analytical skills. Unfortunately for us, John Bingham was no James Madison.

81. *Cong. Globe*, 42nd Cong., 1st Sess., App. 83–84 (1871).

82. Ibid., App. 152.

83. Ibid., App. 151.

84. See, inter alia, his remarks in: *Cong. Globe*, 35th Cong., 2d Sess., 984 (1859); 37th Cong., 2d Sess., 1639 (1862); 39th Cong., 1st Sess. 158 (1866); ibid., 1090.

85. *Cong. Globe,* 39th Cong., 1st Sess., 158 (1866).

86. Charles Fairman, *Does the Fourteenth Amendment Incorporate the Bill of Rights? The Original Understanding*, 2 Stanford L. Rev. 5, 21, 24 (1949). For more details about the framing of the Fourteenth Amendment, see: Joseph B. James, *The Framing of the Fourteenth Amendment* (Urbana: University of Illinois Press, 1965); Benjamin Kendrick, *The Journal of the Joint Committee of Fifteen on Reconstruction* (New York: Columbia University Press, 1914).

87. *Cong. Globe,* 39th Cong., 1st Sess., 1085 (1866).

88. Ibid., 1095.

89. Fairman (supra note 86), at 41–42.

90. Ibid., 42–43.

91. House Report No. 22, 41st Cong., 3rd Sess., appears in Alfred Avins, *The Reconstruction Amendments' Debates: The Legislative History and Contemporary Debates in Congress on the 13th, 14th, and 15th Amendments* (Richmond VA: Virginia Commission on Constitutional Government, 1967), 466–67. Avins' book is a very useful source for many of the relevant reconstruction era debates.

92. See generally Guminski (supra note 3), at 767n8, 781–90. I am grateful to Professor Amar for his citation of my article insofar as I call attention to certain statutes and treaties of the United States, dating before the adoption to the Fourteenth Amendment, which refer to the rights, privileges (or advantages), and immunities of citizens of the United States, and which were understood as including at least some rights specified in

the Bill of Rights. AMAR, 16768n*, 361n12; Guminski (supra note 3), 784–87. It is singularly remarkable that, during and since the incorporation of First Amendment freedoms, jurists and writers commenting on the privileges or immunities clause appear to have almost universally been unaware of the significance of these federal treaties and statutes.

93.   Treaty Between the United States of America and the French Republic, April 30, 1803, 8 Stat. 200, 202. The treaty by which Spain ceded the Floridas to the United States in 1819 used, in Article VI, the term "privileges, rights, and immunities of the citizens of the United States." Treaty of Amity, Settlement and Limits, Between the United States of America, and His Catholic Majesty, February 22, 1819, 8 Stat. 252, 258. The Treaty of Guadalupe Hidalgo of 1848, by which Mexico ceded extensive territory to the United States, used the expression "rights of citizens of the United States" in Article IX. The Treaty of Peace, Friendship, Limits, and Settlement with the Republic of Mexico, February 2, 1848, 9 Stat. 922, 930. The treaty by which Russia ceded Alaska in 1867 referred to "rights, advantages, and immunities of citizens of the United States" in Article III. Treaty concerning the Cession of the Russian Possessions in North America by His Majesty the Emperor of all the Russias to the United States of America, March 30,1867, 15 Stat. 539. See also Act of March 3, 1843, 5 Stat. 645, 647; in which Congress declared that after compliance with certain requirements members of the Stockbridge Tribe of Indians shall then be deemed to be citizens of the United States, "and shall be entitled to all the rights, privileges, and immunities of such citizens."

94.   AMAR, 167–68.

95.   *The Works of Thomas Jefferson*, ed. P.L. Ford (New York: G.P. Putnam's Sons, 1905), 10: 92. In a letter dated November 9, 1803, to Albert Gallatin, his secretary of the treasury, Jefferson wrote: "The existing laws of the country being now in force, the new [territorial] legislature will introduce the trial by jury in *criminal* cases, first; the habeas corpus, the freedom of the press, freedom of religion, etc., as soon as may be, and in general draw their laws and organization to the mould of ours by degrees as they find practicable without exciting too much discontent. In proportion as we find the people there riper for receiving the first principles of freedom, congress may from session to session confirm their enjoyment of them." Ibid., 8: 276. See Guminski (supra note 7), at 784–85, and more extensively Everett Somerville Brown, *The Constitutional History of the Louisiana Purchase 1803-1812* (Berkeley: University of California Press, 1920), 65–67, 72–74, 97–98 for additional evidence of the original understanding that the term "rights, advantages, and immunities of citizens of the United States' in the treaty included the specific rights

of the Bill of Rights. Some more evidences bearing on the thesis that the rights, privileges [advantages], and immunities of the American people include the specific rights of the Bill of Rights, as well as upon the issue of the applicability of the Bill of Rights to the territories and possessions of the United States, may be found in *The Insular Cases: Comprising The Records, Briefs, and Arguments of Counsel in the Insular Cases of the October Term, 1900, in the Supreme Court of the United States, Including the Appendixes Thereto,* ed. Albert H. Howe, House of Representatives, 56th Cong., 2d Sess., Document 509, (Washington: Government Printing Office, 1901).

96.   2 Op. Att'y Gen. 726, 732–33 (opinion of Sept. 21, 1835), cited in Guminski, supra note 3, at 787. As Amar comments: "Butler was of course glossing the [above quoted] language of the Louisiana Purchase Treaty." AMAR, 168 n*. Butler's comments were approvingly mentioned, during the Kansas Affairs debates, by Senator Stephen A. Douglas of Illinois. *Cong. Globe*, 34th Cong., 1st Sess., App. 284 (1856).

97.   *Cong. Globe*, 39th Cong., 1st Sess., 1756 (1866). In his *Bill of Rights*, Amar saw fit not to reference Trumball's allusions to the treaty provisions in question referred to in my article; but instead he wrote: "In debates over the Civil Rights Act of 1866—a precursor of section 1 [of the Fourteenth Amendment]—Senator Lyman Trumball quoted the language of the Stockbridge Tribe Act to his colleagues. *See Cong. Globe*, 39th Cong., 1st Sess. 600 (1866)." AMAR, 168n*. In this exercise of *légerdeparole*, Amar inaccurately refers to the Civil Rights Act of 1866 as a precursor of section 1 of the Fourteenth Amendment, thereby conflating the rights denoted by the privileges or immunities clause with those denoted by section 1 of the Civil Rights Act of 1866, which do not include the First Amendment freedoms. But, more precisely, Trumball's reference to the Stockbridge Tribe Act to his colleagues took place on February 2, 1866, during the course of a discussion of a precursor of the 1866 statute—which concerns itself exclusively with discrimination based upon race, color, or previous condition of slavery.

98.   Fairman, supra note 86, at 41–42.

99.   See, inter alia, *Conner* v. *Elliott*, 59 U.S. (18 How.) 591 (1856); *Paul* v. *Virginia*, 75 U.S. (8 Wall) 168 (1869); *Ward* v. *Maryland*, 79 U.S. (12 Wall.) 418 (1870); *Slaughter-House Cases*, 83 U.S. (16 Wall.) 36 (1873); *Toomer* v. *Witsell*, 334 U.S. 385 (1948); *Austin* v. *New Hampshire*, 420 U.S. 656 (1975); *Hicklin* v. *Orbeck*, 437 U.S. 518 (1978); *Building Trades* v. *Mayor of Camden*, 465 U.S. 208 (1984).

100.   44 U.S. (3 How.) 589 (1845).

101.   Ibid., 591.

102. Ibid., 594–97.

103. Ibid., 606.

104. Ibid., 609.

105. AMAR 172. See also 365n42: "These privileges [i.e., individual rights protected in Bill of Rights] were understood in 1866 to be privileges enjoyed only by citizens because of *Dred Scott.*" Amar accordingly posits the possibility of "this aspect to *Dred Scott* [of being] later abolished vis-à-vis the federal government" and that the "[t]echnical redundancy of the due-process clause is also avoided because the clause would have independent bite until judges repudiated *Dred Scott* on the question of alien rights vis-à-vis the federal government." Ibid. Luckily for aliens, until such judicial repudiation of the alleged doctrine of *Dred Scott,* Amar states that they at least "enjoy against states the full benefit of all procedural rights of the original Bill by dint of the Fourteenth Amendment due process clause and *Murray's Lessee* [v. *Hoboken Land & Development Co....* As to other rights, equal protection principles will require states to justify any discrimination between citizens and aliens. Finally, aliens may sometimes be able to present themselves as third-party beneficiaries of citizen rights." AMAR, 365n42.

106. AMAR, 172.

107. *Orient Insurance Co.* v. *Daggs,* 172 U.S. 557, 561 (1899).

108. The only rights of the Bill of Rights, which could somewhat arguably (but I think unpersuasively) be the rights of *only* American citizens are the freedoms of the First Amendment, perhaps any establishment-clause-entailed immunity, and the specific rights of the second and fourth Amendments, and perhaps whatever individual rights (if any) that are independently secured by the Ninth Amendment. Interestingly enough, Amar argues that the "procedural due process embodied—incorporated, if you will—all the other procedural rules laid down in 'the Constitution itself'" AMAR, 173 (citing *Murray's Lessee v. Hoboken Land & Improvement Co.*) Accordingly, since the framers of the Fourteenth Amendment were entitled to rely on *Murray's Lessee,* "then the due-process clause of the Fourteenth Amendment *by itself* embodied—incorporated—various procedural stafeguards specified in Amendments V–VIII. That leaves only six amendments in the Bill—the first four and the last two—where the privileges-or-immunities clause has independent bite.... The fit between the explicit rights of 'the people' in the original Bill and those provisions where the privileges-or-immunities clause has independent bite may not be perfect, but surely it is close enough to explain why so many in 1866 would naturally have thought of the nonprocedural provisions of the original Bill as rights of citizens."

AMAR, 173-74. Oddly Amar again fails to mention the specific right of the Fourth Amendment.

109. John Hart Ely, in his *Democracy and Distrust: A Theory of Judicial Review* (Cambridge: Harvard University Press, 1980), 25, confused the issue by saying that if the term *the privileges or immunities of citizens of the United States* is one only of description then the states "are not to deny the incorporated rights to anyone." But surely it is possible that the term could mean that any particular right denoted by it is such that either only American citizens are per se entitled to it; or, that it is a right to which all American citizens, and to which some but not all noncitizens, are per se entitled—all other things being equal.

110. AMAR, 234–35. Amar should have also included religious freedom in his listing of the specific rights of the Bill of Rights that were of the greatest concern to the founders of the Fourteenth Amendment.

111. Whatever the substantive aspects of the due process clauses, it would be very odd were the specific right of the due process clause of the Fifth Amendment judicially deemed to include all the components of each First Amendment freedom. According to the Supreme Court's theory, the due process clause of the Fourteenth Amendment incorporates the First Amendment freedoms only because it is unthinkable that the Fourteenth Amendment applies to the states a "watered-down, subjective version" of the fundamental rights specified in the Bill of Rights. *Malloy* v. *Hogan*, 378 U.S. at 10–11. This appears to me to be a patently unpersuasive reason for the Court's selective incorporation theory. But then, *mirabile dictu*, the due process clause of the Fifth Amendment must also incorporate the First Amendment freedoms, and all other specific rights incorporated by the due process clause of the Fourteenth Amendment, because according to one line of cases both clauses are supposed to be equivalent in meaning. See *Hibben* v. *Smith*, 191 U.S. 310, 325 (1903); *Farrington* v. *Tokushige*, 273 U.S. 284, 299 (1927); *Heiner* v. *Donnan*, 295 U.S. 312, 326 (1932); *Paul* v. *Davis*, 424 U.S. 693, 702n3 (1976) ("Surely the Fourteenth Amendment [Due Process Clause] imposes no more stringent requirements upon state officials than does [that of] the Fifth upon their federal counterparts").

112. *Hampton* v. *Mow Sun Wong*, 426 U.S. 88, 100n17 (1976): "Since the Due Process Clause appears in both the Fifth and Fourteenth Amendments, whereas the Equal Protection Clause does not, it is quite clear that the primary office of the latter differs from, and is additive to, the protection guaranteed by the former."

113. See *Malinski* v. *New York*, 324 U.S. 401, 414–15 (1945) (Frankfurter, J., concurring) ("The Due Process Clause of the Fourteenth Amendment thus has potency different from and independent of the

specific provisions in the Bill of Rights"); *Griswold* v. *Connecticut*, 381 U.S. 479, 500 (1965) (Harlan J., concurring) ("The Due Process Clause of the Fourteenth Amendment stands, in my opinion, on its own bottom"). The same things can be said, *mutatis mutandis,* about the Fifth Amendment due process clause.

114. Some rights of American citizens are expressly secured against violations by both the United States and the states independently of the privileges or immunities clause. For example, article I, section 9, clause 3 provides: "No Bill of Attainder or ex post facto Law shall be passed [by Congress]"; whereas section 10, clause 1 provides: "No State shall … pass any Bill of Attainder, ex post facto Law." Similarly, compare the due process clauses of the Fifth and Fourteenth Amendments. Thus the Supreme Court correctly held in a series of cases beginning with *Barron* v. *Baltimore*, 32 U.S. (7 Pet.) 243 (1833) that the provisions of the Bill of Rights as such do not apply to the states.

115. To quote Professor Curtis, see Curtis (1986 (supra note 19), at 117: "If the Fourteenth Amendment had not extended the rights and privileges [and immunities] of [American] citizens 'one iota,' then all of the rights it provides—including equal protection and due process—must have limited the states prior to its passage." He finds this quite puzzling. I, on the other hand, find it quite puzzling that Curtis finds this matter puzzling, for the Bill of Rights (amendments I–VIII) does not apply to the states; but with the Fourteenth Amendment as least some of the specified rights became, as of 1868, became fully secured against state action. Happily, Curtis has come to acknowledge: "The Fourteenth Amendment did not create new privileges. It created a new method of protecting old and inadequately secured privileges." Curtis (1996) (supra note 19), at 25; see also Curtis (1998) (supra note 19), at 1272.

116. A free, noncitizen, neither a resident alien nor resident noncitizen national, is *derivatively* entitled to a component of a specific constitutional right only if this entitlement obtains chiefly because otherwise the citizens' right would be abridged without the entitlement in question. Resident aliens are per se entitled to a privilege of American citizens where the dominant reason for his entitlement is a justice-motivated concern for them. Amar seems to suggest this distinction between *per se* and *derivative* entitlement when he writes that noncitizens "may enjoy certain [constitutional] benefits only insofar as they interact with American citizens, typically because they either live on soil governed by American citizens or do things with important effects on American citizens. Peripheral applications of the Bill should not obscure its core." AMAR, 170. See also ibid., 365n42: "[A]liens may sometimes be able to present themselves as third-party beneficiaries

of citizen rights. Just as a doctor can invoke a female patient's abortion right, so aliens addressing American citizens about national issues should be protected by the *citizens'* right to a free press and freedom of speech—rights which of course go beyond freedom to print and to speak." Here Amar is appears to be speaking of per se entitlement to free speech rights for resident aliens and derivative entitlement for nonresident aliens. Similarly, American citizens in actual or constructive custody may be deemed *derivatively* rather than *per se* entitled to some components of First Amendment freedoms for the same reasons. Curtis astutely points out how corporations are used by citizens for the exercise of their First Amendment freedoms. Curtis (1996) (*supra* note 19), 102–03. In my view, whether a domestic corporation or other artificial person has a per se entitlement to a First Amendment freedom depends upon it being predominantly engaged in public communication. Whether or not some other artificial person has a derivative entitlement to a First Amendment freedom depends upon it being incidentally or occasionally used as an instrumentality by which citizens having per se rights exercise them.

117. *Scott* v. *Sandford,* 60 U.S. (19 How.) 393 (1857).

118. AMAR, 170–71, 365n42.

119. E.g., Curtis (1986) (supra note 19), at 173; Crosskey (supra note 43), 1–10.

120. AMAR, 170, citing at 362n20: "[*Scott* v. *Standford*] 60 U.S. at 449 (emphasis added)."

121. 60 U.S. at 403 (emphasis added.)

122. Ibid., 406 (emphasis added). See also ibid., 403: "The question is simply this: can a negro, whose ancestors were imported into this country and sold as slaves, become a member of the political community formed and brought into existence by the Constitution of the United States, and as such become entitled to all the rights, and privileges, and immunities, guaranteed by that instrument to the citizen."

123. Ibid., 425. And see ibid., 411–12: "It is obvious that they were not even in the minds of the framers of the Constitution when they were conferring special rights and privileges upon the citizens of a State in every other part of the Union."

124. Ibid., 409. It would appear that the phrase "the rights of man and rights of the people" refer to the rights secured and protected by the First, Second, Fourth, and perhaps the Ninth Amendments.

125. 60 U.S. at 449. *Dred Scott* mentions that an Indian, who "leave[s] his nation or tribe, and take[s] up his abode among the white population ... would be entitled to all rights and privileges which would belong to an emigrant from any other foreign people." Ibid., 404. It should

be remembered that *Dred Scott* asserted that the entire human race, except blacks, was embraced within the doctrine of the Declaration of Independence: "[A]ll men are created equal; that they are endowed by their Creator with certain inalienable rights; that among them are life, liberty, and pursuit of happiness; that to secure these rights, governments are instituted, deriving their just powers from the consent of the governed." Ibid., 410. According to the Court's opinion, it would appear that Indians (and nonwhite but nonblack aliens) could be constitutionally naturalized by Congress.

126. 60 U.S. at 409–11. Adherents of the alleged doctrine of *Dred Scott* frequently cite the infamous words from that opinion that blacks, because of their inferior and degraded legal and social status incident to the institution of slavery, "had no rights which the white man was bound to respect." Ibid., 406. Taney, as the entire passage discloses, was referring to the time before the Declaration of Independence and the founding of the Constitution. Earlier he wrote that blacks "had no rights or privileges but such as those who held the power and the government might choose to grant them." Ibid., 405. Ironically, in 1818 Taney (acting as defense counsel) successfully vindicated the right of a white defendant Jacob Gruber (a Methodist minister), charged with having incited slaves to rebellion, for having criticized the institution of African slavery in Maryland by attacking it as inconsistent with the Declaration of Independence. Taney, referred to "the evil of slavery" as "a blot on our national character, and [asserted that] every real lover of freedom confidently hopes that it will be effectually, though it must be gradually, wiped away." He urged that "until it shall be accomplished: until the time shall come when we can point without blush, to the language held in the Declaration of Independence, every friend of humanity will seek to lighten the galling chain of slavery, and better, to the utmost of his power, the wretched condition of the slave." Clement Eaton, *The Freedom-of-Thought Struggle in the Old South* (New York: Harper & Row, 1964), 131–32.

127. 60 U.S. at 409. Thus the Court also asserted (ibid., 416–17) that if blacks were American citizens: "It would exempt them [under the comity clause] from the operation of the special laws and from the police regulations which [the slave states] considered to be necessary for their own safety. It would give to persons of the negro race, who were recognized as citizens in any State of the Union, the right to enter every other State whenever they pleased, singly or in companies, without pass or passport, and without obstruction, to sojourn there as long as they pleased, to go where they pleased at every hour of the day or night without molestation, unless they committed some violation of law for which a white man would

be punished, and it would give them the full liberty of speech in public and in private upon all subjects upon which its own citizens might speak; to hold public meetings upon political affairs, and to keep and carry arms wherever they went."

128. The *Dred Scott* opinion explained: "Besides, we are by no means prepared to say that there are not many cases, civil as well as criminal, in which a circuit court of the United States may exercise jurisdiction, although one of the African race is a party; that broad question is not before the court." Ibid., 425.

129. AMAR, 171. Amar's cites at 362n23 with respect to Bingham: "*Cong. Globe*, 39th Cong., 1st Sess., 430 ([January 25,] 1866) (quoting *Dred Scott*, 60 U.S. at 404)"; and at 362n24 as to Henderson: "*Id.* at 3032 [June 8, 1866] (quoting *Dred Scott*, 60 U.S. at 404)."

130. Amar (2006) (supra note 15), at 388.

131. Ibid. Amar's accompanying at 610n81 reads: "[*Cong. Globe*, 39th Cong., 1st Sess.] 1090 (Bingham, Feb. 28, 1866), 1292 (Bingham, Mar. 9, 1866), 2756–66 (Howard, May 23, 1866)."

132. The proposed amendment continues: "... and to all persons in the several States equal protection in the rights of life, liberty, and property." It is quite clear that the proposed provision was intended by Bingham to be only an improvement on the comity clause, understood to be predicable of only American citizens, by granting the Congress the authority to enforce it against the states. *Cong. Globe*, 39th Cong., 1st Sess., 1034 (Feb. 26, 1866; remarks of Rep. Bingham).

133. Ibid., 39th Cong., 1st Sess. 2542: "The proposed amendment will supply ... the power ... to protect by national law the privileges and immunities of all the citizens of the Republic and the inborn rights of every person within its jurisdiction whenever the same shall be abridged or denied by the unconstitutional acts of any State.... [T]his amendment takes from no State any right that ever pertained to it. No State ever had the right, under the forms of law or otherwise, to deny to any freedom the equal protection of the laws or to abridge the privileges or immunities of any citizen of the Republic, although many of them have assumed and exercised the power, and that without remedy." But if the privileges or immunities clause (as it now reads) is understood to be essentially a remake of the comity clause, it would be natural why Bingham may have thought (if he indeed thought so) why the former's protection protects only American citizens.

134. AMAR, 171. In my article, I rashly asserted that "[t]here is no evidence that the founders of the [F]ourteenth [A]mendment paid any attention to the alleged doctrine of the non-predictability of the Bill of

Rights to persons not citizens of the United States." Guminski (supra note 3), at 778. There is evidently *some* evidence, given Howard's declaration.

135. AMAR, 171, citing *Cong. Globe*, 39th Cong., 1st Sess., 2765 (1866) (bracketed matter supplied by Amar).

136. *Cong. Globe*, 40th Cong., 3rd Sess., 1003 (1869).

137. AMAR, 187.

138. Ibid., 204. See Fairman (supra note 86), at 66–68, for additional evidence of the partisan causes for the paucity of debate in the Senate.

139. AMAR, 182 (citing at 367n4: *Cong. Globe*, 35th Cong., 2d Sess. 983 (1859); and 37th Cong., 2nd Sess. 1638 (1862).

140. AMAR. 182 (citing at 368n6: "*Cong. Globe*, 39th Cong., 1st Sess. 430 (1866) (quoting *Dred Scott*, 60 U.S. U.S. at 404); *id.* at 1090.")

141. *Cong. Globe*, 39th Cong., 1st Sess., 1090 (1866).

142. AMAR at 182 (citing at 368n5): "*Cong. Globe*, 35th Cong., 2d Sess. 983 (1859)."

143. AMAR, 182.

144. Ibid., xiv, 217–23.

145. *Scott* v. *Stanford*, 60 U.S. at 425 (emphasis added).

146. Fehrenbacher (supra note 42), at 336, 430, 439. Fehrenbacher appears to be quite unaware of Amar's alleged doctrine of *Dred Scott.* Fehrenbacher did, however, maintain that *Dred Scott* asserted that African Americans were not entitled to the benefit of any constitutional rights. Fehrenbacher (supra note 42), at 355, 363.

147. The Republican Party platform of 1856 declared: "Resolved: That, with our Republican fathers, we hold it to be a self-evident truth, that all men are endowed with the inalienable right to life, liberty, and the pursuit of happiness, and that the primary object and ulterior design of our Federal Government were to secure these rights to all persons under its exclusive jurisdiction; that, as our Republican fathers, when they had abolished Slavery in all our National Territory, ordained that no person shall be deprived of life, liberty, or property, without due process of law, it becomes our duty to maintain this provision of the Constitution against all attempts to violate it for the purpose of establishing Slavery in the Territories of the United States by positive legislation, prohibiting its existence or extension therein. That we deny the authority of Congress, of a Territorial Legislation, of any individual, or association of individuals, to give legal existence to Slavery in any Territory of the United States, while the present Constitution shall be maintained."(Text available online at http://www.presidency.ucsb.edu/ws/index.php?pid=29619.) The Republican platform of 1860 declared: "That the normal condition of all the territory of the United States is that of freedom: That, as our

Republican fathers, when they had abolished slavery in all our national territory, ordained that 'no person shall be deprived of life, liberty or property without due process of law,' it becomes our duty, by legislation, whenever such legislation is necessary, to maintain this provision of the Constitution against all attempts to violate it; and we deny the authority of Congress, of a territorial legislature, or of any individuals, to give legal existence to slavery in any Territory of the United States." (Text available online at http://www.presidency.ucsb.edu/ws/index.php?pid=29620.)

148. Act of April 16, 1862, ch. 54, 12 Stat. 376 [District of Columbia]; Act of June 19, 1862, ch. 111, 12 Stat. 432 [Territories]. Ferhenbacher (supra note 42), at 575: "Congress ... ignored the Dred Scott decision while defying its most memorable ruling [i.e., that Congress could not exclude slavery from federal territories]. In June 1862, by overwhelming votes, the Senate and House passed a bill abolishing slavery in the federal territories, and Lincoln quickly signed it. Opponents of the measure raised various objections ... But no one mentioned the *Dred Scott* decision throughout the debate."

149. See inter alia his remarks in *Cong. Globe,* 35th Cong., 2d Sess., 983 (1859) ("I invite attention to the significant fact that natural or inherent rights, which belong to all men irrespective of all conventional regulations, are by this constitution guarantied by the broad and comprehensive word 'person,' as contradistinguished from the limited term 'citizen,'—as in the [Fifth Amendment due process and just compensation clauses].... [T]hese wise and beneficent guarantees ... of natural rights to all persons, whether citizens or strangers, may not be infringed."). See also ibid., 36th Cong., lst Sess., App. 83 (1861) ("I say it is the liberty of man that is involved; and that the Constitution, in the administration of justice, in the organization of tribunals for the administration of justice, is no respecter of persons. The word 'citizen' in that connection is not employed in your Constitution. The words 'white man' in that connection, are not employed in the Constitution. On the contrary, the word 'person' is adopted, a term comprehensive enough to embrace all men when the Constitution guarantees life and liberty and trial by jury. The Constitution has the same care for the rights of the stranger within its gates as for the rights of the citizen"). And see ibid., 37th Cong., 2d Sess., 1638 (1862), where Bingham asserted that the Constitution "rejects in its bill of rights the restrictive word 'freeman,' and adopts in its stead the more comprehensive words 'no person,' thus giving its protection to all, whether born free or bond." Incidentally, Bingham in speaking of *Dred Scott,* which he excoriated with commendably strident words, declared: "I recognize the decision of [the Supreme Court] as of binding force only as to the parties and privies

to the suit, and the rights particularly involved and passed upon. The court has no power in deciding the right of Dred Scott and of his children to their liberty, to decide, so as to bind this body, that neither Congress, nor a Territorial Legislature, nor any human power, has authority to prohibit slavery in the Territories; neither has that tribunal the power to decide that five million persons born and domiciled in this land, 'have no rights which we are bound to respect.'" Ibid., 36 Cong., 1st Sess., 1839 (1860).

150. Even *Dred Scott* conceded that "[t]he general words [of the Declaration of Independence concerning the equality of all humans with respect to inalienable rights] would seem to embrace the whole human family, and if they were used in a similar instrument at this day, would be so understood." 60 U.S. at 410. In *Texas* v. *White,* 74 U.S. (7 Wall.) 700, 728 (1869), the Court noted that as an effect of the adoption of the Thirteenth Amendment, "[t]he new freemen necessarily became part of the people, and the people still constituted the State[.]" With the constitutional abolition of slavery and involuntary servitude, there could no longer be any question but that all blacks were entitled to some protection as persons by virtue of the procedural and other kindred rights specified in amendments III–VIII. Devoid from Amar's writings is any evidence that anyone maintained that blacks, after the adoption of the Thirteenth Amendment, were not entitled to the benefit of some rights specified in the Bill of Rights—provided that this *anyone* acknowledged that the Thirteenth Amendment had become part of the law of the land.

151. See, e.g., Paschal, supra note 69: (the term "the people" as used in the Fourth Amendment "embraces all the inhabitants—citizens and aliens—who are entitled to the protection of the law. The slaves were never treated as a party of this 'people'" Ibid., 257); ("Practically the slaves and people of color were never considered as embraced in [the fifth] amendment, as they were often proceeded against without indictment. It meant a free white." Ibid., 258); ("Because the amendments did not apply to the States, the slaves and free persons of color were often deprived of a trial by jury" [i.e., in state criminal prosecutions]. Ibid., 264). For some evidences of the original understanding that the Bill of Rights was not limited in its application to only American citizens, see James Madison's Report on the Virginia Resolutions (1800): "[I]t does not follow, because aliens are not parties to the Constitution, as citizens are parties to it, that whilst they actually conform to it, they have no right to its protection. Aliens are not more parties to the laws than they are parties to the Constitution; yet it will not be disputed that, as they owe, on one hand, a temporary obedience, they are entitled, in return, to their protection and advantage." Jonathan Elliott, *The Debates in the Several State Conventions on the*

Adoption of the Constitution (Philadelphia: J. B. Lippincott & Co., 2d ed. 1836), 4: 556.

152. Paschal (supra note 69), at 228; Thomas M. Cooley, "The Fourteenth Amendment" (supplemental chapter. xlvii), in Joseph Story, *Commentaries on the Constitution of the United States* (T. Cooley 4th ed. 1873) (hereafter Cooley (1873), 2: §1931.

153. 43 U.S. (2 How.) 497.

154. U.S. CONST., art. III, § 2.

155. 43 U.S. at 558.

156. 9 U.S. (5 Cr.) 61, 86.

157. 94 U.S. 444 (1877).

158. 99 U.S. 700, 718–19. In 1877, the Court had already treated corporations as persons within the meaning of the Fifth Amendment due process clause without raising any question as to the question. *Granger Cases*, 94 U.S. 113.

159. 128 S.Ct. 2783 (2008). The opinion of the Court was delivered by J. Scalia with C. J. Roberts, and JJ. Kennedy, Thomas, and Alito concurring. JJ. Stevens, Souter, Ginsburg, and Breyer dissented. (The Second Amendment provides: "A well regulated militia being necessary to the security of a free State, the right of the people to keep and bear arms shall not be infringed.' U.S. CONST. amend. II.)

160. For persuasive accounts of why political rights are not embraced by the privileges or immunities clause, see AMAR, 216–18; Raoul Berger, *Government by Judiciary: The Transformation of the Fourteenth Amendment* (Cambridge, Mass.: Harvard University Press, 1977), 52–68.

161. In Guminski (supra note 3), at 769–70, I erroneously stated that the SAR was held not to be incorporated according to the Court, citing *Presser* v. *Illinois*, 116 U.S. 252 (1886) and *Miller* v. *Texas*, 153 U.S. 535 (1894). These cases, however, only hold that the Second Amendment right is not embraced by the privileges or immunities clause. I perhaps also too swiftly had concluded that the SAR is a political, rather than a civil, right and therefore not a privilege of American citizens within the meaning of the privileges or immunities clause. See Guminski (supra note 3), at 810–11. Accordingly, I rashly asserted that the "the content and predicability of this right varies with the particular laws of each state." Ibid., 811 (note omitted). I am afraid I had with too much docility accepted the deliverances of the great majority of the several circuits of the United States Court of Appeals that the SAR could not be an individual *civil* right unconnected to militia service; although I could not bring myself to thinking that the SAR is a collective or quasi-collective right. I now maintain that the thesis that the SAR is a multi-purposed individual civil right (unconnected to

militia service) is the more probable than not. Nevertheless, I do not think that the SAR includes among its components any right to own assault and semi-assault firearms, or to carry concealed firearms, to carry firearms unto the premises of any dwelling, place of business, or other privately owned enterprise, without the consent of the occupant, or to operate a motor vehicle or boat, or airplane, while impaired because of alcohol or drugs.

162. 128 S.Ct. at 2791.

163. Ibid., 2791–92.

164. Ibid., 2792.

165. Ibid., 2793.

166. Ibid., 2794. As the Court stated: "[T]he 'militia' in colonial America consisted of a subset of 'the people'—those who were male, able bodied, and within a certain age range." Ibid., 2791. "From that pool, Congress has plenary power to organize the units that will make up an effective fighting force.... [T]he adjective 'well-regulated' implies nothing more than the imposition of proper discipline and training." Ibid., 2800. The Court explained: "There are many reasons why the militia was thought to be 'necessary to the security of a free state.'... First, of course, it is useful in repelling invasions and suppressing insurrections. Second, it renders large standing armies unnecessary.... Third, when the able-bodied men of a nation are training in arms and organized, they are better able to resist tyranny." Ibid., 2800–01.

167. Ibid., 2799.

168. Ibid., 2801. In his recently published historical study, *The Founders' Second Amendment: Origins of the Right to Bear Arms* (Chicago: Ivan R. Dee, 2008), Stephen P. Halbrook remarked in commenting upon Madison's initial draft of what was to be the Second Amendment: "This declaration [i.e., the prefatory clause] did not limit the substantive right but gave the chief political reason for guaranteeing the right against governmental infringement." (Ibid., 253).

169. *Heller*, 128 S.Ct. at 2817.

170. Ibid., 2515–16. The Court purports to construe *Miller* v. *United States*. 307 U.S. 174 (1939) on this point; but it is clearly doing so with approval.

171. *Heller*, 128 S.Ct. at 2816. Earlier, the Court remarked that the SAR "was not unlimited, just as the First Amendment's right of free speech was not." The Court's opinion elsewhere makes it abundantly clear that when the Court refers to the SAR as limited, it means that it does not include as a component every conceivable right pertaining to the keeping and bearing of whatever arms; but the government may not

violate any of those rights that are the components of the SAR. Thus, for example, the SAR does not include as a component the right to keep and bear machineguns; not that the SAR includes such a right but that the SAR is not constitutionally infringed by depriving all citizens of the right to have a machinegun.

172. Ibid., 2816–17.

173. Ibid., 2817.

174. Ibid.

175. Ibid., 2812–13.

176. Ibid., 2813n23.

177. Compare the precursors of the First and Second Amendments in James Madison's initial draft of the Bill of Rights presented to the Congress on June 8, 1789: "The people shall not be deprived or abridged of their right to speak, to write, or to publish their sentiments; and the freedom of the press, *as one of the great bulwarks of liberty,* shall be inviolable.... The right of the people to keep and bear arms shall not be infringed; *a well armed and well regulated militia being the best security of a free country*; but no person religiously scrupulous of bearing arms shall be compelled to render military service in person." *Annals of Congress,* 1: 451 (emphasis added.) No state constitution in force during the founding of the Bill of Rights, that contained a provision pertaining to the right to keep and bear arms, described it as being necessary or essential to a free state. Pennsylvania Declaration of Rights, art. IX, § 21 (1790) ; Vermont Constitution, Ch. 1, art. 15 (1777), North Carolina Declaration of Rights, § XVIII (1776), Massachusetts Declaration of Rights, Pt. I, art. 17 (1780), Kentucky Declaration of Rights, art, XII, § 23 (1792). By way of contrast, some state constitutions in force during the founding of the Bill of Rights expressly assigned the liberty of the press as being essential to the security of freedom in a state, or as one of the great or greatest bulwark of liberty, as the reason it was not to be violated (i.e., New Hampshire Constitution, Pt. I, § 22 (1784), Massachusetts Constitution, Pt. I, art. 16 (1780), North Carolina Constitution, Pt. I, art. 15 (1776).

178. *Journal of the Senate,* supra note 60, 1: 63–64.

179. Asserting that the right to be free from unreasonable searches and seizures shall not be infringed is equivalent to asserting that the right to be free from searches and seizures shall not be unreasonably infringed. On the other hand, the First Amendment expressly prohibits any abridgment of any of its freedoms, and the Second Amendment expressly prohibits any infringement of its specific right.

180. Of course, I may have a legal right to be free to advocate a particular doctrine even where I have a moral duty not to do so (e.g.,

advocacy of the restoration of slavery). Another example: as a matter of divine or ecclesiastical law, I may have a moral duty to attend church on Sunday. However, it is a violation of my constitutional freedom-right to attend church if I am legally required to do what I am morally required to do—because I should go to church to satisfy a moral or ecclesiastical duty rather than being compelled to do so by civil authority. There are cases where *A* has a right that *x* by *B* be done because *B* has a legal duty to do *x*. This is an instance of what is frequently called a claim-right. I have a legal right to a speedy trial as an accused because the government has a legal duty to provide me the same—unless I should waive that right. There are other cases where *A* is said to have a right to do *x* because he has a duty to do *x*. This can be called a duty-right.

181. *Wooley* v. *Maynard*, 430 U.S. 705, 714 (1977): "We begin with the proposition that the right of freedom of thought protected by the First Amendment against state action includes both the right to speak freely and the right to refrain from speaking at all"); *West Virginia State Board of Education* v. *Barnette*, 319 U.S. 624, 645 (1941) (Justice Murphy concurring): ("The right of freedom of thought and of religion, as guaranteed by the Constitution against State action, includes both the right to speak freely and the right to refrain from speaking at all, except in so far as essential operations of government may require it for the preservation of orderly society—as in the case of compulsion to give evidence in court"). Where I am constitutionally required to "speak" (such as a witness in court, or as a taxpayer submitting income tax returns), I am to that extent not constitutionally free—hence we have speech-domains to which the First Amendment does not apply per se.

182. See Don B. Kates, Jr., "The Second Amendment: A Dialogue," 49 Law & Cont. Probs. 143, 145, 148 (1986); and Don B. Kates, Jr., *Handgun Prohibition and the Original Meaning of the Second Amendment*, 82 Mich. L. Rev. 204 (1983). The United States Supreme Court in *Miller*, 307 U.S. at 179–182 similarly gives an account of colonial and state legislation obliging citizens to obtain arms at their own expense and to train with them.

183. Kates (1983) (supra note 182), at 214–15 (emphasis in original).

184. Ibid., 216.

185. 307 U.S. 174, 179 (1939) (*held*: no SAR to possess sawed-off shotgun). The opinion proceeds to provide evidences for the last sentence in the quoted text. Ibid., 179–82.

186. Act of May 8, 1792, 1 Stat. 271–72.

187. Act of January 21, 1903, 32 Stat. 775.

188. Frederick Bernays Wiener, "The Militia Clause of the Constitution," 54 Harv. L. Rev. 181, 187 (1940). This is not to say that

the First Militia Act was not, more or less, observed in the states. As Weiner put it: "Annual returns were prescribed, the result of which was that the militia was, in most communities, mustered once a year. At these occasions, so far as can now be ascertained, Mars was less in evidence than Bacchus." Ibid., 187.

189. John K. Mahon, *The American Militia: Decade of Decision*, 1789–1800 (Gainesville: University of Florida Press, 1960), 19.

190. Ibid., 20.

191. Lena London, "The Militia Fine 1830–1860," 15 Military Affairs 133, 134 (1951). For accounts of state laws requiring militiamen to provide their own weapons and the penalties for failure to do so, the failure of militiamen to appear at musters properly armed, and how the system worked in the early national period, see: ibid.; Mahon (1960) (supra note 189), at 38–43, 47–48; John K. Mahon, *History of the Militia and the National Guard* (New York: Macmillan, 1983), 19–22, 26–32, 52–53, 57–60.

192. See London (supra note 191); William H. Riker, *Soldiers of the States: The Role of the National Guard in American Democracy* (Washington, DC: Public Affairs Press, 1957), 21–40; Mahon (1983) (supra note 191), at 78–96.

193. Wiener (supra note 188), at 191. During the Civil War, after the First Bull Run "[t]he militia was left behind, for home guard duty or for sudden emergencies (as in the Gettysburg campaign)." Ibid.

194. Kates (1983) (supra note 182), at 216n49; citing *Hampton & Co. v. United States*, 276 U.S. 394, 412 (1928).

195. Kates (1983) (supra note 182), at 266. See also Glenn Harlan Reynolds, "A Critical Guide to the Second Amendment," 62 Tenn. L. Rev. 461, 487 (1995), where this advocate of the so-called Standard-Model theory of the Second Amendment asserts: "If gun ownership is essential to give the Second Amendment meaning, then simply require everyone to own a gun (and to go through the necessary training to use it responsibly)." However, he does not actually recommend "that individual gun ownership *should* be made mandatory." Ibid., 488.

196. 496 U.S. 334 (1990) (militia clauses held not violated by federal statute's limits on state governor's authority to withhold consent to National Guard training outside the United States because of the Guard's dual enlistment program and where members had been called into active federal service).

197. Ibid., 350 (emphasis added). However, the Court's remark, that the 1792 militia act's "detailed command that every able-bodied male citizen between the ages of 18 and 45 be enrolled therein and equip himself

with appropriate weaponry was virtually ignored for more than a century" (ibid., 341), is rather exaggerated.

198. I.e., ["Congress's] current choice of a dual enlistment system is just as permissible as the 1792 choice to have the members of the militia arm themselves." 496 U.S. at 350.

199. Bernard J. Bordenet, "The Right to Possess Arms: The Intent of the Framers of the Second Amendment," 21 U. West L.A. L. Rev. 1, 22 (1990).

200. Ibid., 24–25. I confidently predict: as the gun control controversy continues it will become increasingly infrequent for holders of strong, individual-rights theories of the Second Amendment to speak of *the right and the duty to keep and bear arms.*

201. Stephen P. Halbrook, *That Every Man Be Armed: The Evolution of a Constitutional Right* (1984), 166 (quoting from 307 U.S. at 179). He also emphasizes, on the same page, the words "general obligation of all adult male inhabitants to possess arms" in a passage from the historian H.L. Osgood quoted by the *Miller* Court (307 U.S. at 179).

202. Halbrook (1984) (supra note 201), at 167.

203. "The Right of the People or the Power of the State: Bearing Arms, Arming Militias, and the Second Amendment," 26 Val. U. Val. Rev. 131, 198 (1991).

204. Ibid., 198.

205. Ibid., 199.

206. Ibid., 203–04.

207. Ibid., 187. Halbrook erroneously quotes the House version, which actually provided: "but no one religiously scrupulous of bearing arms shall be compelled to render military service in person." *Journal of the Senate* (supra note 60), at 1: 63–64. The deletion of the religious scruples clause instead was certainly motivated by the desire to make such an exemption a matter of legislative grace, rather than of constitutional right. See, e.g., *Annals of Cong.* 1: 779 (remarks of Rep. Benson); and ibid., 796 (remarks of Rep. Scott). In his most recent book, Halbrook writes: "The Senate also deleted the phrase that 'no person religiously scrupulous shall be compelled to bear arms'—perhaps because the basic guarantee of the amendment depicted the keeping and bearing of arms as an individual 'right' and not as a duty and also to leave the matter of conscientious objection to the legislature." Halbrook (2008) (supra note 168), at 275. But this explanation is somewhat misleading, quite apart from its inconsistency, because it fails to clearly disclose that the Congress has the constitutional right to oblige members of the active militia to bear arms unless these persons are relieved of that duty upon the ground of conscientious objection.

208. Halbrook (1984) (supra note 201), at 224n159. See the accompanying text at ibid., 79.

209. Halbrook himself provides evidences of congressional awareness of this. See Halbrook (1991) (supra note 203), at 195–97.

210. Act of March 2, 1867, 14 Stat. 423.

211. That requiring militia members to provide weapons at their own expense was widely believed to impose unequal burdens on the rich and poor was well known to some early members of Congress. See also *Annals of Cong.*, 2: 1804–09 (1790); ibid., 3: 420–22, 701–02, 708–11 (1792). See London (supra note 191), at 139–41, for evidence of congressional awareness in 1840 of the oppressive burdens of requiring militia members to procure weapons at their expense.

212. See, e.g., *Annals of Cong.*, 3:709: "Several modes presented themselves. The most obvious is, the furnishing of the arms at the public expense; and another is, the furnishing of the arms to such as might, in the opinion of certain officers, be too poor conveniently to find them" (Remarks of Rep. Murray); ibid., 1804: "[T]he clause which enacts that every man in the United States shall 'provide himself' with military accoutrements would be found impracticable, as it must be well known that there are many persons who are so poor as it is impossible that they should comply with the law. He conceived, therefore, that provisions should be made for arming such persons at the expense of the United States." (Remarks of Rep. Parker—who later altered his motion so that the states would bear the expense. Ibid., 1807.)

213. London (supra note 191), at 135. It should be borne in mind that "[a]bsence from a milita muster or appearing without the specified arms and equipment imposed the penalty of a fine." Ibid., 134.

214. Ibid., 136. See also Mahon (1983) (supra note 191), at 82.

215. Ibid., 83; London (supra note 182), at 138, 141–44; Riker (supra note 191), at 27–29.

216. London (supra note 191), at 137–38, 143–44. See also Riker (supra note 191), at 28–29.

217. London (supra note 191), at 143–44.

218. AMAR, 57. But surely the prefatory clause does not estop the Congress or the Court in determining whether a well-regulated militia is necessary for the security of a free state when either body deliberates about whether the states should be constitutionally prohibited from infringing the right of the people to keep and bear arms.

219. This does not entail, however, that the Court could not properly hold that the imposition of legal duties to keep arms at one's own expense, and to bear such arms for public purposes, is subject to the constraints

of the applicable due process clause—assuming that these clauses have substantive aspects pertaining to firearm-owning-and-carrying.

220. See Wiener (supra note 188), 187–93; Mahon (1983*)*, supra note 191, at 78–96; Riker (supra note 191), at 21–40. The Supreme Court, in *Perpich,* 496 U.S. at 341, noted that since the First Militia Act of 1792 "the militia proved to be a decidedly unreliable fighting force."

221. Joseph Story, *Commentaries on the Constitution of the United States; With a Preliminary Review of the Constitutional History of the United States before the Adoption of the Constitution* (Boston: Hilliard, Gray & Co., 1833), 3: § 1890. (The text of this treatise is available online at http://www.constitution.org/js/js_000.htm.) The court in *Andrews v. State,* 50 Tenn. (3 Heisk.) 141, 152 (1871) described the object of the SAR as "the efficiency of the people as soldiers, when called into actual service for the security of the State, as one end; and in order to this, they were to be allowed to keep arms." But that court also bemoaned "the fact, that what was once deemed a stable and essential bulwark of freedom, 'a well regulated militia,' though the clause still remains in our Constitutions, both State and Federal, has, as an organization, passed away in almost every State of the Union, and only remains to us as a memory of the past, probably never to be revived." Ibid., 158.

222. Halbrook (1984) (supra note 201), at 85–86.

223. Stephen P. Halbrook, *Freedmen, The Fourteenth Amendment, and the Right to bear Arms,* 1855–1876 (Westport, Conn.: Praeger Publishers, 1998), vii. (See ibid., 1–57 and 192–195 (especially pages 39–44) for details and discussion.) Section 14 of the Freedmen's Bureau Act (Act of July 16, 1866, 14 Stat. 173, 176) provides: "That in every State or district where the ordinary course of judicial proceedings has been interrupted by the rebellion, and until the same shall be fully restored, and in every State or district whose constitutional relations to the government have been practically discontinued by the rebellion, and until such State shall have been restored in such relations, and shall be duly represented in the Congress of the United States, the right to make and enforce contracts, to sue, be parties, and give evidence, to inherit, purchase, lease, sell, hold, and convey real and personal property, and have full and equal benefit of all laws and proceedings concerning personal liberty, personal security, and the acquisition, enjoyment, and disposition of estate, real and personal, including the constitutional right to bear arms, shall be secured to and enjoyed by all the citizens of such State or district without respect to race or color or previous condition of slavery. And whenever in either such States or districts the ordinary course of judicial proceedings has been interrupted by the rebellion, and until the same shall have been fully

restored, and until such State shall have been restored in its constitutional relations to the government, and shall be duly represented in the Congress of the United States, the President shall, through the commissioner and the officers of the bureau, and under such rules and regulations as the President, through the Secretary of War, shall prescribe, extend military protection and have military jurisdiction over all cases and questions concerning the free enjoyment of such immunities and rights, and no penalty or punishment for any violation of law shall be imposed or permitted because of race or color, or previous condition of slavery, other or greater than the penalty or punishment to which white persons may be liable by law for the like offense. But the jurisdiction conferred by this section upon the officers of the Bureau shall not exist in any State where the ordinary course of judicial proceedings has not been interrupted by the rebellion, and shall cease in every State when the courts of the State and the United States are not disturbed in the peaceable course of justice, and after such State shall be fully restored in its constitutional relations to the government, and shall be duly represented in the Congress of the United States."

224. In his *Freedom, The Fourteenth Amendment, and the Right to Bear Arms*, Halbrook offers many evidences designed to show that there was a rather widespread original understanding that the privileges or immunities clause incorporates the SAR. But, in my opinion, Halbrook's argument insofar as it is based upon these evidences is weak because most purported supporters of the incorporation thesis appear to me to have maintained either: (1) the erroneous contrarian opinion that the Second Amendment per se also limits the states and that the Court had therefore erred in holding that the Bill of Rights limits only the United States; or (2) that all the specific rights of the Bill of Rights are necessarily denoted by the privileges or immunities clause; or (3) that the essential fundamental rights of free persons includes some substantive rights (unrelated to militia membership) with respect to firearms for protection of person or property; or (4) that the Second Amendment right applies to the states because freedom from racial discrimination was constitutionalized by the adoption of the Thirteenth and/or Fourteenth Amendment and thus all laws and regulations that condition the right of ownership, carrying, or use of firearms upon race, color or previous condition of servitude were nullified. As to the first point, this erroneous view has been and still is very common among many persons who fail to appreciate the profound significance of the differences between parallel provisions in sections 9 and 10 of article I of the Constitution. As to the second point, this erroneous view in question arises because of the neglect of the significance

of the copresence of a due process clause in both the Bill of Rights and the Fourteenth Amendment. As to the third point, the constitutional right asserted sounds more in the substantive aspects of the due process clause rather than in the Second Amendment since the latter bans any infringement because a well-regulated militia is purportedly necessary to the security of a free state. As to the fourth point, the focus of many was on insisting upon the necessary concrete application of the freedom from racial discrimination to firearms control and not upon a freedom-right that the SAR not be infringed by even a color-blind law. Finally, Halbrook's book is seriously flawed because throughout this writing he fails to adequately take into account that the SAR is not a true freedom but rather merely a conditional liberty-right, and that the presence of the prefatory clause of the Second Amendment itself demonstrates that the complete ban on any infringement is grounded on the necessity of a militia for a free state rather than upon the right itself.

225. According to the Court, the privileges or immunities clause does not incorporate the SAR. See *United States* v. *Cruikshank*, 92 U.S. 542, 553 (1876); *Presser* v. *Illinois*, 116 U.S. 252, 265–66 (1886); *Miller* v. *Texas*, 153 U.S. 535, 539 (1894); *Twining* v. *New Jersey*, 211 U.S. 78, 98 (1908). But this doctrine is based upon the erroneous principle that the privileges or immunities clause protects only those rights of American citizens that arise out of the nature or essential character of the national government. On the other hand, the Court stated by way of dictum in *Presser*, 166 U.S. at 265, that "the states cannot, even laying the [Second Amendment] out of view, prohibit the people from keeping and bearing arms, so as to deprive the United States of their rightful resource for maintaining the public security and disable the people from performing their duty to the general government"—this because "all citizens capable of bearing arms constitute the reserved military force or reserve militia of the United States as well of the States, and, in view of this prerogative of the general government, as well as of its general powers." The Court has not, as far as I am aware, adumbrated upon this dictum. However, if the Constitution prohibits a state from forbidding members of the United States militia from possessing firearms that the federal government requires of them, it does not follow that we have thereby a constitutional privilege of American citizens that cannot be abridged by the states. The *Presser* dictum would apply only with respect to such militia members specified by a federal statute that requires them to own and maintain specified arms for militia purposes, and authorizes arm-bearing only when the same takes place during the course of performing militia duties, or in connection with them.

226. Halbrook, a skilled polemicist with keen analytical ability, appears to be quite aware that successful opposition to registration of firearms upon Second Amendment grounds depends upon the SAR being a freedom (rather than a conditional liberty-right). Halbrook (1991) (supra note 203), at 204n330; Stephen P. Halbrook, "What the Framers Intended: A Linguistic Analysis of the Right to 'Bear Arms'" 49 Law & Cont. Probs. 151, 160–62 (1986).

227. AMAR, 297. In a subsequent article, Amar frankly states: "To the extent that the Privileges or Immunities Clause ranges beyond refined incorporation of the first ten amendments, it is, strictly speaking, beyond the scope of my book." "An(other) Afterword on *The Bill of Rights*," 87 Geo. L. J. 2347, 2353 (1999).

228. I had previously discussed the matter in Guminski (supra note 3), at 811–20.

229. Act of April 9, 1866, 14 Stat. 27. Section 1 provided: "[A]ll persons born in the United States and not subject to any foreign power, excluding Indians not taxed, are hereby declared to be citizens of the United States." The constitutionality of this provision was challenged upon the ground that, according to the *Dred Scott* Case, the constitutional authority of Congress to naturalize is limited to aliens (and tribal Indians considered as aliens), and that it can not be deemed as declaratory of preexisting constitutional law in view of the holding of *Dred Scott* concerning the incapacity of native-born blacks for national citizenship. There were three chief grounds advanced for holding that the citizenship clause of the Civil Rights Act was valid: (1) that, despite *Dred Scott*, all free, native-born nationals (even if formerly enslaved) were American citizens; (2) that Congress had the power to naturalize any person who was not a naturalborn citizen of the United States; and (3) the enforcement section of the Thirteenth Amendment empowered Congress to naturalize blacks.

230. The reader is cordially entreated, if he or she so prefers, to substitute "before the adoption of the 1866 Civil Rights Act (assuming arguendo the validity of its citizenship clause)" in lieu of "before the adoption of the Fourteenth Amendment.

231. Some noncitizens, and others, are also *derivatively* entitled to the benefit of some components of the privileges and immunities of American citizens to the extent that such denial of such entitlement would deprive American citizens of their entitlement inn some particular fashion.

232. According to Professor Amar, the adoption of the Fourteenth Amendment had the effect of redefining incorporated rights in terms of the dominant understanding of the founders of the Fourteenth Amendment

rather than that of the founders of the Constitution and the Bill of Rights. AMAR, 236, 256–57, 243–44. One can agree, as I do, with Amar that, for example, the meaning of a First Amendment freedom is to be chiefly determined by recourse to the more sound understanding of that freedom during the founding of the Fourteenth Amendment rather than that which obtained during the founding of the Bill of Rights.

233. AMAR, 171 n*: "This first sentence of the Fourteenth Amendment consciously overruled *Dred Scott*'s holding that blacks could never be 'citizens.'" See also ibid. at 196n*: "It should also be noted that the first sentence of the Civil Rights Act proclaimed blacks to be citizens, and under a strong declaratory vision this proclamation itself carried with it all the privileges and immunities of national citizenship." I do not contend that Amar denies that antebellum national citizenship is paramount. My complaint is that he does not sufficiently consider it in its relationship to the privileges or immunities clause. The Court had earlier held that, for purposes of the diversity clause, a citizen of the United States who resides in a state is a citizen of that state. *Gassies* v. *Ballon,* 31 U.S. (6 Pet.) 761, 762 (1832). Thus that part of the citizenship clause that provides that American citizens are citizens of the state wherein they reside can be considered as declaratory of preexisting law. I do not think that Amar questions this; if he also agrees that the citizenship clause is declaratory of preexisting law concerning the paramountcy of national citizenship.

234. Amar (2006) (supra note 15), at 381.

235. 83 U.S. at 72–73.

236. Ibid., 73.

237. See infra note 344 for text of section 1 of the Civil Rights Act of 1866.

238. 83 U.S. at 79.

239. 73 U.S. (6 Wall.) 36 (1867).

240. 83 U.S. at 79. The Court's opinion in the *Slaughter-House Cases* then noted that the *Crandall* opinion "quote[d] from the language of Chief Justice Taney in another case … 'that, for all the great purposes for which the Federal government was established, we are one people with one common country; we are all citizens of the United States;' and it is as such citizens that their rights are supported in this court in *Crandall* v. *Nevada*." 83 U.S. at 79. The *Crandall* opinion itself declared: "The people of these United States constitute one nation" for federal purposes. 73 U.S. at 43.

241. Interestingly enough, the author of the Court's opinions in both *Crandall* and the *Slaughter-House Cases* was none other than Justice Miller. *Crandall* was decided on March 16, 1868, before the Secretary

of State unreservedly certified on July 28, 1868 that the Fourteenth Amendment had been ratified by the requisite number of states. I surmise that, after the adoption of the Fourteenth Amendment, Justice Miller found it necessary to reexamine what it means to be a citizen of the United States.

242. 48 U.S. (7 How.) 283 (1849).

243. 73 U.S. at 49.

244. 73 U.S. at 48–49 (quoting from 48 U.S. at 492 (dissenting opinion, C.J. Taney) (emphasis added). The emphasized matter is the only portion from the Taney's opinion in the *Passenger Cases* that was quoted in the *Slaughter-House Cases*, 83 U.S. at 79.

245. Thus *Crandall* vindicates the right of interstate travel with respect to all citizens of any given state. *Crandall,* however, did not hold that a state was precluded by the Constitution from abridging the freedom of intrastate travel for its citizens, and therefore (given the comity clause) that of citizens of other states temporarily within its borders, although this liberty is a component of the more general freedom of travel within the United States. However, I maintain that the freedom of travel, as a privilege of American citizens, is not limited to instances of inter-jurisdictional travel within the United States (the District of Columbia, incorporated federal territories (if any) and the states); it also encompasses freedom of travel within any such jurisdiction.

246. I regret appearing to sound so *clinical* in treating of what is an extremely painful subject, that is the inferior and degraded status of persons of color according to then the law of the land. But perhaps we may discover, however, that it may be true, that in some cases good may come from evil.

247. In *United States* v. *Wheeler,* 254 U.S. 281 (1920), the Court stated that the privilege of national citizenship relating to travel as expounded in *Crandall* pertains only to a state statute that "was held to directly burden the performance by the United States of its governmental functions, and also to limit rights of the citizens growing out of such functions." Ibid., 299. The comity clause, the *Wheeler* Court confirmed, prohibits discriminatory action by one state against citizens of other states with respect to interstate travel, including the right of free ingress and regress. Ibid., 298. *Wheeler* also asserted that freedom of interstate ingress and egress was a privilege of state citizenship by virtue of the comity clause. Ibid., 294–98. Justice Douglas, in his concurring opinion in *Edwards* v. *California,* 314 U.S. 160, 178–80 (1941), sharply criticized the narrow reading by *Wheeler* of the doctrine of *Crandall.* According to Justice Douglas, *Crandall* held that the right to move freely from state to state is a right of national citizenship.

Ibid., 178–79. He noted that "the thrust of the Crandall Case is deeper" than as asserted in *Wheeler* since, as he later explains "[t]he statute in that case applied to citizens of Nevada as well as to citizens of other States. That is to say, Nevada was not 'discriminating against citizens of other States in favor of its own.'" Ibid., 180–81.

248. 83 U.S. at 94 (Field, J., dissenting). Justice Curtis, in his dissenting opinion in *Dred Scott*, opined that the true doctrine is "[t]hat it is left to each State to determine what free persons, born within its limits, shall be citizens of each State, and thereby be citizens of the United States." Thus he rejected as false the proposition: "That all free persons, born within the several States, are citizens of the United States." 60 U.S. at 577–78.

249. 83 U.S. at 95. Field continued his description of Taney's doctrine in the *Dred Scott Case*: "[I]t was not in the power of any state to invest any other person with citizenship so that he could enjoy the privileges of a citizen under the Constitution, and that, therefore, the descendants of persons brought to this country and sold as slaves were not, and could not be, citizens within the meaning of the Constitution." Ibid.

250. Ibid., 95. In his separate dissenting opinion, Justice Bradley opined: "The question is now settled by the 14th Amendment itself, that citizenship of the United States is the primary citizenship in this country; and that state citizenship is secondary depending upon the citizen's place of residence. The states have not now, if they ever had, any power to restrict their citizenship to any classes or persons." 83 U.S. at 112.

251. 6 F.Cas. 546 (C. C. E. D. Pa. 1823) (No. 3,230) (Washington, Circuit J.) According to Justice Washington, the rights denoted by the descriptive term of the comity clause "are, in their nature fundamental; which belong, of right, to the citizens of all free government and which have, at all times, been enjoyed by the citizens of the several states which compose this Union, from the time of their becoming free, independent, and sovereign.... [These rights are] subject nevertheless to such restraints as the government may justly prescribe for the general good of the whole." Ibid., 551. In my opinion, so-called fundamental rights "subject ... to such restraints as the government many justly prescribe for the general good of the whole" are not a subset of the constitutional privileges and immunities of the American people constitutionally shielded as they are against all abridgments.

252. 83 U.S. at 97. The term "fundamental rights of citizens in all free governments" should be understood as a term of art to refer, generally, to that class of rights that Justice Washington described in *Corfield v. Coryell* as being the privileges and immunities of citizens in the several

states, within the meaning of the comity clause—which provision has only antidiscriminatory aspects.

253. 83 U.S. at 95.

254. Ibid., 96. It is important to bear in mind that each so-called natural and inalienable right belonging to all citizens is "subject nevertheless to such restraints as the government may justly prescribe for the general good of the whole"—according to Justice Washington. So, assuming the theory of the privileges or immunities clause according to the dissenting justices in the *Slaughter-House Cases,* that clause should only serve to prohibit *unjust* restraints by the states on the rights denoted by the descriptive term of the comity clause. But the ostensible thrust of the dissenting opinions in the *Slaughter-House Cases* was that the numerous rights denoted by the descriptive term of the comity clause are completely protected by the privileges or immunities clause against abridgments by the states.

255. 245 U.S. 366, 389 (1918): "[The Fourteenth Amendment] broadened the national scope of the Government under the Constitution by causing citizenship of the United States to be paramount and dominant instead of being subordinate and derivative." The cases upheld the validity of military conscription during World War I against various claims.

256. 296 U.S. 404 (1935). *Colgate* was overruled by *Madden* v. *Kentucky,* 309 U.S. 83, 92–93 (1940) insofar as *Colgate* held that the right to engage in interstate commerce is a privilege of national citizenship.

257. 296 U.S. at 427.

258. 88 U.S. (21 Wall.) 162 (1985).

259. Ibid., 165.

260. Ibid., 165–67.

261. Ibid., 167 The Court is referring evidently to native-born blacks in the last sentence of this quotation.

262. Ibid., 167–78.

263. The surviving minority justices in the *Slaughter-House Cases* (i.e., Swayne, Field, Bradley), who joined in the *Minor* v. *Happersett* opinion, apparently no longer had the need to be doubtful about the paramountcy of national citizenship before the adoption of the Fourteenth Amendment since they had failed to prevail in that case with their theory that the descriptive term of the privileges or immunities clause denoted the same fundamental rights as that of the comity clause.

264. 169 U.S. 649 (1898).

265. Ibid., 674–75. See also ibid., 693: "The Fourteenth Amendment affirms the ancient and fundamental rules of citizenship by birth within the territory, in the allegiance and under the protection of the country, including all children of resident aliens [except for those not subject to

the jurisdiction of the United States]." The Court pointed out that "[t]o hold that the Fourteenth Amendment of the Constitution excludes from citizenship the children, born in the United States, of citizens or subjects of other countries would be to deny citizenship to thousands of persons of English, Scotch, Irish, German, or other European parentage who have always been considered and treated as citizens of the United States." Ibid., 694.

266. Ibid., 676. In confirmation of the Court's doctrine in *Wong Kim Ark* was an early statute that clearly presupposed that all white native-born American nationals were American citizens. See the Act for the regulation of seamen on board the public and private vessels of the United States, March 3, 1813, 2 Stat. 809: § 1 (prohibiting employment as seamen of "any person or persons not citizens of the United States, or persons of colour, natives of the United States").

267. Accord: *Van Valkenburg* v. *Brown*, 43 Cal. 45, 47 (1872): "No white person born within the limits of the United States, and subject to their jurisdiction ... owes the status of citizenship in the recent amendments to the Federal Constitution"; *State* v. *Gibson*, 36 Ind. 389, 392 (1871): white persons born in the United States before adoption of the Fourteenth Amendment "are by birthright citizens." In *Rogers* v. *Bellei*, 401 U.S. 815, 829–30 (1970), the Court had occasion to observe: "Mr. Justice Gray [speaking for the Court in *United States* v. *Wong Kim Ark*, 169 U.S. at 688] has observed that the first sentence of the Fourteenth Amendment was 'declaratory of existing rights, and affirmative of existing law,' so far as the qualifications of being born in the United States, being naturalized in the United States, and being subject to its jurisdiction are concerned."

268. 74 U.S. (7 Wall.) 700 (1869).

269. Ibid., 724–25.

270. Ibid. at 725.

271. Ibid., 721. Interestingly, the Court related that, as an effect of the adoption of the Thirteenth Amendment, "[t]he new freemen necessarily became part of the people, and the people still constituted the State[.]" Ibid., 728. This innuendo that native-born blacks are citizens was perhaps made in passing because the Court did not yet have the need to construe the Fourteenth Amendment.

272. U.S. CONST. art. I, § 2, cl. 2: "No Person shall be a Representative who shall not have been ... seven Years a Citizen of the United States"; art. I, § 3, cl. 3: "No Person shall be a Senator who shall not have ... been nine Years a Citizen of the United States[.]"

273. What about the citizens of the Northwest Territory?—that territory, as to which several states previously had conflicting claims, was

ceded by them to the United States before the Constitution's adoption. According to the Northwest Ordinance (July 13, 1787), the states had agreed that "[t]he said territory ... shall forever remain a part of this Confederacy" (§ 14, art. 4), out of which "[t]here shall be formed ... not less than three nor more than five States" (§ 14, art. 5). The Constitution required that "[a]ll ... engagements entered into, before the Adoption of this Constitution, shall be valid against the United States, under this Constitution, as under the Confederation." U.S. CONST., art. 6, cl. 1. Before the Constitution's adoption, at least those white Northwest-Territorial citizens who were formerly citizens of some state, and their native-born descendants, were citizens of the United States, in view of the constitutional requirements that senators and representatives must be citizens of the United States for at least nine and seven years respectively.

274. Even some opponents of the Civil Rights Act of 1866 and the Fourteenth Amendment acknowledged that white native-born children of foreign immigrants were American citizens as a matter of preexisting constitutional law. See, e.g., *Cong. Globe*, 39th Cong., 1st Sess., 498 (1866) (remarks of Sen. Edgar Cowan).

275. Justice McClean: "Being born under our Constitution and laws, no naturalization is required, as one of foreign birth, to make him [Dred Scott] a citizen. The most general and appropriate definition of the term 'citizen' is 'a freeman.'" 60 U.S. at 531. But, according to McClean: "If Congress should deem slaves or free persons of color injurious to the population of a free Territory, as conducing to lessen the value of the public lands, or on any other ground connected with the public interest, they have the power to prohibit them from becoming settlers in it." Ibid., 543.

276. Attorney General Edward Bates: "But it is said that African negroes are a degraded race, and that all who are tainted with that degradation are forever disqualified for the functions of citizenship. I can hardly comprehend the thought of the absolute incompatibility of degradation and citizenship. I thought that they often went together." 10 Op. Att'y. Gen., 382, 398 (November 19, 1862). Bates proceeded to point out that individuals are degraded by "the most humiliating punishments ... against persons guilty of certain crimes and misdemeanors." Ibid. Of course, there is a world of difference between the inferior and degraded status of an individual that obtains by virtue of his conviction of a public offense and that which obtains by virtue of membership in a class defined by such natural characteristics as race, color, ethnic origin, caste, or sex, and thus regardless of individual fault or defect of character.

277. The term "national" is used to apply to persons, whether or not citizens, who owe permanent allegiance to the United States. The native-born inhabitants, formerly aliens but not yet naturalized, of unincorporated territory ceded to or otherwise acquired by the United States would be nationals of the United States. According to *Dred Scott*, native-born blacks, whether free or slave, were nationals (to use the modern term), albeit they were not and could not be American citizens, because they "did owe [permanent] allegiance to the government." 60 U.S. at 420.

278. See Guminski (supra note 3), at 812, for my initial exposition of how freedom of travel and migration throughout the United States is a privilege of American citizens in the sense of the privileges or immunities clause.

279. Free resident, noncitizen nationals and permanent resident aliens, and American citizens, are generally entitled insofar as they free persons with the right of permanent residence to at least *some* liberty of travel within the United States by virtue of the due process clauses. See *Williams* v. *Fears*, 179 U.S. 270, 274 (1900); *Truax* v. *Raich*, 239 U.S. 33, 39 (1915). But our discussion in Part II of this book prescinds from issues pertaining to the substantive aspects of the due process clauses since we are now speaking of the privileges or immunities clause.

280. 254 U.S. at 293. It also declared that the right of free interstate travel as a privilege of national citizenship is limited to such rights as grow out of the performance of governmental functions of the United States. Ibid., 299.

281. The right of citizens of a particular state to interstate free ingress and egress can be rightly considered as fundamental only upon the assumption that the state is a member of a confederate or federal union with a common citizenship. Otherwise, the right of a citizen of one state to free ingress into and egress from another state cannot *necessarily*, in my view, be considered as a component of a fundamental right of free persons as such. Absent an organic union of states with a common citizenship, if I as a citizen of state A have the right of free ingress and egress with respect to A, it does not follow that state B, of which I am not a citizen, necessarily has the duty to recognize any right on my part of free ingress or egress with respect to it. Any such duty arises out of comity, treaty, or some other source.

282. See *United States* v. *Guest*, 383 U.S. 745, 759n16 (1966). *Guest* not only ruled that freedom to travel throughout the United States is a basic right under the Constitution (ibid., 758); it also ruled that the federal government had authority to define and punish offenses by private action pertaining to interferences with the federal right of citizens to travel freely

from state to state. Ibid., 757–60. But this book is exclusively concerned with violations of rights by governmental action.

283. Article IV of the Articles of Confederation provides in part: "The better to secure and perpetuate mutual friendship and intercourse among the people of the different States in this Union, the free inhabitants of each of these States, paupers, vagabonds and fugitives excepted, shall be entitled to all the privileges and immunities of free citizens in the several States; and the people of each State shall have free ingress and regress to and from any other State, and shall enjoy therein all the privileges of trade and commerce, subject to the same duties, impositions and restrictions as the inhabitants thereof, respectively." The Articles of Confederation were ratified and in force on March 1, 1781. (The text of the Articles is available online at http://lcweb2.loc.gov/cgi-bin/ampage?collId=llsl&fileName=001/llsl001.db&recNum=127.)

284. The comity clause secured freedom of travel and migration of citizens of state A who enter state B against discriminatory violations by state B; the clause itself did not protect the citizens of state B against substantive violations of such freedom. It also did not protect the citizens of the District of Columbia or the federal territories.

285. For how the Court has failed to definitively identity the source of the freedom of travel and migration of the American people, see, e.g., *United States* v. *Guest*, 383 U.S. at 759 ("Although there have been recurring differences in emphasis within the Court as to the source of the constitutional right of interstate travel, there is no need here to canvass these differences further. All have agreed that the right exists"; and *Saenz* v. *Roe*, 526 U.S. 489, 500–01 (1999) ("For the purposes of this case … we need not identify the source of [the right of free interstate ingress and egress] in the text of the Constitution.… [It] may simply have been 'conceived from the beginning to be a necessary concomitant of the stronger Union the Constitution created'").

286. 314 U.S. 166, 181. The Court in *Edwards* held that a California statute penalizing the bringing or assisting to bring to the state any indigent nonresident knowing him to be an indigent violates the commerce clause of the Constitution.

287. Ibid., 182.

288. This assertion is, admittedly, somewhat inferential because Justice Jackson did not expressly address the issue of free intrastate travel and migration as also being a component of a constitutional privilege pertaining to travel and migration.

289. 314 U.S. at 183 (emphasis added).

290. 314 U.S. at 177 (Justices Blacks and Murphy concurring).

291. 314 U.S. at 179. Justice Douglas rightly observed: "But there is not a shred of evidence in the record of the Crandall Case that the persons there involved were en route on any such mission any more than it appears in this case that Duncan entered California to interview some federal agency." Ibid., 178. He also pointed out that "[t]he [Nevada] statute in [*Crandall*] applied to citizens of Nevada as well as to citizens of other States." Ibid., 180–81.

292. 314 U.S. at 179.

293. 83 U.S. at 79. The Court, in the *Slaughter-House Cases*, however, remarked that one privilege of American citizens conferred by the Fourteenth Amendment "is that a citizen of the United States can, of his own volition, become a citizen of any state of the Union by a bona fide residence therein, with the same rights as other citizens of that state." Ibid., 80.

294. 314 U.S. at 180.

295. 314 U.S. at 181.

296. In the words of the Court: "It would give to persons of the negro race, who were recognized as citizen in any one State of the Union, the right to enter every other State whenever they pleased, singly or in companies, without pass or passport, and without obstruction, to sojourn there as long as they pleased, to go where they pleased at every hour of the day or night without molestation, unless they committed some violation of law for which a white man would be punished." 60 U.S. at 417.

297. Ibid., 422–23.

298. Ibid., 408–09, 413, 416.

299. With respect to bans on immigration of free persons of color in free states see: Paul Finkelman, "Prelude to the Fourteenth Amendment: Black Legal Rights in the Antebellum North," 17 Rutgers L. J. 415, 419–25, 430–43 (1986), and Leon F. Litwack, *North of Slavery: The Negro in the Free States 1790–1860* (Chicago: University of Chicago Press, 1961), 66–74.

300. See, e.g., *Cong. Globe*, 35th Cong., 2d Sess., 970 (1859) (remarks of Rep. John B. Clark); ibid., 39th Cong., 1st Sess., 3211–17 (1866) (remarks of Rep. William E. Niblack).

301. See, e.g., *Cong. Globe*, 35th Cong., 2d Sess., 97475 (1859) (remarks of Rep. Henry L. Dawes); and ibid., 984 (remarks of Rep. John Bingham).

302. See Guminski (supra note 3), at 772–73, 817–819, for my initial exposition of how exemption from racial or ethnic discrimination is an immunity of American citizens in the sense of the privileges or immunities clause.

303. For a very useful general discussion of the legal and practical status of free persons of color in the slave states, see Ira Berlin, *Slaves Without Masters: The Free Negro in the Antebellum South* (New York: Random House, 1976).

304. See *Rabang* v. *Boyd*, 353 U.S. 427 (1957) (*held:* a Filipino admitted to the United States before the date that the Philippines became independent, but convicted of a narcotics violation after such date, was a deportable alien since his status as a noncitizen national of the United States terminated when the Philippines became independent. The Court rejected the contention that noncitizen nationals, residents of unincorporated territory or possessions, had the constitutional right to migrate to the United States, and that Congress could not apply federal laws relating to the immigration, exclusion, or expulsion of aliens to such nationals. For how the Court selectively applied some but not all rights specified in the Bill of Rights to the territories and possessions of the United States, see generally the insular cases: *Hawaii* v. *Mankichi*, 190 U.S. 197 (1901); *Downes* v. *Bidwell*, 182 U.S. 244 (1901); *Dorr* v. *United States*, 195 U.S. 138 (1904); *Ocampo* v. *United States*, 234 U.S. 91 (1914); *Balzac* v. *Porto Rico*, 258 U.S. 298 (1922); see *Examining Board v. Flores de Otero,* 426 U.S. 572, 599n30 (1976). See Howe, *The Insular Cases* (supra note 95).

305. This antebellum notion of paramount national citizenship was maintained, for example, by Justice John McLean in his dissenting opinion in *Dred Scott.* Thus he asserted that a native-born, free person of color was an American citizen. 60 U.S. at 543. McLean, however, also declared: "If Congress should deem slaves or *free colored persons* injurious to the population of a free Territory, as conducing to lessen the value of the public lands, or on any other ground connected with the public interest, they have the power to prohibit them from becoming settlers in it." (Emphasis added.)

306. 17 U.S. (4 Wheat.) 316, 403–04 (1819).

307. Ibid., 404. It is precisely because "[I]n our country ... the people are sovereign and the Government cannot sever its relationship to the people by taking away their citizenship." *Afroyim* v. *Rusk*, 387 U.S. 253, 257 (1967).

308. 60 U.S. at 404. According to the *Dred Scott* opinion, "a person may be a citizen, that is, a member of the community who form the sovereignty, although he exercises no share of the political power, and is incapacitated from holding particular offices." Ibid. at 422.

309. AMAR, 27.

310. Ibid., 119–20.

311. AMAR, 170–71. Amar adds "only" after "their benefit." This gloss by him is an unwarranted reading of the relevant passage in the *Dred Scott* opinion. See 60 U.S. at 410–11. That opinion, I repeat, can best be understood as meaning that a native, freeborn black was not a citizen and therefore was not entitled to those special rights, privileges, and immunities that the Constitution secures for only American citizens. *Dred Scott* does not expressly or impliedly say that only American citizens are entitled to every constitutional right, privilege or immunity secured for them. On the other hand, native, freeborn blacks were determined by the *Dred Scott* opinion to be incapable of national citizenship because of their radical inferior and degraded status as such—a status that precluded constitutional entitlement to First Amendment and other constitutional freedoms. The admittedly vague or ambiguous expression in the opinion must be read in light of its explicitly, and most precisely, expressed declaration that "[t]he question with which we are now dealing is, whether a person of the African race can be a citizen of the United States, and become thereby entitled to a *special* privilege, by virtue to his title to that character, and which, under the Constitution, *no one but a citizen can claim.*" 60 U.S. at 425 (emphasis added).

312. 83 U.S. at 73. This statement appears to implicitly deny that the naturalization of native-born blacks in the 1866 Civil Rights Act was valid. In *Afroyim v. Rusk,* 387 U.S. at 263, the Court declared that, notwithstanding the naturalization of African Americans by the 1866 Civil Rights Act, the "undeniable purpose of the Fourteenth Amendment [was] to make citizenship of Negroes permanent and secure."

313. AMAR, 281.

314. Ibid.

315. AMAR, 281–82 (citing at ibid., 392n189: "[*Plessy*] 163 U.S. 547, 560 (Harlan, J., dissenting)") (emphasis and bracketed matter added by Amar). Harlan claimed in *Plessy* that "[t]he Thirteenth Amendment does not permit the withholding or the deprivation of any right necessarily inhering in freedom. It not only struck down the institution of slavery as previously existing in the United States, but it prevents the imposition of any burdens or disabilities that constitutes badges of slavery or servitude. It decreed universal civil freedom in this country." Harlan further wrote that "the Fourteenth Amendment ... added greatly to the dignity and glory of American citizenship, and to the security of personal liberty [quoting text of Section 1]. These two amendments, if enforced according to their true intent and meaning, will protect all the civil rights that pertain to freedom and citizenship." 163 U.S. at 555. Referring to *Dred Scott,* Harlan declared that "[t]he recent amendments of the Constitution, it was supposed, had

eradicated these principles" [i.e., the doctrine of *Dred Scott* that black Americans were not citizens and could not claim any of the rights and privileges that the Constitution provided for and secured to American citizens]. Ibid., 560.

316. AMAR, 182 (citing at ibid., 393n190: "[*Civil Rights Cases*] 109 U.S. 3, 48 (1883) (Harlan, J., dissenting)").

317. AMAR, 182, 393n191 (citing at ibid., 393n191: *Gibson v. Mississippi*, 162 U.S. 565, 591 (1896). Here Harlan was also speaking for the entire court when he declared: "the Constitution of the United States in its present form forbids, so far as civil and political rights are concerned, discrimination by the general government or by the states against any citizen because of his race. All citizens are equal before the law. The guaranties of life, liberty, and property are for all persons within the jurisdiction of the United States or of any state, without discrimination against any because of their race."

318. *Civil Rights Cases*, 109 U.S. at 36 (1883) (Harlan, J., dissenting).

319. Ibid., 48. Harlan's neglect of the privileges or immunities clause is quite understandable in view of the Court's neutering construction of that clause in the *Slaughter-House Cases*.

320. *Civil Rights Cases*, 109 U.S. at 46. According to Harlan, under the comity clause African Americans visiting from state A in state B became entitled to all such fundamental rights of state citizenship that are accorded by state B to her most favored citizens (i.e., its white citizens). Ibid., 48. The *Dred Scott* opinion took virtually the same point of view: native-and-free-born blacks, were they American citizens, visiting from state A in state B would be entitled to the fundamental rights provided by the law of state B for its white citizens. They could not be limited to only such rights that the law of state B provided for its free persons of color. 60 U.S. at 422–23.

321. *Civil Rights* Cases, 109 U.S. at 50.

322. Ibid., 46

323. Ibid.

324. AMAR, 282–83. Amar elsewhere (ibid., 178) sympathetically discusses John Harrison's "Reconstructing the Privileges or Immunities Clause," 101 Yale L.J. 1385 (1992), wherein Harrison proposes that the descriptive term of the privileges or immunities clause denotes the fundamental rights of citizens of all free governments, but only secures them from discriminatory-type abridgments. Harrison's theory is unduly complex and counterintuitive. One need not posit that the fundamental rights of citizens of all free governments are a subclass of the privileges and immunities of American citizens (within the meaning of the privileges

or immunities clause), but as such are secured only against discriminatory-type violations. It is much more simple to simply posit that exemption from invidious discrimination with respect to the fundamental rights of citizens of all free governments (in the traditional sense of the comity clause) is an immunity of American citizens, which immunity is secured against abridgments by either the United States (implicitly by the original Constitution) or the states (by the privileges or immunities clause). Occam's razor (i.e., entities are not to be multiplied beyond necessity (*entia non sunt multiplicanda praeter necessitatem*) should apply just as well in the domain of law as in philosophy and the sciences. Harrison is correct in noting: "[I]n recent times, the Court has not attempted to carry out the *Corfield* project of determining which categories of rights constitute privileges or immunities of citizens [per the comity clause]. Instead, it now interprets the clause in light of its presumed purpose of interstate harmony and asks whether some particular right is basic to the operation of the Union. [Citing *Baldwin* v. *Fish & Game Commission of Montana*, 436 U.S. 371, 383 (1978)]." Harrison, "Reconstructing," at 1454n267. Harrison immediately adds: "As a result, the Court has developed an interpretation of the concept of privileges and immunities that is adapted to the Comity Clause but that is not useful for interpreting the same words in the 14th Amendment." But not quite—unless one accepts his theory that the descriptive term of the privileges or immunities clause also denotes some common or state law rights but secures them only against discriminatory-type governmental action. I prefer to maintain that such rights are not denoted by the descriptive term of the clause, but rather that an immunity of American citizens against discriminatory action obtains as to them.

325. Harrison's interesting and stimulating article very persuasively shows that the equal protection clause does not provide an intellectually satisfying ground for asserting that the immunity from racial discrimination as to civil rights is a constitutional right. Harrison (supra note 324), at 1433–51. See my critique of the Court's doctrine that freedom from racial discrimination is based upon the equal protection clause of the Fourteenth Amendment and the implicit equal-protection component of the due process clause of the Fifth Amendment in my article. Guminski (supra note 3), at 772–73.

326. We also confront a "puzzlement." The Court presently holds that the Fifth Amendment due process clause includes among its components the right not to be denied equal protection of the laws with respect to racial discrimination. *Bolling* v. *Sharpe*, 347 U.S. 497 (1954): "[I]t would be unthinkable that the same Constitution would impose a lesser duty on the Federal Government. We hold that racial segregation in the public schools

of the District of Columbia is a denial of the due process of law guaranteed by the Fifth Amendment to the Constitution." Ibid., 500. However, the Court noted: "This disposition [i.e., that segregation in public schools violates the equal protection clause] makes unnecessary any discussion whether such segregation also violates the Due Process Clauses of the Fourteenth Amendment." *Brown* v. *Board of Education*, 347 US 483, 495 (1954). Since the Court was quite unwilling to confidently assert that the due process clause of the Fourteenth Amendment itself has an equal-protection component (even though both due process clauses are supposedly equivalent), it is likely to be quite unwilling to confidently assert (again even though both due process clauses are supposedly equivalent), that the Fifth Amendment due process clause incorporates First Amendment freedoms just because the Fourteenth Amendment due process clause does so.

327. Slaughter-*House Cases,* 83 U.S. at 71–72; *Strauder* v. *West Virginia,* 100 U.S. 303, 305–06 (1880) ("[The Thirteenth and Fourteenth Amendments] secur[ed] to a race recently emancipated, a race that, through many generations, had been held in slavery, all the civil rights that the superior race enjoy"); (*Ex Parte Virginia,* 100 U.S. 339, 344–45 (1880) ("One great purpose of [the Thirteenth and Fourteenth] Amendments was to raise the colored race from that condition of inferiority and servitude in which most of them had previously stood into perfect equality of civil rights with all other persons within the jurisdiction of the States. They were intended to take away all possibility of oppression by law because of race or color").

328. John Harrison remarks: "I hesitate to attribute to most participants in the framing and ratification of the Fourteenth Amendment any precise notion of the meaning of Section 1, other than it was designed to forbid Black Codes and constitutionalize the Civil Rights Act of 1866." Harrison (supra note 324), at 1397. I cannot join in Harrison's hesitation; but otherwise agree that section 1 of the Fourteenth Amendment "was designed to forbid Black Codes and constitutionalize the Civil Rights Act of 1866." But the question remains: how?

329. I do not mean to deny, indeed I affirm, that exemption from invidious racial discrimination as to civil rights should also be considered as prohibited by the due process clauses since such exemption should be perceived as implicit in that immunity from discrimination with respect to civil rights brought about by that universal civil freedom established with the abolition of slavery. But this argument necessarily depends upon the premise that the due process clauses have substantive aspects implicating the fundamental rights, privileges, and immunities of free persons as such

and thus grounded in the dignity of their civil freedom. It is very important, I think, to have an alternative but compelling argument that immunity from racial discrimination as to civil rights is a federal constitutional right, as to both the United States and the states, for those who maintain that the due process clauses neither have substantive aspects or that such aspects extend to fully secure the right in question, nor that the equal protection clause and the equal-protection component of the Fifth Amendment due process clause are severally capable of doing so.

330. 388 U.S. 1 (1967).
331. *Cong. Globe*, 39th Cong., 1st Sess., 3211–14 (1866).
332. Ibid., 3214.
333. Ibid., 3211.
334. Ibid., 3213.
335. Ibid., 3216–17. Ironically, the Indiana Supreme Court in *Smith* v. *Moody*, 26 Ind. 299 (1866), held that African Americans were citizens of the United States, and therefore the Indiana legislation banning black immigration was unconstitutional. The court, relying upon *Dred Scott,* asserted that if free native-born black Americans are American citizens, then they are entitled to the right of free interstate travel. 26 Ind. at 303. The court stated that the 1866 Civil Rights Act's citizenship clause was declaratory. 26 Ind. at 307. Moreover, *Dred Scott* "although never formally overruled ... is now disregarded by every department of the government." 26 Ind. at 304. The court appeared to concede that under the comity clause the host state could not limit, or restrict visiting citizens from another state, or place the party in an inferior grade (citing *Dred Scott*, 60 U.S. at 423). 26 Ind. at 303. But the same court in *State* v. *Gibso*n, 36 Ind. 389 (1871) ruled that the Indiana miscegenation statute was valid notwithstanding the Fourteenth Amendment. The court exclaimed that "to assert separateness is not to declare inferiority in either [race]." Ibid., 405. The court declared that native-born whites were born American citizens before the adoption of the citizenship clause, which was needed "to confer the right of citizenship upon persons of the African race, who had previously not been citizens." Ibid., 392. But there is no mention of *Smith* v. *Moody* or of *Dred Scott* in this opinion. The Indiana court concluded that the citizenship clause made black Americans citizens of the United States, but nevertheless they still did not have the right to intermarry with whites in order to avoid "'their intermarriage and that social amalgamation which leads to a corruption of races.'" 36 Ind. at 404. Alas! It is a remarkable phenomenon but "very natural ... for men to embrace those principles by which they find they can best defend their doctrines." David Hume, *Dialogues Concerning Natural Religion* (N. K. Smith ed.) (Indianapolis: Bobbs-Merrill Co., 1947), 140.

336. Some senators, such as Howard, held that Revels had been an American citizen since his birth as a free person; this even in the absence of the Fourteenth Amendment's citizenship clause. *Cong. Globe*, 41st Cong., 2d Sess., 1543 (1870). Others, such as Stewart, maintained that the citizenship clause relates back to birth. Ibid., 1566.

337. Ibid.,1510 (1870).

338. Ibid., 1511. Davis conveniently failed to remember that white Americans were equally not free to "go into a slave State and erect a printing office, and publish his essays against the existence of the institution of slavery, collect together the people of his race and everybody who would come and hear him, and denounce the institution, and tell his race that it was an institution cruel and inhuman, and ought to be overthrown."

339. Ibid., 1558.

340. Ibid., 1559.

341. Ibid.

342. Ibid.

343. Ibid., 40th Cong., 3rd Sess., 691.

344. Section 1 of the this statute (Act of April 9, 1866, 14 Stat. 27) provided: "That all persons born in the United States and not subject to any foreign power, excluding Indians not taxed, are hereby declared to be citizens of the United States; and such citizens, of every race or color, without regard to previous condition of slavery or involuntary servitude, except as a punishment for crime whereof the party shall have been duly convicted, shall have the same right, in every State or Territory in the United States, to make and enforce contracts, to sue, be parties, and give evidence, to inherit, purchase, lease, sell, hold, and convey real and personal property, and to full and equal benefit of all laws and proceedings for the security of person and property, as is enjoyed by white citizens, and shall be subject to like punishment, pains, and penalties, and to none other, any law, statute, ordinance, regulation, or custom, to the contrary notwithstanding."

345. See Berger (supra note 160), at 20–51. (But see Ely (supra note 108), at 30, 198–200, sharply criticizing Berger for holding that the privileges or immunities clause protects only those rights enumerated in the Civil Rights Act of 1866 against discriminatory action. Bergar, in his *The Fourteenth Amendment and the Bill of Rights* [Norman: University of Oklahoma Press, 1989], 41–42, 105–27, 144–45), persisted in the view that the descriptive term of the privileges or immunities clause denoted only the rights specified in the Civil Rights Act of 1866. For statements by some founders of the Fourteenth Amendment that it was needed in order to embody into the Constitution the anti-discriminatory provisions of the

1866 Civil Rights Act with respect to its enumerated rights, see *Cong. Globe*, 39th Cong., 1st Sess., 2459 (1866) (remarks of Rep. Stevens); ibid., 2462 (remarks of Rep. Garfield); ibid., 2465 (remarks of Rep. Thayer); ibid., 2509 (remarks of Rep. Spalding); and ibid. at 2896 (remarks of Sen. Howard).

346. Amar (2006) (supra note 15), at 380–85.

347. Ibid., 382. Amar's accompanying note 69 (ibid., 609) cites *Gibson* v. *Mississippi*, 162 U.S. 565, 591 (1896). See supra note 317.

348. Amar (2006) (supra note 15), at 382.

349. Ibid., 384. I infer that Amar would not maintain that freedom from discrimination based upon sexual orientation is not a constitutional immunity of the American people; although perhaps he maintains that it is a fundamental liberty-from right embraced by the substantive aspects of the due process clauses besides being covered by the equal protection clause. He will have to enlighten us about this matter.

350. In Guminski (supra note 3), at 819–20, I assert that freedom from invidious discrimination as to civil rights based upon gender is a constitutional immunity of American citizens. Amar also discusses freedom from invidious discrimination based upon gender in AMAR , 260–61, and in Amar (2006) (supra note 15), at 384–85. The right to be free from discrimination as to race, color, previous condition of servitude, and sex as to eligibility for the suffrage also is a constitutional immunity of American citizens. But this immunity is one constitutionally protected against abridgment by the states quite independently of the privileges or immunities clause as it concerns a political rather than an individual civil right.

351. 92 U.S. at 555 (1976).

352. U.S. CONST., art. I, § 9, cl. 8: "No Title of Nobility shall be granted by the United States." Id., § 10, cl.1: "No State shall … grant any Title of Nobility."

353. *Osborn* v. *Bank of the United States*, 22 U.S. (9 Wheat.) 738, 827 (1824): "A naturalized citizen is indeed made a citizen under an Act of Congress, but the act does not proceed to give, to regulate, or to prescribe his capacities. He becomes a member of society, possessing all the rights of a native citizen, and standing, in view of the Constitution, on the footing of a native. The constitution does not authorize Congress to enlarge or abridge those rights. The simple power of the national Legislature, is to prescribe a uniform rule of naturalization, and the exercise of this power exhausts it, so far as respects the individual." However, this equality does not extend necessarily to all political rights, such as the qualifications of a representative (U.S. CONST., art. I, § 2,

cl. 2), senator (ibid., § 3, cl. 3), and president (ibid., art. II, § 1, cl. 5). See also *Boyd* v. *Nebraska*, 143 U.S. 135, 170 (1892): "Admission on an equal footing with the original states in all respects whatever involves equality of constitutional right and power, which cannot thereafterwards be controlled, and it also involves the adoption as citizens of the United States of those whom Congress makes members of the political community, and who are recognized as such in the formation of the new state with the consent of Congress."

354. The Commonwealth of Puerto Rico is neither a state nor a territory of the United States. It has the constitutional status of an autonomous commonwealth, although its citizens are American citizens. Nevertheless, "the fundamental protections of the United States Constitution extend to the inhabitants of Puerto Rico." *Rodriguez* v. *Popular Democratic Party*, 457 U.S. 1, 7 (1982). See, *Examining Board* v. *Flores de Otero*, 426 U.S. 572, 600–01 (1976), where the Court leaves undecided whether it is the due process clause of the Fifth or the Fourteenth Amendment that applies to Puerto Rico. Nevertheless, the Court affirms that Puerto Rico may not constitutionally deprive any person of life, liberty, or property, without due process of law. I submit that the Court should squarely hold that, within the meaning of section 1 of the Fourteenth Amendment, Puerto Rico is deemed to be a state because of its commonwealth status is functionally equivalent to that of states for relevant purposes. The privileges or immunities clause should also be held to apply to Puerto Rico, in view of its quasi-state status, because its citizens are citizens of the United States. However, in my view, the privileges or immunities clause would not apply to a territory with commonwealth status but whose native-born inhabitants are not universally American citizens (e.g., the Commonwealth of the Philippines, 1934-46).

355. See Guminski (supra note 3), at 816–17, for my initial exposition that freedom from discrimination with respect to the rights denoted by the descriptive term of the comity clause is an immunity of American citizens in the sense of the privileges or immunities clause.

356. Note that the Court in *Saenz* v. *Roe*, 526 U.S. 489, 502–03 (1999) declared that the privileges or immunities clause protects the right of an American citizen, a citizen of state A, to migrate to state B and enjoy as a new citizen of that state all the rights and privileges enjoyed by the other citizens of state B. However, the Court appears to say that the privileges or immunities clause *conferred* (rather than just secured) the right in question. Hence, this case does not constitute a departure from the doctrine of the *Slaughter-House Cases* that the privileges or immunities clause embraces only those rights that were created by federal law.

357. I mention political freedom in Guminski (supra note 3), at 812–13. Reading, reflecting upon, and reacting to Alexander Meiklejohn's *Political Freedom: The Constitutional Powers of the People* (New York: Oxford University Press, 1965) very much influenced the formation of my views on political freedom as a constitutional privilege of American citizens. Meiklejohn's insights into how popular sovereignty and republican institutions of government relate to political expression helped me discern that what I call political freedom is constitutionally secured independently of the First Amendment. Meiklejohn, however, completely identified political freedom with the First Amendment freedoms of speech and the press. Nevertheless, the dominant original understanding of the founders of the Bill of Rights and the Fourteenth Amendment was that freedom of speech and the press encompassed virtually all subjects. See note 365 below.

358. "The United States shall guarantee to every State in this Union a Republican Form of Government." U.S. Const. art. IV, § 4.

359. 92 U.S. 542, 552 (1876) (emphasis added). Justice Story, referring to the assembly-petition right of the First Amendment, remarked: "This would seem unnecessary to be expressly provided for in a republican government, since it results from the very nature of its structure and institutions. It is impossible that it could be practically denied, until the spirit of liberty had wholly disappeared, and the people had become so servile and debased as to be unfit to exercise any of the privileges of freemen." Story (1833) (supra note 221), at 3: §1887.

360. 283 U.S. 359, 369 (1931).

361. 328 U.S. 654, 658 (1943).

362. *DeJonge* v. *Oregon*, 99 U.S. at 365.

363. Steven G. Calabresi & Sarah E. Agudo, "Individual Rights Under States Constitutions when the Fourteenth Amendment Was Ratified in 1868: What Rights Are Deeply Rooted in American History and Tradition?", 87 Texas L. Rev. 7, 43 (2009). I am very grateful to the authors of this excellent, comprehensive article for sending me an advance copy as well as other useful material. In confirmation of my claim that political freedom has the specific right of the free assembly clause as a component, five of the thirty-seven state constitutions in force in 1868 had a separate provision pertaining to 'political speech' as such; four of this group having each a free speech-free press provision that expressly related to all subjects as well. Del. Const. of 1831, art. 1, § 5: "The press shall be free to every citizen who undertakes to examine the official conduct of men acting in a public capacity, and any citizen may print on any such subject, being responsible for the abuse of that liberty." The following provision or one virtually identical appears in

four state constitutions (PA. CONST. of 1838, art. 9, § 7; ILL. CONST. of 1848, art. 13, § 23; TENN. CONST. of 1834, art. 1, § 19; KY. CONST. OF 1850, art. 13, § 9): "That the printing-presses shall be free to every person who undertakes to examine the proceedings of the legislature or any branch of government; and no law shall ever be made to restrain the right thereof." Vermont was unique in that its analog of the First Amendment free speech-free press provision provided (VT. CONST. of 1793, ch. 1, art. 13): "That the people have the right to freedom of speech, and of writing and publishing their sentiments, concerning the transactions of government, and therefore the freedom of press ought not to be restrained."

364. AMAR, 27.

365. In its address to the people of Quebec, the Continental Congress referred to freedom of the press as relating to "the advancement of truth, science, morality, and arts in general." ("To the Inhabitants of the Province of Quebec," October 24, 1774, in Worthington Chauncey Ford, et al., eds. *Journals of the Continental Congress 1774-1789* (Washington, 1904), 1: 108.) Justice Joseph Story, in writing of freedom of speech and the press, explained: "A little attention to the history of other countries in other ages will teach us the vast importance of this right. It is notorious that even to this day in some foreign countries it is a crime to speak on any subject, religious, philosophical, or political, what is contrary to the received opinions of the government or the institutions of the country, however laudable may be the design, and however virtuous may be the motive.... In some countries no works can be printed at all, whether or science, or literature, or philosophy, without the previous appropriation of government[.]" Story (1833) (supra note 221), at 3: § 1881. Twenty-eight of the thirty-seven state constitutions in force in 1868 (when the Fourteenth Amendment was ratified) expressly related free speech–free press provisions to all subjects; and one additional state constitution expressly related its free press provision to all subjects. According to Article V of the Constitution, proposed constitutional amendments require ratification by three fourths of the states. Hence an Article V consensus obtained with respect to free speech and free press provisions expressly relating to all subjects. I am grateful to Sarah E. Agudo (see note 363 above) for sending me the relevant texts.

366. I most emphatically reject the notion that the specific right of the free exercise clause is redundant upon the ground that religious freedom insofar as it pertains to *expression* encompasses all the freedom-rights in religious matters that are components of freedom of speech (i.e., expression— according to the Court's lexicon). Religious rituals and ceremonies, in my opinion, are not per se within the ambit of *freedom of*

speech or the press even though spoken or written words are involved. A church, temple, synagogue, mosque, and any other structure chiefly devoted to public worship is not just another hall, auditorium, or other public meeting place that from time to time is used for public worship. Compare the majority opinion (religious worship constitutes a form of religious speech) and the dissenting opinion by Justice White (religious worship is different from but overlaps with just religious speech) in *Widmar* v. *Vincent*, 454 U.S. 263 (1981), at 269n6 and 284–89 respectively. But then what should we expect of the Court when it has ruled in several cases that freedom of speech embraces public theatrical and other artistic performances? *Schad* v. *Borough of Mount Ephraim*, 452 U.S. 61, 65 (1981) ("live entertainment such as musical and dramatic works, fall within the First Amendment guarantee"). It is precisely because churches, temples, and other structures are chiefly devoted to public worship (and auxiliary purposes) that nondiscriminatory real property tax exemption for such places had been a historically sanctioned, constitutionally permissible accommodation of religion. (But see *Waltz* v. *Tax Commission*, 397 U.S. 664 (1970), which grounded the real property tax exemption for churches within a broader theoretical structure allowing such exemption for other nonprofit organizations devoted to secular enterprises.) Conversely, it is not a violation of the specific right of the free exercise clause to require that churches and other places chiefly devoted to public worship not be used for electioneering or other partisan purposes in order to qualify for a a real property tax exemption. However, a statute that grants property or other tax exemptions, that are not viewpoint-neutral in religious matters, to halls, auditoria, conferences centers, and other public meeting places (not ordinarily used as places for public worship) would constitute an establishment of religion. (See *Texas Monthly, Inc.* v. *Bullock*, 489 U.S. 1 (1989) (*held*: a state statute providing sales tax exemptions to religious groups for all and only periodicals that consist of writings sacred to a religious faith violates the establishment clause as applied to the states by the Fourteenth Amendment. Justice White, in his concurring opinion, maintained that the statute violated freedom of the press. Ibid., 25–26.) I agree that such viewpoint discriminatory tax exemptions for public meeting places (not chiefly used for religious worship) or the print media violate religious freedom—i.e., freedom of speech and the press in religious matters.

367. Guminski (supra note 3), at 810n157.

368. I maintained the proposition in question for only a fairly brief period of time contemporaneously with the writing and publication of my 1985 article.

369. I explain the essentials of these three leading theories in Chapter D (A Federalist-Accomodationist Theory of the Establishment Clause).

370. The quoted passage appears in the preamble to the statute entitled "An Act for establishing religion freedom" (January 16, 1786). William Waller Hening, ed. *The Statutes at Large; Being a Collection of All the Laws of Virginia* (1823), 12: 84–86 (1823). The statute itself provides in part that "that no man shall be compelled to frequent or support any religious worship, place or ministry whatsoever[.]"

371. In construing the quoted passage from its preamble, it should be noted that the Virginia statute on religious freedom followed the demise by committee inaction in 1784 on the proposed Bill Establishing a Provision for Teachers of the Christian Religion. This bill provided for a tax assessment in the nature of a surtax based on the sum payable as a property tax on property to be paid by each person chargeable with the tax. The specific purpose of the tax purpose was to collect monies to be distributed among the Christian religious societies as named by the taxpayers. The statute required, with certain exceptions in favor of Quakers and "Menonists," the religious societies to appropriate the received monies to support a minister or teacher of the gospel, or for providing places of divine worship, and for no other purpose. Monies collected from taxpayers who failed to appropriate the same were to be deposited in the public treasury, eventually to be used to fund seminaries of learning. Lists of the taxpayers, disclosing their identity and the identity of the religious society designated by him, were to be open for public inspection; as were the lists of taxpayers who did not designate any recipients. The text of the Virginia bill is included in the supplemental appendix to the dissenting opinion by Justice Rutledge in *Everson* v. *Board of Education*, 330 U.S. at 72–74.

372. "An Act for establishing religious freedom," Hening *Statutes* (supra note 370), 12: 86. The statute was originally drafted by Thomas Jefferson in 1779 and adopted, in large part due to James Madison's efforts, in 1786. The operative provision of the statute reads: "That no man shall be compelled to frequent or support any religious worship, place or ministry whatsoever, nor shall be enforced, restrained, molested, or burthened in his body or goods, nor shall otherwise suffer on account of his religious opinions or belief; but that all men shall be free to profess, and by argument to maintain, their opinion in matters of religion, and that the same shall in no wise diminish, enlarge or effect their civil capacities." Ibid. The preamble to the act reads in part: "that to suffer the civil magistrate to intrude his powers into the field of opinion, and to restrain the profession or propagation of principles on supposition of their ill tendency, is a dangerous fallacy, which at once destroys all religious

liberty, because he being of course judge of that tendency will make his opinions the rule of judgment, and approve or condemn the sentiments of others only as they shall square with or differ from his own; that it is time enough for the rightful purposes of civil government, for its officers to interfere when principles break out into overt acts against peace and good order; and finally, that truth is great and will prevail if left to herself, that she is the proper and sufficient antagonist to error, and has nothing to fear from the conflict, unless by human interposition disarmed of her natural weapons, free argument and debate, errors ceasing to be dangerous when it is permitted freely to contradict them." Ibid., 85–86.

373. *Religious freedom* in approximately the same sense as that intended in the Virginia statute of religious freedom was manifested in the Court's opinion in *Minersville School District* v. *Gobitis*, 310 U.S. 586, 593 (1940). Justice Frankfurter wrote for the Court: "Centuries of strife over the erection of particular dogmas as exclusive or all-comprehending faiths led to the inclusion of a guarantee for religious freedom in the Bill of Rights. The First Amendment, and the Fourteenth through its absorption of the First, sought to guard against repetition of those bitter religious struggles by prohibiting the establishment of a state religion and by securing to every sect the free exercise of its faith.… Government may not interfere with organized or individual expression of belief or disbelief. Propagation of belief—or even of disbelief—in the supernatural is protected, whether in church or chapel, mosque or synagogue, tabernacle or meetinghouse. Likewise, the Constitution assures generous immunity to the individual from imposition of penalties for offending, in the course of his own religious activities, the religious views of others, be they a minority or those who are dominant in government." The last sentence in the quoted passage cited *Cantwell* v. *Connecticutt*, 310 U.S. 296 (1940), which overturned on both free exercise and free speech grounds a breach-of-the-peace conviction that involved a Jehovah Witness stopping two men on a street, asking for and receiving permission to play a phonograph record; the playing of which greatly offended and incensed the two men, who were Catholic, because the content of the record attacked their religion and church.

374. Justice Scalia speaking for the Court in *Capital Square Review & Advisory Board.* v. *Pinette*, 515 U.S. 753, 760 (1995) declared: "[P]rivate religious speech, far from being a First Amendment orphan, is as fully protected under the Free Speech Clause as secular private expression. [Citations.] Indeed, in Anglo American history, at least, government suppression of speech has so commonly been directed *precisely* at religious speech that a free speech clause without religion would be *Hamlet*

without the prince. Accordingly, we have not excluded from free speech protections religious proselytizing [citation], or even acts of worship [citation]." But see supra note 366 where I disagree with the Court's view that religious worship is just another kind of religious speech within the scope of freedoms of speech and the press.

375. The Virginia statute on religious freedom consists of a preamble, an operative provision, and a closing declaration. Its operative provision affirms in substance that religious freedom encompasses freedom of opinion in matters of religion. See supra note 372 for the text of the operative provision. This provision was restated in VA. CONST. of 1830, art. III, § 11; and VA. CONST. of 1851, art. IV, § 15. It was also virtually restated in section 3 of the Declaration of Certain Constitutional Rights and Principles, of the Rhode Island Constitution of 1842. In 1799, the Virginia legislature reaffirmed the Virginia statute as being "a true exposition of the principles of the bill of rights and constitution [of Virginia]," and repealed all laws deemed as inconsistent with it. Samuel Shepherd, ed. *The Statutes at Large of Virginia* (1835), 2: 149. Section 16 of the Virginia Bill of Rights of June 12, 1776 (the text of which was later incorporated in the Virginia Constitutions of 1776, 1830, and 1851) reads: "That religion, or the duty which we owe to our Creator, and the manner of discharging it, can be directed only by reason and conviction, nor by force or violence; and therefore all men are equally entitled to the free exercise of religion, according to the dictates of conscience; and that it is the mutual duty of all to practice christian forbearance, love and charity towards each other."

376. In 1940, the Supreme Court held in *Cantwell* v *Connecticutt*, 372 U.S. at 303–04, 307, that the Fourteenth Amendment due process clause fully incorporates "the liberties guaranteed by the first Amendment," specifying the establishment and free exercise clauses. Later that same year in *Minersville School District* v. *Gobitis*, 310 U.S. at 593 (see supra note 365 for quoted matter), the Court again indicated that the Fourteenth Amendment due process clause protects religious freedom (as guaranteed in the Bill of Rights) by virtue of its incorporation of both the establishment and free exercise clauses of the First Amendment. (The unfortunate holding in *Gobitis*, that public school children may be constitutionally compelled to salute the flag, was subsequently overruled in *West Virginia Board of Education* v *Barnette*, 319 U.S. 624 (1943.)

377. 80 U.S. (13 Wall.) 679).

378. In *Kedroff* v. *St. Nicholas Cathedral*, 344 U.S. 94 (1952), an interchurch dispute involving rival Russian Orthodox churches, the Court described *Watson* as follows: "[A]lthough it contains a reference to the relations of church and state under our system of laws, [Watson]

was decided without depending upon prohibition of state interference with the free exercise of religion. It was decided in 1871, before judicial recognition of the coercive power of the Fourteenth Amendment to protect the limitations of the First Amendment against state action. It long antedated the 1938 [decisions in *Erie Railway Co. v. Tompkins*, 304 U.S. 64, and *Ruhlin v. New York Life Insurance Co.*, 304 U.S. 304 (1938), overruling *Swift v. Tyson*, 41 U.S. (16 Pet.) 1 (1842) and its progeny] and, therefore, even though federal jurisdiction in the case depended solely on diversity, the holding was based on general law [i.e., the general principles and doctrines of jurisprudence], rather than Kentucky law. The opinion radiates, however, a spirit of freedom for religious organizations, an independence from secular control or manipulation, in short, power to decide for themselves, free from state interference, matters of church government as well as those of faith and doctrine. Freedom to select the clergy, where no improper methods of choice are proven, we think, must now be said to have federal constitutional protection as a part of the free exercise of religion against state interference." Ibid.,115–16.

379. 80 U.S. at 727–28.

380. Ibid. at 728–29.

381. *Everson v. Board of Education*, 330 U.S. 1 (1947). Recall that although *Cantwell* and *Minersville* relied upon both religion clauses of the First Amendment, each case involved only a claim that religious freedom had been violated. *Everson* pertains to an establishment-of-religion issue not involving religious freedom.

382. 494 U.S. 872, 881–82 (1990). The *Smith* doctrine was affirmed in *City of Bourne v. Flores*, 521 U.S. 507 (1997).

383. 494 U.S. at 879.

384. 394 U.S. at 881–82. The *Smith* Court emphatically rejected the contention "that, even though exemption from generally applicable criminal laws need not automatically be extended to religiously motivated actors, at least the claim for a religious exemption must be evaluated under the balancing test set forth in *Sherbert v. Verner*, 374 U.S. 398 (1963). Under the *Sherbert* test, governmental actions that substantially burden a religious practice must be justified by a compelling governmental interest." 494 U.S. at 882–83. The cases cited in *Smith* to support its doctrine of hybrid-rights, with its apparent neglect of the establishment clause, can be fully explained with greater warrant by either strf-b or strf-c. The one exception, in my view, involves cases upholding the constitutional right of parents to direct the education of their children, (See *Pierce v. Society of Sisters*, 268 U.S. 510 (1925); *Farrington v. Tokushige*, 273 U.S. 284 (1927).) These cases ruled that a law requiring school-age children to

only attend public schools to satisfy compulsory education requirements violates the parental right as protected by the due process clause. But that right must be considered as consistent with "the power of the State reasonably to regulate all schools, to inspect, supervise and examine them, their teachers and pupils; to require that all children of proper age attend some school, that teachers shall be of good moral character and patriotic disposition, that certain studies plainly essential to good citizenship must be taught, and that nothing be taught which is manifestly inimical to the public welfare." (*Pierce*, 268 U.S. at 534). In *Wisconsin* v. *Yoder*, 406 U.S. 205 (1972), the Court held that a compulsory school-attendance law required parents to cause their children to attend public or private school until reaching age 16 was unconstitutionally applied to members of the Old Order Amish religion who declined to send their children, ages 14 and 15, to public school after they completed the eighth grade. The Court, in *Employment Division* v. *Smith*, plausibly linked the parental right regarding the education of children to the free exercise clause to produce a hybrid right. But, it seems to me, the cardinal principle in these cases pertains to the substantive right of parents to freely control (within due limits) the upbringing and education of their children; and that this right encompasses important liberty interests pertaining to religious matters quite independently of the right of religious freedom. Moreover, it seems to me that the establishment clause entails a personal right of parents and their children that such children be exempt in religious matters from proselyting, coercion, undue pressure, or similar exploitation of the presence of children required to be present by law or custom.

385. For example, a law forbidding all buildings or other structures chiefly devoted to public assemblies in predominantly residential neighborhoods would be neutral and generally applicable in the requisite sense of *Smith*. But, quite apart from free speech and assembly, and substantive due process considerations, it would violate the specific right of the free exercise clause and/or that freedom-right entailed by the establishment clause that pertain to building, maintaining, and operating churches or other similar places of public worship in predominantly residential neighborhoods, especially areas in those in which it is lawful to establish and maintain some businesses open to the public.

386. According to that stalwart advocate of the separationist model of the establishment clause, Leonard W. Levy: "The establishment clause of the First Amendment ... does more than buttress freedom of religion, which the same amendment separately protects. Given the extraordinary religious diversity of our nation, the establishment clause functions to depoliticize religion; it thereby helps to defuse a potentially explosive

situation. The clause removes religious issues from the ballot box and from politics.... The establishment clause separates government and religion so that we can maintain civility between believers and unbelievers as well as among the several hundred denominations, sects, and cults that thrive in our nation, all sharing the commitment to liberty and equality that cements us together." *The Establishment Clause: Religion and the First Amendment* (New York: MacMillian Publishing Co., 1986), ix. Levy noted that James Madison, "pointed out [(June 12, 1788) at the Virginia ratification convention] that the Virginia Declaration of Rights (which guaranteed 'the free exercise of religion, according to the dictates of conscience') would not have exempted people 'from paying for the support of one particular sect, if such sect were exclusively established by law.' ... 'Fortunately for this commonwealth' he added, "a majority of the people are decidedly against any exclusive establishment." Levy, *Establishment Clause*, at 70. As Levy notes: "[a]mong the recommended amendments [to the Constitution proffered by the Virginia ratifying convention] was a provision that 'no particular religious set or society ought to be favored or established by law, in preference to others.'" Ibid., 71.

387. See, e.g., Chris Bartolomucci, Note: *"Rethinking the Incorporation of the Establishment Clause: A Federalist View,"* 105 Harv. L. Rev. 1700 (1992), and Jonathan P. Brose, "In Birmingham They Love the Governor: Why the Fourteenth Amendment Does Not Incorporate the Establishment Clause," 24 Ohio N. U. L. Rev. 14 (1998); William K. Lietzau,"Rediscovering the Establishment Clause: Federalism and the Rollback of Incorporation," 39 DePaul L. Rev. 1191 (1990); Joseph M. Snee, "Religious Disestablishment and the Fourteenth Amendment," 1954 Wash. U. L. Q. 371 (1954).

388. *Elk Grove Unified School District* v. *Newdow,* 542 U.S. 1, 49–51 (2004) (Thomas, J., concurring); *Cutter* v. *Wilkinson,* 544 U.S. 709, 766–33 (2005) (Thomas, J., concurring).

389. 330 U.S. at 15.

390. 330 U.S. at 15–16.

391. 330 U.S. at 18. The Court having accepted the separationist theory (with some qualifications) has repeatedly emphasized in different ways that the ban on any law respecting an establishment of religion cuts both ways. Thus, for example in *Abington School District* v. *Schempp,* 374 U.S. 203, 225 (1963) declared "that the State may not establish a 'religion of secularism' in the sense of showing hostility to religion, thus 'preferring those who believe in no religion over those who do believe.'" The *Schempp* Court specified that the establishment clause precludes "the advancement or inhibition of religion ... [and] there must be a secular

legislative purpose and a primary effect that neither advances nor inhibits religion." Ibid., 222.

392. 330 U.S. at 16.

393. 374 U.S. at 224n9.

394. 262 U.S. 447.

395. 392 U.S. 83, 105–06.

396. In *Valley Forge Christian College* v. *Americans United for Separation of Church and State*, 454 U.S. 464 (1982), the Court held in a five-to-four decision that a taxpayers' organization (i.e., Americans United for Separation of Church and State) lacked standing to challenge the constitutionality under the establishment clause of the no-cost transfer of surplus federal property to a religious educational institution due to a decision that, according to the Court, was not in the exercise of the taxing and spending power (art. I, § 8) but rather of the property clause (art. IV, § 3, cl. 2). In *Hein* v. *Freedom From Religion Foundation*, 127 S.Ct. 2553 (2007), the plurality opinion of three justices (by Alito with Roberts and Kennedy concurring) agreed that the *Fast* standing rule should not be extended to allow a federal taxpayer to challenge the constitutionality of expenditures by the executive branch of the government, involving the White House office of faith-based and community initiatives, allegedly in violation of the establishment clause. Two justices (Scalia, Thomas) concurred in the judgment on the ground that the *Flast* standing rule should be overruled. Four justices (Souter, Stevens, Ginsburg, Breyer) dissented, arguing that the *Flast* standing rule in establishment clause cases should have been extended in *Hein* because the federal taxpayer's standing in each case obtains because the injury sufficient to ground standing is the every extraction and spending of tax money in aid of religion.

397. *Hein*, 127 S.Ct. at 2569 (plurality opinion): "We have declined to lower the taxpayer standing bar in suits alleging violations of any constitutional provision apart from the Establishment Clause. See *Tilton* v. *Richardson*, 403 U.S. 672 (1971) (no taxpayer standing to sue under free exercise clause of First Amendment); [other citations and brief summaries omitted]." The dissenting opinion of four justices in *Hein* declared that "[o]utside the Establishment Clause context, as the plurality points out, we have not found the injury to a taxpayer when funds are improperly expended to suffice for standing." 127 S.Ct. at 2587n4. Accordingly, this doctrine limiting the *Flast* rule to establishment clause cases also applies to cases involving alleged violations of the free speech, free press, and assembly-petition clauses.

398. "[T]he injury alleged in Establishment Clause challenges to federal spending is the very extract[ion] and spen[ding] of tax money in

aid of religion" (127 S.Ct. 2584–85; inside quotes omitted); "The three pence [payment of tax money to aid a religion] implicates the conscience, and the injury from Government expenditures on religion is not accurately classified with the 'Psychic Injury' that results whenever a congressional appropriation or executive expenditure raised hackles of disagreement with the policy supported" (ibid., 2585); "[O]nce we recognize the injury [i.e., the expenditure of taxpayer money in identifiable amounts in violation of the establishment clause] as sufficient for Article III, there can be no serious question about the other elements of the standing enquiry: the injury is indisputably 'traceable' to the spending, and 'likely to be redressed by' an injunction prohibiting it" (ibid.); "when the Government spends money for religious purposes a taxpayer's injury is serious and concrete enough to be 'judicially cognizable'" (ibid., 2587).

399. 454 U.S. at 490–513 (1982)." *The taxpayer was the direct and intended beneficiary of the prohibition on financial aid to religion*" (ibid., 504; emphasis in original); "[T]he interest of a taxpayer, even one raising an Establishment Clause claim, was limited to the actions of a government involving the expenditure of funds" (ibid., 507); "Each, and indeed every, federal taxpayer suffers precisely the injury that the Establishment Clause guards against when the Federal Government directs that funds be taken from the pocketbooks of the citizenry and placed into the coffers of the ministry. A taxpayer cannot be asked to raise his objection to such use of his funds at the time he pays his tax.... [T]axpayers could hardly assert that they were being injured until the Government actually lent its support to a religious venture" (ibid., at 509); "[A] taxpayer must have standing at the time that he learns of the Government's alleged Establishment Clause violation to seek equitable relief in order to halt the continuing and intolerable burden on his pocketbook, his conscience, and his constitutional rights" (ibid., 510).

400. 392 U.S. at 114.

401. See *Valley Forge*, 454 U.S. at 502–06 (J. Brennan, dissenting) and *Hein*, 127 S.Ct. at 2585 (J. Souter, dissenting).

402. The third ground of remonstrance in the "Memorial" mentions the "forc[ing] a citizen to contribute three pence only of his property for the support to any one establishment [of religion]." The text of the "Memorial" appears as the appendix to Justice Rutledge's dissenting opinion in *Everson*, 330 U.S. at 63–72. Incidentally it is noteworthy that the Virginia statute of religious freedom, enacted in 1786, which reflects the views of both Jefferson and Madison, began its preamble with: "WHEREAS Almighty God has created the mind free"; and thereafter referred to "the plan of the Holy author of our religion, who being Lord both of body and mind, yet

chose not to propagate it by coercions on either [temporal punishments or burthens, or by civil incapacitations], as was in his Almighty power to do so." These expressions manifest an understanding that some kinds of official endorsements of theological propositions are compatible with the right of religious freedom—assuming that such official professions are incompatible with a ban on an establishment of religion.

403. Justice Harlan in his dissenting opinion in *Flast*, 392 U.S. at 128, declared: "If this case involved a tax specifically designed for the support of religion, as was the Virginia tax opposed by Madison in his Memorial and Remonstrance, I would agree that taxpayers have rights under the religious clauses of the First Amendment that would permit them standing to challenge the tax's validity in the federal courts." He goes on to say: "But this is not such a case, and appellants challenge an expenditure, not a tax. Where no such tax is involved, a taxpayer's complaint can consist only of an allegation that public funds have been, or shortly will be, expended for purposes inconsistent with the Constitution. The taxpayer cannot ask the return of any portion of his previous tax payments, cannot prevent the collection of any existing tax debt, and cannot demand an adjudication of the propriety of any particular level of taxation. His tax payments are received for the general purposes of the United States, and are, upon proper receipt, lost in the general revenues."

404. 392 U.S. at 131.

405. 459 U.S. 116 (1982).

406. Ibid., 126.

407. *Board of Education of Kiryas Joel Village School District* v. *Grumet*, 512 U.S. 687, 698 (1994) (*held*: establishment of the Kiryas Joel Village School District by the New York legislature violated the establishment clause (as applied to the states via the Fourteenth Amendment) in that the statute provided that the territory of the village shall be a separate school district, with its own locally-elected board of directors, where the population of the village was composed of only members of Satmar Hasidem, a fundamentalist Jewish sect, and the village itself owned by the Satmars. The only publicly funded program run by the school district was for the benefit of handicapped children. Otherwise, the children of the village went to private Jewish schools.

408. U.S. Const., art. VI.

409. 366 U.S. 420 (1961). A Maryland Sunday closing law, as applied to defendant employees of a large discount department store convicted and fined for violating the law insofar as it prohibited retail sale of merchandise with inapplicable exceptions, violated neither the equal protection clause nor the establishment clause (as applied to states by the Fourteenth

Amendment) because the purpose and effect of the statutes was not to aid religion but to set aside Sunday as a day of rest and recreation despite the religious origins of the statute. The defendant employees were held to lack standing to allege free exercise violations because they did not allege any infringement of their own religious freedom due to Sunday closing but only economic injury.

410. 366 U.S. 582 (1961). Pennsylvania Sunday closing laws, which prohibited the retail sale of certain enumerated commodities but with many exceptions as applied to a corporate operator of a large discount department store on a highway, violated neither the equal protection clause nor the establishment clause (as applied to the states by the Fourteenth Amendment) because neither the purpose nor the effect of the statute was religious. The corporate operator of the store had no standing to allege a violation of the free exercise clause, as applied to the states by the Fourteenth Amendment, where it alleged only an economic injury to itself; but it had standing to attack the statute on establishment clause grounds.

411. 366 U.S. 599 (1961). The very same Pennsylvania Sunday closing laws considered in *Two Guys* did not violate the free exercise clause, as applied to the states by the Fourteenth Amendment, with respect to retail merchants who were Orthodox Jewish retail merchants; whose religion obliges them to not operate their places of business and abstain from all manner of work during the Sabbath although enforcement of the statute would impair the ability of each such merchant to earn a livelihood or would render him unable to continue in his business, thereby losing his capital investment.

412. 366 U.S. 617 (1961). Massachusetts Sunday closing law, which prohibited (with inapplicable exceptions) the keeping open of shops as applied to a market that sold almost exclusively kosher food products, as applied to Orthodox Jewish customers of the market, the corporate owner of the market, and some stockholders, violated neither the equal protection clause nor either of the religion clauses of the First Amendment (as applied to the states by the Fourteenth Amendment) because of the predominant secular purpose and effect of the law even though the Orthodox Jews were religiously obliged not to operate the kosher market, or to shop there, from sundown Friday to sundown Saturday, and despite the law complicating the task of Orthodox rabbis to supervise the production of kosher meat.

413. *McGowan*, 366 U.S. at 429-30.

414. Ibid., 430–31.

415. Cf. Ibid., 430n8.

416. These models are described in chapter D below. Although some writers consider the terms accomodationist and nonpreferentialist as synonyms, I think it is more useful to have these two different terms denote two different notions.

417. With a few changes, the substance of this hypothetical statute is similar to an Alabama statute held in *Wallace* v. *Jaffree,* 472 U.S. 38 (1985) as violative of the establishment clause (as applied to the states by the Fourteenth Amendment). Since the Court held that the Alabama statute violated the establishment clause despite its having authorized an announced period of silence during which either silent prayer or meditation could be engaged in, it follows a fortiori that our hypothetical statute is unconstitutional according to the Court's current doctrine.

418. The substance of this hypothetical statute is similar to a Pennsylvania statute that the Court held as violative of the establishment clause (as applied to the states by the Fourteenth Amendment) in *Abington School District* v. *Schempp,* 374 U.S. 203 (1963). Only Justice Stewart dissented from the judgment and opinion of the Court.

419. But, in my opinion, the delivery of a nondenominational prayer at a public middle-school or high-school graduation ceremony (attended by parents and other adult guests), where those attending are free to not participate, would not violate a freedom-from right even assuming that the establishment clause was violated. But see *Lee* v. *Weisman,* 505 U.S. 577 (1992), where the Court held (five-to-four) that the establishment clause (as applied to the states by the Fourteenth Amendment) was violated in this factual scenario. The Court implausibly asserted that peer pressure and school supervision, in combination, effectively requires students to stand or at least maintain respectful silence, and this is tantamount to requiring them to participate in the religious exercise during a public ceremony. As Justice Scalia, in his dissenting opinion, aptly remarked: "our school prayer cases turn in part on the fact that the classroom is inherently an instructional setting, and daily prayer there — where parents are not present to counter 'the students' emulation of teachers as role models and the children's susceptibility to peer pressure,' [citation]— might be thought to raise special concerns regarding state interference with the liberty of parents to direct the religious upbringing of their children: 'Families entrust public schools with the education of their children, but condition their trust on the understanding that the classroom will not purposely be used to advance religious views that may conflict with the private beliefs of the student and his or her family.' [Citations.] Voluntary prayer at graduation — a one time ceremony at which parents, friends and relatives are present — can hardly be thought to raise the same concerns." Ibid., 643.

As Scalia further noted, in order to avoid any appearance of coercion or pressure, "[a]ll that is seemingly needed is an announcement, or perhaps a written insertion at the beginning of the graduation program, to the effect that, while all are asked to rise for the invocation and benediction, none is compelled to join in them, nor will be assumed, by rising, to have done so." Ibid., 645.

420. *Raines* v. *Byrd*, 521 U.S. 811, 818–19 (1997); *Lujan* v. *Defenders of Wildlife*, 504 U.S. 555, 560–61 (1992).

421. The First Amendment reads in relevant part: "Congress shall make no law respecting an establishment of religion, or prohibiting the free exercise thereof[.]" The term *Congress* in connection with the First Amendment is to be understood as also encompassing actions of any legislative, executive, or judicial body or person acting on behalf or as an agent of the United States.

422. The description of the separationist model in the accompanying text is distilled from study of the opinions in such cases as *Everson* v. *Board of Education*, 330 U.S. 1 (1947); *Abington School District* v. *Schempp*, 374 U.S. 203 (1963); *Lemon* v. *Kurtzman*, 403 U.S. 602 (1971); *Wallace* v. *Jaffree*, 472 U.S. 38 (1985); *Allegheney County* v. *American Civil Liberties Union*, 492 U.S. 573 (1989); *Lee* v. *Weisman*, 505 U.S. 577 (1992); *Capital Square Review & Advisory Board* v. *Pinette*, 515 U.S. 753 (1995); *Santa Fe School District* v. *Doe*, 530 U.S. 290 (2000): *McCreary County* v. *American Civil Liberties Union*, 545 U.S. 844 (2005), and is reasonably accurate for our purposes. To be sure, plausible models of the establishment clause come in different versions, just as the quarks of theoretical physics come in different colors. The devil is in the details of the unitary separationist model as is the case with any special theory of the establishment clause.

423. This argument has been vigorously expounded by Levy. See Levy (supra note 386), at 65–66, 72–74, 89, 93, 115.

424. 330 U.S. at 16. However as the Court declared in *Lemon* v. *Kurtzman*, 403 U.S. at 614: "Our prior holdings do not call for total separation between church and state; total separation is not possible in an absolute sense. Some relationship between government and religious organizations is inevitable.... Judicial caveats against entanglement must recognize that the line of separation, far from being a 'wall,' is a blurred, indistinct, and variable barrier depending on all the circumstances of a particular relationship."

425. Levy (supra note 386), at 93.

426. Ibid., 74.

427. Ibid. 93.

428. Gaillard Hunt, ed., *The Writings of James Madison, comprising his Public Papers and his Private Correspondence, including his numerous letters and documents now for the first time printed,* (New York: G.P. Putnam's Sons, 1910), 9: 191–92.

429. U.S. Const. art. I, § 8, cl. 13: "To make Rules for the Government and Regulation of the land and naval Forces[.]"

430. *Kendall* v. *United States ex rel. Stokes,* 37 U.S. (12 Pet.) 524, 619 (1838): "There is in this District [of Columbia] no division of powers between the general and state governments. Congress has the entire control over the District for every purpose of government[.]"

431. Article I, section 8, cl. 16 of the Constitution provides that the Congress shall have power "[t]o exercise exclusive Legislation in all Cases whatsoever, over such District ... as may ... become the Seat of the Government of the United States, and to exercise like Authority over all Places purchased by the Consent of the legislature of the State in which the Same shall be[.]"

432. Article IV, section 3, clause 2 provides: "The Congress shall have Power to dispose of and make all needful Rules and Regulations respecting the Territory or other Property belonging to the United States[.]" *Simms* v. *Simms,* 175 U.S. 162, 168 (1899): "In the territories of the United States, Congress has the entire dominion and sovereignty, national and local, federal and state, and has full legislative power over all subjects upon which the legislature of a state might legislate within the state, and may, at its discretion, entrust that power to the legislative assembly of a territory."

433. An Act to Provide for the Government of the Territory Northwest of the River Ohio, Act of August 7, 1789, 1 Stat. 50.

434. An Act for raising and adding another Regiment to the Military Establishment of the United States, and for making further provision for the protection of the frontiers, Act of March 3, 1791, 1 Stat. 222.

435. 403 U.S. at 612.

436. It is no wonder that Justice Stewart, in his dissenting opinion in *Abington School District* v. *Schempp*, found himself able to "accept ... the proposition that the Fourteenth Amendment has somehow absorbed the Establishment Clause," but remarked how "although it is not without irony that a constitutional provision evidently designed to leave the States free to go their own way should now have become a restriction upon their autonomy." 374 U.S. at 310.

437. 403 U.S. at 612–613. The first and second prongs of the three-fold *Lemon* test were first stated in *Abington School District v. Schempp*, 374 U.S. at 223 (1963); the third prong was added in *Waltz* v. *Tax Commission*, 397 U.S. 664, 674 (1970).

438. *Abington School District v. Schempp*, 374 U.S. at 222.

439. The Court's decisions over the years have been marked by a inflation of the meaning of *religion* from the time when it declared in *Davis v. Beason*, 133 U.S. 333, 342 (1890): "The term 'religion' has reference to one's views of his relations to his Creator, and to the obligations they impose of reverence for his being and character, and of obedience to his will. It is often confounded with the *cultus* or form of worship of a particular sect, but is distinguishable from the latter." This notion of *religion* is essentially a restatement of the opening words of section 15 of the Virginia Bill of Rights of 1776: "That religion, or the duty which we owe to our Creator, and the manner of discharging it[.]" However in *Torcaso* v. Watkins, 367 U.S. 488, 495 (1961), the Court, while "reaffirm[ing] that neither a State nor the Federal Government can constitutionally ... aid those religions based on a belief in the existence of God as against those religions founded on different beliefs," mentioned in the accompanying note that "[a]mong religions in this country which do not teach what would generally be considered a belief in the existence of God are Buddhism, Taoism, Ethical Culture, Secular Humanism and others."

440. The nonpreferentialist model was expounded and defended by (then) Associate Justice Rehnquist in his dissenting opinion in *Wallace* v. *Jaffree*, 472 U.S. at 91.

441. See, e.g., Levy (supra note 386), at 60–62, 91–119 and Thomas J. Curry, *The First Freedoms: Church and State in America to the Passage of the First Amendment* (New York: Oxford University Press, 1986), 199–222, for persuasive historical explanations of why the establishment clause precludes a multiple but nonpreferential establishment of religion as well as an exclusive one.

442. Virginia (1788) and New York (1788) proposed: "that no particular religious sect or society ought to be favored or established by law in preference to others." Elliot *Debates in the Several State Conventions* (supra note 151), 3: 659 and 4: 244 (a comma precedes and follows "by law" in the Virginia proposal); and New York (1787) proposed: "that no religious sect or society ought to be favored or established by law in preference to others" Elliot *Debates*, 1: 328. See *Journal of the Senate* (supra note 60), (September 3, 1789) 1: 70: "On motion, To amend the third Article, to read thus—'Congress shall make no law establishing any particular denomination of religion in preference to another, or prohibiting the free exercise thereof, nor shall the rights of conscience be infringed.'— It passed in the Negative."

443. Robert L. Cord, *Separation of Church and State* (Grand Rapids MI: Baker Book House, 1988), 57–80.

444. As I pointed out in my article (Guminski (supra note 3), at 785): "The Congress consistently legislated with respect to the territory, ceded by France and Spain by the treaties of 1803 and 1819, respectively, upon the principle that the provisions of the Bill of Rights did not apply *ex proprio vigore* [i.e., by their own force] to such territory." Similar remarks should be made, *mutatis mutandis*, concerning congressional policy pertaining to the Northwest Territory and the Indian nations and tribes, and the territories acquired from Mexico in 1848 and Russia in 1867. The evolution of constitutional doctrine by the Court about which provisions in the Bill of Rights apply *ex proprio vigore* to territories and possessions of the United States was something that chiefly took place after the annexation of the Hawaiian Islands and the treaty of peace concluding the Spanish-American War in 1898.

445. The essentials of accomodationist model described in this section are chiefly drawn (with some modification) from concurring or dissenting opinions in); *Allegheney County* v. *American Civil Liberties Union*, 492 U.S. 573, 655 (1989) (Kennedy, with Rehnquist, White, and Scalia, joining); *Lee* v. *Weisman*, 505 U.S. 577, 631 (1992) (Scalia, with Rehnquist, White, Thomas, joining); *Capital Square Review & Advisory Board* v. *Pinette*, 515 U.S. 753, 763 (1995) (Scalia, concurring as to part IV, with Rehnquist, Kennedy, Thomas, joining); *Santa Fe School District v. Doe*, 530 U.S. 290, 378 (2000) (Rehnquist, with Scalia, Thomas, joining): *McCreary County* v. *American Civil Liberties Union*, 545 U.S. 844, 885 (2005) (Scalia, with Rehnquist, Thomas, joining, and Kennedy joining in parts II and III).

446. Presently there does not currently appear to be any judicially recognized applicable "historically sanctioned exception of narrow scope" of the kind referred to in the accompanying text, especially given the Court's decision in the famous *Burstyn* v. *Wilson,* 343 U.S. 495 (1952). *Burstyn* ruled that the freedoms of speech and of the press encompass motion picture plays and shows, and that the film "The Miracle" could not be banned upon the ground that it is *sacrilegious* (i.e., [as defined by the Court of Appeals of New York] "no religion, as that word is understood by the ordinary, reasonable person, shall be treated with contempt, mockery, scorn and ridicule") As the *Burstyn* Court declared: "It is not the business of government in our nation to suppress real or imagined attacks upon a particular religious doctrine, whether they appear in publications, speeches, or motion pictures." 343 U.S. at 504. The Court, however, did not address the issue whether either religion clause (as applied to the states) was violated by the "Miracle" ban. Quite independently of the freedom of speech or the press, in my opinion the Miracle ban violated a freedom-

right entailed by the establishment clause because its exhibition in a movie theater cannot reasonably be deemed to be a profound offense in the sense explained by Joel Feinberg (*Offense to Others: The Moral Limits of the Criminal Law* (New York: Oxford University Press, 1985), 50–96). Besides what Feinberg calls *profound offense* (which does not presuppose captive or semi-captive auditors or spectators), there can also be instances of the commission of public or private nuisances concerning religious matters that involves captive or semi-captive auditors or spectators subjected to expression or other conduct that is calculated to outrage religious and moral sentiments. Ibid., 1–49. The statutory definition of *profound offenses* or *public nuisances* in religious matters must be so defined as to exclude the vigorous and aggressive exposition and advocacy by the written or spoken word of opinions on religious or moral issues that may be very offensive to people willing to expose themselves to the hearing or reading of such matter and not to those who in no way assumed the risk of being offended or from whom, having been exposed to the offending matter, it is unduly burdensome to discontinue such exposure.

447. *Robertson* v. *Baldwin*, 165 U.S. 275, 282 (1897).

448. *The American Commonwealth* (New York: Macmillan and Co, 1883), 3: 473. Lord Bryce (1838–1922), a British jurist, historian, politician and diplomat, was ambassador to the United States from 1907 to 1913. The passage from which this quotation is taken continues thus: "Each House of Congress has a chaplain, and opens its proceedings each day with prayers. The President annually after the end of harvest issues a proclamation ordering a general thanksgiving, and occasionally appoints a day of fasting and humiliation. So prayers are offered in the State legislatures, and State governors issue proclamations for days of religious observance. Congress in the crisis of the Civil War (July 1863) requested the President to appoint a day for humiliation and prayer. In the army and navy provision is made for religious services, conducted by chaplains of various denominations, and no difficulty seems to have been found in reconciling their claims. In most States there exist laws punishing blasphemy or profane swearing by the name of God (laws which however are in some places openly transgressed and in few or none enforced), laws restricting or forbidding trade or labour on the Sabbath, as well as laws protecting assemblages for religious procession, from being disturbed. The Bible is read in the public State-supported schools, and though controversies have arisen on this head, the practice is evidently in accord with the general sentiment of the people." Other than a few issues (especially pertaining to the participation of public school teachers and students in the daily recitation of prayers) that require some appropriate

tweaking and poking, Lord Bryce's account of American practices during the time of his sojourn in the United States is very instructive. The reader should, with respect to Bryce's remarks about blasphemy, take into account his later remark concerning persons holding irreligious views: "Except in small places in the West or South, where aggressive skepticism would rouse displeasure and might affect a man's position in society, everybody is as free in America as in London to hold and express any views he pleases [about religious matters]." Ibid., 493.

449. *A Treatise on the Constitutional Limitations Which Rest Upon the Legislative Powers of The States of the American Union* (Boston: Little, Brown, & Co., 1868). Thomas M. Cooley (1824–1898) was a member of the Michigan Supreme Court (1865–85). A celebrated legal scholar, his *Constitutional Limitations* was very influential for many decades. Justice Scalia (writing for the Court in *District of Columbia* v. *Heller*, 128 S.Ct. at 2811) refers to Cooley's work as "massively popular."

450. Cooley (1868) (supra note 449), at 470–71. It is significant that "[f]ully twenty-seven, or two-thirds, of the 1868 state constitutions contained an explicit reference to God in their preambles" (Calabresi & Agudo (supra note 263), at 37; and that, furthermore, "in addition to these references to God in the preambles of state constitutions, thirty state constitutions in 1868, or more than three-fourths of the total, contained references to God that can only be described as a state constitutional 'endorsement' of what U.S. Supreme Court [justices] in recent years has sometimes (and somewhat misleadingly) called 'ceremonial deism'" (ibid., at 38). As Calabresi and Agudo remark: "There was thus an Article V, three-quarters-of-the-states consensus in 1868 that ceremonial deism was perfectly consistent with the nonestablishment and free exercise principles" (ibid., at 39). The term *ceremonial deism* is to be understood as being consistent with the theism of positive religions, such as Christianity, Judaism, and Islam, which include doctrines based upon supernatural (or according to another usage, special) revelation vouchsafed by miracles and fulfilled prophecies.

451. Ibid., 477–78.

452. The persistence of this rationale has been evidenced in many ways including but not limited to: the declaration in article III of the Northwest Ordinance of 1787 beginning with "[r]eligion, morality, and knowledge being necessary to good government and the happiness of mankind"; the Court's assertion in *Church of the Holy Trinity* v. *United States*, 143 U.S. 457, 465 (1892) that "[n]o purpose of action against religion can be imputed to any legislation, State or national, because this is a religious people"; and the Court's declaration in *Zorach* v. *Clauson*, 343 U.S. 306, 313 (1952) that "[w]e are a religious people whose institutions presuppose a Supreme

Being"—which I think is putting it a bit too strongly. That Congress discontinues a historically sanctioned practice deemed consistent with the constitutional ban of an establishment of religion is not action that per se endorses or purposively promotes irreligion or any particular form of irreligion. Whether to continue or discontinue, or to re-establish some historically sanctioned accommodation according to the accomodationist model constitutes a legislative public policy issue to be determined on its individual merits.

453. Ibid., 33.

454. Again I express my thanks to Sarah Agudo for supplying me with the relevant constitutional texts. Calabresi and Agudo, however, look at things somewhat quite differently than I do on the question at hand. They write (Calabresi & Agudo (supra note 363), at 31–32: "Twenty-seven states—of two-thirds of the thirty-seven states that formed the United States in 1868—had clauses in their constitutions that, in our view, explicitly prohibited the establishment of a state religion. Typical establishment clauses provided, 'No subordination nor preference of any one sect or denomination to another shall ever be established by law.' Some clauses were less explicit, prohibiting establishment by preventing the government from forcing citizens to financially support any specific religion." But the majority of the state constitutions prohibited the establishment of one religion in preference to another rather than more broadly prohibiting the establishment of religion.

455. AMAR, 34.

456. *Passenger Cases*, 48 U.S. at 492 (Taney, C.J., dissenting opinion); quoted approvingly in *Crandall* v *United States,* 73 U.S. at 48.

457. Somewhat similar sentiments were expressed in Bartolomucci (supra note 387, at 1715: "Perhaps the most important value to be served in restoring state authority over religion would be the federalist value of decentralized decisionmaking. This method of political organization confers two principal benefits. First, states and localities can better respond to the needs and interests of the majority of their citizens than the national government because they can tailor their laws to suit local conditions and preferences.... A second advantage of a federalist scheme of government is that it allows for experimentation by and competition among the states."

458. Astute foreign observers were much impressed by the beneficial consequences of the establishment clause and its analogs in state constitutions for civil society and religion. See, e.g., Alexis de Tocqueville, *Democracy in America* (1835) (tr. Henry Reeves 1899) book I, ch. 17 (Principal Causes Maintaining The Democratic Republic—Part

III): "In France I had almost always seen the spirit of religion and the spirit of freedom pursuing courses diametrically opposed to each other; but in America I found that they were intimately united, and that they reigned in common over the same country. My desire to discover the causes of this phenomenon increased from day to day. In order to satisfy it I questioned the members of all the different sects; and I more especially sought the society of the clergy, who are the depositaries of the different persuasions, and who are more especially interested in their duration. As a member of the Roman Catholic Church I was more particularly brought into contact with several of its priests, with whom I became intimately acquainted. To each of these men I expressed my astonishment and I explained my doubts; I found that they differed upon matters of detail alone; and that they mainly attributed the peaceful dominion of religion in their country to the separation of Church and State. I do not hesitate to affirm that during my stay in America I did not meet with a single individual, of the clergy or of the laity, who was not of the same opinion upon this point." Available online at http://www.gutenberg.org/etext/815.) See also Bryce (supra note 448), at 3: 483: "So far from suffering from want of State support, religion seems in the United States to stand all the firmer because, standing alone, she is seen to stand by her own strength."

459. 110 U.S. 516, 535 (1884). The Court's decision in the infamous *Dred Scott* Case, 60 U.S. at 450 (1857), to the effect that the Congress could not constitutionally prohibit slavery in the federal territories, was the one and only (and an ignominious one at that) realization of the substantive aspects of the due process clause in the Court's jurisprudence before the adoption of the Fourteenth Amendment.

460. In *Hurtado*, the Court held that the specific right of the grand jury clause of the Fifth Amendment is not a component of the specific right of the Fourteenth Amendment due process clause. See also *Mugler* v. *Kansas*, 123 U.S. 623 (1887) (*held*: a statute which prohibits the manufacture of spirituous, malt, vinous, fermented, or other intoxicating liquors within the limits of the State, to be there sold or bartered for general use as a beverage, does not violate the due process clause). The Court declared (ibid., 661): "It does not at all follow that every statute enacted ostensibly for the promotion of these ends [i.e., the protection of the public morals, the public health, or the public safety] is to be accepted as a legitimate exertion of the police powers of the State. There are, of necessity, limits beyond which legislation cannot rightfully go.... If, therefore, a statute purporting to have been enacted to protect the public health, the public morals, or the public safety has no real or substantial relation to those objects, or is a palpable invasion of rights secured by the fundamental law,

it is the duty of the courts to so adjudge, and thereby give effect to the Constitution." Justice Miller joined in the Court's opinion in *Mugler*.

461. 165 U.S. 578 (*held*: there is a deprivation of liberty without due process of law when a statute forbids an assured from directly contracting with a maritime insurance company licensed in another state for coverage of property within his own state). The Court declared (ibid., 589): "The 'liberty' mentioned in [due process clause] means not only the right of the citizen to be free from the mere physical restraint of his person, as by incarceration, but the term is deemed to embrace the right of the citizen to be free in the enjoyment of all his faculties, to be free to use them in all lawful ways, to live and work where he will, to earn his livelihood by any lawful calling, to pursue any livelihood or avocation, and for that purpose to enter into all contracts which may be proper, necessary, and essential to his carrying out to a successful conclusion the purposes above mentioned." The liberty of contract was eventually demoted to a right subject to the rational basis test of validity in *West Coast Hotel Co. v. Parrish*, 300 U.S. 379 (1937), when the Court (overruling *Adkins* v. *Children's Hospital*, 261 U.S. 525 (1923)) held that a statute requiring minimum wages for women did not violate the due process clause. The liberty of contract, and other economic liberties, went off the radar screen with *Ferguson* v. *Skrupa*, 372 U.S. 726 (1963) and *Griswold* v. *Connecticut*, 381 U.S. 479 (1965). However, they subsequently resurfaced and now barely survive as nonfundamental rights to which a weak version of the rational basis test applies. See, e.g., *Usery v. Turner Elkhorn Mining Co.*, 428 U.S. 1, 15 (1976); and *Williamson v. Lee Optical Co.*, 348 U.S. 483, 477–78 (1955). Although this book emphasizes noneconomic liberty-interests, I should not want to be understood as implying that there are no economic or property liberty-interests that should not be deemed fundamental in the requisite sense.

462. The preferred status of the right of liberty of contract reached its high-water mark in *Lochner* v. *New York* 198 U.S. 45 (1905), when the Court held that the due process clause violated by statute limiting the number of hours a baker could work to only 60 hours per week or 10 hours per day. In *Adkins,* 261 U.S. at 546, the Court explained: "There is … no such thing as absolute freedom of contract. It is subject to a great variety of restraints. But freedom of contract is, nevertheless, the general rule and restraint the exception; and the exercise of legislative authority to abridge it can be justified only by the existence of exceptional circumstances."

463. 179 U.S. 270, 274 (1900).
464. 245 U.S. 60 (1917).

465. 262 U.S. 390 (1923).

466. 268 U.S. 510 (1925).

467. 268 U.S. 652 (1925): (criminal anarchy statute, prohibiting advocacy of overthrow of organized government by force, violence and unlawful means ruled valid as applied to such advocacy for the accomplishment of that purpose). See *Fiske* v. *Kansas*, 274 U.S. 380 (1927): criminal syndicalism statute held as invalid as applied to teaching the inevitability of the class struggle without any charge or evidence that crime, violence, or other unlawful acts or methods were advocated as a means of effecting industrial or political changes or revolution. But it was only three years before the *Gitlow* decision that the Court in *Prudential Insurance Co.* v. *Cheek*, 259 U.S. 530, 543 (1922) stated as dictum that "neither the Fourteenth Amendment nor any other provision of the Constitution of the United States imposes upon the States any restriction about 'freedom of speech' or the 'liberty of silence;' nor, we may add, does it confer any right of privacy upon either persons or corporations." In his dissenting opinion in *Gilbert* v. *Minnesota*, 254 U.S. 325, 343 (1920), Justice Brandeis chastised his brethren by remarking: "But I have difficulty in believing that the liberty guaranteed by the Constitution ... does not include the liberty to teach, either in the privacy of the home or publicly, the doctrine of pacifism; so long, at least, as Congress has not declared that the public safety demands its suppression. I cannot believe that the liberty guaranteed by the Fourteenth Amendment includes only liberty to acquire and to enjoy property."

468. It was not until 1936 that the Court, for the first time, declared in effect that the Fourteenth Amendment due process clause protected freedom of speech and of the press against all abridgments by the states. *Grosjean* v. *American Press Co.*, 297 U.S. 233, 243.

469. C. D. Broad, "Relations of Science and Religion," in his *Reason, Philosophy and Psychical Research* (New York; Harcourt, Brace & Co., 1953), 243.

470. Recall that to say that, for example, *the specific right of the due process clause incorporates freedom of speech* is to say that *the specific right of the due process clause includes as a component the right that freedom of speech is not to be abridged.* There are some writers who do not classify First Amendment freedoms as substantive rights. But they are clearly wrong because there is nothing more substantive than a First Amendment freedom.

471. *Malloy* v. *Hogan*, 378 U.S. at 10–11; *Pointer* v. *Texas*, 380 U.S. at 406; *Benton* v. *Maryland*, 395 U.S. at 794–95.

472. *Palko* v. *Connecticut*, 302 U.S. 319, 325 (1937).

473. *DeJonge* v. *Oregon*, 299 U.S 353, 364 (1937). The Court expounded in *Washington* v. *Glucksberg*, 521 U.S. 702, 722 (1997) the thesis that the due process clause treats only those rights as *fundamental* that are "found to be deeply rooted in our legal tradition.... [B]y establishing a threshold requirement—that a challenged state action implicates a fundamental right—before requiring more than a reasonable relation to a legitimate state interest to justify the action, it avoids the need for complex balancing of competing interests in every case." However, this thesis cannot safely be regarded as part of the Court's current doctrine given its decision and opinion in *Lawrence* v. *Texas*, 539 U.S. 558 (2003) (*held*: a statute which prohibits two adults of the same sex from consensually and privately engaging in noncommercial oral or anal intercourse violates the due process clause). I agree with the *Lawrence* decision (understood rather strictly) for reasons that I present below in Chapter C.

474. The First Amendment, it should be recalled, does not prohibit the enactment of a law that abridges speech. Nor does it only prohibit laws that unreasonably abridge freedom of speech. Rather, it prohibits the enactment of any law, reasonable or not, that abridges freedom of speech. But not all logically conceivable substantive freedom-rights with respect to speech (e.g., the right to solicit the murder of specific persons) are components of the right of freedom of speech. Many important components of freedom of speech necessarily presuppose the absence of extraordinary background conditions—such as those, for example, that would justify the proportionate suspension of the writ of habeas corpus or the imposition of martial law.

475. Sui generis in the Court's current jurisprudence is its de facto doctrine in abortion cases found in the plurality opinion in *Planned Parenthood of Southeastern Pennsylvania* v. *Casey*, 505 U.S. 833 (1992). In *Casey* two justices (Stevens and Blackmun) voted to completely reaffirm *Roe* v. *Wade*, 410 U.S. 113 (1973); four justices (Rehnquist, White, Scalia and Thomas) voted to completely overturn *Roe;* three justices (O'Conner, Souter and Kennedy) voted to reaffirm the central principle and essential holding of *Roe*; but they rejected the three-trimester analysis of *Roe*, replacing it with before-and-after viability approach. The plurality opinion rejects the strict scrutiny test in previability abortion cases. It postulates in its place an *undue burden* test, (i.e., "[o]nly where state regulation imposes an undue burden on a woman's ability to make [the decision whether to have her nonviable fetus aborted] does the State reach into the heart of liberty protected by the Due Process Clause.") *Planned Parenthood*, 505 U.S. at 874. According to the plurality opinion: "An undue burden exists, and therefore a provision of law is invalid, if its purpose or effect is to

place a substantial obstacle in the path of a woman seeking an abortion before the fetus attains viability." 505 U.S. at 878. The undue burden test, limited presently to abortion cases, appears to me to offer a much better general approach to understanding what constitutes a fundamental right for substantive due process purposes than the Court's current approach in nonabortion cases—an approach that involves the use of the strict scrutiny standard.

476. 17 U.S. (4 Wheat.) 235, 244.

477. 59 U.S. (18 How.) 272, 276. The Court's opinion in this case reflects the view that the Fifth Amendment due process clause has only procedural aspects and thereby confirms the dominant original understanding of that clause.

478. *The Constitution and what it means today* (New York: Atheneum, 1963), 217–18. The Taney opinion in *Dred Scott* emphatically confirmed that "the right of property in a slave is distinctly and expressly affirmed in the Constitution." 60 U.S. at 451. The dissenting opinion by Justice Curtis (ibid., 623–33) refutes the opinion of the Court that due process of law is violated by a congressional statute that bars slavery in federal territory. But nowhere in Justice Curtis's opinion is it expressly or impliedly maintained that the due process clause has only procedural aspects. And it appears that the principal ground for Justice Curtis's conclusion is that "[s]lavery being contrary to natural right, [it] is created only by municipal law." Ibid., 624.

479. *Cong. Globe*, 39 Cong., 1st Sess., 2542.

480. Bingham claimed in the following paragraph: "this amendment takes from no State any right that ever pertained to it." He explained: "No State ever had the right, under the forms of law or otherwise, to deny to any freeman the equal protection of the laws or to abridge the privileges or immunities of any citizen of the Republic, although many of them have assumed and exercised the power, and that without remedy." Bingham here again disclosed his gross misunderstanding of the Constitution in that he thought at the time that the provisions of the Bill of Rights are binding on the states; and he repeated his thesis that the privileges or immunities clause denotes the same rights as those denoted by the descriptive term of the comity clause.

481. *Cong. Globe*, 35th Cong., 2d Sess., 983 (February 11, 1859).

482. Ibid., 985. Bingham had occasion to condemn a statute of the Territory of Kansas that made it a felony for any free person, by speaking or writing, to assert that persons have not the right to hold slaves in Kansas, or to circulate there any book containing any denial of the right of any person to hold slaves in that territory. Bingham, noting that the

Kansas territorial legislature was bound by the organic act to conform to the Constitution, maintained that the statute in question abridged the freedom of speech and of the press as well as the due process clause. *Cong. Globe*, 34th Cong., 1st Sess., App. 124 (1856). I do not understand Bingham to have meant that the due process clause per se prohibits all abridgments of freedom of speech and of the press. In any event, he did not explicitly or implicitly assert that—although he apparently attributed some liberty-rights pertaining to speech and the press to the due process clause.

483. Ibid., 35 Cong., 1d Sess., 985 (1859). But Senator Trumball (the author of the Civil Rights Act of 1866) stated during the debate about the admission of Oregon: "I have never contended for giving the negro equal privileges with the white man. That is a doctrine I do not advocate. I have believed that negro slavery was an evil. Now, in regard to the clause in the constitution of Oregon, which her citizens have thought proper to adopt, excluding the settlement of free negroes in the State, I am not prepared to say they may not adopt such a clause." Ibid., 1st Sess., 1965 (1858). Quite clearly, Bingham's views of what are the essential natural rights of free persons were more extensive than those of Trumball. But even Trumball appeared at times to have at times a broader view of what are the essential natural rights of free persons besides those enumerated in section 1 of the Civil Rights Act of 1866. See, e.g.: *Cong. Globe*, 39th Cong., 1st Sess., 475 (January 29, 1866): "[I]t is perhaps difficult to draw the precise line, to say where freedom ceases and slavery begins, but a law that does not allow a colored person to go from one county to another is certainly a law in derogation of the rights of a freeman. A law that does not allow a colored person to hold property, does not allow him to teach, does not allow him to preach, is certainly a law in violation of the rights of a freeman, and being so may property be declared void." Trumball, it should be noted, took a very broad view of the scope of the Thirteenth Amendment to the effect that it empowered Congress to enact the Civil Rights Act of 1866.

484. Cooley (1873) (supra note 152), at 2: § 1950. Cooley's edition of Story's treatise was published after the adoption of the Fourteenth Amendment in 1866 but before its judicial construction in the *Slaughter-House Cases* in 1873. Cooley's view (Cooley (1873), at 2: § 1937) of the meaning of the privileges or immunities clause appears to have been substantially identical to that adopted by the Court in the *Slaughter-House Cases*. Hence he was obliged to look upon the equal protection and due process clauses as providing the basis for vindicating the freedom for invidious discrimination based upon race, color, or other similar birth status as constitutionally protected against infringement by the states.

485. Cooley (1873) (supra note 152), at 2: § 1950

486. That Cooley denies that the due process clause provides no protection for the freedom of speech and religious worship does not entail that the clause prohibits all abridgments of these freedoms.

487. Ibid., § 1939. I write of the per se potency of the due process clause to substantively limit governmental legislative power because in one sense the clause is also violated if, for example, a person is deprived of his liberty because he is convicted of violating a statute that violates another constitutional provision (e.g., the free press clause of the First Amendment) or a statute, rule or regulation. So in this book, whenever I write of a liberty-right (whether fundamental or not) being protected by the due process clause, unless otherwise indicated, I am writing of a liberty right that the clause protects independently of its protection by any other constitutional provision.

488. The author of this maxim was Carveth Read, in his *Logic: Deductive and Inductive* (London: Alexander Moring Ltd., 1914), 351. Read went on to say: "In the criticism of manners, of fine art, or of literature, in politics, religion and moral philosophy, what we are anxious to say is often far from clear to ourselves; and it is better to indicate our meaning approximately, or as we feel about it, than to convey a false meaning, or to lose the warmth and colour that are the life of such reflections."

489. Cooley (1873) (supra note 152), at 2: § 1945. The bottom line, however, is that the due process clause, insofar as it has an independent per se potency of its own with respect to both its substantive and procedural aspects, intrinsically embodies an unwritten miniconstitution—and "[a *constitution*] would be, that body of rules and maxims in accordance with which the powers of sovereignty are habitually exercised" Cooley (1868) (supra note 449), at 2.

490. 96 U.S. 97, 104.

491. 83 U.S. at 80–81. The Court recited how "notwithstanding the formal recognition by those states [formerly in the Confederate States of America] of the abolition of slavery, the condition of the slave race would, without further protection of the Federal government, be almost as bad as it was before. *Among the first acts of legislation adopted by several of the states in the legislative bodies which claimed to be in their normal relations with the Federal government, were laws which imposed upon the colored race onerous disabilities and burdens and curtailed their rights in the pursuit of life, liberty, and property, to such an extent that their freedom was of little value,* while they had lost the protection which they had received from their former owners from motives both of interest and humanity." 83 U.S. at 70 (emphasis added). So had the Court declared that

the due process clause has substantive aspects pertaining to both liberty and liberty-from rights, then these should be "rights in the pursuit of life, liberty, and property to such an extent that [the] freedom [from servitude] of [all free persons, including 'the colored race,' would not be] of little value."

492. 83 U.S. at 122 (J. Bradley, dissenting): "In my view, a law which prohibits a large class of citizens from adopting a lawful employment, or from following a lawful employment previously adopted, does deprive them of liberty as well as property, without due process of law. Their right of choice is a portion of their liberty; their occupation is their property." Justice Swayne concurred in the views expressed by Bradley on this head. Ibid., 124, 128.

493. 87 U.S. (20 Wall.) 655, 662–63. This declaration was made by the Court in the course of reviewing a judgment in a federal diversity civil case in which it was determined that a tax must be for a public benefit. Justice Clifford was the only member of the Court who took issue with the above-quoted declaration.

494. 92 U.S. at 554.

495. 96 U.S. at 104.

496. However, later in *Chicago, Burlington & Quincy Railroad Co.* v. *Chicago*, 166 U.S. 226 (1897), the Court ruled in effect that it violates due process of law to deprive a person of his property without just compensation.

497. 110 U.S. at 536–37: "This court, speaking by Mr. Justice Miller in [*Loan Assocation* v. *Topeka*, 87 U.S. at 662–63] said: 'It must be conceded that there are such rights in every free government beyond the control of the State. A government which recognized no such rights, which held the lives, the liberty, and the property of its citizens subject at all times to the absolute disposition and unlimited control of even the most democratic depository of power, is, after all, but a despotism. It is true, it is a despotism of the many, of the majority, if you choose to call it so, but it is nevertheless a despotism. It may be doubted, if a man is to hold all that he is accustomed to call his own, all in which he has placed his happiness and the security of which is essential to that happiness, under the unlimited dominion of others, whether it is not wiser that this power should be exercised by one man than by many.'"

498. 41 U.S. 1. See supra note 378.

499. (Edward S. Corwin, ed.) *The Constitution of the United States of America: Analyis and Interpretation* (Washington, D.C.: U.S. Government Printing Office, 1952), 974.

500. 109 U.S. at 20 (emphasis added).

501. The Fugitive Slave Act of 1850 (Act of September 18, 1850, 9 Stat. 462), for example, authorized the putative slave owner to take possession of an alleged fugitive slave on the strength of an affidavit; with the alleged slave having no right to jury trial or a judicial hearing. The text of this infamous statute is available online at http://lcweb2.loc. gov/ammem/amlaw/lwsllink.html. For a thorough account of the federal fugitive slave acts and their enforcement, see Don E. Fehrenbacher, *The Slaveholding Republic: An Accont of the United States Government's Relations to Slavery* (ed. & completed by Ward M. McAfee) (New York: Oxford University Press, 2001), 205–251.

502. CAL. CONST. of 1849, art. I, § 1; ILL. CONST. of 1818, art. XIII, § 1; IND. CONST. of 1851, art. I, § 1; IOWA CONST. of 1846, art. II, § 1; KAN. CONST. of 1859, Bill of Rights, § 1; N.H. CONST. of 1792, Part I, §§ 1, 2; MASS. CONST. of 1790, Pt. I, art. I. ME. CONST. of 1820, art. I, § 1; N.J. CONST. of 1844, art. I, § 1; OHIO CONST. of 1851, art. I, § 1; PA. CONST. of 1838, art. IX, § 1; VT. CONST. of 1793, ch. I, art. 1; WIS. CONST. of 1848, art. I, § 1.

503. VA. CONST. of 1851, Bill of Rights, art. I, § 1. It is noteworthy that eight antebellum state constitutions had provisions grounding equality of rights of freemen upon the social compact. Of these six were slave states (ALA. CONST. of 1831, Declaration of Rights, art. I, § 1; ARK. CONST. of 1836, Art. II, § 1; FLA. CONST. of 1845, Art. I, § 1; KY. CONST. of 1845, Art. XIII, § 1; MISS. CONST. of 1831, Art. I, § 1; TEX. CONST. of 1845, Art. I, § 2;); two were free states (CONN. CONST. of 1792, Art. I, § 1; OR. CONST. of 1859, Art. I, § 1). There were eleven antebellum state constitutions each of which lacked an equal natural rights or a social compact equal rights provision.

504. Elliot, *Debates in the Several State Conventions* (supra note 151), 4: 316.

505. This is according to my own count of the relevant constitutional texts. But see Calabresi & Agudo (supra note 363), at 88: "Twenty-seven out of thirty-seven state constitutions in 1868—or two-thirds of the states but not an Article V consensus—declared as a matter of positive state constitutional law the existence of natural, inalienable, inviolable, or inherent rights."

506. Cooley (1873) (supra note 152), at 2: § 1940.

507. Ibid. But note that Cooley's exposition of the equal protection clause, despite its declaration "that this clause, of its own force, neither confers rights nor gives privileges: its sole office is to insure impartial legal protection to such as under the laws may exist" (ibid., § 1960), arguably appears to also attribute to the equal protection clause the office of prohibiting the making or enforcement of laws that "would assail the

very foundations of a government whose fundamental idea is, the equality of all its citizens." Ibid., § 1961. He asserts: "And now that it has become a settled rule of constitutional law that color or race is no longer a badge of inferiority and no test of capacity to participate in government, we doubt if any distinction whatever either in right or in privilege, which has color or race for its sole basis, can either be established in the law or enforced where it had been previously established." Ibid. But by virtue of what constitutional provision does this principle of racial equality obtain with respect to the United States unless it is by virtue of the Fifth Amendment due process clause—assuming a narrow construction of the privileges or immunities clause that is substantially identical to that adopted in the *Slaughter-House Cases*?

508. The Court declared (83 U.S. at 71): "[N]o one can fail to be impressed with the one pervading purpose found in them all [i.e., the three reconstruction amendments], lying at the foundation of each, and without each none of them would have been even suggested; we mean the freedom of the slave race, the security and firm establishment of that freedom, and the protection of the newly made freemen and citizen from the oppressions of those who had formerly exercised unlimited dominion over him.... [I]n any fair and just construction of any section or phrase of these amendments, it is necessary to look to the purpose which we have said was the pervading spirit of them all, the evil which they were designed to remedy; and the process of continued addition to the Constitution until that purpose was supposed to be accomplished, as far as constitutional law can accomplish it."

509. 262 U.S. at 399–400.

510. Francis Lieber, *Manual of Political Ethics* (ed. Theodore D. Woolsey, 2d ed. rev'd) (Philadelphia: J. B. Lippincott Co., 1890), 1: 68. Lieber unfortunately defines the term *ethics* or *moral law* as "treat[ing], among other subjects, of the duties of man, and secondarily of his rights derivable from his duties; the term *natural law*, on the other hand, [as] treat[ing], as the fundamental and primary subject, of man's rights, and secondarily of his obligations flowing from the fact of each man's being possessed of the same rights." Ibid., 69 (emphasis added). I prefer to use the term *natural morality* or *natural moral law* as embracing both what Lieber terms the *natural law* and *ethics* or the *moral law*. *Natural morality*, in my view, embraces what are commonly understood among rational men and women of good will to be basic moral principles, and moral precepts and norms universally binding on humans for reasons other than being required by customary mores, or human or divine positive law, or as having been supernaturally revealed.

511. Ibid., 68–69.

512. Ibid., 202. Lieber criticizes the term *absolute rights* because "[t]his is not a very apt term, for ... there are no absolute rights, if this term mean either than they cannot be abridged, or that men cannot agree to give them up." Ibid., 200. Similarly, he criticizes the term *inalienable rights* as "an expression which would not have been so freely adopted had not those who used it started from the idea that the state is produced by contract, in which certain rights are given up for higher considerations.... Does inalienable mean that those rights cannot be alienated? Facts speak against it." Ibid., 201. I do not see Lieber as doing more than demanding more precision in speaking of certain *natural rights* as inalienable.

513. Ibid.,178.

514. Because an American citizen of the age of 18 years or older cannot be denied the right to vote because of age by virtue of the Twenty-sixth Amendment, a person of the age of eighteen years or older, even if not technically an adult for all purposes, is no longer a minor.

515. Russell Kirk, *Academic Freedom: An Essay in Definition* (Chicago: Henry Regnery Co., 1955), 4. He also explained: "Our dearest liberties and privileges are conferred upon us much more by immemorial usage and the dictates of conscience than by statutory enactment." Ibid., 5.

516. 106 U.S. 583 (*held*: state statute that criminalized interracial marriage and made interracial adultery and fornication subject to greater punishment than when parties were of the same race did not violate equal protection of the laws); overruled in *McLaughlin* v. *Florida*, 379 U.S. 184 (1964).

517. 163 U.S. 537 (*held*: a state statute that required equal but separate accommodations for the white and colored races does not violate equal protection of the laws).

518. 388 U.S. 1, 12.

519. 100 U.S. 303, 307–08 (1880).

520. 83 U.S. at 81.

521. Ely (supra note 108), at 32.

522. Since, given *Bolling*, 347 U.S. at 500, the Fifth Amendment due process clause incorporates the specific right of the equal protection clause, does the Fourteenth Amendment due process clause incorporate the specific right of the equal protection clause? The Court in *Brown* v. *Board of Education*, 347 U.S. at 495 (1954), declined to rule whether school segregation, condemned as violative of the equal protection clause, "also violates the Due Process Clause of the Fourteenth Amendment."

523. There was much concern in the Congress and elsewhere as to whether section 2 of the Thirteenth Amendment authorized the enactment of the Civil Rights Act of 1866. See, e.g., *Cong. Globe*, 39th Cong., 1st Sess., 2459, 2462 (May 8, 1866) (remarks of Congressmen Stevens and Garfield). The Thirteenth and Fourteenth Amendments were ratified respectively on December 18, 1865 and July 9, 1868. The Civil Rights Act of 1866 was enacted on April 9, 1866. See note 344 for the text of section 1 of that Act.

524. The concurring opinion of Justice Souter in *Washington v. Glucksberg*, 521 U.S. at 755–73, contains a valuable exposition of a philosophy of the fundamental rights protected by the due process clause and makes many commonsensible points. My regret is that he joined in the Court's opinion in *Lawrence* v. *Texas* (see supra note 473) instead of joining in the judgment and issuing a concurring opinion in harmony with views expressed by him in *Glucksberg*.

525. 539 U.S. at 567.

526. Ibid., 578. The Court further announced that "liberty presumes an autonomy of self that includes freedom of thought, believe, expression, and certain intimate conduct. The instant case involves liberty of the person both in its spatial and more transcendent dimensions." Ibid., 562. The Court also approvingly quoted (at ibid., 574) from *Planned Parenthood of Southeastern Pa.* v. *Casey*, 505 U.S. 833, 851 (1992): "These matters, involving the most intimate and personal choices a person may make in a lifetime, choices central to personal dignity and autonomy, are central to the liberty protected by the Fourteenth Amendment. At the heart of liberty is the right to define one's own concept of existence, of meaning, of the universe, and of the mystery of human life." According to the *Lawrence* Court "Persons in a homosexual relationship may seek autonomy for these purposes, just as heterosexual persons do." 539 U.S. at 574. The Court appears to be adverting to a notion of *liberty* that encompasses much more than the civil right to be legally free to form and express a particular belief, or not to do so, as a necessary foundation for persons to hold beliefs as rational, moral and social beings. The Court also declared in *Planned Parenthood*, 505 U.S. at 851: "Beliefs about these matters could not define the attributes of personhood were they formed under compulsion of the State." Of course, the issue of being legally free to form, profess, and advocate one's beliefs about these lofty matters is quite different from overtly acting out one's beliefs.

527. *Lawrence*, 539 U.S. at 571.

528. 478 U.S. 186, 216 (1986). In *Bowers* the Court upheld as not violative of the due process of law a statute making it a crime for persons,

whether or not of the same sex, to engage in oral or anal intercourse, as applied to a openly gay male in the privacy of his home.

529. Quoted in 539 U.S. at 577. The Court's reference to miscegenation displays its abject failure to effectually realize how the adoption of the Thirteenth Amendment had radically changed the fundamental law of the land embodied in the Fifth Amendment due process clause with respect to persons of color. Racial or ethnic identity, unlike homosexual conduct, is not determined by choices or preferences manifested in behavior—even if, as it appears to be the case, a homosexual orientation for many individuals is due to a genetic predisposition. See supra, part II, section 3 ("The freedom from invidious gender and other similar kinds of discrimination as to civil rights based upon birth status").

530. 539 U.S. at 578.

531. The Court indeed stated (ibid., 578): "The present case does not involve minors. It does not involve persons who might be injured or coerced or who are situated in relationships where consent might not easily be refused. It does not involve public conduct or prostitution. It does not involve whether the government must give formal recognition to any relationship that homosexual persons seek to enter. The case does involve two adults who, with full and mutual consent from each other, engaged in sexual practices common to a homosexual lifestyle." However, given the Court's rationale in *Lawrence* and its judgment and opinion in *Romer* v. *Evans,* 517 U.S. 620 (1996), it appears to me that the Court as presently constituted would likely rule in some future case that the Texas-type statute is not valid as applied to residential same-sex intercourse involving multiple parties or as noncommercial entertainment for other consenting adults since the statute does not also encompass opposite-sex intercourse. As the *Lawrence* court explained: "the Court [in *Romer*] struck down class-based legislation directed at homosexuals as a violation of the Equal Protection Clause. *Romer* invalidated an amendment to Colorado's Constitution that named as a solitary class persons who were homosexuals, lesbians, or bisexual either by 'orientation, conduct, practices or relationships,' ... and deprived them of protection under state antidiscrimination laws. We concluded that the provision was 'born of animosity toward the class of persons affected" and further that it had no rational relation to a legitimate governmental purpose." 539 U.S. at 574. In my opinion, otherwise constitutionally permissible statutes criminalizing oral or anal intercourse in certain scenarios should be equally applicable to couples of the same or opposite gender as a matter of public policy rather than being constitutionally required by the equal protection components of the due process clauses.

532. See *United States* v. *Williams*, 128 S.Ct. 1830, 1838 (2008): "According to our First Amendment overbreadth doctrine, a statute is facially invalid if it prohibits a substantial amount of protected speech.... [W]e have vigorously enforced the requirement that a statute's overbreadth be *substantial*, not only in an absolute sense, but also relative to the statute's plainly legitimate sweep." The Court declared in *Bates* v. *State Bar of Arizona*, 433 U.S. 350, 579–81 (1977) that the overbreadth doctrine does not apply to so-called commercial speech. For an interesting case illustrative of the ordinary rule that a statute may be constitutionally applied to the facts of the case despite its substantial overbreadth, see *Connecticut* v. *Munillo*, 423 U.S. 9 (1975). The *Munillo* Court held that a criminal statute forbidding an attempted abortion by any person could continue to be validly enforced against nonphysicians notwithstanding the decision in *Roe* v. *Wade*, 410 U.S. 113 (1973) that a state may not constitutionally prohibit a woman from having an abortion performed by her physician during the first trimester.

533. 478 U.S. at 196.

534. Arguably there are exceptions to this general statement (e.g., regulations of college and other school dormitories, military barracks, rooms in hospitals or other similar institutions, or prisons or jails). But then it is questionable whether any of these places amount to what should be regarded as a dwelling or its functional equivalent (e.g., a hotel room or suite).

535. The FLVC as does FSP-VC encompasses auxiliary rights such as involve the incidental use of pictures and nonverbal graphs as visual aids or adjuncts, subject to reasonable viewpoint-neutral regulation. Visually or auditorily recorded lectures, speeches, conversations, debates, etc., are also embraced within the scope of the FLVC and the FSP-VC. And so also would be verbal communication via the electronic mass media. I do not, however, use the term FLVC or FSP-VC to include live, recorded, or transmitted motion pictures, whether presented via the electronic media or on a film screen, that are predominantly visual in the sense of being substantially more graphic than the recording or transmission of a lecture, speech, etc. with or without incidental use of visual aids. It would take us too far afield to discuss even in a general way the particular substantive rights that pertain to predominantly visual communication (whether as components of FSP or political freedom, some other freedom, or as components of the specific right of the due process clause), since admittedly the constitutional power to regulate predominantly visual communication is somewhat broader than that with respect to predominantly verbal communication.

536. *Schneider* v. *State*, 308 U.S. 147, 163 (1939) "[O]ne is not to have the exercise of his liberty of expression in appropriate places abridged on the plea that it may be exercised in some other place." In *Schneider* and its progeny on this point, the Court is speaking of abridgments that are viewpoint or content (other than obscene) biased. For example, the Court holds that the First Amendment equally protects the solicited and unsolicited mailing of nonobscene commercial expression concerning contraceptives. *Bolger* v. *Youngs Drug Products Corp.*, 463 U.S. 60 (1983). According to the *Bolger* Court (ibid. at 71): "In striking down a state prohibition of contraceptive advertisements in *Carey v. Population Services International* [431 U.S. 678, 701 (1977)], we stated that offensiveness was 'classically not [a] justificatio[n] validating the suppression of expression protected by the First Amendment. At least where obscenity is not involved, we have consistently held that the fact that protected speech may be offensive to some does not justify its suppression.'" (Bracketed matter in original.)

537. The Court implicitly maintains that the FSP includes as a component the right to freely propagate white supremacist doctrines in any appropriate form or channel of public communication. See *Brandenburg* v. *Ohio*, 395 U.S. 444 (1969), *R. A. V.* v. *City of St. Paul*. 505 U.S. 377 (1992); and *Virginia* v. *Black*, 538 U.S. 343 (2003). The opinions in these cases, as well as in *New York Times* v. *Sullivan*, 376 U.S. 254 (1654), presuppose that *Beauharnais* v. *Illinois*, 343 U.S. 250 (1952), which upheld a statute criminalizing a group libel statute prohibiting the making of false defamatory statements about racial groups, is no longer good law.

538. It would be absurd were the Court to hold that the so-called fundamental right of privacy does not encompass some substantive rights of expression in some forms and channels of essentially private communication, such as personal conversations or individualized personal correspondence. Of course, if one has a right encompassed by the FSP to freely advocate **T** in all appropriate forms and channels of public communication then he also has a right encompassed by the FSP to freely advocate **T** in virtually all appropriate forms and channels of private communication.

539. The absorption of commercial expression within the ambit of FSP was initiated with *Virginia Pharmacy Board* v. *Virginia Consumer Council*, 425 U.S. 748 (1976). In *Ohralik* v. *Ohio State Bar Association*, 436 U.S. 447, 455–56 (1978), the Court noted "the 'common sense' distinction between speech proposing a commercial transaction, which occurs in an area traditionally subject to governmental regulation, and other varieties of speech." Accordingly, the Court assigned commercial expression "a limited measure of protection, commensurate with its subordinate

position in the scale of First Amendment values, while allowing modes of regulation that might be impermissible in the realm of non-commercial expression." Ibid. In my view, substantive rights pertaining to commercial expression are generally (but not exceptionlessly) not per se components of the FSP. Other substantive rights pertaining to commercial expression are derivative components of the FSP because the mass and print media are characterized by much commercial advertising. Therefore an unreasonable regulation of commercial advertising in the mass and print journalistic media could in some contexts constitute an abridgment of FSP. On the other hand, I would say that some liberty interests in commercial expression are per se components of the FLVC.

540. 527 U.S. 173 (1999).

541. *Paris Adult Theatre I* v. *Slaton*, 413 U.S. 49, 65 (1973) (citing *"Griswold v. Connecticut*, 381 U.S. 479, 482 (1965). *See Ferguson v. Skrupa*, 372 U.S. [726,] 731 [1963]; *Day-Brite Lighting, Inc. v. Missouri*, 342 U.S. 421, 423 (1952).")

542. Ernst Freund, *The Police Power: Public Policy and Constitutional Rights* (Chicago: Callaghan & Co., 1904), 224.

543. Ibid., 224–25.

544. I shall suppose that the statute provides for some exceptions such as for personal correspondence, mail addressed to governmental agencies and officers, academic institutions, submissions of manuscripts to publishing houses, and bona fide individualized business correspondence. I further suppose that the statute is in accord with the procedural aspects of the due process clause. Finally, I suppose that the intended recipient has not already communicated his demand that he not receive printed or similar matter from the sender.

545. According to current doctrine, pictorial or textual hard-core pornography without serious literary, artistic, political, or scientific value is legally obscene for constitutional purposes and is completely unprotected by the First Amendment free speech and free press provisions (and as applied to the states via the Fourteenth Amendment due process clause). The Court has rejected the notion that the fundamental right of privacy, which encompasses the right to freely possess obscene matter in one's home, also encompasses any correlative rights to receive, transport, or distribute legally obscene matter. *Stanley v. Georgia*, 394 U.S. 557 (1969); *Miller v. California*, 413 U.S. 15 (1973); *Paris Adult Theatre I v. Slaton*, 413 U.S. 49 (1973); *Kaplan v. California*, 413 U.S. 115 (1973); *United States v. 12 200-Ft. Reels of Film*, 413 U.S. 123 (1973); *United States v. Orito*, 413 U.S. 139 (1973).

546. In *Memoirs* v. *Massachusetts,* 383 U.S. 413 (1966), the judgment of in a civil equity action that *Fanny Hill* is obscene was reversed by the Court; although the majority could not agree upon the grounds for the decision. The plurality opinion maintained that a book is not obscene despite it being patently offensive and having the requisite prurient interest unless it is utterly without socially redeeming value; and this could not be said of *Fanny Hill.* The plurality doctrine became the de facto rule of decision for the Court in obscenity cases until 1973 when the Court disclosed in *Miller* v. *California* that only hard-core pornography that, on the whole, lacks serious literary, artistic, political, or scientific value constitutes sexual obscenity.

547. The book is so described in *Kaplan* v. *California,* 413 U.S. at 116–17. The Court in *Kaplan* ruled that publication to only consenting adults of a textually pornographic book (without pictorial content) and lacking serious value is not constitutionally protected. I believe that *Kaplan* was erroneously decided.

548. See the very useful discussion in Charles Rembar, *The End of Obscenity: The Trials of Lady Chatterley, Tropic of Cancer, and Fanny Hill* (New York: Random House, 1968), 443–448, concerning what should be the constitutionally privileged status of the printed (or, I would add, recorded) word in writings chiefly designed for individual reading (or, I would add, hearing) by a free adult individual. What in part has made the Court's jurisprudence concerning obscenity a shambles is that the introduction of the *serious literary, artistic, political, or scientific value* rubric introduces serious 'First Amendment' issues concerning statutory vagueness and overbreadth. (See the several opinions in *Pope* v. *Illinois,* 481 U.S. 497 (1987).

549. I believe that political freedom, considered as a constitutional privilege quite independently of the FSP, includes component rights pertaining to journalistic freedom in the predominantly visual media— including pictorial news broadcasts and documentaries—about public affairs and politically relevant matters of public concern.

550. Acts 22: 25–30 (RSV): "But when they had tied him up with thongs, Paul said to the centurian who was standing by, 'Is it lawful for you to scourge a man who is a Roman citizen, and uncondemned?' When the centurian heard that, he went to the tribune and said to him, 'What are you about to do? For this man is a Roman citizen.' So the tribune came and said to him, 'Tell me, are you a Roman citizen?' And he said, 'Yes.' The tribune answered, 'I bought this citizenship for a large sum.' Paul said, 'But I was born a citizen.' So those who were about to examine him withdrew from him instantly; and the tribune also was afraid, for

he realized that Paul was a Roman citizen and that he had bound him." Justice Robert Jackson referred to this incident, in his concurring opinion in *Edwards* v. *California*, 314 U.S. at 182, in the course of his argument that the right of interstate travel and migration is one of the constitutional privileges of American citizens.

551. AMAR, 296

552. Ibid., 181.

553. There may, however, be overlapping with respect to the components of the respective specific rights. For example, as I have already pointed out, some components of the FSP-VC may be components of the specific right of the due process clause—the right of the person not to be deprived of life, liberty, or property, without due process of law.

554. Shifting alliances among the justices in *Apodaca* v. *Oregon*, 406 U.S. 404 (1972) and *Johnson* v. *Louisiana*, 406 U.S. 356 (1972) have resulted in the anomalous situation that the supposedly incorporated Sixth Amendment right to trial by jury requires unanimity in federal trials but not so in state criminal trials.

555. That the true ancestral line of the privileges or immunities clause is found in such public acts as federal treaties and statutes should, I think, be given much more weight that the incidental remarks of legislators, jurists, and other writers that the privileges or immunities clause is based upon the comity clause. Whatever the merits of my theory of selective incorporation, I believe that my 1985 article will have enduring value in having called attention to the true ancestral line of the privileges or immunities clause.

556. Michael Kent Curtis asserts: "Unless one is willing to disregard virtually all the evidence, however, the contest is between selective and full application of the provisions of the Bill of Rights to the states.... I have found over thirty examples of statements by Republicans during the Thirty-eighth and Thirty-ninth Congresses indicating that they believed that at least some Bill of Rights liberties [i.e., rights in the generic sense] limited the states." Curtis (1986) (supra note 19), at 112. Charles Fairman, in his famous article, *Does the Fourteenth Amendment Incorporate the Bill of Rights? The Original Understanding* (supra note 86), at 139, concluded: "Brooding over the matter in the writing of this article has, however, slowly bought the conclusion that Justice Cardozo's gloss on the due process clause—what is "implicit in the concept of ordered liberty"—comes as close as one can to catching the vague aspirations that were hung upon the privileges and [sic!] immunities clause. This accommodates the fact that freedom of speech was mentioned in the discussion of 1866, and the conclusion that, according to the contemporary

understanding, surely the federal requirements as to juries were not included." Amar inaccurately makes Fairman as imputing the selective incorporation function to section 1 of the Fourteenth Amendment as a whole. AMAR, 188. See also Earl M. Maltz, Civil Rights, *The Constitution and Congress, 1863-1869* (Lawrence: University Press of Kansas, 1990), 117: "[T]here can be little doubt that the privileges and immunities clause has incorporated some of the Bill of Rights." Ibid. (emphasis in original). He remarked: "the evidence impressively demonstrates that the basic guarantees of the First Amendment were understood to be included in the concept of privileges and immunities.' Ibid. But after initially writing that "the full incorporation theory, though not refuted, must be classified as not proven beyond a reasonable doubt," Maltz nevertheless ultimately "conclude[d] that contemporaries must have understood the privileges and immunities clause to embody most of the Bill if Rights, and they probably viewed the first eight amendments as incorporated in their entirety." Ibid., 118–19. Jacobus tenBroek, in his well-regarded study on the antislavery origins of the Fourteenth Amendment, concluded: "Certain of the rights in the first eight amendments received well-nigh universal abolitionist attention. They were the rights mentioned in the due process clause of the Fifth Amendment and in the First and Fourth amendments. The rights in the other amendments received only casual, incidental, and infrequent inference.... It is an overstatement to say that an integral part of the abolitionist movement was the application of all the first eight amendment to the states." *Equal Under Law* (New York: Collier Books, 1965), 127.

557. AMAR, 181.

558. Ibid., 235. Amar's omission of religious freedom in this list is evidently an oversight. See ibid., 257: "For the men and women who reglossed our Bill of Rights in the 1860's, *our* First Amendment was *their* First Amendment—first in the text, and first in their hearts. The antebellum experience had indeed dramatized for them the substantive firstness of the First Amendment; in the minds of *these* forefathers—and foremothers, too—religion and expression stood as the nation's first freedoms, the paradigmatic 'privileges' and 'immunities' of citizens of the United States." (Emphasis in original.) It is, by the way, of probative value to our inquiry that only "[t]wenty-two state constitutions in 1868—a majority but not an Article V, federal-constitutional-law-making consensus—had language that explicitly guaranteed the right of the people to keep and bear arms." Calabresi & Agudo (supra note 363), at 50. Even assuming that each provision pertaining to an individual civil right, it does not follow that most provisions respectively secured a true freedom rather than just a conditional liberty-right. On the other hand, every specific right of the

First Amendment was supported by an Article V consensus. Calabresi & Agudo, 33–35 (free exercise); ibid., 41–42 (free press); ibid., 42–43 (free speech); ibid., 43–44 (assembly-petition).

559. AMAR, 204.

560. Curtis (1986) (supra note 19), at 217.

561. *The Birth of a New Physics* (Anchor Books, 1960), 44–45. The heliocentric system of Nicholas Copernicus (1473–1543) reduced the number of epicycles from over eighty to thirty-four. The system of Johannes Kepler (1571–1630), which inter alia postulated an elliptical rather than a circular orbit for each planet, succeeded in eliminating epicycles altogether.

562. From roughly *Allgeyer v. Lousiana*, 165 U.S. 578 (1896) until *West Coast Hotel Co., v. Parrish*, 300 U.S. 379 (1937).

563. I Corinthians 13: 11 (KJV).

564. Justice Thomas, in his dissenting opinion in *Saenz v. Roe*, 526 U.S. at 527–28 wrote: "I believe that the demise of the Privileges or Immunities Clause has contributed in no small part to the current disarray of our Fourteenth Amendment jurisprudence, I would be open to reevaluating its meaning in an appropriate case. Before invoking the Clause, however, we should endeavor to understand what the framers [why not the other founders?] of the Fourteenth Amendment thought that it meant. We should also consider whether the Clause should displace, rather than augment, portions of our equal protection and substantive due process jurisprudence."

565. *The Slaughter-House Cases*, 83 U.S. at 96 (Field, J., dissenting).

566. Although, for my purposes, this book focuses upon how blacks have been the victims of racial discrimination, I do not intend at all to minimize the extent and severity of the unjust treatment of other persons of color because of the racism that characterized our legal and social institutions before and following the adoption of the reconstruction amendments in 1868. For example, the mass expulsion of American citizens of Japanese birth or ancestry from the west coast states during World War II and its vindication by the Court in *Korematsu v. United States*, 323 U.S. 214 (1944) would not have been constitutionally possible had the Court firmly adopted and adhered to an exalted notion of what it means to be an American citizen.

567. *An nescis, mi fili, quantilla prudentia mundus regatur.*

568. [Original in Polish: "Więc tobie, wielka, święta przeszłości, i tobie, krwi ofiarnia, niech będzie chwała i cześć po wszystkie czasy!"] These powerful words are the concluding lines of the penultimate chapter from the historical novel *The Knights of the Cross* [*Krzyżacy*] [(trans.

Jeremiah Curtin) (Boston: Little, Brown & Co., 1900), 2: 344] by Henryk Sienkiewicz (1846–1916), Polish author and Nobel laureate, better known to the American public as the author of *Quo Vadis*. The historical backdrop of *The Knights of the Cross* pertains to the great stuggle of the Polish and Lithuanian nations with the territorially greedy German crusading order, the Teutonic Knights (i.e., The Order of the Teutonic Knights of St. Mary's Hospital in Jerusalem). The struggle reached its climax in 1410 when Polish and Lithuanian forces (under the leadership of the Władysław II Jagiełło, King of Poland and Grand Duke of Lithuania) decisively defeated the Teutonic Knights in the great battle of Grunwald. For a new edition and translation of Sienkiewicz's work, see *The Teutonic Knights*, ed. & rev'd by Mirosław Lipinski, trans. by Alicia Tyszkiewicz (New York: Hippocrene Books, 1993).

Appendix: Relevant Provisions of The Constitution of the United States of America

[In effect on September 13, 1788]
Preamble: We the People of the United States, in Order to form a more perfect Union, establish Justice, insure domestic Tranquillity, provide for the common defense, promote the general Welfare, and secure the Blessings of Liberty to ourselves and our Posterity, do ordain and establish this Constitution for the United States of America.

Article. I.
Section. 1. All legislative Powers herein granted shall be vested in a Congress of the United States, which shall consist of a Senate and House of Representatives.
[Sections 2–7 omitted.]
Section. 8. The Congress shall have Power To lay and collect Taxes, Duties, Imposts and Excises, to pay the Debts and provide for the common Defence and general Welfare of the United States; but all Duties, Imposts and Excises shall be uniform throughout the United States;

To borrow Money on the credit of the United States;

To regulate Commerce with foreign Nations, and among the several States, and with the Indian Tribes;

To establish an uniform Rule of Naturalization, and uniform Laws on the subject of Bankruptcies throughout the United States;

To coin Money, regulate the Value thereof, and of foreign Coin, and fix the Standard of Weights and Measures;

To provide for the Punishment of counterfeiting the Securities and current Coin of the United States;

To establish post Offices and post Roads;

To promote the Progress of Science and useful Arts, by securing for limited Times to Authors and Inventors the exclusive Right to their respective Writings and Discoveries;

To constitute Tribunals inferior to the supreme Court;

To define and punish Piracies and Felonies committed on the high Seas, and Offences against the Law of Nations;

To declare War, grant Letters of Marque and Reprisal, and make Rules concerning Captures on Land and Water;

To raise and support Armies, but no Appropriation of Money to that Use shall be for a longer Term than two Years;

To provide and maintain a Navy;

To make Rules for the Government and Regulation of the land and naval Forces;

To provide for calling forth the Militia to execute the Laws of the Union, suppress Insurrections and repeal Invasions;

To provide for organizing, arming, and disciplining, the Militia, and for governing such Part of them as may be employed in the Service of the United States, reserving to the States respectively, the Appointment of the Officers, and the Authority of training the Militia according to the discipline prescribed by Congress;

To exercise exclusive Legislation in all Cases whatsoever, over such District (not exceeding ten Miles square) as may, by Cession of Particular States, and the Acceptance of Congress, become the Seat of the Government of the United States, and to exercise like Authority over all Places purchased by the Consent of the Legislature of the State in which the Same shall be, for the Erection of Forts, Magazines, Arsenals, dock-Yards and other needful Buildings;—And

To make all Laws which shall be necessary and proper for carrying into Execution the foregoing Powers and all other Powers vested by this Constitution in the Government of the United States, or in any Department or Officer thereof.

Section. 9. The Migration or Importation of such Persons as any of the States now existing shall think proper to admit, shall not be prohibited by the Congress prior to the Year one thousand eight hundred and eight, but a Tax or duty may be imposed on such Importation, not exceeding ten dollars for each Person.

The Privilege of the Writ of Habeas Corpus shall not be suspended, unless when in Cases of Rebellion or Invasion the public Safety may require it.

No Bill of Attainder or ex post facto Law shall be passed.

No Capitation, or other direct, Tax shall be laid, unless in Proportion to the Census of Enumeration herein before directed to be taken.

No Tax or Duty shall be laid on Articles exported from any State.

No Preference shall be given by any Regulation of Commerce or Revenue to the Ports of one State over those of another: nor shall Vessels bound to, or from, one State, be obliged to enter, clear or pay Duties in another.

No Money shall be drawn from the Treasury, but in Consequence of Appropriations made by Law; and a regular Statement and Account of the Receipts and Expenditures of all public Money shall be published from time to time.

No Title of Nobility shall be granted by the United States: And no Person holding any Office of Profit or Trust under them, shall, without the Consent of the Congress, accept of any present, Emolument, Office, or Title, of any kind whatever, from any King, Prince or foreign State.

Section. 10. No State shall enter into any Treaty, Alliance, or Confederation; grant Letters of Marque and Reprisal; coin Money; emit Bills of Credit; make any Thing but gold and silver Coin a Tender in Payment of Debts; pass any Bill of Attainder, ex post facto Law, or Law impairing the Obligation of Contracts, or grant any Title of Nobility.

No State shall, without the Consent of the Congress, lay any Imposts or Duties on Imports or Exports, except what may be absolutely necessary for executing its inspection Laws: and the net Produce of all Duties and Imposts, laid by any State on Imports or Exports, shall be for the Use of the Treasury of the United States; and all such Laws shall be subject to the Revision and Controul of the Congress.

[Further text omitted.]

Article. II.

Section 1. The executive Power shall be vested in a President of the United States of America. [Further text omitted.]

Section. 2. The President shall be Commander in Chief of the Army and Navy of the United States, and of the Militia of the several States, when called into the actual Service of the United States; [further text omitted].

Article III.

Section. 1. The judicial Power of the United States, shall be vested in one supreme Court, and in such inferior Courts as the Congress may from time to time ordain and establish. [Further text omitted.]

Section. 2. The judicial Power shall extend to all Cases, in Law and Equity, arising under this Constitution, the Laws of the United States, and Treaties made, or which shall be made, under their Authority;—to all Cases affecting Ambassadors, other public ministers and Consuls;—to all Cases of admiralty and maritime Jurisdiction;—to Controversies to which the United States shall be a Party;—to Controversies between two or more States;—between a State and Citizens of another State;—between Citizens of different States;—between Citizens of the same State claiming Lands under Grants of different States, and between a State, or the Citizens thereof, and foreign States, Citizens or Subjects.

In all Cases affecting Ambassadors, other public Ministers and Consuls, and those in which a State shall be Party, the supreme Court shall have original Jurisdiction. In all the other Cases before mentioned, the supreme Court shall have appellate Jurisdiction, both as to Law and Fact, with such Exceptions, and under such Regulations as the Congress shall make.

The Trial of all Crimes, except in Cases of Impeachment, shall be by Jury; and such Trial shall be held in the State where the said Crimes shall have been committed; but when not committed within any State, the Trial shall be at such Place or Places as the Congress may by Law have directed.

Section. 3. Treason against the United States, shall consist only in levying War against them, or in adhering to their Enemies, giving them Aid and Comfort. No Person shall be convicted of Treason unless on the Testimony of two Witnesses to the same overt Act, or on Confession in open Court.

The Congress shall have Power to declare the Punishment of Treason, but no Attainder of Treason shall work Corruption of Blood, or Forfeiture except during the Life of the Person attainted.

Article. IV.

Section.1. [Text omitted.]

Section. 2. The Citizens of each State shall be entitled to all Privileges and Immunities of Citizens in the several States.

A Person charged in any State with Treason, Felony, or other Crime, who shall flee from Justice, and be found in another State, shall on Demand of the executive Authority of the State from which he fled, be delivered up, to be removed to the State having Jurisdiction of the Crime.

No Person held to Service or Labour in one State, under the Laws thereof, escaping into another, shall, in Consequence of any Law or Regulation therein, be discharged from such Service or Labour, but shall be delivered up on Claim of the Party to whom such Service or Labour may be due.

Section. 3. New States may be admitted by the Congress into this Union; but no new State shall be formed or erected within the Jurisdiction of any other State; nor any State be formed by the Junction of two or more States, or Parts of States, without the Consent of the Legislatures of the States concerned as well as of the Congress.

The Congress shall have Power to dispose of and make all needful Rules and Regulations respecting the Territory or other Property belonging to the United States; and nothing in this Constitution shall be so construed as to Prejudice any Claims of the United States, or of any particular State.

Section. 4. The United States shall guarantee to every State in this Union a Republican Form of Government, and shall protect each of them against Invasion; and on Application of the Legislature, or of the Executive (when the Legislature cannot be convened) against domestic Violence.

Article. V. [Text omitted.]

Article. VI. [Opening text omitted.] This Constitution, and the Laws of the United States which shall be made in Pursuance thereof; and all Treaties made, or which shall be made, under the Authority of the United States, shall be the supreme Law of the Land; and the Judges in every State shall be bound thereby, any Thing in the Constitution or Laws of any state to the Contrary notwithstanding.

[Further text omitted.]

Amendments I–X) [December 15, 1791]:

Amendment I. Congress shall make no law respecting an establishment of religion, or prohibiting the free exercise thereof; or abridging the freedom of speech, or of the press; or the right of the people peaceably to assemble, and to petition the Government for a redress of grievances.

Amendment II. A well regulated Militia, being necessary to the security of a free State, the right of the people to keep and bear Arms, shall not be infringed.

Amendment III. No Soldier shall, in time of peace be quartered in any house, without the consent of the Owner, nor in time of war, but in a manner to be prescribed by law.

Amendment IV. The right of the people to be secure in their persons, houses, papers, and effects, against unreasonable searches and seizures, shall not be violated, and no Warrants shall issue, but upon probable cause, supported by Oath or affirmation, and particularly describing the place to be searched, and the persons or things to be seized.

Amendment V. No person shall be held to answer for a capital, or otherwise infamous crime, unless on a presentment or indictment of a Grand Jury, except in cases arising in the land or naval forces, or in the Militia, when in actual service in time of War or public danger; nor shall any person be subject for the same offence to be twice put in jeopardy of life or limb; nor shall be compelled in any criminal case to be a witness against himself, nor be deprived of life, liberty, or property, without due process of law; nor shall private property be taken for public use, without just compensation.

Amendment VI. In all criminal prosecutions, the accused shall enjoy the right to a speedy and public trial, by an impartial jury of the State and district wherein the crime shall have been committed, which district shall have been previously ascertained by law, and to be informed of the nature and cause of the accusation; to be confronted with the witnesses against him; to have compulsory process for obtaining witnesses in his favor, and to have the Assistance of Counsel for his defence.

Amendment VII. In Suits at common law, where the value in controversy shall exceed twenty dollars, the right of trial by jury shall be preserved, and no fact tried by a jury, shall be otherwise re-examined in any Court of the United States, than according to the rules of the common law.

Amendment VIII. Excessive bail shall not be required, nor excessive fines imposed, nor cruel and unusual punishments inflicted.

Amendment IX. The enumeration in the Constitution, of certain rights, shall not be construed to deny or disparage others retained by the people.

Amendment X. The powers not delegated to the United States by the Constitution, nor prohibited by it to the States, are reserved to the States respectively, or to the people.

[Amendments XI and XII omitted.]

Amendment XIII. Section 1. Neither slavery nor involuntary servitude, except as a punishment for crime whereof the party shall have been duly convicted, shall exist within the United States, or any place subject to their jurisdiction.

Section 2. Congress shall have power to enforce this article by appropriate legislation. [18 December 1865]

Amendment XIV. Section. 1. All persons born or naturalized in the United States and subject to the jurisdiction thereof, are citizens of the United States and of the State wherein they reside. No State shall make or enforce any law which shall abridge the privileges or immunities of citizens of the United States; nor shall any State deprive any person of life, liberty, or property, without due process of law; nor deny to any person within its jurisdiction the equal protection of the laws.

[Sections 2. 3, and 4 omitted.].

Section 5. The Congress shall have power to enforce, by appropriate legislation, the provisions of this article. [28 July 1868]

Amendment XV. Section. 1. The right of citizens of the United States to vote shall not be denied or abridged by the United States or by any State on account of race, color, or previous condition of servitude. [Section 2 omitted.]. [March 30, 1870]

[Amendments XVI-XVIII omitted.]

Amendment XIX. The right of citizens of the United States to vote shall not be denied or abridged by the United States or by any State on account of sex. Congress shall have power to enforce this article by appropriate legislation. [August 26, 1920]

[Amendments XX-XXIII omitted.]

Amendment XXIV. Section. 1. The right of citizens of the United States to vote in any primary or other election for President or Vice President, for electors for President or Vice President, or for Senator or Representative in Congress, shall not be denied or abridged by the United States or any State by reason of failure to pay any poll tax or other tax. [Section. 2 omitted.]. [August 27, 1964]

[Amendment XXV omitted.]

Amendment XXVI. Section. 1. The right of citizens of the United States, who are eighteen years of age or older, to vote shall not be denied or abridged by the United States or by any State on account of age. [Section. 2 omitted.] [July 1, 1971]

[Amendment XXVII omitted.]

Supreme Court Cases with Endnote Citations for Parts I–IV

Opinions of the United States Supreme Court are conveniently available online at http://supreme.justia.com/us/

Abington School District v. *Schempp*, 374 U.S. 203, 225 (1963): nn 391, 393, 418, 422, 436–38

Adkins v. *Children's Hospital*, 261 U.S. 525 (1923): nn 461–62

Afroyim v. *Rusk*, 387 U.S. 253, 257 (1967): nn 307, 312

Allegheny County of Allegheny v. *American Civil Liberties Union*, 492 U.S. 573 (1989): nn 422, 445

Allgeyer v. *Louisiana*, 165 U.S. 578 (1896): nn 461, 562

Apodaca v. *Oregon*, 406 U.S. 404 (1972): n 554

Austin v. *New Hampshire*, 420 U.S. 656 (1975): n 99

Baker v. *Carr*, 369 U.S. 186 (1962): n 16

Baldwin v. *Fish & Game Commission of Montana*, 436 U.S. 371 (1978): n 324

Balzac v. *Porto Rico*, 258 U.S. 298 (1922): n 304

Bank of Columbia v. *Okely*, 17 U.S. (4 Wheat.) 235 (1819): n 476

Bank of United States v. *Deveaux*, 9 U.S. (5 Cr.) 61 (1809): n 156

Barron v. *Baltimore*, 32 U.S. (7 Pet.) 243 (1833): nn 1, 114

Bates v. *State Bar of Arizona*, 433 U.S. 350 (1977): n 532

Beauharnais v. *Illinois*, 343 U.S. 250 (1952): n 537

Benton v. *Maryland*, 395 U.S. 784 (1969): nn 5, 9, 23, 471

Bolger v. *Youngs Drug Products Corp.*, 463 U.S. 60 (1983): n 536

Bolling v. *Sharpe*, 347 U.S. 497 (1954): nn 326, 522

Board of Education of Kiryas Joel Village School District v. *Grumet*, 512 U.S. 687 (1994): n 407

Bowers v. *Hardwick*, 478 U.S. 186 (1986): nn 528, 533

Boyd v. *Nebraska*, 143 U.S. 135 (1892): n 353

Brandenburg v. *Ohio*, 395 U.S. 444 (1969): n 537

Braunfeld v. *Brown*, 366 U.S. 599 (1961): n 411

Brown v. *Board of Education*, 347 U.S. 483 (1954): nn 326, 522

Browning-Ferris v. *Kelco Disposal*, 492 U.S. 257 (1989): n 11

Buchanan v. *Warley*, 245 U.S. 60 (1917): n 464

Building Trades v. *Mayor of Camden*, 465 U.S. 208 (1984): n 99

Ex Parte Virginia, 100 U.S. 313 (1880): n 327

Examining Board v. Flores de Otero, 426 U.S. 572 (1976): nn 304, 354

Farrington v. Tokushige, 273 U.S. 284 (1927): nn 111, 384

Ferguson v. Skrupa, 372 U.S. 726 (1963): nn 461, 541

Fiske v. Kansas, 274 U.S. 380 (1927): n 467

Flast v. Cohen, 392 U.S. 83 (1968): nn 395–96, 400, 403–04

Fong Yue Ting v. United States, 149 U.S. 698 (1893): n 151

Frothingham v. Mellon, 262 U.S. 447 (1923): n 394

Gallager v. Crown Kosher Super Market: 366 U.S. 617 (1961): n 412

Gassies v. Ballon, 31 U.S. (6 Pet.) 761 (1832): n 233

Gibson v. Mississippi, 162 U.S. 565 (1896): nn 317, 347.

Gideon v. Wainwright, 372 U.S. 335 (1963): n 10

Gilbert v. Minnesota, 254 U.S. 325, 343 (1920): n 467

Gitlow v. New York, 268 U.S. 652 (1925) nn 7, 467

Granger Cases, 94 U.S. 113 (1877): n 158

Greater New Orleans Broadcasting Association v. United States, 527 U.S. 173 (1999): n 540

Griswold v. Connecticut, 381 U.S. 479 (1965): nn 7, 14, 113, 461, 468, 541

Grosjean v. American Press Co., 297 U.S. 233 (1936): nn 7, 468

Hampton v. Mow Sun Wong, 426 U.S. 88 (1976): n 112

Hampton & Co. v. United States, 276 U.S. 394 (1928): n 194

Harper v. Virginia State Board of Elections, 383 U.S. 663 (1966): n 16

Hawaii v. Mankichi, 190 U.S. 197 (1901): n 304

Hebert v. Louisiana, 272 U.S. 312 (1926): n 6

Hein v. Freedom From Religion Foundation, 127 S.Ct. 2553 (2007): nn 396–98, 401

Heiner v. Donnan, 285 U.S. 312 (1932): n 111

Hibben v. Smith, 191 U.S. 310 (1903): n 111

Hicklin v. Orbeck, 437 U.S. 518 (1978): n 99

Hurtado v. California, 110 U.S. 516 (1884): nn 12, 459–60, 497

In re Oliver, 333 U.S. 257 (1948): n 10

Irvin v. Dowd, 366 U.S. 717 (1961): n 10

Johnson v. Louisiana, 406 U.S. 356 (1972): n 554

Kaplan v. California, 413 U.S. 115 (1973): nn 545, 547

Kendall v. United States ex rel. Stokes, 37 U.S. (12 Pet.) 524 (1838): n 430

Murray's Lessee v. *Hoboken Land & Improvement Co.*, 59 U.S. (18 How) 272 (1856): nn 34, 105, 109, 477

New York Times v. *Sullivan*, 376 U.S. 254 (1964): n 537

Ocampo v. *United States*, 234 U.S. 91 (1914): n 304

Ohralik v. *Ohio State Bar Association*, 436 U.S. 447 (1978): n 539

Orient Insurance Co. v. *Daggs*, 172 U.S. 557, 561 (1899): n 107

Osborn v. *Bank of the United States*, 22 U.S. (9 Wheat.) 738 (1824): n 353

Pace v. Alabama, 106 U.S. 583 (1893): n 516

Palko v. *Connecticut*, 302 U.S. 319 (1937): n 472.

Paris Adult Theatre I v. *Slaton*, 413 U.S. 49 (1973): nn 541, 545

Passenger Cases, 48 U.S. (7 How.) 283 (1849): nn 242, 456

Paul v. *Davis*, 424 U.S. 693 (1976): n 111

Paul v. *Virginia*, 75 U.S. (8 Wall.) 168 (1869): n 99

Permoli v. *New Orleans*, 44 U.S. (3 How.) 589 (1845): nn 1, 100–04

Perpich v. *Department of Defense*, 496 U.S. 334 (1990): nn 196–98, 220

Pierce v. *Society of Sisters*, 268 U.S. 510 (1925): nn 384, 466

Planned Parenthood of Southeastern Pennsylvania v. *Casey*, 505 U.S. 833 (1992): nn 475, 526

Plessy v. *Ferguson*, 163 U.S. 537 (1896): nn 315, 517

Pointer v. *Texas*, 380 U.S. 400 (1965): nn 10, 471

Pope v. *Illinois*, 481 U.S. 497 (1987): n 548

Powell v. *Alabama*, 287 U.S. 45 (1932): n 6

Presser v. *Illinois*, 116 U.S. 252 (1886): nn 161, 225

Prudential Insurance Co. v. *Cheek*, 259 U.S. 530, 543 (1922): n 467

R. A. V. v. *City of St. Paul*, 505 U.S. 377 (1992): n 537

Rabang v. *Boyd*, 353 U.S. 427 (1957): n 304

Raines v. *Byrd*, 521 U.S. 811 (1997): n 420

Reynolds v. *Sims*, 377 U.S. 533 (1964): n 16

Rodriguez v. *Popular Democratic Party*, 457 U.S. 1, 7 (1982): n 354

Robertson v. *Baldwin*, 165 U.S. 275 (1897): n 447

Robinson v. *California*, 370 U.S. 660 (1962): n 11

Roe v. *Wade*, 410 U.S. 113 (1973): nn 475, 532

Rogers v. *Bellei*, 401 U.S. 815 (1970): n 267

Romer v. *Evans*, 517 U.S. 620 (1996): n 531

Ruhlin v. *New York Life Insurance Co.*, 304 U.S. 304 (1938): n 378

Saenz v. *Roe*, 526 U.S. 489 (1999): nn 285, 356, 564

San Antonio School District v. *Rodriquez,* 411 U.S. 1 (1973): n 16
Santa Fe School District v. *Doe,* 530 U.S. 290 (2000): nn 422, 445
Schad v. *Borough of Mount Ephraim,* 452 U.S. 61 (1981): n 366
Schlib v. *Kuebel,* 404 U.S. 357 (1971): n 11
Schneider v. *State,* 308 U.S. 147, 163 (1939): n 536
Scott v. *Sandford,* 60 U.S. (19 How.) 393 (1857): nn 42–43, 76, 105, 117, 120–28, 145, 150, 229, 248–49, 275, 277, 296–98, 305, 308, 311, 315, 320, 335, 459, 478
Selective Draft Law Cases, 245 U.S. 366 (1918): n 255
Sherbert v. *Verner,* 374 U.S. 398 (1963): n 384
Simms v. *Simms,* 175 U.S. 162, 168 (1899): n 432
Sinking Fund Cases, 99 U.S. 700 (1878): n 158
Slaughter-House Cases, 83 U.S. (16 Wall.) 36 (1873): nn 4, 99, 235–36, 238, 240–41, 244, 248–50, 252–54, 263, 293, 327, 312, 319, 356, 484, 491–92, 508, 520, 565
Stanley v. *Georgia,* 394 U.S. 557 (1969): n 545
Strauder v. *West Virginia,* 100 U.S. 303 (1880): nn 16, 327, 519
Stromberg v. *California,* 283 U.S. 359, 369 (1931): n 360
Swift v. *Tyson,* 41 U.S. (16 Pet.) 1 (1842): nn 378, 498
Texas v. *White,* 74 U.S. (7 Wall.) 700 (1869): nn 150, 268–71
Texas Monthly, Inc. v. *Bullock,* 489 U.S. 1 (1989): n 366
Tilton v. *Richardson,* 403 U.S. 672 (1971): n 397
Toomer v. *Witsell,* 334 U.S. 385 (1948): n 99
Torcaso v. Watkins, 367 U.S. 488, 495 (1961): n 439
Truax v. *Raich,* 239 U.S. 33, 39 (1915): n 279
Twining v. *New Jersey,* 211 U.S. 78, (1908): nn 4, 225.
Two Guys From Harrison-Allentown v. *McGinley,* 366 U.S. 582 (1961): n 410
United States v. *Cruikshank,* 92 U.S. 542 (1876): nn 225, 351, 359, 494
United States v. *Guest,* 383 U.S. 745 (1966): nn 282, 285
United States v. *Hudson,* 11 U.S. (7 Cran.) 32 (1812): n 53
United States v. *Miller,* 307 U.S. 174 (1939): nn 170, 182, 185, 201
United States v. Orito, 413 U.S. 139 (1973): n 545
United States v. *Verdugo-Urquidez,* 494 U.S. 259 (1990): n 304
United States v. *Wheeler,* 254 U.S. 281 (1920): nn 247, 280
United States v. *Williams,* 128 S. Ct. 1830 (2008): n 532
United States v. *Wong Kim Ark,* 169 U.S. 649 (1898): nn 264–67

United States v. *12 200-Ft. Reels of Film,* 413 U.S. 123 (1973): n 545

Usery v. Turner Elkhorn Mining Co., 428 U.S. 1 (1976): n 461

Valley Forge Christian College v. *Americans United for Separation of Church and State,* 454 U.S. 464 (1982): nn 396, 399, 401

Virginia v. *Black,* 538 U.S. 343 (2003): n 537

Virginia Pharmacy Board v. *Virginia Consumer Council,* 425 U.S. 748 (1976): n 539

Walker v. *Sauvinet,* 92 U.S. 90 (1876): n 13

Wallace v. *Jaffree,* 472 U.S. 38 (1985): nn 417, 422, 440

Waltz v. *Tax Commission,* 397 U.S. 664 (1970): nn 366, 437

Ward v. *Maryland,* 79 U.S. (12 Wall.) 418 (1870): n 99

Washington v. *Glucksberg,* 521 U.S. 702, 719–722 (1997): nn 473, 524

Washington v. *Texas,* 388 U.S. 14 (1967): n 10

Watson v. *Jones,* 80 U.S. (13 Wall.) 679 (1872): nn 377–80

West Coast Hotel Co. v. *Parrish,* 300 U.S. 379 (1937): nn 461, 562

West Virginia State Board of Education v. *Barnette,* 319 U.S. 624 (1941): nn 181, 376

Widmar v. *Vincent,* 454 U.S. 263 (1981): n 366

Williams v. *Fears,* 179 U.S. 270 (1900): nn 279, 463

Williamson v. *Lee Optical Co.,* 348 U.S. 483 (1955): n 461

Wisconsin v. *Yoder,* 406 U.S. 205 (1972): n 384

Wooley v. *Maynard,* 430 U.S. 705, 714 (1977): n 181

Zorach v. *Clauson,* 343 U.S. 306 (1952): n 452

Select Bibliography with Endnote Citations for Parts I–IV

Amar, Akhil Reed. *The Bill of Rights: Creation and Reconstruction* (New Haven:Yale University Press, 1998): nn 15–22, 25–27, 29–36, 38, 41, 43–52, 56–56, 58, 61, 63–67, 70, 72, 74–76, 80, 92, 94, 96–97, 105–106, 109–10, 116, 118, 120, 129, 134–35, 137–140, 142–44, 160, 218, 227, 232–33, 309–11, 313–17, 324, 350, 364, 453, 455, 551–52, 556–59

——. *America's Constitution: A Biography* (New York: Random House, 2005): nn 15, 37, 76, 130–31, 234, 346–50

——. "The Bill of Rights as a Constitution," 100 Yale L. J. 1131–1210 (1991): nn 21, 66

——. "The Bill of Rights and the Fourteenth Amendment," 101 Yale L. J. 1193–1284 (1992): nn 21

——. "An(other) Afterword on *The Bill of Rights*," 87 Geo. L. J. 2347–62 (1999); n 227

Annals of Congress (official title: *The Debates and Proceedings in the Congress of the United States) 1789*–1824), http://lcweb2.loc.gov/ammem/amlaw/lwac.html: nn 28, 59–60, 177, 207, 211–212

Avins, Alfred. *The Reconstruction Amendments' Debates: The Legislative History and Contemporary Debates in Congress on the 13th, 14th, and 15th Amendments* (Richmond VA: Virginia Commission on Constitutional Government, 1967): n 91

Bartolomucci, Chris. Note: "*Rethinking the Incorporation of the Establishment Clause: A Federalist View*," 105 Harv. L. Rev. 1700–19 (1992): nn 387, 457

Berger, Raoul. *Government by Judiciary: The Transformation of the Fourteenth Amendment* (Cambridge, Mass.: Harvard University Press, 1977): nn 160, 345

———. *The Fourteenth Amendment and the Bill of Rights* (Norman: University of Oklahoma Press, 1989): n 345

Berlin, Ira. *Slaves Without Masters: The Free Negro in the Antebellum South* (New York: Random House Vintage Books, 1976): n 303

Bordenet, Bernard J. "The Right to Possess Arms: The Intent of the Framers of the Second Amendment," 21 U. West L.A. L. Rev. 1–30 (1990): nn 199–200

Bradley, Gerard V. *Church-State Relationships in America* (New York: Greenwood Press, 1987): n 59

Broad, C. D. "Relations of Science and Religion," in his *Reason, Philosophy and Psychical Research* (New York; Harcourt, Brace & Co., 1953): n 469

Brose, Jonathan P. "In Birmingham They Love the Governor: Why the Fourteenth Amendment Does Not Incorporate the Establishment Clause," 24 Ohio N. U. L. Rev. 14–30 (1998): n 387

Brown, Everett Somerville. *The Constitutional History of the Louisiana Purchase 1803–1812* (Berkeley: University of California Press, 1920): n 95

Bryce, James. *The American Commonwealth* (New York: Macmillan and Co, 1883): nn 448, 458

Calabresi, Steven G. & Agudo, Sarah E. "Individual Rights Under States Constitutions when the Fourteenth Amendment Was Ratified in 1868: What Rights Are Deeply Rooted in American History and Tradition?", 87 Texas L. Rev. 7–120 (2008): nn 363, 450, 454, 505, 558

Cohen, I. Bernard. *The Birth of a New Physics* (Anchor Books, 1960): n 561

Congressional Globe (1833–73), http://lcweb2.loc.gov/ammen/amlaw/lwcg.html: nn 57, 68–69, 78, 81–85, 87–88, 96–97, 129, 131–33, 135–36, 139–42, 149, 274, 300–01, 331–43, 345, 479–83, 523

Cooley, Thomas M. *A Treatise on the Constitutional Limitations Which Rest Upon the Legislative Powers of The States of the American Union* (Boston, Little, Brown, & Co., 1868): nn 449–51, 489

———. "The Fourteenth Amendment" (supplemental chapter xlvii), in Joseph Story, *Commentaries on the Constitution of the United States*, ed. Thomas M. Cooley (Boston: Little, Brown, & Co., 1873), 2: §§ 1929–69: nn 152, 365, 484–87, 489, 506–07

Cord, Robert L. *Separation of Church and State* (Grand Rapids, MI: Baker Book House, 1988): n 443

Corwin, Edward S. *The Constitution and what it means today* (New York: Atheneum, 1963): n 478

———, ed. *The Constitution of the United States of America: Analysis and Interpretation* (Washington, D.C.: U.S. Government Printing Office, 1952): n 499

Crosskey, W. W. "Charles Fairman, 'Legislative History,' and the Constitutional Limitations on State Authority," 22 U. Chi. L. Rev. 1–143 (1954): nn 43, 119

Curry, Thomas J. *The First Freedoms: Church and State in America to the Passage of the First Amendment* (New York: Oxford University Press, 1986): n 441

Curtis, Michael Kent. *No State Shall Abridge: The Fourteenth Amendment And The Bill Of Rights* (Durham, Duke University Press, 1986): nn 19, 43, 115–16, 119, 556, 560

————. *Free Speech, "The People's Darling Privilege"*: *Struggles for Freedom of Expression in American History* (Durham: Duke University Press, 2000): nn 24, 54

————."Resurrecting the Privileges or Immunities Clause and Revising the Slaughter-House Cases Without Exhuming Lochner: Individual Rights and the Fourteenth Amendment," 38 B. C. L. Rev.1–106 (1996): nn 19, 73, 80, 115–16

————. "Two Textual Adventures: Thoughts on Reading Jeffrey Rosen's Paper," 66 Geo. Wash. L. Rev. 1269–92 (1998): nn 19, 21, 115,

————. "Historical Linguistics, Inkblots, and Life after Death: The Privileges or Immunities Clause of the Fourteenth Amendment," 78 N.C.L. Rev. 1071–1151 (2000): n 19

————. "John A. Bingham and the Story of American Liberty," 36 *U. Akron L. Rev.* 617–69 (2003): n 19

DeTocqueville, Alexis. *Democracy in America* (1835) (trans. Henry Reeves 1899) http://www.gutenberg.org/etext/815: n 458

Eaton, Clement. *The Freedom-of-Thought Struggle in the Old South* (revised and enlarged edition) (New York: Harper & Row, 1964): n 126

Elliot, Jonathan, ed. *Debates in the Several State Conventions on the Adoption of the Federal Constitution* (Philadelphia: J. B. Lippincott, 1836), http://lcweb2.loc.gov/ammem/amlaw/lwed.html: nn 151, 442, 504

Ely, John Hart. *Democracy and Distrust: A Theory of Judicial Review* (Cambridge: Harvard University Press, 1980): nn 108, 345, 521

Fairman, Charles. *Does the Fourteenth Amendment Incorporate the Bill of Rights? The Original Understanding*, 2 Stanford L. Rev. 5–139 (1949): nn 86, 89–90, 98, 138, 556

Fehrenbacher, Don E. *The Dred Scott Case: Its Significance in American Law and Politics* (New York: Oxford University Press, 1978): nn 42, 146, 148

——. *The Slaveholding Republic: An Account of the United States Government's Relations to Slavery* (ed. & completed by Ward M. McAfee) (New York: Oxford University Press, 2001): n 501

Feinberg, Joel. *Offense to Others: The Moral Limits of the Criminal Law* (New York: Oxford University Press, 1985): n 446

Finkelman, Paul. "Prelude to the Fourteenth Amendment: Black Legal Rights in the Antebellum North," 17 Rutgers L. J. 415–82 (1986): n 299

Freund, Ernst. *The Police Power: Public Policy and Constitutional Rights* (Chicago: Callaghan & Co., 1904): n 542–43

Guminski, Arnold T. "The Rights, Privileges, and Immunities of the American People: A Disjunctive Theory of Selective Incorporation of the Bill of Rights." 7 Whittier L. Rev. 765–626 (1985): nn 3, 17, 73, 80, 92, 95–96, 134, 161, 228, 278, 302, 325, 350, 355, 357, 367, 444

[The addendum below contains the corrigenda pertaining to this article.]

Halbrook, Stephen P. *That Every Man Be Armed: The Evolution of a Constitutional Right* (1984): nn 201–02, 208, 222

——. *Freedmen, The Fourteenth Amendment, and the Right to bear Arms*, 1855–1876 (Westport, Conn.: Praeger Publishers, 1998): nn 223–24

——. *The Founders' Second Amendment: Origins of the Right to Bear Arms* (Chicago: Ivan R. Dee, 2008): nn 168, 207

———. "What the Framers Intended: A Linguistic Analysis of the Right to 'Bear Arms'" 49 Law & Cont. Probs. 151–62 (1986): n 226

———. "The Right of the People or the Power of the State: Bearing Arms, Arming Militias, and the Second Amendment," 26 Val. U. Val. Rev. 131–207 (1991): nn 203–07, 209, 226

Harrison, John. "Reconstructing the Privileges or Immunities Clause," 101 Yale L.J. 1385–1427 (1992): nn 324–25, 328

Hening, William Waller, ed. *The Statutes at Large; Being a Collection of All the Laws of Virginia* (1823), 12: 84–86 (1823), http://vagenweb. org/hening/vol12–04.htm: nn 370, 372,

Hohfeld, Wesley N. *Fundamental Legal Conceptions As Applied In Judicial Reasoning And Other Legal Essays* (ed. W.W. Cook) (New Haven: Yale University Press, 1923): n 70

Howe, Albert H., ed. *The Insular Cases: Comprising The Records, Briefs, and Arguments of Counsel in the Insular Cases of the October Term, 1900, in the Supreme Court of the United States, Including the Appendixes Thereto*, House of Representatives, 56th Cong., 2d Sess., Document 509, (Washington: Government Printing Office, 1901): nn. 95, 304

Hume, David. *Dialogues Concerning Natural Religion* (N. K. Smith ed.) (Indianapolis: Bobbs-Merrill Co., 1947): n 335

James, Joseph B. *The Framing of the Fourteenth Amendment* (Urbana: University of Illinois Press, 1965): n 86

Jefferson, Thomas. *The Works of Thomas Jefferson*, ed. P.L. Ford (New York: G.P. Putnam's Sons, 1905): n 95

Journal of the Senate of the United States, http://lcweb2.loc.gov/ ammem/amlaw/lwsj.html: nn 60, 178, 207, 442

Kacourek, Albert. *Jural Relations* (Indianapolis: Bobs-Merrill Co., 2d ed. 1928): n 70

Kates, Jr., Don B. "The Second Amendment: A Dialogue," 49 Law & Cont. Probs. 143–50 (1986): n 182

———. *Handgun Prohibition and the Original Meaning of the Second Amendment*. 82 Mich. L. Rev. 204–73 (1983): nn 182–84, 194–195

Kendrick, Benjamin. *The Journal of the Joint Committee of Fifteen on Reconstruction* (New York: Columbia University Press, 1914): n 86

Kirk, Russell. *Academic Freedom: An Essay in Definition* (Chicago: Henry Regnery Co., 1955): n 515

Larsh, Kurt. "The Second Adoption of the Free Exercise Clause: Religious Exemptions Under the Fourteenth Amendment," 88 Nw. U. L. Rev. 1106–56 (1994): n 21

Levy, Leonard W. *The Establishment Clause: Religion and the First Amendment* (New York: MacMillian Publishing Co., 1986): nn 386, 423, 425–27, 441

Lieber, Francis. *Manual of Political Ethics* (ed. Theodore D. Woolsey, 2d ed. rev'd) (Philadelphia: J. B. Lippincott Co., 1890): nn 510–13

Lietzau, William K. "Rediscovering the Establishment Clause: Federalism and the Rollback of Incorporation," 39 DePaul L. Rev. 1191–1234 (1990): n 387

Litwack, Leon F. *North of Slavery: The Negro in the Free States 1790–1860* (Chicago: University of Chicago Press, 1961): n 299

London, Lena. "The Militia Fine 1830–1860," 15 Military Affairs 133–44 (1951): nn 191–92, 211, 213–17

Mahon, John K. *The American Militia: Decade of Decision*, 1789–1800 (Gainesville: University of Florida Press, 1960): nn 189–91

——. *History of the Militia and the National Guard* (New York: Macmillan, 1983): nn 191–92, 214, 220, 330

Maltz, Earl M. Civil Rights, *The Constitution and Congress, 1863–1869* (Lawrence: University Press of Kansas, 1990): n 556

Meiklejohn, Alexander. *Political Freedom: The Constitutional Powers of the People* (New York: Oxford University Press, 1965): n 357

Miller, Samuel F. *Lectures on the Constitution of the United States* (1893): n 14

Paschal, George W. *The Constitution of the United States: Defined and Carefully Annotated* (Washington, DC: W.H. & O.H. Morrison, Law Booksellers, 1868): nn 69, 151–52,

Read, Carveth. *Logic: Deductive and Inductive* (London: Alexander Moring Ltd., 1914): n 488

Rembar, Charles. *The End of Obscenity: The Trials of Lady Chatterley, Tropic of Cancer, and Fanny Hill* (New York: Random House, 1968): n 548

Reynolds, Glenn Harlan. "A Critical Guide to the Second Amendment," 62 Tenn. L. Rev. 461–512 (1995): n 195

Riker, William H. *Soldiers of the States: The Role of the National Guard in American Democracy* (Washington, DC: Public Affairs Press, 1957): nn 192, 215–16, 220

Salmond, John. *Jurisprudence* (G.L. Williams 10th ed.) (London: Street & Maxwell, 1947): n 70

Sienkiewicz, Henryk (*Krzyżacy*) *Knights of the Cross*, tr. Jeremiah Curtin (Boston: Little, Brown & Co., 1900): n 568

Snee, Joseph M. "Religious Disestablishment and the Fourteenth Amendment," 1954 Wash. U. L. Q. 371–407: n 387

Story, Joseph. *Commentaries on the Constitution; With a Preliminary Review of the Constitutional History of the United States before the Adoption of the Constitution* (Boston: Hilliard, Gray & Co., 1833), http://www.constitution.org/js/js_000.htm: nn 221, 359, 365

tenBroek, Jacobus. *Equal Under Law* (New York: Collier Books, 1965): n 556

Thorpe, Francis Newton. *The Federal And State Constitutions, Colonial Charters, And Other Laws, of the States, Territories, and Colonies Now Or Heretofore Forming The United States Of America* (Washington: Government Printing Office, 1909): n 71

Wiener, Frederick Bernays. "The Militia Clause of the Constitution," 54 Harv. L. Rev. 181–220 (1940): nn 188, 193, 220

Addendum—Corrigenda pertaining to Arnold T. Guminski, "The Rights, Privileges, and Immunities of the American People: A Disjunctive Theory of Selective Incorporation of the Bill of Rights," 7 Whittier L. Rev. 765–626 (1985):
p. 765: 2nd line of n. *: "1965" should read "1956"
p. 765: 7th line of n. *: "Sandheim" should read "Sondheim"
p. 769: last line of n. 12: "*in re* Oliver" should read "*In re Oliver*"
p 769: last sentence on page (and continued on p. 770) should begin: "The right specified in the second amendment, . . ." and citations to *Presser* and *Miller* in note 13 should be deleted
p. 772: 5th line of text: insert "or deflating" after "inflating"
p. 776: n. 33: "National" should read "Second"
p. 783: 2d par. of text: omit "article IV of the Articles of Confederation as well as"

p. 783: 3rd line of n. 61: "*Id.* At 211. Act" should read "*Id.* at 211, Act"

p. 788: 5th line of 2d par. of text: delete comma after "Buchanan"

p. 790: 6th line of 3rd par. of text: add "on April 4, 1866" after "noted"; p. 792, 1st line of 1st full par. of text: add double quotation after "noticed" delete comma after privilege", and substitute single for double quotation marks around "privilege"

p. 792: 1st line of 2nd full par. of text: "Hohfeld's insistence" should read "Hohfield insisted"

p. 795: "Complimentaries" in the second heading should read "Complementaries"

p. 796: 3rd line of 1st full par. of text: "complimentaries" should read "complementaries"

p. 797: 10th line of text: omit ellipsis

p. 809: 5th line of 3rd par.: "fourteenthth" should read "fourteenth"

p. 812: 4th line of 1st full par. of text: Political freedom" should begin new par.

p. 814: 2nd line of 1st full par. of text: "1879" should read "1789"

p. 815: 2nd, 3rd, and 4th lines of 3rd full par: "complimentaries" should read "complementaries"

p. 817: 4th line of 2nd full par. of text: "is" should read "are"

p. 820: 1st line of n. 178: "note 76" should read "note 75"

p. 825: 4th line of n. 189: "note 156" should read "note 155"

About The Author

Arnold T. Guminski was born in Buffalo, New York in 1932. He graduated in 1952 from the University of Buffalo with a B.A. degree in history and philosophy. He graduated with a juris doctorate from the University of California at Los Angeles School of Law in 1956, and was admitted to the California State Bar in 1957. Guminski was on active duty with the United States Army from 1957 to 1963, serving three years in France as an officer with the Judge Advocate General's Corps. From 1963 to 1993, he was a deputy district attorney for Los Angeles County, and was assigned to the Appellate Division for the last twenty years of his service. During that time, he argued many cases before state and federal appellate courts in California, including the California Supreme Court and the United States Court of Appeals for the Ninth Circuit. He has twice argued before the United States Supreme Court. After his retirement in January 1993, he and Annegret, his wife, moved to Boulder, Colorado, where they have since resided. Guminski is an independent scholar. Besides constitutional-rights theory, he is also very interested in the philosophy of religion, ethics, and law; and has authored peer-reviewed articles for *Faith & Reason*, *Philo*, and *Philosophia Christi*, as well as for the Secular Web. (See http:// www.infidels.org/library/modern/arnold_guminski/ and http://www. infidels.org/library/modern/arnold_guminski/bio.shtml for access to or citations for his articles.) The Guminski's enjoy traveling at home and abroad. They heartily engage in social dancing of various kinds— including Greek and other international folk dancing, ballroom, and ragtime dancing.